HISTORICAL VIEWPOINTS

NINTH EDITION

VOLUME TWO ■ SINCE 1865

EDITOR

John A. Garraty

Gouverneur Morris Professor of History

Columbia University

Longman

New York San Francisco Boston
London Toronto Sydney Tokyo Singapore Madrid
Mexico City Munich Paris Cape Town Hong Kong Montreal

Vice President and Publisher: Priscilla McGeehon
Acquisitions Editor: Ashley Dodge
Executive Marketing Manager: Sue Westmoreland
Project Coordination,Text Design, and Electronic Page Makeup: Nesbitt Graphics, Inc.
Cover Designer/Manager: Wendy Ann Fredericks
Cover Illustration: © Franklin McMahon/CORBIS
Photo Researcher: Photosearch, Inc.
Senior Manufacturing Buyer: Dennis J. Para
Printer and Binder: Hamilton Printing Co.
Cover Printer: Lehigh Press, Inc.

Library of Congress Cataloging-in-Publication Data

Historical viewpoints / editor, John A. Garraty.—9th ed.
   p. cm.
  Includes bibliographical references.
  Contents: v. 1. To 1877—v. 2. Since 1865.
  ISBN 0-321-10299-1 (v. 1)—ISBN 0-321-10211-8 (v. 2)
   1. United States—History.   I. Garraty, John Arthur, 1920–   II. American heritage.

E178.6 .H67 2003
973—dc21   2002069479

Please visit our website at http://www.ablongman.com

ISBN 0-321–10211–8

1 2 3 4 5 6 7 8 9 10—HT—05 04 03 02

CONTENTS

INTRODUCTION

Thirteen Books You Must Read to Understand America

Arthur M. Schlesinger, Jr.

Arthur M. Schlesinger, Jr. won the Pulitzer Prize for *The Age of Jackson* (1945). In addition to serving as a special consultant to President John F. Kennedy, Schlesinger has written many important works of history, including his three-volume *Age of Roosevelt* (1957–1960), *A Thousand Days: John F. Kennedy in the White House* (1965), *The Imperial Presidency* (1973), *Robert Kennedy and His Times* (1978), *Disuniting of America* (1991), and, most recently, the first volume of his memoirs (2000).

When Drake McFeely of W. W. Norton proposed an updated and enlarged edition of my book *The Disuniting of America,* he thought it might be a good idea to add an all-American reading list. What are the dozen or so books, he wondered, that everyone should know in order to have a sense of the American experience? McFeely, as the son of the Pulitzer Prize–winning biographer of Ulysses S. Grant and Frederick Douglass, has a special interest in American history; and as the son of another eminent historian, I appreciated both the value and the challenge of his invitation.

A dozen books? A hundred—or a thousand—books would not do the job. All countries are hard to understand, and despite its brief history, the United States of America is harder to understand than most, because of its size in dreams, because of its obstreperousness, and because of its heterogeneity. Still, for all this, the United States has an unmistakable national identity. Here, in chronological order, are books that have described, defined, and enriched America's sense of itself. I am dismayed at all the significant works so brief a list must leave out, but I do think that these particular choices illuminate in a major way what Ralph Ellison called "the mystery of American identity": how we Americans are at once many and one.

THE FEDERALIST (1787–88) originated as an explanation and defense of the American Constitution. It survives as a brilliant exposition of the first principles of democratic government. Written mostly by **Alexander Hamilton** and **James Madison,** the eighty-five *Federalist* papers were published between October 1787 and May 1788 in New York City newspapers, were reprinted throughout the thirteen states, and were read avidly during the debates over the ratification of the Constitution—and have been read avidly ever since. Can one imagine any newspaper today, even the august *New York Times,* running a series of such length and weight?

WRITINGS, **Thomas Jefferson** (Library of America, 1984). Jefferson embodied much of American versatility within himself. He was an architect, an educator, an inventor, a paleontologist, an oenophile, a fiddler, an astute diplomat, a crafty politician, and a luminous prophet of liberty in words that light the human way through the centuries. President John F. Kennedy once called a dinner of Nobel Prize winners the most extraordinary collection of human knowledge ever to be gathered together at the White House "with the possible exception of when Thomas Jefferson dined alone."

But Jefferson was a man of contradictions: a champion of human freedom who did not, as George Washington had done, set his slaves free at his death; a champion of the free press who favored prosecuting editors for seditious libel; a champion of the strict construction of the Constitution who bent the sacred document for the sake of the Louisiana Purchase. Other early Presidents, observed Henry Adams, our most brilliant historian, could be painted with broad brushstrokes, but Jefferson "could be painted only touch by touch, with a fine pencil, and the perfection of the likeness depended upon the shifting and uncertain flicker of its semi-transparent shadows." That invaluable publishing project the Library of America brings together in a single volume Jefferson's most notable writings, including his *Autobiography*, his major addresses, and a selection of his letters.

DEMOCRACY IN AMERICA, **Alexis de Tocqueville** (two volumes, 1835, 1840). The concept of "national character" has been under a cloud in scholarly circles, but can anyone really deny that Englishmen tend to be different from Frenchmen, and Germans from Italians? And can anyone read this extraordinary book about a country of thirteen million people along the Atlantic seaboard without seeing how much of the description and analysis still applies to the nation of 265 million stretching from sea to sea?

When Tocqueville, a twenty-five-year-old French nobleman, arrived in the United States in 1831, he was more interested in democracy than he was in America—or rather he was interested in America as a test case of the "great democratic revolution" that, he felt, was "universal and irresistible" and destined to transform the world. The grand question was whether this revolution would lead to "democratic tyranny." Though concerned about the "tyranny of the majority," Tocqueville believed that the power of voluntary associations and intermediate institutions had put America on the road to democratic liberty. He traveled around the country from May 1831 to February 1832 (and never came back). But in those nine months he saw more deeply into American institutions and the American character than anyone before or since. More than a century and a half later, his great work still illuminates American society.

ESSAYS AND LECTURE, **Ralph Waldo Emerson** (Library of America, 1983). No one has expressed the American faith in the sovereignty of the individual more brilliantly, lyrically, and sardonically than Emerson. Born in 1803, trained for the Unitarian ministry, he left the pulpit for the lecture platform, from which he expounded his transcendentalist philosophy in crackling aphorisms.

Some critics have decried what they see as Emerson's shallow optimism, but underneath his alleged disregard of the problem of evil and his allegedly guileless faith in intuition lie shrewd, skeptical, hard-edged, almost ruthless Yankee insights into human nature. "For every benefit you receive," Emerson said, "a tax is levied." It is this tough side of Emerson that appealed in the nineteenth century to Hawthorne, Carlyle, and Nietzsche and that appeals to postmodernists today. The

Ralph Waldo Emerson was largely responsible for generating the transcendentalist movement and in a broader sense for fostering romantic thought in the United States.

Library of America volume contains his masterly study of national character *English Traits,* the penetrating biographical portraits in *Representative Men,* and his essays. For the tough-minded Emerson, read "History," "Self-Reliance," "Experience," and, in *The Conduct of Life,* "Power" and "Fate."

UNCLE TOM'S CABIN, Harriet Beecher Stowe (1852). She was forty years old, the wife of a professor of biblical literature, the mother of seven children, when her indignation over the forced return of slaves to bondage under the Fugitive Slave Act led her to write the most influential novel in American history. The book sold three hundred thousand copies in its first year—equivalent to a sale of three million copies in the 1990s. "So this is the little lady who made this big war," Lincoln is supposed to have said to her.

Uncle Tom's Cabin is remembered for its vivid depiction of the horrors of slavery—and often misremembered, because so many images derive from the stage versions rather than from the novel itself. *Uncle Tom's Cabin* is far more than the sentimental melodrama of "the Tom shows." It is a wonderfully shrewd and nuanced panorama of American life in the decade before the Civil War, rich in its variety of characters, settings, and perceptions. Mrs. Stowe may not in every respect meet contemporary standards of political correctness, but she was radical for her time in her insights and sympathies—one of the first, for example, to use the term *human rights*. Frederick Douglass called *Uncle Tom's Cabin* a book "plainly marked by the finger of God."

SPEECHES AND WRITINGS, Abraham Lincoln (two volumes, Library of America, 1989). The most miraculous of Presidents, he was the best writer and the most intense moralist, with the most disciplined intelligence and the greatest strength of purpose, and yet he sprang out of the bleakest and most unpromising of circumstances. Confronting the supreme test and tragedy of American nationhood, he saw the crisis in perspective—"with malice toward none, with charity for all"—but never let perspective sever the nerve of action.

His Gettysburg Address amended the work of the Founding Fathers by leaving no doubt that the United States was a single nation based on the proposition that all men are created equal. And his Second Inaugural affirmed human limitations by declaring that "the Almighty has His own purposes"—purposes that erring mortals could never ascertain. "Men are not flattered," he later wrote, "by being shown that there has been a difference of purpose between the Almighty and them. To deny it, however . . . is to deny that there is a God governing the world."

ADVENTURES OF HUCKLEBERRY FINN, Mark Twain (Samuel Langhorne Clemens) (1884). What piece of imaginative writing best expresses the spirit of America? A strong case can be made for Herman Melville's *Moby-Dick*, for Walt Whitman's *Leaves of Grass*, for Nathaniel Hawthorne's *The Scarlet Letter*. But in the end one is compelled to go for *Huck Finn*.

This is because of the mordant way Mark Twain depicts antebellum America and the corruptions encouraged by a system in which people owned other people as private property—the hypocrisy, the sanctimoniousness, the humbuggery, the murderous feuds, the lynch mobs, the overhanging climate of brutality and violence.

It is also because of the language; *Huck Finn* is the first purely American novel. In it Mark Twain shows how the colloquial idiom spoken by an uneducated boy can express the most subtle perceptions and exquisite appreciations. The book liberated American writers. "All modern American literature," Ernest Hemingway wrote in *The Green Hills of Africa*, "comes from one book by Mark Twain called *Huckleberry Finn*. . . . All American writing comes from that. There was nothing before. There has been nothing so good since."

And it is because the novel's climactic scene so wonderfully dramatizes the essential American struggle of the individual against absolutes. Huck, responding for a moment to conventional morality, decides that the "plain hand of Providence" requires him to tell Miss Watson where she can locate Jim, her runaway slave and Huck's companion on the Mississippi raft. Huck feels suddenly virtuous, "all washed clean of sin for the first time I had ever felt so in my life." He reflects on his narrow escape: "How near I come to being lost and going to hell."

Then Huck begins to remember Jim and the rush of the great river and the singing and the laughing and the comradeship. He takes up the letter to Miss Watson, the letter of betrayal, and holds it in his hand. "I was a-trembling because I'd got to decide, forever, betwixt two things, and I knowed it. I studied a minute, sort of holding my breath, and then says to myself; 'All right, then, I'll go to hell,'—and tore it up."

That, it may be said, is what America is all about. No wonder William Dean Howells called Mark Twain "the Lincoln of our literature."

THE AMERICAN COMMONWEALTH, James Bryce (two volumes, 1888). Bryce, a Scotsman born in Belfast in 1838, was one of those Victorian figures of fantastic energy, curiosity, versatility, and fluency, an expert in law, politics, diplomacy, history, literature, and mountaineering. He made his first visit to America in 1870 and, unlike Tocqueville, often came back, serving from 1907 to 1913 as British ambassador in Washington.

Bryce's mind was less probing and philosophical than Tocqueville's. His passion for facts has had the ironic effect of making *The American Commonwealth* more dated than *Democracy in America,* since facts in America change all the time. But Bryce was a canny observer of institutions, and his observations have great value for historians. He spent much more time than Tocqueville on the party system and on state and local government. His chapters on "Why Great Men Are Not Chosen President" and "Why the Best Men Do Not Go Into Politics" strike chords today. His analysis of the role of public opinion, "the great central point of the whole American polity," opened a new field of investigation. His aphorisms still reverberate: The Constitution "is the work of men who believed in original sin, and were resolved to leave open for transgressors no door which they could possibly shut." "The student of institutions, as well as the lawyer, is apt to overrate the effect of mechanical contrivances in politics." And, above all, "Perhaps no form of government needs great leaders so much as democracy."

WRITINGS, William James (two volumes, Library of America, 1987, 1992). The most American of philosophers, a wonderfully relaxed, humane, and engaging writer (his brother, Henry, people used to say, wrote novels like a psychologist, while William wrote psychology like a novelist), he moved on from psychology to philosophy. James's pragmatism, with its argument that the meaning of ideas lies in their practical consequences, could not have been more in the American vein.

So, too, was his argument for pluralism and an open universe against those who contend for a monist system and a closed universe. People, James wrote, can discover partial and limited truths, truths that work for them, but no one can discover absolute truths. He rejected the notion that the world can be understood from a single point of view, as he rejected the assumption that all virtuous principles are in the end reconcilable and "the great single-word answers to the world's riddle" and "the pretense of finality in truth." He had an exhilarating faith in the adventure of an unfinished universe.

THE EDUCATION OF HENRY ADAMS, Henry Adams (1918). Where William James saw the future as a great adventure, his friend and contemporary Henry Adams looked on it with foreboding. Oppressed by the exponential rate of scientific and technological change, Adams doubted that the human mind could keep abreast of the relentless transformations wrought by the increasing velocity of history.

The challenge, as Adams saw it, was to control the new energies created and unleashed by science and technology. This required education, and looking back at his own education, Adams believed that "in essentials like religion, ethics, philosophy; in history, literature, art; in the concepts of all science, except perhaps mathematics, the American boy of 1854 [when he went to Harvard, at the age of sixteen] stood nearer the year 1 than to the year 1900. The education he had received bore little relation to the education he needed."

The *Education* describes Adams's attempts to grapple with the emerging era. Along the way he distributes fascinating portraits of politicians and writers, fascinating accounts of historical episodes, fascinating reflections on the changing world. "The new Americans," he said, "must, whether they were fit or unfit, create a world of their own, a science, a society, a philosophy, a universe, where they had not yet created a road or even learned to dig their own iron." Could the new Americans rise to the challenge?

"Man has mounted science and is now run away with," he had written in 1862, when the *Monitor* and the *Merrimack* were foreshadowing new technologies in the instrumentation of war. "I firmly believe that before many centuries more, science will be the master of man. The engines he will have invented will be beyond his strength to control. Some day science shall have the existence of mankind in its power, and the human race shall commit suicide by blowing up the world."

THE AMERICAN LANGUAGE, **H. L. Mencken** (1936; supplements 1945, 1948). Mencken, of course (but why do I write "of course"? He is very likely a forgotten man today), was one of the literary heroes of the 1920s. He was a master of exuberant irreverence, and he presented a satirical take on America with swashbuckling vigor of style and a liberating polemical tone. But in the 1930s Mencken fell out of sync with the national mood. The great cultural heretic of the twenties, he was a libertarian, not a democrat, and suddenly confronted by the harsh political antagonisms of the thirties, he seemed sour and mean spirited.

But to his fans he redeemed himself by *The American Language,* his shrewd, copious, quite scholarly, highly entertaining account of the way a new language evolved out of the English spoken across the sea. This rich and readable book is a wonderful compendium of Americana. It shows, among other things, that assimilation, far from an unconditional surrender to Anglocentrism, has been a two-way street in which non-Anglo newcomers play an active part in transforming the English into the American language.

AN AMERICAN DILEMMA, **Gunnar Myrdal** (1944). Racism has been an organic element in American life from the start. Jefferson had mixed views on the subject of race; Tocqueville had prescient comments along with mistaken prophecies; Mark Twain was haunted by the enigma of race; for Lincoln it was a central issue. But most of the time the race question has been ignored or denied. It took a Swedish economist commissioned by an American foundation to undertake the first full-dress, comprehensive study of black-white relations. Heading a team that included such black scholars as Ralph Bunche and Kenneth B. Clark, Gunnar Myrdal produced *An American Dilemma* in 1944, eighty-one years after Lincoln's Emancipation Proclamation.

This powerful work was not only an analysis: It was a challenge. Written during the war against Hitler and his theory of a master race, it called on Americans to discard their own theories of racial superiority and live up to the promises of equality

Journalist and critic H. L. Mencken made a lasting contribution to American scholarship with The American Language, *published in 1919.*

implicit in what Myrdal termed the American Creed. Myrdal was unduly optimistic in thinking that the American Creed by itself could overcome the pathologies of racism. But his work encouraged the activism of blacks, and it pricked the consciences of whites. And the account it offers of the conditions under which black Americans lived, worked, and died half a century ago provides a heartening measure of the changes that have taken place since its publication.

THE IRONY OF AMERICAN HISTORY, **Reinhold Niebuhr** (1952). The most influential American theologian of the century, Niebuhr approached American history from a neo-orthodox religious perspective—that is, from a tempered, nonfundamentalist belief in original sin (defined as the self-pride that mistakes the relative for the absolute), in the ambiguities of human nature, in divine judgment on human pretensions, and in the incompleteness of life within history. It is necessary, he wrote in this book, to understand "the limits of all human striving, the fragmentariness of all human wisdom, the precariousness of all historic configurations of power, and the mixture of good and evil in all human virtue."

Like William James, Niebuhr was a relativist and a pluralist who scorned monists and absolutists. Like Lincoln, he was especially critical of those whose vainglory leads them to suppose they grasp the purposes of the Almighty. By irony Niebuhr meant the situation that arises when the consequences of an action are contrary to the intentions of the actors because of weaknesses inherent in the actors themselves. This concept informed his reading of American history. Americans, Niebuhr felt, are too much inclined to believe in their own innocence and righteousness and too reluctant to recognize the self-regard in their own souls. He deplored the national inability "to comprehend the depth of evil to which individuals and communities may sink, particularly when they try to play the role of God to history."

Niebuhr's interpretation of the American past is wise and chastening, and it is deep in the American tradition. His conception of democracy is akin to that of the men who made the Constitution. "Man's capacity for justice makes democracy possible," he wrote in *The Children of Light and the Children of Darkness,* "but man's inclination to injustice makes democracy necessary."

1 Impact of Industrialism

The Corliss engine, a "mechanical marvel" at the Centennial Exposition, was a prime example of the giantism so admired by the public.

The Making of Men: Fraternal Orders in the Nineteenth Century

Mark C. Carnes

In the 1870s and 1880s, American men spent as much on initiation rites as their government did on defense. This essay chronicles the invention and diffusion of fraternal rituals in the 19th century and draws a parallel to the men's movement of the 1990s.

Mark C. Carnes is Ann Whitney Olin Professor of History at Barnard College. His *Secret Ritual and Manhood in Victorian America* (1989) and *Meanings for Manhood: Constructions of Masculinity in Victorian America* (1990) stimulated interest in the subject, and the study of masculinity emerged as a major topic within the profession during the 1990s. Although many subsequent scholars endorsed "men's history" as a means of complementing the proliferation of work in women's history during the 1970s and 1980s, Carnes contends that neither sex could be understood apart from the other. He calls instead for a unitary scholarly enterprise under the rubric of gender history. The present essay shows that women were part of the story even when they were excluded from participating in it directly. That manhood should need to be "constructed" in the late 19th century—and even today—suggests that gender "identity" remains problematic.

"The Almighty dollar," Washington Irving wrote, was the "great object of universal devotion" among Americans. Tocqueville described moneymaking as their "prevailing passion." And though the object of their craving sometimes changed, Tocqueville noticed that the emotional intensity persisted. This was why tightfisted Yankee merchants would break down in penitential tears and convert to Christ, why sober Ohio farmers would abandon their homesteads and join utopian communes. Because Americans were so bound up in the struggle to get ahead, Tocqueville concluded, they rushed "unrestrained beyond the range of common sense" when cut loose. Thus did a materialistic nation beget so many "strange sects," each striking out on such "extraordinary paths to eternal happiness."

Yet even Tocqueville might have flinched at the spectacle of thousands of adult men, most of them well-to-do and college-educated, chanting before bonfires and pounding on drums, growling and cavorting in imitation of foxes and bears, plunging naked into baptismal mudholes, and smudging their faces with ashes—all of them following a path blazed by the poet Robert Bly in the final decade of the twentieth century.

What set them in motion was Bly's 1990 *Iron John: A Book About Men.* Manhood had seldom been of much interest to general readers, and the book's odd amalgam of romantic poetry, esoteric philosophy, and popular psychology, all bolted to a little-known myth by the Grimm brothers, seemed unlikely to appeal to the masses. But *Iron John* clambered onto the best-seller list and remained there for more than a year.

The book's success confirmed its central premise: that American men who had renounced the Vietnam War and embraced feminism now fear they have become too soft. Having drifted far from traditional manhood, they need help finding their way back. Such men are drawn to Iron John—a Wildman who led boys from the suffocating confines of childhood into the liberating expanses of manhood. Bly believes the story outlines the initiatory process by which boys become men in most societies. Though deprived of such guidance, American men need not despair, for the requisite rituals are too deeply embedded in the human psyche to be forever lost, or so Bly maintains.

Some of Bly's readers, calling themselves mythopoets, resolved to exhume those rituals and breathe into them new life. They scoured the works of Joseph Campbell and Mary Stewart for mythological or historical examples of men's rituals that could be "adapted" for modern usage. Other Bly enthusiasts published magazines and placed ads in newspapers to attract like-minded men to share the experience. Still others—some one hundred thousand strong—sought to identify with their hoary male forebears by attending weekend "mancamps" in the woods (or in suitably bucolic convention centers). Soon the mythopoetic army overran the tiny outposts of "pro-feminist" academics and men's-rights activists, each of which until then had claimed the men's movement as its own.

But as Bly's boys tried to create and perform initiatory rituals dating back to the Bronze Age, they overlooked a less remote source: the Gilded Age of nineteenth-century America, when literally millions of men—members of the Freemasons, Odd Fellows, Knights of Pythias, and hundreds of similar societies—each week performed elaborate initiatory rituals.

The oldest and most imitated of the fraternal orders was Freemasonry. Founded in late-seventeenth-century England as a stonemasons' guild, the group evolved into a drinking and eating club for tradesmen, merchants, and some noblemen. Its special cachet was secrecy. Members used hand signals and passwords to identify one another; soon they devised a legend about Hiram Abiff, the master mason of Solomon's Temple who was assassinated by rivals and "raised" back to life. Eventually new members underwent a simple initiation, during which they learned the secret signals and heard Abiff's story. Then everyone hastened to the wine steward.

By the mid-1700s Freemasonry had diffused through much of the Western world. In France it was taken up by free-thinkers and evolved into a shadowy political force that attached itself to various conspiracies against church and monarchy. In Germany it served as the inspiration among a group of intellectuals for an elevated mysticism that culminated in Mozart's *The Magic Flute*.

But it was chiefly as a drinking society that Freemasonry crossed the Atlantic and took root in the English colonies. In America nearly all the lodges were located in taverns. Often the three "degrees," or ritual ranks, were conferred in a single evening by members who, having lingered too long at the punch bowl, stumbled over the oaths, passwords, and whatever else they happened upon. Their revelries commonly spilled beyond the tavern, and constables learned to exercise special vigilance on nights the "merry Masons" were abroad.

The character of American Freemasonry changed after 1826. That year William Morgan, who had joined a Masonic lodge in Rochester, New York, moved to Batavia, New York, but was denied admission to the lodge there. Disdaining his oath of secrecy, Morgan announced plans to publish the Masonic signs and lectures. Several weeks later some mysterious strangers showed up, told Morgan that he was under arrest for unpaid debts, and took him to Fort Niagara. Then he disappeared, never to be seen again. Rumors abounded that he had been tossed into the rapids by Freemasons; members of the order suggested that Morgan had fled town and changed his name to avoid creditors.

What happened next is beyond dispute: Two dozen Masons were indicted for conspiring to abduct Morgan, conspiracy being the most serious charge that could be lodged in the absence of a body. Though the evidence against the defendants was damning, only a handful were convicted, and their sentences were brief. But a public tumult ensued when it was learned that Gov. De Witt Clinton, as well as some of the prosecutors, judges, and jurors, were members of the order. Ministers raged against Freemasonry. Politicians, insisting that both political parties had been tainted by the order, founded the nation's first third party, the Anti-Masonic party.

Tens of thousands of Masons withdrew from the order, many lodges ceased meeting, and some officials closed their doors for what they assumed would be the final time. But the Morgan debacle indirectly reinvigorated the fraternal movement by turning it over to an emerging middle class of businessmen, clerks, lawyers, and doctors. Many ex-Freemasons flocked to the Odd Fellows, formerly a working-class club, and took control of it. They sold the punch bowls and banned alcohol, they investigated the morals of prospective initiates and hauled wayward members before lodge tribunals, and they ceased passing the hat for needy members and established an insurance system based on fixed weekly assessments. These, however, were simply the means to promote the order's chief new purpose: initiation.

The ceremonies were drafted by a special committee on ritual, which included several former Freemasons. They wrote an hour-long pageant based loosely on the story of Genesis, with the initiate playing Adam. Because Adam was naked, the initiate's shirt was removed. "Thou art dust," he was told, and chains were wound around his body to symbolize his "guilty soul." He was led blindfolded around the lodge room four or five times as officers lectured on mortality, God, and the meaning of life. Suddenly the blindfolds were snatched away. A skeleton loomed in the torchlight. "Contemplate that dismal, ghastly emblem of what thou art sure to be, and what thou mayst soon become," an officer intoned.

Odd Fellows found this ritual inspiring and craved more like it. But English officials, who had chartered the first American lodges, were dumbfounded. To them the lodge was a place for workers to unwind, perhaps over a tankard of beer, and to help one another when times were bad. Workers needed tangible assistance and support, not long-winded lectures on morality and religion. Relations between American and English branches smoldered as droves of bibulous English emigrants knocked on the doors of the American lodges, took seats in awe-inspiring "tem-

MASTERS CARPET

The prestige of fraternal orders centered around secrecy; rituals, symbols, hand signals, and passwords. The symbols shown here are associated with Freemasonry, the oldest fraternal order.

ples," and stared in disbelief as lamps were extinguished, torches lit, and robes, altars, and skeletons prepared. As speakers droned on, with no one stirring to prepare libations, the Englishmen's wonder turned to anger. During the 1840s English officials demanded that the Americans abandon the new rituals on pain of having their charters revoked. The Americans refused, explaining that Odd Fellowship had grown in America only after it had discarded "conviviality" and instituted religious rituals. "Our career affords an example not unworthy of your imitation," American officials noted pointedly.

In 1844 the Americans broke loose and established the "Independent" Order of Odd Fellows. Free to develop on its own terms, American Odd Fellowship created a sequence of nine elaborate rituals, most of them derived from the Old Testament. In one, for example, the initiate became Isaac, the son of Abraham, who journeyed across a desert wilderness to Mount Moriah (several blind-folded circuits of the lodge room). Then he was tied up and placed upon an altar. Firewood was piled beneath it, a torch was lit, and the Twenty-third Psalm read. After explaining that Isaac was to be sacrificed, Abraham struck a match and leaned toward the wood. Then a gong sounded. God, Abraham announced, had decided to save Isaac and had commanded that he be admitted as a patriarch of Abraham's family. Odd Fellows reported that such a rite "fully satisfied" their "desire" and elevated their order "almost to the dignity of a religion." The Odd Fellows grew from some thirty thousand members in 1843, just prior to the new rituals, to two hundred thousand by 1860 and nearly a million by 1900.

American Freemasonry developed along similar lines, especially the Scottish Rite, the most prestigious branch of the fraternity, which greatly expanded its twenty-nine rituals during the 1850s and 1860s; the new sequence filled eight hundred printed pages. Although a few traditionalists claimed that Freemasonry had been "murderously perverted" by the revisions, most credited the new rituals for the order's growth from forty thousand members in the 1830s to nearly three-quarters of a million by the close of the nineteenth century.

During the 1860s and 1870s hundreds of fraternal organizers imitated the Odd Fellows and Freemasons. The Knights of Pythias, founded in 1864, devised a set of five wildly eclectic rituals: Roman senators sauntered through Hades, and crusaders through medieval castles. Within a decade membership in the order exceeded a quarter of a million, a figure that doubled by the end of the century. An official in 1887 attributed the order's growth to a ritual that had "taken hold of the hearts of men."

The craving was so widespread that entrepreneurs proffered initiatory ritual rather like the way Publishers' Clearinghouse exploits the gambling itch to sell magazines. Victorian insurance promoters, recognizing that men would more likely buy a policy if it came with evenings of initiation, created scores of ritualistic beneficiary societies. One syndicate approached Lew Wallace to transform his best-selling novel into a ritual for the Knights of Ben-Hur. After eliminating the anachronism, Wallace agreed, and within a decade more than a hundred thousand men—initiates of the Tribe of Ben-Hur—had raced "chariots," done time on "Roman" galleys, and forked over substantial premiums for the Tribe's life insurance. Life insurance companies, lacking such rituals, fought hard to gain control of the market. But as late as 1900 a half-million more Americans were insured by fraternal societies than by insurance companies.

Wherever Victorian men came together, someone, it seemed, would propose formal initiations. The Grand Army of the Republic, a veterans' organization, offered three separate rituals, much to the dismay of politically ambitious men such as Oliver Wilson of Indiana who complained that GAR members cared more about the "bauble of ritualism" than pensions. The Knights of Labor, the largest of the post–Civil War labor organizations, provided its membership with three lengthy ceremonies. When Terence Powderly took charge of the Knights, he fought to eliminate the rituals. "The best part of each meeting was taken up in initiating new members, in instructing them in the use of symbols, in hymns and formula that could not be put in the interest of labor outside the meeting room," he complained in his autobiography. But the Knights refused to give up their ceremonies.

At the turn of the century observers estimated that from 20 to 40 percent of all adult men belonged to at least one of the nation's seventy-thousand lodges. Because only the highest-paid manual workers could afford the dues, paraphernalia, and initiation fees, and because Catholic lodge members were threatened with excommunication, the fraternal movement was chiefly an activity of middle-class Protestant men, many of whom belonged to several orders. Initiation was arguably their chief leisure activity.

The money spent on ritual, though incalculable, was by any standard staggering. During the last third of the nineteenth century the Odd Fellows' total revenue was about $150 million; the Freemasons, far more affluent, surely took in several times this amount. The insurance industry estimated the revenue of beneficiary societies at $650 million. All told, fraternal income perhaps approached $2 billion, about what federal government spent on defense during the same period.

Some of this wealth went into costumes, pensions, charity, or the pockets of unscrupulous officials, but much was expended on the temples themselves. In nearly every community the temple of the Masons, Odd Fellows, or Knights of Pythias was a landmark. The spectacular Masonic Temple in Philadelphia, built during the 1870s at a cost of $1.5 million, rivaled Wanamaker's across the street. The Masonic Temple in Chicago, completed in time for the world's fair in 1893, was the tallest building in the world.

We neglect fraternal orders partly because they declined so rapidly in the twentieth century. A new generation of men, when dragged to the lodge by their bosses or fathers-in-law, choked down laughter as the neighborhood grocer, donning the miter of a Jewish high priest, fumbled through an Old Testament lesson for the Odd Fellows or as the superintendent of the ironworks, wearing the headdress of an Iroquois sagamore, brandished a tomahawk and challenged the initiate's fitness for the Improved Order of Red Men. Many young men regaled friends with hilarious accounts of what had transpired at the lodge, and they never went back. Hundreds of smaller orders quietly passed out of existence. Most beneficiary societies, financially dependent on an infusion of young members, were in serious trouble by the 1920s. The Depression finished them off and also wiped out thousands of lodges that could no longer make the mortgage payments on their temples. Within a few years most Americans would associate the orders with Ralph Kramden and Ed Norton of the Loyal Order of Raccoons.

The historical profession came of age during these skeptical years, and academics saw no reason to pay much attention to institutions that were intentionally behind the times. Scholars who bothered to look at the rituals dismissed them as hokum; they assumed that businessmen joined to make contacts, workers to acquire insurance, and others because there was not much else to do. With the development of trade associations and businessmen's clubs, private and governmental insurance, and movies and television, most of the orders expired out of sheer inanity.

But historians erred in thinking of the orders as yet another manifestation of the backwardness of small-town America. The orders in fact thrived especially in large cities. And the businessmen, engineers, and lawyers who spent evenings pretending to be medieval knights or Indian chiefs were by day transforming the United States into an urban-industrial nation.

The popularity of *Iron John* in recent years further confirms that male rituals are not incompatible with modernity. At first glance the slouching, dungareed participants at Bly's mancamps little resemble the somber, stiff faces that stare out from nineteenth-century lodge photographs. But the rituals invented by Bly's mythopoets are uncannily similar to those performed in fraternal lodges more than a century ago.

Both sets of rituals attempted to establish a link to primitive or ancient peoples. Bly proposes that the story of Iron John, though based on a tale the Grimm brothers set down in 1820, may have originated twenty thousand years earlier. Men's movement enthusiasts exalt drumming as an "ancient ritual" and carve wooden masks in honor of "old gods" such as Pan, Orpheus, Shiva, and Dionysus.

More than a hundred years ago Albert Pike—poet, lawyer, Confederate general, and Masonic ritualist—similarly called for a return to the primitive truths that "faded out from men's souls before the world grew old." He viewed Freemasonry as a faint echo of rites practiced by druidic shamans, Eleusinian mystics, and Zoroastrian priests. The Ancient Order of United Workmen and the Improved Order of Red Men in their very names suggested a link to the distant past. They did so not from any romantic attachment to Noble Savages—Native Americans who sought admission to the Red Men were turned away—but to lay claim to rites of prehistoric origin. For much the same reason the Knights of Pythias identified Pythagoras as the first member of their order.

Once they had settled into their tribal sweat lodge, Solomonic temple, or medieval castle, initiates for both the fraternal orders and modern men's groups underwent an initiatory sequence with comparable motifs. After being depicted as deficient or immature, they embarked on arduous journeys revealing the knowledge necessary for self-transformation. Fraternal initiates, their shirts removed or disarranged, were blindfolded and prodded around the lodge. The ritual climaxed when the blindfolds were snatched away. "God said, 'Let there be light,'" Masons were informed.

Men's movement initiates, also blindfolded and their faces smudged or covered with masks, are carried over the heads of members or obliged to crawl on hands and knees. As the drumming reaches a crescendo, the blindfolds are removed. Newcomers to one men's group, after scrambling through a tunnel, are told, "Go. The light is gold."

All fraternal initiates swore themselves to secrecy on pain of allowing brethren to "thrust my tongue through with a red-hot iron" or words to that effect. Fearsome oaths notwithstanding, the orders were remarkably lax. Some, fearing that another would steal an affecting ritual, copyrighted their "secret" work. Everyone recognized that meaningful secrets could not be kept among a million members. Secrecy was chiefly symbolic, a means of strengthening the bond among men by underscoring the exclusion of women. Indeed, no offense was more serious than to tell one's wife the "concerns of the order." Women, for their part, resented the large sums spent on dues and paraphernalia and chafed at their husbands' absence on the frequent lodge nights. In the 1850s the Odd Fellows, seeking to "lessen and ultimately destroy the prejudice of the fairer sex," created a women's auxiliary called the Degree of Rebekah. Still, women were to have no part in men's initiations. "The simple truth is this," one official explained in 1867: "Woman is not entitled to and seeks not a place among us."

Bly's mythopoets initially took a more moderate stand. Because some men's groups met in family rooms or booked events in public facilities, women came and went pretty much as they wished. But it soon became apparent that even their fleeting presence somehow interfered with the proceedings. "Don't have a woman near the meeting space," men's organizers warned. The need for secrecy and exclusion was driven home after one exuberant group invited the media to a weekend mancamp. Bly telegrammed a warning: The mythopoetic movement was still in its "infancy," and its rituals would be ridiculed by the public. But by then a small army of freelance journalists had already filled their notebooks with arch accounts of what they had seen. "A luscious hologram of multilayered idiocy," Joe Queenan of *GQ* wrote. Now most men's groups exclude women and outsiders. Many swear participants to secrecy—one reason less has been heard of them in recent months.

If women were conspicuous by their absence, "fathers" were omnipresent—in both fraternal and men's groups. The central drama of fraternal rituals derived from the hostility of "elderly" officers—patriarchs with flowing white beards or sachems leaning upon walking sticks—toward the callow initiates—"squaws," "pages," "children." Tension between surrogate father and son rose to a climax. Suddenly, usually on completion of the initiatory journey, the officer embraced the initiate. Father and son had become brothers.

Bly's goal is similar. Young men today do not know what it means to be a man because their fathers—"enfeebled, dejected, paltry"—failed to teach them. Bly's hairy Wildman serves as a surrogate for the clean-shaven (or absent) male cipher of the modern family. Some men's groups place an empty "Spirit Chair" at the front of the room, a mute reminder (and perhaps indictment) of the missing fathers.

Rituals such as these, abstracted from a "sacred" context and a community of shared sentiment, seem so artificial as to verge on fraud. (Some wags during the nineteenth century said that the orders had been invented by novelty companies; today critics propose that men's group organizers have a stake in drum companies). Many find it hard not to agree with Lance Morrow of *Time,* who called the men's movement a "depthless happening in the goofy circus of America," language reminiscent of the nineteenth-century criticisms of the lodges.

But though contrived, the rituals—then and now—are not without effect. Mancamp participants are commonly convulsed with sobs. A reporter for *Esquire,* while sniggering at what he described as a "Three Stooges skit," was taken aback by the "murderously authentic" moans and weeping around him. In 1877 the *Voice of Masonry* observed that fraternal initiates became "so wrought upon and their feelings so excited that they shed tears." The National Christian Association, founded in 1867 to rid the nation of the orders, acknowledged the mysterious power of the rituals and identified Satan as their source. Members took degree after degree "as a charmed frog goes into a snake's mouth."

To what, indeed, can we attribute the enduring attraction of men's rituals? Bly, whose views matter if only because he predicted the movement his book inspired, responds that all men possess an intuitive attraction to the requisite rituals of manhood, which are "still very much alive in our genetic structure." But until scientists find a peptide chain curled along the Y chromosome that impels men to caper in mudholes or don outlandish headgear, his argument will persuade few who are not already wedded to Jung's notion that some ideas are factory-installed in the brain. Moreover, Bly's belief that men are predisposed to such rituals fails to explain why American men had to invent them in the first place or why so many of their great-grandchildren scorned their vaunted rites.

Some social scientists regard male rites as attempts by men to assert their fading power over women. In this vein, many feminists view the mythopoets as part of a backlash against their movement, a longing for the good old days when men were Wildmen and women chattel; they brush aside the pro-feminist protestations of Bly and his followers as little more than a smoke screen.

Many women in the nineteenth century, particularly those active in reform and women's rights, had similar misgivings about what transpired behind the lodge's thick veil of secrecy. If, as defenders of the orders claimed, fraternal rituals were designed to make initiates "gentle, charitable, and tender as a woman," why weren't women permitted to see what went on? If the purpose of the orders were laudable, why were they so elaborately cloaked in secrecy? The charge that men's rituals are a male reaction against the advances of women has surfaced repeatedly; it is probably not far from wrong.

By the first few decades of the nineteenth century, women were assuming a new place within the homes of the emerging middle classes. At a time when lawyers and merchants—not to mention legions of ambitious inventors and clerks—fastened their attention upon the prospects of making money within the rapidly expanding national economy, they all but abandoned patriarchal traditions of men's religious and moral guidance. And women, delivered from many of the crushing burdens of farm life, eagerly filled the void left by men's withdrawal from the "domestic sphere." Their special task, women now proclaimed, was to redeem the nation from a hardhearted materialism by instilling in children the gentle and self-effacing virtues of Christ.

When the men who had been reared in such homes came of age, they found themselves inhabiting a competitive world where the government safety net was but a few filaments in the imaginations of the likes of Edward Bellamy and Henry George. How were these young men to reconcile the demands of bosses and the remorseless workings of the market with the lessons of love learned at a mother's knee? How reconcile the Darwinian world of adult men with the peaceable promises of childhood?

Fraternal rituals offered psychological guidance by leading men from the precepts and enticements of childhood into a closer affinity with bosses and bankers, customers and colleagues. It did so by attenuating adult men's associations with childhood and women and by strengthening the ties amongst themselves. The rituals provided a religious experience antithetical to what they had learned as youths and supplanted the familial bonds of childhood with the brotherhood of the lodge.

Lodge officials insisted that their rites accorded with Christianity. There was seemingly no reason for initiates to view the religion of the lodge with suspicion: lodge meetings usually began with a minister offering a prayer, all initiates were obliged to profess belief in God, most rituals were drawn from the Bible, and the setting itself resembled nothing so much as the church. But the altars, chalices, coffins, and flickering candles, when used as props to enact the destruction of King Solomon's Temple (Royal Arch Masonry), the execution of a spy (Grand Army of the Republic), or a sojourn through the "calcined wastes" of Hades (Knights of Pythias), conveyed lessons far different from what ministers imparted to their flocks on Sunday. The deity of the lodge was distant and impersonal, totally unlike the loving God that then prevailed in Protestant churches.

The rituals, too, provided a family psychodrama that drew initiates from the feminine attachments of childhood and brought them, by means of an initiatory "rebirth," into a new family of brothers. This transference climaxed with the reconciliation of the initiate—the son—with his new father.

The rituals of Bly's mythopoets seem to function much the same way, evoking the "old gods" of patriarchal tradition, imitating the warrior rites of tribal societies, enshrining ancient kings and heroes. From these imaginative realms women are almost entirely absent. Modern men cling tightly to Iron John partly because he carries them into a world where manhood is unencumbered by gender-role ambiguities.

The leaders of fraternal orders nowadays take unabashed pride in the "masculine" character of their rites and express misgivings over what they regard as the "feminine" inventions of the men's movement: the "touchy-feely" quality of the steam baths, naked romps in the woods, the self-revelatory discussions that stretch deep into the night. Such experiences may well be therapeutic, states Harry E. Echols, a lawyer and prominent Odd Fellow and Freemason in Washington, D.C., but they lack the ongoing fellowship of the lodge and meaningful rituals that, burnished by the passage of time, reflect the wisdom of the past.

Echols's statement points out that more than gender is involved in the appeal of men's rituals. The orders and the men's groups seize upon the distant past because it offers something of an antidote to the modern world. Victorian men, driven by sales and production quotas, buffeted by the vagaries of distant markets, and trapped in widening webs of corporate bureaucracies, retreated on lodge nights into a mystic wonderland inhabited by gods and heroes, kings and knights, a place where identity was conferred rather than imperiled. The unreality of the lodge was its chief attraction.

The same may be true of the mancamps. When one participant complained that its rituals were ridiculous, an organizer explained that the weekend's purpose was to let people "get beyond the logical world." The rational demands of the modern world for system, regularity, and order may spawn an antithetical world of fantasy and emotional expression. Tocqueville put it somewhat differently: The material satisfactions of life notwithstanding, "the soul has needs that must be fulfilled."

The emergence of Bly and of the Wildman he brought back from the primordial depths of the human soul serves as a reminder that the road to the future may take some strange detours. The enduring appeal of compensatory anachronisms—not to mention the resurgence of religious fundamentalism and ethnic nationalism—shows the emotional power of pre-modern values and beliefs. When we finally arrive at the year 2001, it may bear less resemblance to the aseptic and androgynous landscapes of Stanley Kubrick than to terrain through which we passed centuries ago.

Butte, America

Dan Baum

In the 1920s Butte, Montana, with a population of nearly 100,000, was the biggest and wealthiest inland city of the Northwest. By the end of the century, the population was less than 40,000, and only the hard-core boosters could claim distinction for the declining town. In this essay Dan Baum calls Butte "one of American history's great disappearing acts." The statement was even literally true, because Butte's economy was built on the nearby metal ores its inhabitants mined: when a large seam of copper was found beneath the city itself during the 1950s, entire neighborhoods were dug up and destroyed, leaving great gashes in the downtown. As the ores subsequently disappeared, so did many of Butte's inhabitants. Economic decline was followed by environmental calamity. With a natural storyteller's delight, Baum recalls Butte in its heyday, inhabited by rough men and loose women. He also recounts the titanic struggle between the Anaconda Copper Mining Company, which controlled all of Montana, and "Big Bill" Haywood's radical Western Federation of Mineworkers. But Baum's searing critique of 20th-century Butte is tempered by his obvious love for the place, which he calls "a beguiling collection of elegant buildings wrapped in mountains and glowing in mile-high sunlight." More, it is a place made rich by its past. Baum's most recent book is *Citizen Coors: An American Dynasty* (2000).

It's spooky up here on the top floor of the Metals Bank & Trust Building. Shards of glass and crumbled plaster crunch underfoot, obscuring the elegant tile pattern of the corridor floor. Heavy oak doors with pebbled windows and missing knobs stand open to the hallway. Inside what used to be plush offices, the hardwood floors are buckling under porcelain washstands flecked with pigeon droppings. At one time this was some of the most exclusive real estate within a thousand miles. Now it gives me the creeps.

Still, I've hiked up seven flights for the view. Bracing myself in the frame of a broken window, I peer down on what was once the "richest hill on earth." Majestic offices and apartment blocks rise below me, thick with terra-cotta embroidery. The Curtis Music Hall across the street, built in 1892, could be a fairytale castle. Beyond it, turreted mansions with broad verandas dot the hillside, rising from a dense jumble of cottages, brownstones, stores, and churches. The whole scene evokes a city in the long-inhabited, densely packed East—Boston perhaps, or Baltimore. Until, that is, I look out just a little farther to see the empty Montana prairie and beyond that a horizon of jagged, snowy mountains. The effect is disorienting.

And where are all the people? It's rush hour, but the traffic lights are blinking uselessly at one another along the grand avenues. Few storefronts are boarded, but most of the windows above them are dark. A handful of people are making their way along sidewalks built wide enough for throngs. What happened here?

Butte, Montana, has been one of American history's great disappearing acts. In the time that it took the United States to move in and out of the industrial age, a major city blossomed on the Continental Divide, flourished, withered, dried up, and blew away. During the early years of the century, Butte was a big, noisy cog in our national machinery, greater in population than Houston, Dallas, or Phoenix and as crucial to the economy for the copper it mined as Detroit was for engines or Pittsburgh for steel. It was a major vaudeville stop, a place no presidential candidate could miss, a daily destination for the thirty-eight passenger trains on five separate railroads. More than five hundred miles from the nearest ocean, Butte had among its thousands whole communities of people who led their entire lives speaking nothing but Serbian or Chinese, Croatian or Italian, Finnish, Spanish, German. By the time the 1920s began, Butte was the biggest and wealthiest city in a vast region stretching from Minnesota on the east and Spokane on the west and Salt Lake City on the south, the center of politics, culture, and finance for the entire inland Northwest. There was a time when you didn't have to say, "Butte, Montana," just "Butte."

Now that city is gone. All that is left is a small town rattling along inside the corpse of a great one. Barely a third of Butte's former population remains, and most of it has abandoned the majestic city on the hill for a flossy commercial suburb spread across the valley below. The Butte mines, which once produced half the country's copper, are long dead, although everywhere you look you can see their black derricks, perched over the silent shafts. The good times in Butte were fleeting. Copper prices started sliding with the last shot of the Great War, and all through the decades that followed, Butte spiraled slowly and fitfully downward as technology pushed copper aside. Electric utilities no longer needed the metal for their transmission wires; they had lighter and cheaper aluminum. Telephone conversations could travel via fiber optics and, eventually, satellite relays. Foreign mines and scrap could supply what little copper American industry needed.

Other American cities have suffered—Flint, Michigan, and Lowell, Massachusetts, come to mind—but they were components of the automobile and textile archipelagoes, not economic giants unto themselves. They also grew up short buggy rides away from sister cities, while Butte stood alone on the vast old bison range—"an island in a sea of land," locals called it. "In terms of its size and architecture," says the University of Montana historian David Emmons, "Butte is like no place else I know."

The top floor of the Metals Bank & Trust Building offers an overview, but to understand Butte, a visitor also needs an underview, a peek at the tunnels that worm their way for hundreds of miles beneath the hill to the sources of the city's bygone riches.

On a January morning five years ago, Joe Driscoll, a stout young engineer of Irish descent, loaded me into an ore car, and we slid, Jonah-like, down the cold gullet of the earth. That day Driscoll was the last man working underground in Butte, pulling out old equipment for salvage.

"I can't stand to see it end," he shouted over the clatter of the ore car. The tunnel was damp and cramped and palpably dangerous, with boulders hanging low overhead and rusted equipment reaching out to gouge us at every turn. This was

At the turn of the century Miner's Union Day brought throngs out into Butte's streets.

how Butte's men went to work for four generations, spending themselves against dark rock for wages unheard of in the Old World. As we stared up into an old stope, a hollowed-out vein of ore thirty feet across and so high my headlamp couldn't find where it stopped, voices returned to us as the mutter of ghosts. I could barely wait to get back to the surface, but Driscoll wanted to linger. "My last day is a week from tomorrow," he said, idly fingering the jagged rock wall beside him. "Then I'll be an artist for the state—drawing unemployment."

Most of the shafts closed in the 1950s, when Butte made a Pyrrhic stab at modernizing by digging an open-pit mine right inside the city limits. As the Montana writer Ivan Doig puts it, the city spent three decades willingly "eating its own guts," razing block after block of vibrant ethnic neighborhoods. Finntown; the Italian stronghold of Meaderville; "Dublin Gulch"; and the McQueen Addition, home to Croatians who called themselves Austrians, met the wrecking ball to make way for the Pit. For a while it looked as though the entire business district would go under too, but the Pit played out before that could happen, leaving behind, when it closed in 1983, a mile-and-a-half square that, viewed from the visitors' platform on the southwest rim, almost defies belief. It's one of the biggest man-made holes on earth, an inverted monument to human labor.

Among Butte's first prospectors were itinerant Chinese, sprung from the railroads and scratching up bits of gold and silver as they sought a new livelihood. But the discovery of copper there in 1876—the year of the first telephone conversation, the year of the Philadelphia Centennial Exhibition with its array of inventions animated by copper-conducted electricity—changed everything. In a matter of weeks the squalid nomadic miners' settlement around the shark-fin-shaped Big Butte became the center of the mining universe.

An old tent city of three hundred men exploded into a boomtown of five banks, seven breweries, three cigar factories, and more than one hundred saloons. By 1890 the area's population had grown nearly a hundredfold to some twenty-three thousand people, and the newly incorporated Butte City was churning out more than a million dollars' worth of ore a month. Butte had the nation's first electrified train and the first labor union west of the Mississippi River, and World War I raised it even higher: Every rifle cartridge fired in the war contained an ounce of pure copper, and 1917 was Butte's high-water mark. That year's city directory lists more than ninety-six thousand souls, and considering the additional hordes of journeymen miners migrating through, the number present in Butte at any one time was likely much higher.

In an ironic stroke of luck for urban historians and architecture buffs, a fire wiped out the Butte business district in 1879, inspiring the new city council to pass as its tenth ordinance a ban on wood-frame structures in the center of town. Many of the exuberant stone and brick buildings remaining in uptown Butte rose soon after. Opulently frosted with cornice and gargoyle, they recall the same era and mentality that built the mansions on New York's upper Fifth Avenue when industrialists strove to outdo one another in the architectural expression of their wealth.

Butte's savage winters dictated the city's peculiar layout. Nobody wanted to walk far through Montana's shearing arctic winds, so the houses and stores were clustered tightly around the mines. People dug mineshafts in back yards, schoolyards, alleys, even basements. The proximity of mines to homes had some odd repercussions. "When I was growing up, you'd hear it in the walls: a whup-whup-whup—carumph!" remembers sixty-year-old Jiggsie Elphison. "The miners would ask my mother, 'Dja hear us last night? We had a feeling we were near your house.' Sometimes a family would feel the *carumph!* and look out the window to find a hole where the sidewalk used to be." To this day uptown Butte feels like no other city in the West. It is darker, grittier, more vertical and compact. "The density here is what makes Butte so unusual for the West and much more like an Eastern city," says Bob Corbett, a Butte native and architect whose own futuristic house is a hundred-foot concrete cube that once served as an ore bin.

Butte drew miners and laborers from every corner of the globe. The discovery of copper also brought Chinese and Jewish merchants to the town; indeed, the city's first mayor was Jewish. And by the turn of the century, the government's fourth-largest immigration office was in Butte. A 1918 survey revealed that Butte families had origins in thirty-eight different countries. The seven slender smokestacks of Butte's Neversweat Mine were such a well-known image around the world that immigrants would arrive at Ellis Island speaking no English, clutching only a picture of the Neversweat. Immigration officers would recognize it and help get them on the proper train.

The historian David Emmons has studied thousands of antique Butte photos and says that he has never once seen a man wearing a cowboy hat. "People in Butte never thought of themselves as Montanans," he says. "They identified first with Butte and then with places overseas—the countries they came from or other places where copper was mined." Still popular on baseball caps and bumper stickers here is the legend "Butte, America."

The city began as a polyglot oddity and remains one today, retaining an intense ethnic flavor unusual not only in Montana but anywhere in rural America. Butte's ethnic neighborhoods are gone, but this is still the only place within five hundred miles—outside of an Indian reservation—where you're likely to hear any language besides English. Some 150 Serbian families gather every Sunday in an ornate Eastern Orthodox church for a service in the language of the old country. Mexicans celebrate the Festival of Guadalupe in Spanish. The Jewish community is big enough to maintain the city's elegantly restored 1903-vintage synagogue and to fly a rabbi up from Los Angeles once a month for Sabbath services in Hebrew. Frank Mandic still speaks "Austrian" to the old customers at his Terminal Meat Market on Park Street, and Michael Mazzolini, a forty-two-year-old restaurateur and preservation activist born in Meaderville, hardly spoke English until he went to first grade. Even in the early 1960s, he says, Italian would get you by. "It's like something from the last century, isn't it?"

Although Finntown was almost entirely bulldozed to make way for the open-pit mine, Envin Niemi's Helsinki bar was spared; today it overlooks a field of weeds that was once a Scandinavian neighborhood. When the earth behind Niemi's subsided into an abandoned mining tunnel many years ago, the owner took advantage of the sudden topographical change to build into the bar's underside one of Butte's most cherished institutions: round-the-clock saunas. (IT'S PRONOUNCED SOW-NA, barks the sign above the bar, NOT SAW-NA.)

Emerging dusty and cold from my tour of the mine, I headed for the Helsinki, feeling as badly in need of a sweat as any Finnish ore mucker. The saunas aren't elegant, but they're clean and roaring hot. Once thoroughly smelted, I followed tradition back into the bar, where the idea is to start repoisoning oneself immediately with beer, vodka, and a bottle of homemade pickled herring that moves along the counter with a communal fork. The sign above the stuffed bison head reminds me I'm in Butte: BROKEN ENGLISH UNDERSTOOD HERE.

Since the first mineshaft was dug, the people of Butte have endured a series of plagues with remarkable humor. Miners who inhaled the dust from broken rock contracted silicosis, a slow killer also known as miner's "con," or consumption. Pneumonia, too, claimed many miners ascending to a Butte winter from a hundred-degree tunnel. ("When my father was a boy, he used to watch the miners explode—really explode—in a cloud of steam as they hit the cold air," says Jim Harrington, a retired Butte High School history teacher.) Then there were the cave-ins and other catastrophes. Nobody knows exactly how many men died in the Speculator Mine fire on June 8, 1917, but it was American history's worst hard-rock mining disaster, claiming at least 169 lives. "On average, one miner died in an accident every other day for the thirty-year stretch that ended in 1925," says Harrington, who conducted research for a monument to the Speculator Mine victims that was dedicated last summer. "And everybody wondered why the workers fought back," he adds.

Fight they did. Butte was the battlefield where one of the world's biggest corporations took on one of the world's toughest unions. The Anaconda Copper Mining Company, the fourth-largest company on earth during Butte's zenith, owned virtually every mine on the hill by 1927 and ruled not only Butte but all Montana. "The great Commonwealth of Montana is a dual entity," wrote Oswald Garrison Villard in *The Nation* in 1930. "There is the State, supposedly a free and independent part of the Union, and there is 'the Company,' otherwise [known as] the Anaconda Copper Mining Company. It is not always easy to differentiate between the two . . . ."

Against the Anaconda colossus stood a city full of workers so thoroughly organized that the labor hero "Big Bill" Haywood called it "the greatest single social force of the working class in the western part of America." Every trade had its union backed by the muscle of Local Number One of the Western Federation of Miners, perhaps the strongest American union ever. Solidarity among unions in Butte was legendary. "You couldn't paint your own storefront without getting picketed," remembers Frank Mandic. . . .

It was in Butte that company goons lynched Frank Little, an organizer for the radical Industrial Workers of the World. His gravestone at the bottom of Butte Hill reads like an IWW call to arms:

Frank Little
1879–1917
SLAIN BY CAPITALIST
INTERESTS
FOR ORGANIZING AND
INSPIRING
HIS FELLOW MEN

Clashes between Anaconda and the unions were fought in the streets and in the mines with rocks and bottles, even guns and dynamite. Every few years Butte suffered grueling months of shutdown owing to strikes, low copper prices, or company efforts to break the unions. Butte's work was hard and dangerous but barely more so than its play.

The mines worked every hour of the day, so every eight hours another shift of miners and smeltermen would flood the bars and brothels. Although the rest of the state had closing laws, Butte tradition required barkeeps to unlock their shops on opening day and throw the keys into the gutter. The brothels were famous throughout the West, from the "parlors" to the low-rent "cribs"—individual rooms just big enough for a cot and a door opening onto the street. (One such row of cribs is now an electrical shop on Mercury Street; across the way is the old Dumas, once a famous brothel and now an antiques shop.) It was Butte that introduced keno to America, adapting it from a Chinese gambling game, and it was Butte that ended the antiliquor crusading career of Carry Nation.

Nation showed up with her ax in 1910, having busted up saloons and whiskey barrels from New York to Chicago. But on her first foray in Butte, she ran into May Maloy, a barkeep and madam who beat her so badly that Nation fled town and retired from her jihad for good.

Life in Butte has never been for the meek. Maybe because the present is so diminished and the future so uncertain, Butte tends to live in the past; people talk about copper barons a century dead as though they still walked the streets. Butte's is a thoroughly disreputable history, and that's exactly how Butte likes it. The visitor is shown the old whorehouses of Mercury Street and the bullet hole in the judge's bench long before anyone gets around to mentioning the art museum. Even civic boosters recount with positive nostalgia events other cities would soon forget, like the nadir of corruption when a junkie cop held up a drugstore with his service revolver. ("How many kids does it take to play cops and robbers in Butte?" goes the joke. "One.")

As if financial calamity weren't enough, Butte is the nation's number one environmental disaster. After a century of gouging and smelting the earth into giving up its riches, Butte stands coated with heavy-metal tailings and arsenic-laden smelter soot. The water is barely drinkable, the slag heaps that tower everywhere are eroding into back yards, and the Pit, which is filling with water at a rate of more than five million gallons a day, already contains an eight-hundred-foot-deep acid lake. The Environmental Protection Agency (EPA) expects the cleanup here to take years, if not decades, and millions, if not billions, of dollars.

But somehow, even this seems only to make Butte's citizens fonder of their town. There's civic pride—half inspiring, half perverse—in being weird enough to love with all your heart a place as wrecked, raw, and inhospitable as Butte, America. Even in 1902 Butte was such a god-forsaken place that the local writer Mary MacLane called it "near the perfection of ugliness." And the Butte poet Berton Braley wrote in 1905:

> *She's beautiful too, in her fashion,*
> *In her wonderful, strange old ways;*
> *With her chimneys and throbbing engines,*
> *Her hillsides marred and gray.*

Only those who absolutely had to leave when the Pit closed did so. The city lost forty-four hundred jobs in the eighties, and it's a measure of how many people cherish Butte that only about that many packed up and left town. (While there's no exact formula, the loss of one job in a city usually results in several people leaving as entire families pack their bags.) But in an era when people across the country are fretting about the erosion of community, it's common in Butte to find three or even four generations living within walking distance of one another in Old World intimacy, often sharing meager paychecks and pensions. "Butte people have a real sense of living," says Dan Dysinger, a Reno, Nevada, metallurgist who had to leave Butte nearly twenty years ago, "a good sense of priorities. Money is not an overriding concern. It's being near their families, their friends, and having fun. My parents and two sisters still live there, and I'm trying to get back, 'cause I want my kids to know what that's about."

Having indentured itself to "the Company," endangered its physical health, and eaten the very earth from under its feet to stay alive, Butte is now beginning to make a living off its history. The six square miles of uptown Butte—what the EPA calls the biggest Superfund site in America—is also the second-biggest National

Historic Landmark District, after downtown Lowell, Massachusetts. And now that the mines are silent and the arsenic smoke has cleared, Butte is a beguiling collection of elegant buildings wrapped in mountains and glowing in mile-high sunlight. Butte's residents see all that and point to Montana's growing allure as a vacation and retirement haven, and Mark Reavis, Butte's historic preservation officer, wants more of the thousands of tourists who seek out Montana to explore this strange and vibrant chapter of American history. After all, as he asks, "Where else can you see what you see in Butte?"

Reavis, an imposing six feet five with bright red hair, can work himself into a beard-pulling, arm-waving lather extolling his town's architecture and history. "The finest example of industrial American architecture in the country," he exclaims during a conversation in the 1910-vintage courthouse that's grandiose enough to be an opera house. "What took place here happened nowhere else!" . . .

The Age of the Bosses

William V. Shannon

The rapid industrialization of the United States after the Civil War, which produced great tycoons such as Andrew Carnegie and encouraged millions of work-hungry Europeans to migrate, changed the shape of society in a variety of ways. One of the most obvious and important of these was industrialization's effect on where and how people lived. Huge industrial concerns brought together masses of workers in one place; commercial and service enterprises sprang up alongside the factories; in short, great cities rapidly developed and America was on its way to becoming an urban nation.

The advantages of urbanization were great—new wealth, better educational opportunities, a wide range of amusements; soon a more refined and complex culture emerged. But great problems also appeared—crowded, unhealthy living conditions, crime and vice, and countless others. Not the least of these was the problem of how to govern these gigantic agglomerations. More government was essential to run a city, yet the nation had lived for the better part of a century by the motto: "that government is best which governs least." New kinds of government were necessary—building and sanitary codes, social services, a system of representation suited to a mass but atomized society—for which no precedents existed.

It was this situation, as William V. Shannon explains, that produced the big-city political machines and the bosses who ran them. Shannon shows that the bosses served a function; they filled a gap in the political system created by the changes resulting from swift industrialization and urban growth. Eventually better machinery than the "machine" was devised to perform that function, although the proper government of cities still eludes us today. As a former editor of the New York Times, Mr. Shannon brings to this subject a thorough knowledge of modern urban politics and, as the author of The American Irish, an equally solid understanding of the old boss system.

The big cities and the political bosses grew up together in America. Bossism, with all its color and corruption and human drama, was a natural, perhaps even a necessary accompaniment to the rapid development of cities. The new urban communities did not grow slowly and according to plan; on the contrary, huge conglomerations of people from all over the world and from widely varying backgrounds came together suddenly, and in an unplanned, unorganized fashion fumbled their way toward communal relationships and a common identity. The political bosses emerged to cope with this chaotic change and growth. Acting out of greed, a ruthless will for mastery, and an imperfect understanding of what they were about, the bosses imposed upon these conglomerations called cities a certain feudal order and direction.

By 1890 virtually every sizable city had a political boss or was in the process of developing one. By 1950, sixty years later, almost every urban political machine was in an advanced state of obsolescence and its boss in trouble. The reason is not hard to find. Some of the cities kept growing and all of them kept changing, but the bosses, natural products of a specific era, could not grow or change beyond a certain point. The cities became essentially different, and as they did, the old-style organizations, like all organisms which cannot adapt, began to die. The dates vary from city to city. The system began earlier and died sooner in New York. Here or there, an old-timer made one last comeback. In Chicago, the organization and its boss still survive. But exceptions aside, the late nineteenth century saw the beginning, and the middle twentieth, the end, of the Age of the Bosses. What follows is a brief history of how it began, flourished, and passed away.

Soft-spoken Irish farmers from County Mayo and bearded Jews from Poland, country boys from Ohio and sturdy peasants from Calabria, gangling Swedes from near the Arctic Circle and Chinese from Canton, laconic Yankees from Vermont villages and Negro freedmen putting distance between themselves and the old plantation—all these and many other varieties of human beings from every national and religious and cultural tradition poured into America's cities in the decades after the Civil War.

Rome and Alexandria in the ancient world had probably been as polyglot, but in modern times the diversity of American cities was unique. Everywhere in the Western world, cities were growing rapidly in the late nineteenth century; but the Germans from the countryside who migrated to Hamburg and Berlin, the English who moved to Birmingham and London, and the French who flocked to Paris stayed among fellow nationals. They might be mocked as country bumpkins and their clothes might be unfashionable, but everyone they met spoke the same language as themselves, observed the same religious and secular holidays, ate the same kind of food, voted—if they had the franchise at all—in the same elections, and shared the same sentiments and expectations. To move from farm or village to a big European city was an adventure, but one still remained within the reassuring circle of the known and the familiar.

In American cities, however, the newcomers had nothing in common with one another except their poverty and their hopes. They were truly "the up-rooted." The foreign-born, unless they came from the British Isles, could not speak the language of their new homeland. The food, the customs, the holidays, the politics, were alien. Native Americans migrating to the cities from the countryside experienced their own kind of cultural shock: they found themselves competing not with other Americans but with recently arrived foreigners, so that despite their native birth they, too, felt displaced, strangers in their own country.

It was natural for members of each group to come together to try to find human warmth and protection in Little Italy or Cork Hill or Chinatown or Harlem. These feelings of clannish solidarity were one basis of strength for the political bosses. A man will more readily give his vote to a candidate because he is a neighbor from the old country or has some easily identifiable relationship, if only a similar name or the same religion, than because of agreement on some impersonal issue. Voters can take vicarious satisfaction from his success: "One of our boys is making good."

With so many different races and nationalities living together, however, mutual antagonisms were present, and the opportunity for hostility to flare into open violence was never far away. Ambitious, unscrupulous politicians could have exploited these antagonisms for their own political advantage, but the bosses and the political organizations which they developed did not function that way. If a man could vote and would "vote right," he was accepted, and that was the end of the matter. What lasting profit was there in attacking his religion or deriding his background?

Tammany early set the pattern of cultivating every bloc and faction and making an appeal as broad-based as possible. Of one precinct captain on the Lower East Side it was said: "He eats corned beef and kosher meat with equal nonchalance, and it's all the same to him whether he takes off his hat in the church or pulls it down over his ears in the synagogue."

Bosses elsewhere instinctively followed the same practice. George B. Cox, the turn-of-the-century Republican boss of Cincinnati, pasted together a coalition of Germans, Negroes, and old families like the Tafts and the Longworths. James M. Curley, who was mayor of Boston on and off for thirty-six years and was its closest approximation to a political boss, ran as well in the Lithuanian neighborhood of South Boston and the Italian section of East Boston as he did in the working-class Irish wards. In his last term in City Hall, he conferred minor patronage on the growing Negro community and joined the N.A.A.C.P.

The bosses organized neighborhoods, smoothed out antagonisms, arranged ethnically balanced tickets, and distributed patronage in accordance with voting strength as part of their effort to win and hold power. They blurred divisive issues and buried racial and religious hostility with blarney and buncombe. They were not aware that they were actually performing a mediating, pacifying function. They did not realize that by trying to please as many people as possible they were helping to hold raw new cities together, providing for inexperienced citizens a common meeting ground in politics and an experience in working together that would not have been available if the cities had been governed by apolitical bureaucracies. Bossism was usually corrupt and was decidedly inefficient, but in the 1960s, when antipoverty planners try to stimulate "community action organizations" to break through the apathy and disorganization of the slums, we can appreciate that the old-style machines had their usefulness.

When William Marcy Tweed, the first and most famous of the big-city bosses, died in jail in 1878, several hundred workingmen showed up for his funeral. The *Nation* wrote the following week:

> Let us remember that he fell without loss of reputation among the bulk of his supporters. The bulk of the poorer voters of this city today revere his memory, and look on him as the victim of rich men's malice; as, in short, a friend of the needy who applied the public funds, with as little waste as was possible under the circumstances, to the purposes to which they ought to be applied—and that is to the making of work for the working man. The odium heaped on him in the pulpits last Sunday does not exist in the lower stratum of New York society.

This split in attitude toward political bosses between the impoverished many and the prosperous middle classes lingers today and still colors historical writing.

To respectable people, the boss was an exotic, even grotesque figure. They found it hard to understand why anyone would vote for him or what the sources of his popularity were. To the urban poor, those sources were self-evident. The boss ran a kind of ramshackle welfare state. He helped the unemployed find jobs, interceded in court for boys in trouble, wrote letters home to the old country for the illiterate; he provided free coal and baskets of food to tide a widow over an emergency, and organized parades, excursions to the beach, and other forms of free entertainment. Some bosses, such as Frank Hague in Jersey City and Curley in Boston, were energetic patrons of their respective city hospitals, spending public funds lavishly on new construction, providing maternity and children's clinics, and arranging medical care for the indigent. In an era when social security, Blue Cross, unemployment compensation, and other public and private arrangements to cushion life's shocks did not exist, these benefactions from a political boss were important.

In every city, the boss had his base in the poorer, older, shabbier section of town. Historians have dubbed this section the "walking city" because it developed in the eighteenth and early nineteenth centuries, when houses and businesses were jumbled together, usually near the waterfront, and businessmen and laborers alike had to live within walking distance of their work. As transportation improved, people were able to live farther and farther from their place of work. Population dispersed in rough concentric circles: the financially most successful lived in the outer ring, where land was plentiful and the air was clean; the middle classes lived in intermediate neighborhoods; and the poorest and the latest arrivals from Europe crowded into the now-rundown neighborhoods in the center, where rents were lowest. Politics in most cities reflected a struggle between the old, boss-run wards downtown and the more prosperous neighborhoods farther out, which did not need a boss's services and which championed reform. The more skilled workingmen and the white-collar workers who lived in the intermediate neighborhoods generally held the balance of power between the machine and the reformers. A skillful boss could hold enough of these swing voters on the basis of ethnic loyalty or shared support of a particular issue. At times, he might work out alliances with business leaders who found that an understanding with a boss was literally more businesslike than dependence upon the vagaries of reform.

But always it was the poorest and most insecure who provided the boss with the base of his political power. Their only strength, as Professor Richard C. Wade of the University of Chicago has observed, was in their numbers.

> These numbers were in most cases a curse; housing never caught up with demand, the job market was always flooded, the breadwinner had too many mouths to feed. Yet in politics such a liability could be turned into an asset. If the residents could be mobilized, their combined strength would be able to do what none could do alone. Soon the "boss" and the "machine" arose to organize this potential. The boss system was simply the political expression of inner city life.

At a time when many newcomers to the city were seeking unskilled work, and when many families had a precarious economic footing, the ability to dispense jobs was crucial to the bosses. First, there were jobs to be filled on the city payroll. Just as vital, and far more numerous, were jobs on municipal construction projects. When the machine controlled a city, public funds were always being spent for more schools, hospitals, libraries, courthouses, and orphanages. The growing cities had to have more sewer lines, gas lines, and waterworks, more paved streets and trolley tracks. Even if these utilities were privately owned, the managers needed the good-will of city hall and were responsive to suggestions about whom to hire.

The payrolls of these public works projects were often padded, but to those seeking a job, it was better to be on a padded payroll than on no payroll. By contrast, the municipal reformers usually cut back on public spending, stopped projects to in-vestigate for graft, and pruned payrolls. Middle- and upper-income taxpayers wel-comed these reforms, but they were distinctly unpopular in working-class wards.

Another issue that strengthened the bosses was the regulation of the sale of liquor. Most women in the nineteenth century did not drink, and with their back-ing, the movement to ban entirely the manufacture and sale of liquor grew steadily stronger. It had its greatest support among Protestants with a rural or small-town background. To them the cities, with their saloons, dance halls, cheap theatres, and red-light districts, were becoming latter-day versions of Sodom and Gomorrah.

Many of the European immigrants in the cities, however, had entirely different values. Quite respectable Germans took their wives to beer gardens on Sundays. In the eyes of the Irish, keeping a "public house" was an honorable occupation. Some Irish women drank beer and saw no harm in going to the saloon or sending an older child for a bucketful—"rushing the growler," they called it. Poles, Czechs, Italians, and others also failed to share the rage of the Prohibitionists against sa-loons. Unable to entertain in their cramped tenements, they liked to congregate in neighborhood bars.

The machine also appealed successfully on the liquor issue to many middle-class ethnic voters who had no need of the machine's economic assistance. Thus, in New York in 1897, Tammany scored a sweeping victory over an incumbent reform administration that had tried to enforce a state law permitting only hotels to sell liquor on Sundays. As one of the city's three police commissioners, Theodore Roosevelt became famous prowling the tougher neighborhoods on the hunt for sa-loon violations, but on the vaudeville stage the singers were giving forth with the hit song, "I Want What I Want When I Want It!" As a character in Alfred Henry Lewis' *The Boss* explained it, the reformers had made a serious mistake: "They got between the people and its beer!"

In 1902, Lincoln Steffens, the muckraker who made a name for himself writing about political bossism, visited St. Louis to interview Joseph W. Folk, a crusading district attorney. "It is good businessmen that are corrupting our bad politicians," Folk told him. "It is good business that causes bad government in St. Louis." Thirty-five years later, Boss Tom Pendergast was running the entire state of Missouri on that same reciprocal relationship.

Although many factory owners could be indifferent to politics, other business-men were dependent upon the goodwill and the efficiency of the municipal gov-ernment. The railroads that wanted to build their freight terminals and extend their lines into the cities, the contractors who erected the office buildings, the banks that held mortgages on the land and loaned money for the construction, the utility and transit companies, and the department stores were all in need of li-censes, franchises, rights of way, or favorable rulings from city inspectors and agencies. These were the businesses that made the big pay-offs to political bosses in cash, blocks of stock, or tips on land about to be developed.

In another sense, profound, impersonal, and not corrupt, the business community needed the boss. Because the Industrial Revolution hit this country when it was still thinly populated and most of its cities were overgrown towns, American cities expanded with astonishing speed. For example, in the single decade from 1880 to 1890, Chicago's population more than doubled, from a half million to over a million. Minneapolis and St. Paul tripled in size. New York City increased from a million to a million and a half; Detroit, Milwaukee, Columbus, and Cleveland grew by sixty to eighty per cent.

Municipal governments, however, were unprepared for this astonishing growth. Planning and budgeting were unknown arts. City charters had restrictive provisions envisaged for much smaller, simpler communities. The mayor and the important commissioners were usually amateurs serving a term or two as a civic duty. Authority was dispersed among numerous boards and special agencies. A typical city would have a board of police commissioners, a board of health, a board of tax assessors, a water board, and many others. The ostensible governing body was a city council or board of aldermen which might have thirty, fifty, or even a hundred members. Under these circumstances, it was difficult to get a prompt decision, harder still to coordinate decisions taken by different bodies acting on different premises, and easy for delays and anomalies to develop.

In theory, the cities could have met their need for increased services by municipal socialism, but the conventional wisdom condemned that as too radical, although here and there a city did experiment with publicly owned utilities. In theory also, the cities could have financed public buildings and huge projects such as water and sewer systems by frankly raising taxes or floating bonds. But both taxes and debt were no more popular then than they are now. Moreover, the laissez-faire doctrine which holds that "that government is best which governs least" was enshrined orthodoxy in America from the 1870s down to the 1930s.

As men clung to such orthodox philosophies, the structures of government became obsolete; they strained to meet unexpected demands as a swelling number of citizens in every class clamored for more services. In this climate the bosses emerged. They had no scruples about taking shortcuts through old procedures or manipulating independent boards and agencies in ways that the original city fathers had never intended. They had no inhibiting commitment to any theory of limited government. They were willing to spend, tax, and build—and to take the opprobrium along with the graft. Sometimes, like Hague in Jersey City, Curley in Boston, and Big Bill Thompson in Chicago, they got themselves elected mayor and openly assumed responsibility. More often, like Pendergast in Kansas City, Cox in Cincinnati, the leaders of Tammany, and the successive Republican bosses of Philadelphia, they held minor offices or none, stayed out of the limelight, and ran city government through their iron control of the party organization. In ruling Memphis for forty years, Ed Crump followed one pattern and then the other. Impeached on a technicality after being elected three times as mayor, Crump retreated to the back rooms and became even more powerful as the city's political boss.

What manner of men became political bosses? They were men of little education and no social background, often of immigrant parentage. A college-educated boss like Edward Flynn of The Bronx was a rarity. Bosses often began as saloonkeepers, because the saloon was a natural meeting place in poorer neighborhoods in the days before Prohibition. They were physically strong and no strangers to violence. Seventy-five years ago, most men made their living with brawn rather than brain, and a man who expected to be a leader of men had to be tough as well as shrewd. Open violence used to be common at polling places on Election Day, and gangs of repeaters roamed from one precinct to another. Although the typical boss made his way up through that roughneck system, the logic of his career led him to suppress violence. Bloody heads make bad publicity, and it is hard for any political organization to maintain a monopoly on violence. Bosses grew to prefer quieter, more lawful, less dangerous methods of control. Ballot-box stuffing and overt intimidation never disappeared entirely, but gradually they receded to weapons of last resort.

Political bosses varied in their idiosyncrasies and styles. A few, like Curley, became polished orators; others, like the legendary Charles Murphy of Tammany Hall, never made speeches. They were temperate, businesslike types; among them a drunk was as rare as a Phi Beta Kappa. If they had a generic failing it was for horses and gambling. Essentially they were hardheaded men of executive temper and genuine organizing talents; many, in other circumstances and with more education, might have become successful businessmen.

They have disappeared now, most of them. Education has produced a more sophisticated electorate; it has also encouraged potential bosses to turn away from politics toward more secure, prestigious, and profitable careers. A young man who had the energy, persistence, and skill in 1899 to become a successful political boss would in 1969 go to college and end up in an executive suite.

The urban population has also changed. The great flood of bewildered foreigners has dwindled to a trickle. In place of the European immigrants of the past, today's cities receive an influx of Negroes from the rural South, Puerto Ricans, Mexicans, and the white poor from Appalachia. As they overcome the language barrier and widen their experience, the Puerto Ricans are making themselves felt in urban politics. New York City, where they are most heavily concentrated, may have a Puerto Rican mayor in the not too distant future.

But the other groups are too isolated from the rest of the community to put together a winning political coalition of have-nots. The Mexicans and the ex-hillbillies from Appalachia are isolated by their unique cultural backgrounds, the Negroes by the giant fact of their race. Inasmuch as they make up a quarter to a third of the population in many cities, are a cohesive group, and still have a high proportion of poor who have to look to government for direct help, the Negroes might have produced several bosses and functioning political machines had they been of white European ancestry. But until Negroes attain a clear numerical majority, they find it difficult to take political power in any city because various white factions are reluctant to coalesce with them.

Regardless of the race or background of the voters, however, there are factors which work against the old-style machines. Civil service regulations make it harder to create a job or pad a payroll. Federal income taxes and federal accounting requirements make it more difficult to hide the rewards of graft. Television, public relations, and polling have created a whole new set of political techniques and undermined the personal ties and neighborhood loyalties on which the old organizations depended.

In this contemporary cartoon, Michael Ramus has pictured Chicago Mayor Richard J. Daley as "The Last Leaf" on the blasted tree of old-style urban bosses.

The new political style has brought an increase in municipal government efficiency and probably some decline in political corruption and misrule. But the politics of the television age puts a premium on hypocrisy. Candor has gone out the window with the spoils system. There is still a lot of self-seeking in politics and always will be. But gone are the days of Tammany's Boss Richard Croker, who when asked by an investigating committee if he was "working for his own pocket," shot back: "All the time—same as you." Today's politicians are so busy tending their images that they have become incapable of even a mildly derogatory remark such as Jim Curley's: "The term 'codfish aristocracy' is a reflection on the fish."

Curley entitled his memoirs *I'd Do It Again.* But the rough-and-tumble days when two-fisted, rough-tongued politicians came roaring out of the slums to take charge of America's young cities are not to come again.

Learning to Go to the Movies

David Nasaw

Modern parents worry about how the Internet affects children. They are concerned less about the content of the Internet—young people need not surf the Net to encounter pornography or expressions of hate and violence—than by the unfamiliar *experience* of the technology: the meeting of strangers in "chat rooms" where words and pictures and who-knows-what-else can be exchanged. Parents have understandably called for public authorities to police the unsettling "virtual reality" of the Internet. In this essay historian David Nasaw finds a remarkably similar response among the first generation that grew up with the movies. People initially worried less about what appeared on screen than the experience of being in a totally dark room with electrical "sparks" zapping through the air, confined in a large crowd of strangers, many of them poor, where they breathed foul air saturated with germs. Nasaw recounts how people adapted to the strange world of the movie theatre, and how the movie industry itself changed to address their concerns. Nasaw is author most recently of *Chief: The Life of William Randolph Hearst* (2000).

On July 5, 1896, the Los Angeles *Times* greeted the imminent arrival of Thomas Alva Edison's moving-picture projector with enormous enthusiasm: "The vitascope is coming to town. It is safe to predict that when it is set up at the Orpheum and set a-going, it will cause a sensation as the city has not known for many a long day."

Thousands of city residents had already viewed moving pictures by peering into the eyeholes of peep-show machines on display in saloons, railroad terminals, and amusement parlors, but these images were no bigger than a postcard. Never before had anyone seen moving pictures projected big as life on a screen.

The commercial possibilities of such an exhibition seemed boundless, and inventors, electricians, and showmen on two continents had been hard at work on a "screen machine" for several years. That the one about to make its debut at the Orpheum vaudeville theater had not actually been invented by Edison was kept secret by its promoters. The Edison name was much too valuable to compromise by suggesting that there might be others who were the Wizard's equal in imagination and technical skill.

The projector that bore Edison's name had, in fact, been invented by Thomas Armat, a Washington, D.C., bookkeeper, and his partner, C. Francis Jenkins, a government stenographer. After months of tinkering, separately and together, the two men had in the summer of 1895 put together a workable projector, named it the Phantoscope, and arranged to exhibit it at the Cotton States and International Exposition in Atlanta, Georgia, in September of the same year.

A kinetoscope arcade in San Francisco circa 1899.

The partners borrowed money from relatives to erect an outdoor tent theater on the fairgrounds, arranged for a series of newspaper articles on their wondrous invention, and printed complimentary tickets. When the expected crowds failed to materialize, in large part because fairgoers were not willing to pay a quarter for an amusement they knew nothing about, Armat and Jenkins hired a barker who invited visitors to enter free and pay at the exit only if they were satisfied. The offer worked, but the customers it attracted entered the theater with only the vaguest idea of what they were going to see. Never having viewed projected moving pictures before, they did not know that the theater had to be darkened. "The moment the lights were turned off for the beginning of the show a panic ensued," wrote the film historian Terry Ramsaye some thirty years later. "The visitors had a notion that expositions were dangerous places where pickpockets might be expected on every side. This was, the movie audience thought, just a new dodge for trapping the unwary in the dark."

Jenkins and Armat never did figure out how to introduce their moving pictures to prospective audiences. They ended up losing the fifteen hundred dollars they had borrowed, and the rights to their projector were eventually sold to the company that licensed and distributed Edison's peep-show machines.

The Los Angeles debut of the Phantoscope, renamed Edison's Vitascope, went off without a hitch. The Orpheum Theater was filled with vaudeville patrons who, though not accustomed to sitting in the dark, had no reason to fear that they would be assaulted by those seated next to them. The Los Angeles *Times* carried a complete description of the exhibition for those who had been unfortunate or unadventurous enough not to buy tickets in advance or to secure standing room at the last minute:

"The theatre was darkened until it was as black as midnight. Suddenly a strange whirling sound was heard. Upon a huge white sheet flashed forth the figure of Anna Belle Sun, [a dancer whose real name was Annabelle Whitford] whirling through the mazes of the serpentine dance. She swayed and nodded and tripped it lightly, the filmy draperies rising and falling and floating this way and that, all reproduced with startling reality, and the whole without a break except that now and then one could see swift electric sparks. . . . Then, without warning, darkness and the roar of applause that shook the theater; and knew no pause till the next picture was flashed on the screen. This was long, lanky Uncle Sam who was defending Venezuela from fat little John Bull, and forcing the bully to his knees. Next came a representation of Herald Square in New York with streetcars and vans moving up and down, then Cissy Fitzgerald's dance and last of all a representation of the way May Irwin and John C. Rice kiss. [*The May Irwin Kiss,* perhaps the most popular of the early films, was a fifteen-second close-up of the embrace in the closing scene of the musical comedy *The Widow Jones.*] Their smiles and glances and expressive gestures and the final joyous, overpowering, luscious osculation was repeated again and again, while the audience fairly shrieked and howled approval. The vitascope is a wonder, a marvel, an outstanding example of human ingenuity and it had an instantaneous success on this, its first exhibition in Los Angeles."

It was through lengthy newspaper descriptions like this one that prospective customers first learned about the magic of moving pictures. Note how the article begins with mention of the darkened theater and refers to the darkness again in mid-paragraph. Note too the reference to "swift electric sparks." Neither audiences nor critics understood how the projectors worked, nor were they convinced that the electricity used to project the pictures was harmless.

After two weeks of sold-out performances, the projector and its operators left the Orpheum for a tour of nearby vaudeville houses. But it turned out that theaters outside Los Angeles could not provide the electrical power needed to run the projector, so the machine was hauled back to Los Angeles and installed in the back of Thomas Tally's amusement parlor.

In the front of his store, Tally had set up automatic phonograph and peepshow machines that provided customers, for a nickel a play, with a few minutes of scratchy recorded sound or a few seconds of flickering moving images. Tally now partitioned off the back of his parlor for a "vitascope" room. To acquaint the public with what he billed as the "Wizard's latest wonder," he took out ads in the Los Angeles newspapers: "Tonight at Tally's Phonograph Parlor, 311 South Spring St, for the first time in Los Angeles, the great Corbett and Courtney prize fight will be reproduced upon a great screen through the medium of this great and marvelous invention. The men will be seen on the stage, life size, and every movement made by them in this great fight will be reproduced as seen in actual life."

Tally's back room was arguably the nation's first moving-picture theater. But although the technology for projecting moving images was in place, people turned out to be reluctant to enter a dark room to see pictures projected on a sheet. Unable to lure customers into his "theater," Tally did the next best thing. He punched holes in the partition separating the larger storefront from the vitascope room and, according to Terry Ramsaye, invited customers to "peer in at the screen while standing in the comfortable security of the well lighted phonograph parlor. . . . Three peep holes were at chair level for seated spectators, and four somewhat higher for standees—standing room only after three admissions, total capacity seven. The price per peep hole was fifteen cents."

As Tally and other storefront proprietors quickly discovered, it was not going to be easy to assemble an audience for moving pictures. Projectors were difficult to run and impossible to repair; the electrical current or batteries they ran on seldom worked properly; and the films were expensive, of poor quality, and few. But most important, customers balked at entering darkened rooms to see a few minutes of moving pictures. In April 1902 Tally tried again to open an "Electric Theater" but was forced to convert it to vaudeville after six months.

It was the same story everywhere. As a disgusted Oswego, New York, operator reported, at first the vitascope drew "crowded houses on account of its novelty. Now everybody has seen it, and, to use the vernacular of the 'foyer,' it does not 'draw flies.'"

Although projected films failed to attract customers to storefront theaters during their first decade of life, they were nonetheless being introduced to millions of vaudeville fans. "Dumb" acts—animals, puppets, pantomimists, magic-lantern slides, and *tableaux vivants*—had traditionally opened and closed the show because, being silent, they would not be disturbed by late arrivals or early departures. The movies were, the managers now discovered, the perfect dumb acts: they were popular, cheaper than most live performers, didn't talk back or complain about the accommodations, and could be replaced weekly.

Most of the early projectors held only fifty feet, or sixteen seconds, of film, which if looped and repeated five or six times could be stretched out to almost two minutes. Seven or eight films, displayed one after another in this fashion, lasted fifteen to twenty minutes, the perfect length for a vaudeville "turn."

The first moving pictures, shot in Edison's Black Maria studio in New Jersey, had been of vaudeville, musical theater, and circus acts. But audiences turned out to prefer pictures that moved across the frame: waves crashing onto a beach, trains barreling down their tracks, soldiers parading, horses racing. At the vitascope's debut performance at Koster & Bial's vaudeville theater in New York City, the crowd cheered loudest on seeing *Rough Sea at Dover,* the one picture shot outside the studio. Still, in the vaudeville halls the "living pictures" constituted one act among many.

Only in the middle of the first decade of the 1900s, after enormous improvements in the quality of the projectors and the production and distribution of films, was a new generation in show business ready to try again to lure customers into a moving-picture theater. What made the moment right was the fact that after 1903 the manufacturers—as the film producers referred to themselves—grew concerned that their customers were weary of the same old "actualities" and began to make pictures that told stories.

Although it was not possible to tell much of a story in a few silent minutes, audiences were captivated by the new films. As demand increased, the manufacturers developed assembly-line production methods, distributors streamlined the process of getting the films to exhibitors, and businessmen opened storefront theaters to exhibit the increasingly sophisticated product.

The first freestanding moving-picture theater was probably the work of Harry Davis, Pittsburgh's most prosperous showman. In April of 1904 Davis opened an amusement arcade near his Grand Opera House. When a fire burned it down, he rented a larger storefront, but instead of outfitting it as an arcade, he filled the room with chairs, gaily decorated the exterior, and, attaching the high-toned Greek word for theater to the lowly five-cent coin, advertised the opening of a "nickelodeon." It was an instant success.

Although Davis was certainly the first exhibitor to use the name *nickelodeon,* similar experiments were taking place in other parts of the country. Marcus Loew on a visit to his Cincinnati arcade in 1905 learned from his manager that a rival across the river in Covington, Kentucky, had come up with a marvelous new "idea in entertainment. . . . I went over with my general manager—it was on Sunday . . . and I never got such a thrill in my life. The show was given in an old-fashioned brownstone house, and the proprietor had the hallways partitioned off with dry goods cases. He used to go to the window and sell the tickets to the children, then he went to the door and took the tickets, and after he did that he locked the door and went up and operated the machine. . . . I said to my companion, 'This is the most remarkable thing I have ever seen.' The place was packed to suffocation." Loew returned to Cincinnati and opened his own screen show the following Sunday. "The first day we played I believe there were seven or eight people short of five thousand and we did not advertise at all. The people simply poured into the arcade. That showed me the great possibilities of this new form of entertainment." Back in New York City, Loew rented space for similar picture-show theaters alongside each of his arcades.

Across the country arcade owners shut off the backs of their storefronts or rented additional space for picture shows, while vaudeville managers, traveling exhibitors, and show businessmen left their jobs to set up their own nickel picture shows.

There was a great deal of money to be made in the fledgling business, but nickelodeon owners had to work hard to introduce their product. They could not afford to advertise heavily in the papers, but they could and did design their storefront facades to call attention to their shows—with oversized entrances, attraction boards, posters, and as many light bulbs as they had room for. To draw the attention of passersby, they set up phonographs on the street outside and hired live barkers: "It is only five cents! See the moving-picture show, see the wonders of Port Said tonight, and a shrieking comedy from real life, all for five cents. Step in this way and learn to laugh!"

The din became such that local shopkeepers complained it was interfering with business. In Paterson, New Jersey, the Board of Aldermen outlawed "phonographic barkers" after complaints from storekeepers, among them M. L. Rogowski, who claimed that the "rasping music, ground out for hours at a time, annoyed his milliners until they became nervous."

With the aural accompaniment of the barkers, the visual displays of glittering light bulbs, and word of mouth, city residents began to throng the new theaters.

The opening-night movie audience throngs the rather spartan Rex in Hannibal, Missouri, 1912.

Contemporary commentators used terms like *madness, frenzy, fever,* and *craze* to describe the rapidity with which nickel theaters went up after about 1905. By November of 1907, a little more than two years after the opening of the first one, there were already, according to Joseph Medill Patterson of *The Saturday Evening Post,* "between four and five thousand [nickel shows] running and solvent, and the number is still increasing rapidly. This is the boom time in the moving-picture business. Everybody is making money . . . as one press-agent said enthusiastically, 'this line is a Klondike.'"

It is, from our vantage point in the 1990s—suffused as we are by television, radio, CD players, and VCRs—difficult to recapture the excitement caused by the appearance of these first nickel theaters. For the bulk of the city's population, until now shut out of its theaters and commercial amusements, the sudden emergence of not one but five or ten nickel shows within walking distance must have been nothing short of extraordinary.

Imagine for a moment what it must have meant to be able to attend a show for a nickel in your neighborhood. City folk who had never been to the theater or, indeed, to any commercial amusement (even the upper balcony at a vaudeville hall cost a quarter) could now, on their way home from work or shopping or on a Saturday evening or Sunday afternoon, enter the darkened auditorium, take a seat, and witness the latest technological wonders, all for five cents.

One understands the passion of the early commentators as they described in the purplest of prose what the moving-picture theater meant to the city's working people. Mary Heaton Vorse concluded a 1911 article in *The Outlook* by referring to the picture-show audiences she had observed on Bleecker Street and the Bowery in New York City, "You see what it means to them; it means Opportunity—a chance to glimpse the beautiful and strange things in the world that you haven't in your life; the gratification of the higher side of your nature; opportunity which, except for the big moving picture book, would be forever closed to you."

The nickelodeon's unprecedented expansion did not go unnoticed by the critics of commercialized popular culture who had for a century complained about and organized against the evils of saloons, bawdy houses, honky-tonks, prizefights, and variety theaters. For the anti-vice crusaders and child savers, the nickel shows presented an unparalleled threat to civic morality, precisely because they were so popular with the city's young and poor.

Although they grossly exaggerated the "immorality" of the pictures and the danger to those who saw them, the anti-vice crusaders and reformers were correct in claiming that never before had so many women, men, and children, most of them strangers to one another, been brought together to sit in the closest physical proximity in the dark for twenty to thirty minutes. The Vice Commission of Chicago believed that "many liberties are taken with young girls within the theater during the performance when the place is in total or semi-darkness. Boys and men slyly embrace the girls near them and offer certain indignities." The New York Society for the Prevention of Cruelty to Children presented case after case of such depravities. "This new form of entertainment," it claimed in its 1909 annual report, "has gone far to blast maidenhood. . . . Depraved adults with candies and pennies beguile children with the inevitable result. The Society has prosecuted many for leading girls astray through these picture shows, but GOD alone knows how many are leading dissolute lives begun at the 'moving pictures.'"

While the anti-vice crusaders complained about the moral dangers, other reformers and a number of industry spokesmen worried about the physical conditions inside the "nickel dumps." Not only were the storefront theaters dark, dirty, and congested, but the stench inside was often overpowering. Investigators hired by the Cleveland commission investigating local movie theaters claimed that the "foul air" in the theaters was so bad that even a short stay was bound to result in "sneezing, coughing and the contraction of serious colds."

The Independent reported in early 1910 that the city's "moving picture places" had "become foci for the dissemination of tubercle bacilli," and *Moving Picture World* warned exhibitors to clean up their theaters before it was too late. "Should a malignant epidemic strike New York City, and these conditions prevail, the result might be a wholesale closing down of these germ factories."

Tuberculosis and head colds were not the only, or even the most serious, threats to the safety of movie patrons. In the early years of the storefront theaters, the danger of fire breaking out in the projection booth and sweeping through houses that lacked adequate exits was ever-present, especially since the film stock was highly flammable. There were close to one thousand theater fires in 1907 alone.

While nickelodeon owners and operators were reaping a bonanza, it had become apparent to manufacturers, distributors, and trade-journal editors that the industry had to do something about conditions inside the theaters to forestall government action and broaden the audience base. Homer W. Sibley of *Moving Picture World* warned his colleagues in August of 1911, "the 'dump' is doomed, and the sooner the cheap, ill-smelling, poorly ventilated, badly managed rendezvous for the masher and tough makes way for the better class of popular family theater the better it will be for the business and all concerned."

The enormous success of the nickelodeon was, paradoxically, blocking future growth of the moving-picture business. Potential customers who preferred not to mingle with the lower orders stayed away. In the vaudeville theaters the "refined" could, if they chose, sit safe from the rabble in the more expensive box and orchestra seats. There were no such sanctuaries in the nickel and dime theaters, where customers could sit wherever they pleased.

Nickelodeon owners began to realize that to attract an audience large enough to fill and refill their theaters twenty to thirty times a day, they would have to meld into one institutional space the openness of the saloon and the selectivity of the hotel. They had to welcome all who sought entrance to their amusements, while simultaneously "appearing" to screen their customers and admit only those who were, as Henry James had described the clientele of the American hotel, "presumably 'respectable,' . . . that is, not discoverably anything else."

The trick of remaining open to the street and its passersby while keeping out the riffraff was accomplished by designing an imposing exterior and entrance. The penny arcades had opened their fronts to encourage passersby to "drop in." The nickel theaters re-enclosed them, pulling back their doors about six feet from the sidewalk, in effect extending the distance between the theater and the street. This recessed, sheltered entrance functioned as a buffer or filter between the inside of the theater and the tumult outside. Framing this recessed entrasnce, massive arches or oversized columns jutted out onto the sidewalk. Thus the nickelodeon owners colonized the sidewalks in front of their establishments, shortening—while emphasizing—the distance between the amusements within and the workday world outside.

Theater owners did all they could to convince customers that they would be safe inside, no matter whom they sat next to in the dark. To guarantee their customers' good behavior, the exhibitors began to hire and parade uniformed ushers through the largest theaters and flashed signs on the screen warning patrons that those who misbehaved would quickly be banished from the house and prosecuted by the law.

The industry also accepted new fire-safety legislation, but perhaps the most important step the exhibitors took to allay the public's anxieties about health hazards was to install new and expensive ventilation systems that, they claimed, removed not only bad odors but germs as well. A. L. Shakman, owner of a Broadway theater, proudly proclaimed that there were "no clothing or body odors noticeable even during the capacity hours of the 81st Street Theater, for the simple reason that the air is changed by dome ventilators every twenty minutes. The air is just as sweet and pure in the balcony as it is downstairs." The Butterfly Theater in Milwaukee advertised that its "Perfect Ventilation" system provided customers with a "Complete Change of Air Every Three Minutes."

To convince the city's respectable folk that the movie theaters, though cheap, were safe and comfortable, the exhibitors assiduously courted the local gentry, businessmen, and politicians and invited them to their opening celebrations. The Saxe brothers of Milwaukee launched their Princess Theatre in 1909 with a gala invitation-only theater party, organized, as the owners told the Milwaukee *Sentinel,* "in the effort to secure the patronage of a better class of people." Mayor David S. Rose not only attended but gave the dedicatory address.

Gala openings like this had become routine occurrences by the late 1910s. Just as Barnum propelled Tom Thumb into the rank of first-class attractions by arranging and publicizing the midget's audience with the Queen of England, so did the exhibitors signify that their theaters were first-class entertainment sites by celebrating the patronage of the crowned heads of their communities.

Even though the moving pictures would not reach the pinnacle of their respectability until the early twenties, with the building of the movie palaces, the industry had by the middle 1910s educated a huge and heterogeneous urban public that they could visit movie theaters without danger to their pocketbooks, their reputations, or their health.

When the social researcher George Bevans was writing *How Workingmen Spend Their Spare Time* in late 1912 and early 1913, he discovered that no matter what the men's particular jobs, how many hours a week they worked, whether they were single or married, native-born or immigrant, earned less than ten dollars or more than thirty-five, they unfailingly spent more of their spare time at the picture show than anywhere else. William Fox claimed that the saloons in the vicinity of his theaters "found the business so unprofitable that they closed their doors. . . . If we had never had prohibition," he later told Upton Sinclair, "the motion pictures would have wiped out the saloon."

More and more what drew these audiences was the emergence of the movie star from the ranks of the wholly anonymous players of a decade earlier. Actors in the early story films had borrowed their gestures, poses, grins, and grimaces from melodrama and pantomime. Villains all dressed, acted, and moved the same way, as did the other stock characters: the heroes, heroines, and aged mothers. Any child in the audience could tell who the villain was (the man in the long black coat), why he acted as he did (he was evil), and what he was going to do next. By 1909 or so critics and audiences alike appeared to be growing weary of these histrionics, and players adopted instead a "more natural" or "slower" acting style. As cameras moved in closer to capture increasingly subtle and personalized expressions, audiences began to distinguish the players from one another. Since the manufacturers never divulged their actors' given names, the fans had to refer to them by their brand names—the Vitagraph Girl, or the Biograph Girl.

It didn't take long for manufacturers to recognize the benefits of exploiting their audience's curiosity. Kalem was the first to identify its actors and actresses by name, in a group photograph published as an advertisement in the January 15, 1910, *Moving Picture World* and made available to exhibitors for posting in their lobbies. In that same year, Carl Laemmle, a distributor who was preparing to manufacture his own films, hired Florence Lawrence to star in them for the then exorbitant salary of fifteen thousand dollars a year. To make sure the public knew that the Biograph Girl would now be appearing exclusively in IMP pictures, Laemmle engineered the first publicity coup. In March of 1910 he leaked the rumor that Miss Lawrence had been killed in a St. Louis streetcar accident and then took out a huge ad in *Moving Picture World* to announce that the story of her demise was the "blackest and at the same time the silliest lie yet circulated by enemies of the 'Imp.'"

It took only a few years for the picture players to ascend from anonymity to omnipresence. The best evidence we have of the stars' new-found importance is the salaries the producers were willing to pay them. On Broadway Mary Pickford had earned $25 a week. In 1910 Carl Laemmle lured her away from Biograph, her first movie home, with an offer of $175 a week. Her starting salary with Adolph Zukor at Famous Players in 1914 was $20,000 a year, soon raised to $1,000 a week and then, in January of 1915, to $2,000 a week and half the profits from her pictures. In June of 1916 another contract raised her compensation to 50 percent of the profits of her films against a guaranteed minimum of $1,040,000 a year, including at least $10,000 every week, a bonus of $300,000 for signing the contract, and an additional $40,000 for the time she had spent reading scripts during contract negotiations. And this was only the beginning.

The stars were worth the money because their appearance in films not only boosted receipts but added a degree of predictability to the business, a predictability that was welcomed by the banks and financiers that in the 1920s would assume a larger role in the picture business. The most reliable, perhaps the only, predictor of success for any given film was the presence of an established star.

The stars were not only bringing new customers into the theaters but incorporating a movie audience scattered over thousands of different sites into a vast unified public. "Stars" were by definition actors or actresses whose appeal transcended every social category, with the possible exception of gender. As the theater and now film critic Walter Prichard Eaton explained in 1915, "The smallest town . . . sees the same motion-picture players as the largest. . . . John Bunny and Mary Pickford 'star' in a hundred towns at once."

The reception accorded *The Birth of a Nation* that same year marked the distance the movies had traveled since their disastrous debut in Armat and Jenkins's tent just twenty years earlier. While African-Americans and their supporters strenuously protested the film's appalling portrayal of blacks and succeeded in forcing state and municipal censors to cut many scenes, white Americans of every age group, economic status, neighborhood, and ethnicity lined up at the box offices to see D. W. Griffith's Civil War epic.

The Birth of a Nation would eventually make more money than any film of its time and be seen by an audience that extended from prosperous theatergoers who paid two dollars in the first-class legitimate theaters to the women, children, and men who viewed it at regular prices in their neighborhood moving-picture houses. Even the President of the United States, as the promotions for the film asserted, had seen *The Birth of a Nation* and was now a moving-picture fan.

The ultimate confirmation of a picture show's respectability came only a few years later, during World War I, when the federal government, concerned that its propaganda messages might not reach the largest possible audience through the available print media, decided to send its "Four-Minute Men" into the nation's movie theaters. (The speakers were so named to reassure audiences and theater owners that their talks would be brisk.)

As President Wilson proclaimed in an open letter to the nation's moviegoers in April 1918, the picture house had become a "great democratic meeting place of the people, where within twenty-four hours it is possible to reach eight million citizens of all classes." There was nothing wrong with going to the movies while a war was being fought across the Atlantic, the President declared in his letter: "The Government recognizes that a reasonable amount of amusement, *especially* in war time, is not a luxury but a necessity."

2 Minorities and Race Relations

In this 1897 photograph a black woman with her child and dog watches her husband, cane in hand, leave for work.

A Road They Did Not Know

Larry McMurtry

Larry McMurtry, author of the *Lonesome Dove* tetralogy and many other novels, has
an uncanny ability to see the Old West through many different perspectives: an
Indian girl, a Mexican vacquero, an aging rancher. In this essay McMurtry applies
these imaginative skills to the Battle of Bighorn, about which remarkably little is
known with certainty, except that on June 25, 1876, George Armstrong Custer and
the 250 men of his 7th Cavalry were surrounded and annihilated when they attacked an enormous encampment of Sioux and Cheyenne Indians. What accounted for the Indian resolve? McMurtry suggests that the Indians were "highly
psyched" by a recent victory against another contingent of federal troops, by the
experience of the glorious encampment itself, culminating in a moving Great Sun
Dance. And why did Custer embark on so suicidal a mission? Perhaps, as some
have suggested, he wanted to be President. But McMurtry concludes that the erratic cavalryman "did what he had always done: push ahead, disregard orders,
start a fight, win it unassisted if possible, then start another fight." In the end,
what McMurtry imagines was the great swirl of dust the thousands of horses must
have thrown into the air, a fitting metaphor for a battle that looms large, if indistinct, in the historical imagination.

By the summer of 1875 the crisis over the Black Hills could no longer be post-
poned. Custer's grand announcement caught the nation's attention: after that the
miners could not be held back. The government was obviously going to find a way
to take back the Black Hills; but just as obviously, they were not going to be able to
do so without difficulty and without criticism. The whites in the peace party were
vocal; they and others of various parties thought the government ought to at least
try to honor its agreements, particularly those made as solemnly and as publicly as
this one. So there ensued a period of wiggling and squirming, on both the part of
the government and the part of the Sioux, many of whom had become agency Indians by this time. The free life of the hunting Sioux was still just possible, but only
in certain areas: the Powder River, parts of Montana, and the Dakotas, where the
buffalo still existed in some numbers.

By this time most of the major Indian leaders had made a realistic assessment
of the situation and drawn the obvious conclusion, which was that their old way of
life was rapidly coming to an end. One way or another they were going to have to
walk the white man's road—or else fight until they were all killed. Crazy Horse and
Sitting Bull were among the most determined of the hostiles; Red Cloud and Spotted Tail, rivals at this point, both had settled constituencies. They were administrators essentially, struggling to get more food and better goods out of their respective
agents. As more and more Indians came in and enrollment lists swelled, this became a full-time job, and a vexing and frustrating one at that.

There were of course many Indians who tried to walk a middle road, unwilling to completely give up the old ways but recognizing that the presence of whites in what had once been their country was now a fact of life. Young Man Afraid, son of the revered Old Man Afraid, was one of the middle-of-the-roaders.

The whites at first tried pomp and circumstance, bringing the usual suspects yet again to Washington, hoping to tempt them—Red Cloud, Spotted Tail, anyone—to sell the Black Hills. They would have liked to have Sitting Bull and Crazy Horse at this grand parley, or even a moderate such as Young Man Afraid, but none of these men nor any of the principal hostiles wanted anything to do with this mini-summit. Red Cloud and Spotted Tail had no authority to sell the Black Hills, or to do anything about them at all, a fact the white authorities should have realized by this time. There were still thousands of Sioux on the northern plains who had not given their consent to anything. The mini-summit fizzled.

Red Cloud and Spotted Tail had probably long since concluded that the whites were going to take the Black Hills: When had they not taken land they wanted? The two leaders, for a time, probably hoped to get the best obtainable price rather than see their land taken for nothing, which is what eventually happened. But most Sioux had not achieved this level of realism, or cynicism, yet. They thought the Black Hills were theirs forever.

Parade diplomacy having failed in Washington, the government decided to take its roadshow west. In the early fall of 1875 they staged a big conclave at a place carefully chosen to be midway between Red Cloud's agency and Spotted Tail's—they knew they couldn't afford to further inflame that rivalry. Historians who argue that either the Fort Laramie council of 1851 or the massing at the Little Bighorn was the greatest gathering of Plains Indians ever tend to forget the Black Hills council of 1875, which was at least a challenger. I don't think anyone can present an accurate count of how many Indians came, or at least hovered in the vicinity, but all agree there were a lot. The Blackfeet came, and the Cheyennes, and at least seven or eight of the major bands of the Sioux. Sitting Bull held aloof, as did Crazy Horse, meaning that both the Hunkpapas and the Oglalas were without their most resolute resisters. Just as Red Cloud was getting ready to deliver one of his lengthy orations, a very great many warriors, by one reckoning seven thousand (here again I can't imagine who was counting), rode out of the hills and circled the council tent. Then Little Big Man made his dramatic charge right up to the feet of the peace commissioners, threatening to shoot anyone who wanted to sell the Black Hills. Whether Little Big Man was really speaking for Crazy Horse is hard to say, but all witnesses agree that his entrance made for a touchy situation. The warriors were very stirred up; there was danger, for a time, of serious violence.

Fortunately, Young Man Afraid—he was by this time an Indian policeman—stepped forward and managed to quiet the situation. Thanks both to his valor and to his irreproachable character, he enjoyed an authority almost equal to his father's; the warriors, much to the peace commissioner's relief, would not go against him. The hostiles soon mostly left and the seasoned bargainers got down to business. Various sums were bruited about, but in the end nobody agreed to anything, though soon afterward, miners poured into the Black Hills so rapidly that the land that was to have been the Sioux's forever had more whites on it than

Indians; the same thing happened in Oklahoma, where the citizens of the Five Civilized Tribes were soon outnumbered three to one on their own land.

The best the government could do at this time was to establish, by fiat, a reservation system and to criminalize the Indians who didn't feel like parking themselves within the boundaries of whichever reservation they were assigned to. In the fall of 1871, Grant ordered them to hurry on in and get themselves enrolled by January, ignoring the fact that few Indians cared to move their camps in the wintertime.

No officer in the field—and this now included the redoubtable George Crook, Three Stars to the Indians—supposed that the nonagency Sioux would simply hurry in and sign up. Crazy Horse, who was then riding with Black Twin (No Water's brother), sent back word that it was a particularly inconvenient time to move; perhaps he would look more favorably on the proposal in the spring. The hostile Sioux didn't take Grant's order seriously, and neither did the military men who marched off, confidently for the most part, to whip them into submission. The Indians stayed wherever they happened to be, and the army got on the move, though in fact it didn't fight much that winter of 1875–76. It proved no more convenient for General Crook to march on Crazy Horse than it would have for Crazy Horse to come in.

Many Indians by this time had taken to wintering in the agencies and then drifting off again once the weather improved. Thousands came in, but when spring came, many of them went out again.

Crazy Horse, meanwhile, was enjoying what was to be his last more or less unharassed winter as a free Indian. How well or how clearly he realized that his time was ending, we don't know. Perhaps he still thought that if the people fought fiercely and didn't relent they could beat back the whites, not all the way to the Platte perhaps, but at least out of the Powder River country. We don't really know what he was thinking and should be cautious about making him more geopolitically attuned than he may have been. At this juncture nobody had really agreed to anything, but as the spring of 1876 approached, the army directed a number of its major players toward the northern plains. To the south, on the plains of Texas, the so-called Red River War was over. The holdouts among the Comanches and the Kiowas had been defeated and their horse herd destroyed. Ranald Mackenzie and Nelson A. Miles both distinguished themselves in the Red River War and were soon sent north to help subdue the Cheyennes and the northern Sioux. General Crook was already in the field, and Gibbon, Terry, and, of course, Custer were soon on their way.

By March of 1876 a great many Indians were moving north, toward Sitting Bull and the Hunkpapas, ready for a big hunt and possibly for a big fight with the whites, if the whites insisted on it, as in fact they did. The Little Bighorn in eastern Montana was the place chosen for this great gathering of native peoples, which swelled with more and more Indians as warmer weather came.

General Crook—Three Stars, or the Grey Fox—struck first. He located what the scout Frank Grouard assured him was Crazy Horse's village, made a dawn attack, captured the village, destroyed the ample provender it contained (some of which his own hungry men could happily have eaten), but killed few Indians. Where Crazy Horse actually was at this time is a matter much debated, but the camp Crook destroyed seems not to have been his. It may have been He Dog's, who was apparently on his way to the Red Cloud agency, hoping to avoid trouble. For Crook the encounter was more vexation than triumph. The Sioux regrouped that night and got back most of their horses, and the fight drove these peace-seeking Indians back north toward Sitting Bull. Crook continued to suppose that he had destroyed Crazy Horse's village; no doubt some of his friends were there, but the man himself was elsewhere.

A vast amount has been written about the great gathering of Indians who assembled in Montana in the early summer of 1876. It was to be the last mighty grouping of native peoples on the Great Plains of America. For the older people it evoked memories of summer gatherings before—reunions of a sort—such as had once been held at Bear Butte, near Crazy Horse's birthplace. Many of these Indians probably knew that what was occurring was in the nature of a last fling: there might be no opportunity for such a grand occasion again. Most of the Indians who gathered knew that the soldiers were coming, but they didn't care: their numbers were so great that they considered themselves invincible. Many Indians, from many tribes, remembered it as a last great meeting and mingling, a last good time. Historically, from this point on, there is a swelling body of reminiscence about the events of the spring and summer of 1876. Indeed, from the time the armies went into the field in 1876 to the end of the conflict there is a voluminous memoir literature to be sifted through—most of it military memoirs written by whites. Much of this found its way into the small-town newspapers that by then dotted the plains. These memoirs are still emerging. In 1996 four letters written by the wife of a captain who was at Fort Robinson when Crazy Horse was killed were discovered and published. The woman's name was Angie Johnson. It had taken more than a century for this literature to trickle out of the attics and scrapbooks of America, and it is still trickling. Of course it didn't take that long for the stately memoirs of Sheridan and Sherman and Miles and the rest to be published.

Though the bulk of this memoir literature is by white soldiers, quite a few of the Sioux and the Cheyennes who fought at the Little Bighorn managed to get themselves interviewed here and there. It is part of the wonder of *Son of the Morning Star* that Evan S. Connell Jr. has patiently located many of these obscurely published reminiscences from both sides of the fight and placed them in his narrative in such a way as to create a kind of mosaic of firsthand comment. These memoirs don't answer all the questions, or even very many of them, but it is still nice to know what the participants *thought* happened, even if what we're left with is a kind of mesquite thicket of opinion, dense with guessing, theory, and speculation. Any great military conflict—Waterloo, Gettysburg, etc.—leaves behind a similar confusion, a museum of memories but an extremely untidy one. Did the general say that or do this? Was Gall behind Custer or in front of him or nowhere near him? The mind that is troubled by unanswered and perhaps unanswerable questions should perhaps avoid military history entirely. Battles are messy things. Military historians have often to resort to such locutions as "it would at this juncture probably be safe to assume. . . ." Stephen Ambrose is precisely right (and uncommonly frank) when he says plainly that much of the fun of studying the Battle of the Little Bighorn is the free rein it offers to the imagination. Once pointed toward this battle, the historical imagination tends to bolt, like the uncheckable horse that carried poor Lieutenant Collins to his death near the Platte Bridge. Certainly the field of battle that the Indians called the Greasy Grass has caused many imaginations to bolt.

What we know for sure is that when June rolled around in 1876 there were a great many Indians, of several tribes, camped in southern Montana, with a fair number of soldiers moving west and north to fight them. Early June of that year may have been a last moment of confidence for the Plains Indians: they were many, they had meat, and they were in *their* place: let the soldiers come.

This buildup of confidence was capped by what was probably the best-reported dream vision in native American history—namely, Sitting Bull's vision of soldiers falling upside down into camp. This important vision did not come to the great Hunkpapa spontaneously; instead, it was elaborately prepared for. Sitting Bull allowed a friend to cut one hundred small pieces of flesh from his arms, after which he danced, staring at the sun until he fainted. When he came out of his swoon he heard a voice and had a vision of soldiers as numerous as grasshoppers falling upside down into camp. There were some who were skeptical of Sitting Bull—he could be a difficult sort—but this vision, coming as it did at the end of a great sundance, convinced most of his people that if the soldier did come they would fall. (It is worth mentioning that Sitting Bull had mixed luck with visions: not long before his death a meadowlark, speaking in Sioux, told him that his own people would kill him—which is what occurred.)

Shortly after this great vision of soldiers falling had been reported and considered, some Cheyenne scouts arrived with the news that the great General Crook was coming from the south with a lot of soldiers and also a considerable body of Crow and Shoshone scouts. This was a sign that Sitting Bull had not danced in vain, although Crook never got very close to the great encampment, because Crazy Horse, Sitting Bull, and a large force immediately went south to challenge him on the Rosebud, where the first of the two famous battles fought that summer was joined.

When the Indians attacked, Crook's thousand-man force was very strung out, with soldiers on both sides of the river, in terrain that was broken and difficult. Crow scouts were the first to spot the great party from the north; by common agreement the Crows and Shoshones fought their hearts out that day, probably saving Crook from the embarrassment of an absolute rout. But Crazy Horse, Black Twin, Bad Heart Bull, and many others were just as determined. Once or twice Crook almost succeeded in forming an effective battle line, but Crazy Horse and the others kept dashing right into it, fragmenting Crook's force and preventing a serious counter-attack. There was much close-quarter, hand-to-hand fighting. In a rare anticipation of women-in-combat, a Cheyenne woman rushed in at some point and saved her brother, who was surrounded. (The Cheyennes afterward referred to the Battle of the Rosebud as the Battle Where the Girl Saved Her Brother.) Crook struggled all day, trying to mount a strong offensive, but the attackers were so persistent that they thwarted him. Finally the day waned and shadows began to fall across the Rosebud. The Indians, having enjoyed a glorious day of battle, went home. They had turned Three Stars back, allowing him nowhere near the great gathering on the Little Bighorn.

Because the Indians left the field when the day was over, Crook claimed a victory, but nobody believed him, including (probably) himself. The Battle of the Rosebud was one of his most frustrating memories. It was indeed a remarkable battle between forces almost equally matched; in some ways it was more interesting than the fight at the Little Bighorn eight days later. Neither side could mount a fully decisive offensive, and both sides suffered unusually high casualties but kept fighting. The whites had no choice, of course; their adversaries in this case fought with extreme determination. The body count for the two sides varies with the commentator: George Hyde puts Crook's loss as high as fifty-seven men, a number that presumably includes many Crows and Shoshones who fell that day; Stephen Ambrose says it was twenty-eight men; Stanley Vestal says it was ten; and Robert Utley and Evan S. Connell Jr. claim it was nine. The attacking Sioux and Cheyennes may themselves have lost over thirty men, an enormous casualty rate for a native force. Accustomed as we are to the wholesale slaughter of the two world wars, or even of the Civil War, it is hard to keep in mind that when Indian fought Indian a death count of more than three or four was unusual.

At the end of the day General Crook at last accepted the advice his scouts had offered him earlier, which was that there were too many Indians up ahead for him to fight.

Had the full extent of Crook's difficulties on the Rosebud been known to the forces moving west into Montana, the sensible officers—that is, Gibbon and Terry—would have then proceeded with extreme caution; but it is unlikely that any trouble of Crook's would have slowed Custer one whit. Even if he had known that the Indians had sent Crook packing, it is hard to imagine that he would have proceeded differently. He had plenty of explicit—and, at the last, desperate—warnings from his own scouts, but he brushed these aside as he hurried the 7th Cavalry on to its doom. He plainly did not want to give his pessimistic scouts the time of day. He wanted to whip the Indians and, besides that, he wanted to do it by himself, with just the 7th Cavalry. He refused the offer of extra troops and also refused a Gatling gun, for fear that it might slow him down and allow the Indians to get away. It was only in the last minutes of his life that Custer finally realized that the Indians were fighting, not running. Custer was as convinced as Fetterman that he could whip whatever body of Indians he could persuade to face him. He meant to win, he meant to win alone, and he meant to win rapidly, before any other officers arrived to dilute his glory.

This book is about Crazy Horse, not Custer. That erratic egotist has been studied more than enough; he has even been the subject of one of the best books written about the west, Evan S. Connell Jr.'s *Son of the Morning Star*. Historians have speculated endlessly about why he did what he did at the Little Bighorn, on the twenty-fifth of June, 1876; and yet what he did was perfectly in keeping with his nature. He did what he had always done: push ahead, disregard orders, start a fight, win it unassisted if possible, then start another fight. He had seldom done otherwise, and there was no reason at all to expect him to do otherwise in Montana.

It may be true, as several writers have suggested, that he was covertly running for president that summer. The Democratic convention was just convening: a flashy victory and a timely telegram might have put him in contention for the nomination. Maybe, as Connell suggests, he thought he could mop up on the Sioux, race down to the Yellowstone, hop on the steamer *Far West,* and make it to the big Centennial parade on July fourth. So he marched his men most of the night and flung them into battle when—as a number of Indians noted—they were so tired their legs shook when they dismounted. As usual, he did only minimal reconnaissance, and convinced himself on no evidence whatever that the Indians must be running away from him, not toward him. The highly experienced scouts who were with him—the half-breed Mitch Bouyer and the Crows Bloody Knife and Half Yellow Face—all told Custer that they would die if they descended into the valley where the Indians were. None of them, in all their many years on the plains, had ever seen anything to match this great encampment. All the scouts knew that the valley ahead was for them the valley of death. Half Yellow Face, poetically, told Custer that they would all go home that day by a road they did not know. The fatalism of these scouts is a story in itself. Mitch Bouyer, who knew exactly what was coming, sent the young scout Curly away, but then himself rode on with Custer, to his death.

Whatever they said, what wisdom they offered, Custer ignored. It may be that he *was* running for president, but it is hard to believe that he would have done anything differently even if it had been an off year politically. Reno and Benteen, whom he had forced to split off, both testified much later that they didn't believe Custer had any plan when he pressed his attack. He was—and long had been—the most aggressive general in the American army. It didn't matter to him how many Indians there were. When he saw an enemy, he attacked, and would likely have done so even if he had no political prospects.

In the week between the fight on the Rosebud and the one at the Little Bighorn, Crazy Horse went back to the big party. The great General Crook had been whipped—the Indians felt invincible again, though some commentators have suggested that a sense of doom and foreboding hung over the northern plains during this fatal week: Indian and soldier alike were said to have felt it. Something dark and terrible was about to happen—and yet it was high summer in one of the most beautiful places in Montana, the one time when that vast plain is usually free of rain clouds or snow clouds. But this summer, Death was coming to a feast, and many felt his approach. On the morning of the battle, when most of the Sioux and Cheyennes were happily and securely going about their domestic business, never supposing that any soldiers would be foolish enough to attack them, Crazy Horse, it is said, marked, in red pigment, a Bloody Hand on both of his horse's hips, and drew an arrow and a bloody red hand on both sides of his horse's neck. Oglala scouts had been keeping watch on Custer, following his movements closely. Crazy Horse either knew or sensed that the fatal day had come.

The Battle of the Little Bighorn, June 25 and 26, 1876, is one of the most famous battles in world history. I doubt that any other American battle—not the Alamo, not Gettysburg—has spawned a more extensive or more diverse literature. There are books, journals, newsletters, one or another of which has by now printed every scrap of reminiscence that has been dredged up. Historians of both the professional and the amateur persuasions have poured forth voluminous speculations, wondering what would have happened if somebody—usually the unfortunate Major Reno—had done something differently, or if Custer hadn't foolishly split his command, or if and if and if. Though the battle took place more than one hundred and twenty years ago, debate has not much slackened. In fact, the sudden rise in Native American studies has resulted in increased reprinting of Indian as opposed to white reminiscences; now the Sioux and the Cheyennes are pressing the debate.

A number of white historians have argued that one or another Indian leader made the decisive moves that doomed Custer and the 7th; for these historians the battle was decided by strategy and generalship, not numbers. Both Stephen Ambrose and Mari Sandoz have written many pages about the brilliance of Crazy Horse in flanking Custer and seizing the high ground—today called Custer Hill—thus ending Custer's last hope of establishing a defensive position that might have held until reinforcements arrived. Others argue for their favorite chief, whether Gall, Two Moon, or another. Evan Connell, in his lengthy account of the battle, scarcely mentions Crazy Horse's part in it. All these arguments, of course, depend on Indian memory, plus study of the battleground itself. To me they seem to be permanently ambiguous, potent rather than conclusive. It is indeed an area of study where historians can give free rein to their imaginations; what Stephen Ambrose doesn't mention is that the Sioux and the Cheyennes, in remembering this battle, might be giving *their* imaginations a little running room as well. A world in which all whites are poets and all Indians sober reporters is not the world as most of us know it.

We are likely never to know for sure who killed Custer. He had cut his famous hair short for this campaign; had it still been long, many Indians might have recognized him. It is as well to keep in mind that as many as two thousand horses may have been in motion during this battle; between the dust they raised and the gunsmoke the scene would soon have become phantasmagorical; it would have been difficult for anyone to see well, or far. It is thus little wonder that no one recognized Custer. At some sharp moment Custer must have realized that his reasoning had been flawed. The Indians he had assumed were running away were actually coming to kill him, and there were a lot of them. Whether he much regretted his error is doubtful. Fighting was what Custer did, battle thrilled him, and now he was right in the dead thick of the biggest Indian fight of all. He may have enjoyed himself right up to the moment he fell.

For his men, of course, it was a different story. They had been marching since the middle of the night; a lot of them were so tired they could barely lift their guns. For them it was dust, weariness, terror, and death.

No one knows for sure how many Indians fought in this battle, but two thousand is a fair estimate, give or take a few hundred. Besides their overpowering numbers they were also highly psyched by the great sundance and their recent victory over Crook. When Major Reno and his men appeared at the south end of the great four-mile village, the Indians were primed. Reno might have charged them and produced, at least, disarray, but he didn't; the Indians soon chased him back across the Little Bighorn and up a bluff, where he survived, just barely. A lucky shot hit Bloody Knife, the Crow scout, square in the head; Major Reno, standing near, was splattered with his brain matter—some think this gory accident undid Major Reno, but we will never know the state of his undoneness, if any. Gall, the Hunkpapa warrior who, by common agreement, was a major factor in this battle, soon had fifteen hundred warriors mounted and ready to fight. If Major Reno *had* charged the south end of the village, he might have been massacred as thoroughly as Custer.

Exactly when Crazy Horse entered the battle is a matter of debate. Some say he rode out and skirmished a little with Reno's men; others believe he was still in his lodge when Reno arrived and that he was only interested in the larger fight with Custer. Most students of the battle think that when it dawned on Custer that he was in a fight for survival, not glory, he turned north, toward the high ground, hoping to establish a defensive redoubt on the hill, or rise, that is now named for him. But Crazy Horse, perhaps at the head of as many as a thousand warriors himself, flanked him and seized that high ground, sealing Custer's doom while, incidentally, making an excellent movie role for Errol Flynn and a number of other leading men.

So Crazy Horse may have done, but it was Gall and *his* thousand or so warriors who turned back Reno and then harried Custer so hard that the 7th Cavalry—the soldiers who fell into camp, as in Sitting Bull's vision—could never really establish *any* position. If Crazy Horse did flank Custer, it was of course good quarterbacking, but it hardly seems possible now to insist that any one move was decisive. Gall and his men might have finished Custer without much help from anyone—Gall had lost his wife and daughter early in the battle and was fighting out his anger and his grief.

From this distance of years the historians can argue until their teeth rot that one man or another was decisive in this battle, but all these arguments are unprovable now. What's certain is that George Armstrong Custer was very foolish, a glory hound who ignored orders, skipped or disregarded his reconnaissance, and charged, all but blindly, into a situation in which, whatever the quality of Indian generalship, he was quickly overwhelmed by numbers.

What I think of when I walk that battleground is dust. Once or twice in my life I rode out with as many as thirty cowboys—I remember the dust that small, unhurried group made. The dust of two thousand milling, charging horses would have been something else altogether; the battleground would soon have been a hell of dust, smoke, shooting, hacking; once the two groups of fighting men closed with one another, visibility could not have been good. Custer received a wound in the breast and one in the temple, either of which would have been fatal. His corpse was neither scalped nor mutilated. Bad Soup, a Hunkpapa, is said to have pointed out Custer's corpse to White Bull. "There he lies," he said. "He thought he was going to be the greatest man in the world. But there he is."

Most of the poetic remarks that come to us from this battle are the work of writers who interviewed Indians, or those who knew Indians, who thought they remembered Bad Soup saying something, or Half Yellow Face making (probably in sign) the remark about the road we do not know, or Bloody Knife staring long at the sun that morning, knowing that he would not be alive to see it go down behind the hills that evening. All we can conclude now is that Bloody Knife and Bad Soup and Half Yellow Face were right, even if they didn't say the words that have been attributed to them.

Hundreds of commentators, from survivors who fought in the battle to historians who would not be born until long years after the dust had settled in the valley of the Little Bighorn, have developed opinions about scores of issues which remain, in the end, completely opaque. Possibly Crazy Horse fought as brilliantly as some think—we will never really know. But he and Sitting Bull and Two Moon survived the battle and Custer didn't. General Grant, no sentimentalist, put the blame for the defeat squarely on Custer, and said so bluntly. The Indians made no serious attempt to root out and destroy Reno, though they could have. Victory over Long Hair was enough; Black Kettle was well revenged.

The next day, to Major Reno's vast relief, the great gathering broke up, the Indians melting away into the sheltering vastness of the plains.

What did the Sioux and Cheyenne leaders think at this point? What did they feel? Several commentators have suggested that once the jubilation of victory subsided, a mood of foreboding returned. Perhaps the tribes recognized that they were likely never to be so unified again—and they were not. Probably the leaders knew that they were likely never to have such a one-sided military victory again, either—a victory that was thrown them because of the vaingloriousness of one white officer.

Or perhaps they didn't think in these terms at all—not yet. With the great rally over, the great battle won, they broke up and got on with their hunting. Perhaps a few did reckon that something was over now, but it is doubtful that many experienced the sense of climax and decline as poetically as Old Lodge Skins in Thomas Berger's *Little Big Man*: "Yes, my son," he says,

> it is finished now, because what more can you do to an enemy than beat him? Were we fighting red man against red man—the way we used to, because that is a man's profession, and besides it is enjoyable—it would now be the turn of the other side to whip us. We would fight as hard as ever and perhaps would win again, but they would definitely start with an advantage, because that is the *right* way. There is no permanent winning or losing when things move, as they should, in a circle....
>
> But the white men, who live in straight lines and squares, do not believe as I do ... With them it is everything or nothing, Washita or Greasy Grass ... Winning is all they care about, and if they can do that by scratching a pen across a paper or saying something into the wind, they are much happier....

Old Lodge Skins was right about the army wanting to win. Crook's defeat at the Rosebud had embarrassed the army, and the debacle at the Little Bighorn shamed it. The nation, of course, was outraged. By August of 1876 Crook and Terry were lumbering around with a reassuring force of some four thousand soldiers. Naturally they found few Indians. Crazy Horse was somewhere near Bear Butte, harrying the miners in the Black Hills pretty much as the mood struck him. There was a minor engagement or two, of little note. The Indians were not suicidal—they left the massive force alone. Crook and Terry were such respecters now that they were bogged down by their own might.

In the fall of that year the whites, having failed to buy the Black Hills, simply took them. There was a travesty of a treaty council at which the theme of farming was again accented. Young Man Afraid, after hearing a great deal about farming, sarcastically ventured the view that it might take him one hundred years to learn how to do such work—he wanted to make sure that the government meant to take care of his people well during this learning period. With this disgraceful treaty the Indians lost not only the Black Hills but the Powder River, the Yellowstone, the Bighorns. There was even talk of moving the settled Sioux at the Red Cloud and Spotted Tail agencies to a reservation on the Missouri River, a move they all bitterly resisted. Crook, at this point, wanted to depose Red Cloud, insisting that he had not been forceful enough when it came to bringing in the hostiles. He wanted to promote Spotted Tail, not because he was better about the hostiles but because he was somewhat easier to deal with than the argumentative Bad Face.

From this point in 1876 on, the bitter factionalism of agency politics—in the Sioux's case, the factionalism of the defeated—has a place in the story. Everyone was getting more than a little tired of Red Cloud, but he was both tenacious and smart. He was to be one of the very few Plains Indian leaders of this period who survived everything, dying of old age in 1909.

By the late fall of 1876 General Crook had been in the field for almost a year, with no significant victories and one embarrassing defeat, the Rosebud. In November he finally had a victory, hitting the Cheyennes under Dull Knife and Little Wolf in their winter camp in the Bighorns. The Cheyennes who got away struggled north in weather so terrible that eleven babies froze in one night; when the survivors finally reached Crazy Horse, he took them in and provided for them as best he could.

By the end of what was in some ways a year of glory, 1876, Crazy Horse had to face the fact that his people had come to a desperate pass. It was a terrible winter, with subzero temperatures day after day. The Indians were ragged and hungry; the soldiers who opposed them were warmly clothed and well equipped. The victories of the previous summer were, to the Sioux and the Cheyennes, now just memories. They had little ammunition and were hard pressed to find game enough to feed themselves.

Colonel Nelson A. Miles, then camped on the Tongue River, badly wanted Crazy Horse's surrender. (Though he couldn't have known it at the time, if he could have persuaded Crazy Horse to come in to his camp he would have ended up claiming three great surrenders, the other two being Chief Joseph and Geronimo.) To entice Crazy Horse, Miles sent many runners promising fair treatment for himself and his people.

Near the end of the year Crazy Horse apparently decided he had better consider this offer. He approached, but stopped well short of Miles's camp and sent a number of emissaries ahead to discuss the matter. Unfortunately, some of Miles's Crow scouts saw the Oglalas coming and attacked them, killing several. Miles was furious when he heard of this and tried to make amends, but the damage was done. Crazy Horse turned back.

When the New Year came, Miles attacked and kept attacking until the weather finally stopped him. Crazy Horse moved north and hung on. It was during this time that he is said to have shot the horses of Sioux who wanted to give up and go to the agencies, a charge that is still debated.

During this hard period, with the soldiers just waiting for spring to begin another series of attacks, Sitting Bull decided to take himself and his people to Canada. Crazy Horse perhaps considered this option, but rejected it. It may have been because in Canada it was even colder—or it may have been because he just didn't want to leave home.

The Winter of 1876–77 was very hard. The fact that the soldiers had been willing to fight until the middle of January was evidence of a new determination on the part of the military to finish the job and subdue the Plains Indians once and for all. Only a few of the Indian leaders still holding out were much to be feared, Crazy Horse being one of these. In general, that long, bitter winter was a time of wearing down.

Very probably, during these months, Crazy Horse finally realized that he would not be able to live out his life as a free man—a resister. During these months he wandered off alone so often that He Dog reproached him for it, reminding him that there were people who depended on him. Crazy Horse was not a chief in the sense that Old Man Afraid had been a chief, but he did have followers, several hundred cold, ill-clad people who looked to him for guidance and provision. When he tried a second time to come in, in early May of 1877, he had nine hundred people with him, and more than two thousand horses.

It was a surrender, of a sort, but only of a sort. Crook claimed it, though Crazy Horse actually first sat down with Lieutenant Philo Clark. Even so, it was not a full or normal surrender, and neither the agency Indians (whether Red Cloud's or Spotted Tail's) nor the generals nor, probably, Crazy Horse himself ever quite believed that a true surrender had taken place. They may all have intuited an essential truth, which was that Crazy Horse was not tamable, not a man of politics. He could only assist his people as warrior and hunter—a bureaucrat he was not. Had there not been those nine hundred people looking to him for help, he might have elected to do what Geronimo did for so long: take a few warriors and a few women and stay out. He might have gone deep into the hills with a few men and fought as a guerrilla until someone betrayed him or at least outshot him. But it was true that these nine hundred people depended on him, so he brought them in and sat down, for the first time, in council with the white men.

He came into Red Cloud's agency, at Fort Robinson in northwestern Nebraska. I think it is fair to say that neither Red Cloud nor Spotted Tail nor any of the leading agency Indians were happy to see him. Perhaps Crook, who soon arrived, was the one happy person. With Sitting Bull in Canada and Crazy Horse settled near an agency, Three Stars could wipe his brow in relief. Also, Crook, not Miles, got credit for the surrender, which made up a little for the embarrassment on the Rosebud.

This august event, the surrender of "Chief" Crazy Horse, was reported in *The New York Times*, May 8, 1877.

———————————

The Diaspora in America:
A Study of Jewish Immigration

David Boroff

Except for Indians, all Americans are themselves at least the descendants of immigrants; thus, it is perhaps not surprising that "native born" citizens have often displayed a kind of love–hate attitude toward newcomers. They recognize in these newcomers their own successes and failures, their pride in what they have forgotten or rejected in their heritage. This ambivalence has been exacerbated by the very real conflicts that immigration has caused. On the one hand, immigrants have always been a national asset—their labor and intelligence add to the productivity and wealth of society; their culture enriches and diversifies American civilization. On the other hand, the immigrant has represented competition, strangeness, unsettling change. Most immigrants have been poor and many upon arrival have been ill-adjusted to American values and habits. Social and economic problems have frequently resulted, especially when large numbers have flooded into the country in relatively short periods of time. This last point explains why the late nineteenth and early twentieth centuries produced the movement to restrict immigration, for the influx was greater then than at any other time.

In this essay the late David Boroff of New York University discusses the impact of Jewish immigrants on the United States and the impact of the nation on these immigrants. He focuses chiefly on the period after 1880, when Jewish immigration was heaviest. His account provides a vivid picture of the life of these people and helps explain both why they, as well as other immigrants, were sometimes disliked and why they were themselves at times ambivalent in their reactions to America.

It started with a tiny trickle and ended in a roaring flood. The first to come were just twenty-three Jews from Brazil who landed in New Amsterdam in 1654, in flight from a country no longer hospitable to them. They were, in origin, Spanish and Portuguese Jews (many with grandiloquent Iberian names) whose families had been wandering for a century and a half. New Amsterdam provided a chilly reception. Governor Peter Stuyvesant at first asked them to leave, but kinder hearts in the Dutch West India Company granted them the right to stay, "provided the poor among them . . . be supported by their own nation." By the end of the century, there were perhaps one hundred Jews; by the middle of the eighteenth century, there were about three hundred in New York, and smaller communities in Newport, Philadelphia, and Charleston.

Because of their literacy, zeal, and overseas connections, colonial Jews prospered as merchants, though there were artisans and laborers among them. The

Jewish community was tightly knit, but there was a serious shortage of trained religious functionaries. There wasn't a single American rabbi, for example, until the nineteenth century. Jews were well regarded, particularly in New England. Puritan culture leaned heavily on the Old Testament, and Harvard students learned Hebrew; indeed, during the American Revolution, the suggestion was advanced that Hebrew replace English as the official language of the new country. The absence of an established national religion made it possible for Judaism to be regarded as merely another religion in a pluralistic society. The early days of the new republic were thus a happy time for Jews. Prosperous and productive, they were admitted to American communal life with few restrictions. It is little wonder that a Jewish spokesman asked rhetorically in 1820: "On what spot in this habitable Globe does an Israelite enjoy more blessings, more privileges?"

The second wave of immigration during the nineteenth century is often described as German, but that is misleading. Actually, there were many East European Jews among the immigrants who came in the half century before 1870. However, the German influence was strong, and there was a powerful undercurrent of Western enlightenment at work. These Jews came because economic depression and the Industrial Revolution had made their lot as artisans and small merchants intolerable. For some there was also the threatening backwash of the failure of the Revolution of 1848. Moreover, in Germany at this time Jews were largely disfranchised and discriminated against. During this period, between 200,000 and 400,000 Jews emigrated to this country, and the Jewish population had risen to about half a million by 1870.

This was the colorful era of the peddler and his pack. Peddling was an easy way to get started—it required little capital—and it often rewarded enterprise and daring. Jewish peddlers fanned out through the young country into farmland and mining camp, frontier and Indian territory. The more successful peddlers ultimately settled in one place as storekeepers. (Some proud businesses—including that of Senator Goldwater's family—made their start this way.) Feeling somewhat alienated from the older, settled Jews, who had a reputation for declining piety, the new immigrants organized their own synagogues and community facilities, such as cemeteries and hospitals. In general, these immigrants were amiably received by native Americans, who, unsophisticated about differences that were crucial to the immigrants themselves, regarded all Central Europeans as "Germans."

Essentially, the emigration route was the same between 1820 and 1870 as it would be in the post-1880 exodus. The travellers stayed in emigration inns while awaiting their ship, and since they had all their resources with them, they were in danger of being robbed. The journey itself was hazardous and, in the days of the sailing vessels when a good wind was indispensable, almost interminable. Nor were the appointments very comfortable even for the relatively well to do. A German Jew who made the journey in 1856 reported that his cabin, little more than six feet by six feet, housed six passengers in triple-decker bunks. When a storm raged, the passengers had to retire to their cabins lest they be washed off the deck by waves. "Deprived of air," he wrote, "it soon became unbearable in the cabins in which six seasick persons breathed." On this particular journey, sea water began to trickle into the cabins, and the planks had to be retarred.

Still, the emigration experience was a good deal easier than it would be later. For one thing, the immigrants were better educated and better acquainted with modern political and social attitudes than the oppressed and bewildered East European multitudes who came after 1880. Fewer in number, they were treated courteously by ships' captains. (On a journey in 1839, described by David Mayer, the ship's captain turned over his own cabin to the Jewish passengers for their prayers and regularly visited those Jews who were ill.) Moreover, there was still the bloom of adventure about the overseas voyage. Ships left Europe amid the booming of cannon, while on shore ladies enthusiastically waved their handkerchiefs. On the way over, there was a holiday atmosphere despite the hazards, and there was great jubilation when land was sighted.

There were, however, rude shocks when the voyagers arrived in this country. The anguish of Castle Garden and Ellis Island was well in the future when immigration first began to swell. But New York seemed inhospitable, its pace frantic, the outlook not entirely hopeful. Isaac M. Wise, a distinguished rabbi who made the journey in 1846, was appalled. "The whole city appeared to me like a large shop," he wrote, "where everyone buys or sells, cheats or is cheated. I had never before seen a city so bare of all art and of every trace of good taste; likewise I had never witnessed anywhere such rushing, hurrying, chasing, running. . . . Everything seemed so pitifully small and paltry; and I had had so exalted an idea of the land of freedom." Moreover, he no sooner landed in New York than he was abused by a German drayman whose services he had declined. "Aha! thought I," he later wrote, "you have left home and kindred in order to get away from the disgusting Judaeophobia and here the first German greeting that sounds in your ears is hep! hep!" (The expletive was a Central European equivalent of "Kike.") Another German Jew who worked as a clothing salesman was affronted by the way customers were to be "lured" into buying ("I did not think this occupation corresponded in any way to my views of a merchant's dignity").

After 1880, Jewish immigration into the United States was in flood tide. And the source was principally East Europe, where by 1880 three quarters of the world's 7.7 million Jews were living. In all, over two million Jews came to these shores in little more than three decades—about one third of Europe's Jewry. Some of them came, as their predecessors had come, because of shrinking economic opportunities. In Russia and in the Austro-Hungarian empire, the growth of large-scale agriculture squeezed out Jewish middlemen as it destroyed the independent peasantry, while in the cities the development of manufacturing reduced the need for Jewish artisans. Vast numbers of Jews became petty tradesmen or even *luftmenschen* (men without visible means of support who drifted from one thing to another). In Galicia, around 1900, there was a Jewish trader for every ten peasants, and the average value of his stock came to only twenty dollars.

Savage discrimination and pogroms also incited Jews to emigrate. The Barefoot Brigades—bands of marauding Russian peasants—brought devastation and bloodshed to Jewish towns and cities. On a higher social level, there was the "cold pogrom," a government policy calculated to destroy Jewish life. The official hope was that one third of Russia's Jews would die out, one third would emigrate, and one third would be converted to the Orthodox Church. Crushing restrictions were imposed. Jews were required to live within the Pale of Settlement in western Russia, they could not Russify their names, and they were subjected to rigorous quotas for schooling and professional training. Nor could general studies be included in the curriculum of Jewish religious schools. It was a life of poverty and fear.

Nevertheless, the *shtetl*, the typical small Jewish town, was a triumph of endurance and spiritual integrity. It was a place where degradation and squalor could not wipe out dignity, where learning flourished in the face of hopelessness, and where a tough, sardonic humor provided catharsis for the tribulations of an existence that was barely endurable. The abrasions and humiliations of everyday life were healed by a rich heritage of custom and ceremony. And there was always Sabbath—"The Bride of the Sabbath," as the Jews called the day of rest—to bring repose and exaltation to a life always sorely tried.

To be sure, even this world showed signs of disintegration. Secular learning, long resisted by East European Jews and officially denied to them, began to make inroads. Piety gave way to revolutionary fervor, and Jews began to play a heroic role in Czarist Russia's bloody history of insurrection and suppression.

This was the bleak, airless milieu from which the emigrants came. A typical expression of the Jewish attitude toward emigration from Russia—both its hopefulness and the absence of remorse—was provided by Dr. George Price, who had come to this country in one of the waves of East European emigration:

> Should this Jewish emigrant regret his leave-taking of his native land which fails to appreciate him? No! A thousand times no! He must not regret fleeing the clutches of the blood-thirsty crocodile. Sympathy for this country? How ironical it sounds! Am I not despised? Am I not urged to leave? Do I not hear the word *Zhid* constantly? . . . Be thou cursed forever my wicked homeland, because you remind me of the Inquisition . . . May you rue the day when you exiled the people who worked for your welfare.

After 1880, going to America—no other country really lured—became the great drama of redemption for the masses of East European Jews. (For some, of course, Palestine had that role even in the late nineteenth century, but these were an undaunted Zionist cadre prepared to endure the severest hardships.) The assassination of Czar Alexander II in 1881, and the subsequent pogrom, marked the beginning of the new influx. By the end of the century, 700,000 Jews had arrived, about one quarter of them totally illiterate, almost all of them impoverished. Throughout East Europe, Jews talked longingly about America as the "goldene medinah" (the golden province), and biblical imagery—"the land of milk and honey"—came easily to their lips. Those who could write were kept busy composing letters to distant kin—or even to husbands—in America. (Much of the time, the husband went first, and by abstemious living saved enough to fetch wife and children from the old country.) Children played at "emigrating games," and for the entire *shtetl* it was an exciting moment when the mail-carrier announced how many letters had arrived from America.

German steamship companies assiduously advertised the glories of the new land and provided a one-price rate from *shtetl* to New York. Emigration inns were established in Brody (in the Ukraine) and in the port cities of Bremen and Hamburg, where emigrants would gather for the trip. There were rumors that groups of prosperous German Jews would underwrite their migration to America; and in fact such people often did help their co-religionists when they were stranded without funds in the port cities of Germany. Within Russia itself, the government after 1880 more or less acquiesced in the emigration of Jews, and connived in the vast business of "stealing the border" (smuggling emigrants across). After 1892, emigration was legal—except for those of draft age—but large numbers left with forged papers, because that proved to be far easier than getting tangled in the red tape of the Czarist bureaucracy. Forged documents, to be sure, were expensive—they cost twenty-five rubles, for many Jews the equivalent of five weeks' wages. Nor was the departure from home entirely a happy event. There were the uncertainties of the new life, the fear that in America "one became a gentile." Given the Jewish aptitude for lugubriousness, a family's departure was often like a funeral, lachrymose and anguished, with the neighbors carting off the furniture that would no longer be needed.

For people who had rarely ventured beyond the boundaries of their own village, going to America was an epic adventure. They travelled with pitifully little money; the average immigrant arrived in New York with only about twenty dollars. With their domestic impedimenta—bedding, brass candlesticks, samovars—they would proceed to the port cities by rail, cart, and even on foot. At the emigration inns, they had to wait their turn. Thousands milled around, entreating officials for departure cards. There were scenes of near chaos—mothers shrieking, children crying; battered wicker trunks, bedding, utensils in wild disarray. At Hamburg, arriving emigrants were put in the "unclean" section of the *Auswandererhallen* until examined by physicians who decided whether their clothing and baggage had to be disinfected. After examination, Jews could not leave the center; other emigrants could.

The ocean voyage provided little respite. (Some elected to sail by way of Liverpool at a reduction of nine dollars from the usual rate of thirty-four dollars.) Immigrants long remembered the "smell of ship," a distillation of many putrescences. Those who went in steerage slept on mattresses filled with straw and kept their clothes on to keep warm. The berth itself was generally six feet long, two feet wide, and two and a half feet high, and it had to accommodate the passenger's luggage. Food was another problem. Many Orthodox Jews subsisted on herring, black bread, and tea which they brought because they did not trust the dietary purity of the ship's food. Some ships actually maintained a separate galley for kosher food, which was coveted by non-Jewish passengers because it was allegedly better.

Unsophisticated about travel and faced by genuine dangers, Jewish emigrants found the overseas trip a long and terrifying experience. But when land was finally sighted, the passengers often began to cheer and shout. "I looked up at the sky," an immigrant wrote years later. "It seemed much bluer and the sun much brighter than in the old country. It reminded me on [*sic*] the Garden of Eden."

Unhappily, the friendly reception that most immigrants envisioned in the new land rarely materialized. Castle Garden in the Battery, at the foot of Manhattan—and later Ellis Island in New York Harbor—proved to be almost as traumatic as the journey itself. "Castle Garden," an immigrant wrote, "is a large building, a Gehenna, through which all Jewish arrivals must pass to be cleansed before they are considered worthy of breathing freely the air of the land of the almighty dollar. . . . If in Brody, thousands crowded about, here tens of thousands thronged about; if there they were starving, here they were dying; if there they were crushed, here they were simply beaten."

One must make allowances for the impassioned hyperbole of the suffering immigrant, but there is little doubt that the immigration officials were harassed, overworked, and often unsympathetic. Authorized to pass on the admissibility of the newcomers, immigration officers struck terror into their hearts by asking questions designed to reveal their literacy and social attitudes. "How much is six times six?" an inspector asked a woman in the grip of nervousness, then casually asked the next man, "Have you ever been in jail?"

There were, of course, representatives of Jewish defense groups present, especially from the Hebrew Immigrant Aid Society. But by this time, the immigrants, out of patience and exhausted, tended to view them balefully. The Jewish officials tended to be highhanded, and the temporary barracks which they administered on Ward's Island for those not yet settled became notorious. Discontent culminated in a riot over food; one day the director—called The Father—had to swim ashore for his life, and the police were hastily summoned.

Most immigrants went directly from Castle Garden or Ellis Island to the teeming streets of Manhattan, where they sought relatives or *landsleit* (fellow townsmen) who had gone before them. Easy marks for hucksters and swindlers, they were overcharged by draymen for carrying their paltry possessions, engaged as strikebreakers, or hired at shamelessly low wages.

"Greenhorn" or "greener" was their common name. A term of vilification, the source of a thousand cruel jokes, it was their shame and their destiny. On top of everything else, the immigrants had to abide the contempt of their co-religionists who had preceded them to America by forty or fifty years. By the time the heavy East European immigration set in, German Jews had achieved high mercantile status and an uneasy integration into American society. They did not want to be reminded of their kinship with these uncouth and impoverished Jews who were regarded vaguely as a kind of Oriental influx. There was a good deal of sentiment against "aiding such paupers to emigrate to these shores." One charitable organization declared: "Organized immigration from Russia, Roumania, and other semi-barbarous countries is a mistake and has proved to be a failure. It is no relief to the Jews of Russia, Poland, etc., and it jeopardizes the well-being of the American Jews."

A genuine uptown-downtown split soon developed, with condescension on one side and resentment on the other. The German Jews objected as bitterly to the rigid, old-world Orthodoxy of the immigrants as they did to their new involvement in trade unions. They were fearful, too, of the competition they would offer in the needle trades. (Indeed, the East Europeans ultimately forced the uptown Jews out of the industry.) On the other side of the barricades, Russian Jews complained that at the hands of their uptown brethren, "every man is questioned like a criminal, is looked down upon . . . just as if he were standing before a Russian official." Nevertheless, many German Jews responded to the call of conscience by providing funds for needy immigrants and setting up preparatory schools for immigrant children for whom no room was yet available in the hopelessly overcrowded public schools.

Many comfortably settled German Jews saw dispersion as the answer to the problem. Efforts were made to divert immigrants to small towns in other parts of the country, but these were largely ineffective. There were also some gallant adventures with farming in such remote places as South Dakota, Oregon, and Louisiana. Though the Jewish pioneers were brave and idealistic, drought, disease, and ineptitude conspired against them. (In Oregon, for example, they tried to raise corn in cattle country, while in Louisiana they found themselves in malarial terrain.) Only chicken farming in New Jersey proved to be successful to any great degree. Farm jobs for Jews were available, but as one immigrant said: "I have no desire to be a farm hand to an ignorant Yankee at the end of the world. I would rather work here at half the price in a factory; for then I would at least be able to spend my free evenings with my friends."

It was in New York, then, that the bulk of the immigrants settled—in the swarming, tumultuous Lower East Side—with smaller concentrations in Boston, Philadelphia, and Chicago. Far less adaptable than the German Jews who were now lording it over them, disoriented and frightened, the East European immigrants constituted a vast and exploited proletariat. According to a survey in 1890, 60 percent of all immigrant Jews worked in the needle trades. This industry had gone through a process of decentralization in which contractors carried out the bulk of production, receiving merely the cut goods from the manufacturer. Contracting establishments were everywhere in the Lower East Side, including the contractors' homes, where pressers warmed their irons on the very stove on which the boss's wife was preparing supper. The contractors also gave out "section" work to families and *landsleit* who would struggle to meet the quotas at home. The bondage of the sewing machine was therefore extended into the tenements, with entire families enslaved by the machine's voracious demands. The Hester Street "pig market," where one could buy anything, became the labor exchange; there tailors, operators, finishers, basters, and pressers would congregate on Saturday in the hope of being hired by contractors.

Life in the sweatshops of the Lower East Side was hard, but it made immigrants employable from the start, and a weekly wage of five dollars—the equivalent of ten rubles—looked good in immigrant eyes. Moreover, they were among their own kin and kind, and the sweatshops, noisome as they were, were still the scene of lively political and even literary discussions. (In some cigar-making shops, in fact, the bosses hired "readers" to keep the minds of the workers occupied with classic and Yiddish literature as they performed their repetitive chores.) East European Jews, near the end of the century, made up a large part of the skilled labor force in New York, ranking first in twenty-six out of forty-seven trades, and serving, for example, as bakers, building-trade workers, painters, furriers, jewellers, and tinsmiths.

Almost one quarter of all the immigrants tried their hands as tradesmen—largely as peddlers or as pushcart vendors in the madhouse bazaar of the Lower East Side. For some it was an apprenticeship in low-toned commerce that would lead to more elegant careers. For others it was merely a martyrdom that enabled them to subsist. It was a modest enough investment—five dollars for a license, one dollar for a basket, and four dollars for wares. They stocked up on pins and needles, shoe laces, polish, and handkerchiefs, learned some basic expressions ("You wanna buy somethin'?"), and were on their hapless way.

It was the professions, of course, that exerted the keenest attraction to Jews, with their reverence for learning. For most of them it was too late; they had to reconcile themselves to more humble callings. But it was not too late for their children, and between 1897 and 1907, the number of Jewish physicians in Manhattan rose from 450 to 1,000. Of all the professions it was medicine that excited the greatest veneration. (Some of this veneration spilled over into pharmacy, and "druggists" were highly respected figures who were called upon to prescribe for minor—and even major—ills, and to serve as scribes for the letters that the immigrants were unable to read and write themselves.) There were Jewish lawyers on the Lower East Side and by 1901 over 140 Jewish policemen, recruited in part by Theodore Roosevelt, who, as police commissioner, had issued a call for "the Maccabee or fighting Jewish type."

The Lower East Side was the American counterpart of the ghetto for Jewish immigrants, as well as their glittering capital. At its peak, around 1910, it packed over 350,000 people into a comparatively small area—roughly from Canal Street to Fourteenth Street—with as many as 523 people per acre, so that Arnold Bennett was moved to remark that "the architecture seemed to sweat humanity at every window and door." The most densely populated part of the city, it held one sixth of Manhattan's population and most of New York's office buildings and factories. "Uptowners" used to delight in visiting it (as a later generation would visit Harlem) to taste its exotic flavor. But the great mass of Jews lived there because the living was cheap, and there was a vital Jewish community that gave solace to the lonely and comfort to the pious.

A single man could find lodgings of a sort, including coffee morning and night, for three dollars a month. For a family, rent was about ten dollars a month, milk was four cents a quart, kosher meat twelve cents a pound, bread two cents a pound, herring a penny or two. A kitchen table could be bought for a dollar, chairs at thirty-five cents each. One managed, but the life was oppressive. Most families lived in the notorious "dumbbell" flats of old-law tenements (built prior to 1901). Congested, often dirty and unsanitary, these tenements were six or seven stories high and had four apartments on each floor. Only one room in each three or four room apartment received direct air and sunlight, and the families on each floor shared a toilet in the hall.

Many families not only used their flats as workshops but also took in boarders to make ends meet. Jacob Riis tells of a two-room apartment on Allen Street which housed parents, six children, and six boarders. "Two daughters sewed clothes at home. The elevator railway passed by the window. The cantor rehearses, a train passes, the shoemaker bangs, ten brats run around like goats, the wife putters. . . . At night we all try to get some sleep in the stifling, roach-infested two rooms." In the summer, the tenants spilled out into fire escapes and rooftops, which were converted into bedrooms.

Nevertheless, life on the Lower East Side had surprising vitality. Despite the highest population density in the city, the Tenth Ward had one of the lowest death

The immigrants' new home: a crowded, noisy, but friendly street on New York's Lower East Side.

rates. In part, this was because of the strenuous personal cleanliness of Jews, dictated by their religion. Though only 8 percent of the East European Jews had baths, bathhouses and steam rooms on the Lower East Side did a booming business. There was, of course, a heavy incidence of tuberculosis—"the white plague." Those who were afflicted could be heard crying out, *"Luft! Gib mir luft!"* ("Air! Give me air!"). It was, in fact, this terror of "consumption" that impelled some East Side Jews to become farmers in the Catskills at the turn of the century, thus forerunning the gaudy career of the Catskill Borscht Belt resort hotels. The same fear impelled Jews on the Lower East Side to move to Washington Heights and the Bronx, where the altitude was higher, the air presumably purer.

Alcoholism, a prime affliction of most immigrant groups, was almost unknown among Jews. They drank ritualistically on holidays but almost never to excess. They were, instead, addicted to seltzer or soda water—Harry Golden's "2¢ plain"—which they viewed as "the worker's champagne." The suicide rate was relatively low, though higher than in the *shtetl,* and there was always a shudder of sympathy when the Yiddish press announced that someone had *genumen di ges* (taken gas).

The Lower East Side was from the start the scene of considerable crime. But its inhabitants became concerned when the crime rate among the young people seemed to rise steeply around 1910. There was a good deal of prostitution. The dancing academies, which achieved popularity early in this century, became recruiting centers for prostitutes. In 1908–9, of 581 foreign women arrested for prostitution, 225 were Jewish. There was the notorious Max Hochstim Association, which actively recruited girls, while the New York Independent Benevolent Association—an organization of pimps—provided sick benefits, burial privileges, bail, and protection money for prostitutes. The membership was even summoned to funerals with a two-dollar fine imposed on those who did not attend. Prostitution was so taken for granted that Canal Street had stores on one side featuring sacerdotal articles, while brothels were housed on the other.

Family life on the Lower East Side was cohesive and warm, though there was an edge of shrillness and hysteria to it. Marriages were not always happy, but if wives were viewed as an affliction, children were regarded as a blessing. The kitchen was the center of the household, and food was almost always being served to either family or visitors. No matter how poor they were, Jewish families ate well—even to excess—and mothers considered their children woefully underweight unless they were well cushioned with fat.

It was a life with few conventional graces. Handkerchiefs were barely known, and the Yiddish newspapers had to propagandize for their use. Old men smelled of snuff, and in spite of bathing, children often had lice in their hair and were sent home from school by the visiting nurse for a kerosene bath. Bedbugs were considered an inevitability, and pajamas were viewed as an upper-class affectation. Parents quarrelled bitterly—with passionate and resourceful invective—in the presence of their children. Telephones were virtually unknown, and a telegram surely meant disaster from afar.

The zeal of the immigrants on behalf of their children was no less than awe-inspiring. Parents yearned for lofty careers for their offspring, with medicine at the pinnacle. In better-off homes, there was always a piano ("solid mahogany"), and parents often spent their precious reserves to arrange a "concert" for their precocious youngsters, followed by a ball in one of the Lower East Side's many halls.

To be sure, the children inspired a full measure of anxiety in their parents. "Amerikane kinder" was the rueful plaint of the elders, who could not fathom the baffling new ways of the young. Parents were nervous about their daughters' chastity, and younger brothers—often six or seven years old—would be dispatched as chaperones when the girls met their boy friends. There was uneasiness about Jewish street gangs and the growing problem of delinquency. The old folks were vexed by the new tides of secularism and political radicalism that were weaning their children from traditional pieties. But most of all, they feared that their sons would not achieve the success that would redeem their own efforts, humiliations, and failures in the harsh new land. Pressure on their children was relentless. But on the whole the children did well, astonishingly well. "The ease and rapidity with which they learn," Jacob Riis wrote, "is equalled only by their good behavior and close attention while in school. There is no whispering and no rioting at these desks." Samuel Chotzinoff, the music critic, tells a story which reveals the attitude of the Jewish schoolboy. When an altercation threatened between Chotzinoff and a classmate, his antagonist's reaction was to challenge him to spell "combustible."

The Lower East Side was a striking demonstration that financial want does not necessarily mean cultural poverty. The immigrant Jews were nearly always poor and often illiterate, but they were not culturally deprived. In fact, between 1890 and World War I, the Jewish community provides a remarkable chapter in American cultural history. Liberated from the constrictions of European captivity, immigrant Jews experienced a great surge of intellectual vitality. Yiddish, the Hebrew-German dialect which some people had casually dismissed as a barbarous "jargon," became the vehicle of this cultural renascence. Between 1885 and 1914, over 150 publications of all kinds made their appearance. But the new Yiddish journalism reached its apogee with the *Jewish Daily Forward* under the long editorial reign of Abraham Cahan. The *Forward* was humanitarian, prolabor, and socialistic. But it was also an instrument for acclimatizing immigrants in the new environment. It provided practical hints on how to deal with the new world, letters from the troubled *(Bintel Brief)*, and even, at one time, a primer on baseball ("explained to non-sports"). The *Forward* also published and fostered an enormous amount of literature in Yiddish—both original works by writers of considerable talent, and translations of classic writers.

In this cultural ferment, immigrants studied English in dozens of night schools and ransacked the resources of the Aguilar Free Library on East Broadway. "When I had [a] book in my hand," an immigrant wrote, "I pressed it to my heart and wanted to kiss it." The Educational Alliance, also on East Broadway, had a rich program designed to make immigrant Jews more American and their sons more Jewish. And there were scores of settlement houses, debating clubs, ethical societies, and literary circles which attracted the young. In fact, courtships were carried on in a rarefied atmosphere full of lofty talk about art, politics, and philosophy. And though there was much venturesome palaver about sexual freedom, actual behavior tended to be quite strait-laced.

But the most popular cultural institution was the café or coffee house, which served as the Jewish saloon. There were about 250 of them, each with its own following. Here the litterateurs sat for hours over steaming glasses of tea; revolutionaries and Bohemians gathered to make their pronouncements or raise money for causes; actors and playwrights came to hold court. For immigrant Jews, talk was the breath of life itself. The passion for music and theatre knew no bounds. When Beethoven's Ninth Symphony was performed one summer night in 1915, mounted police had to be summoned to keep order outside Lewisohn Stadium, so heavy was the press of crowds eager for the twenty-five-cent stone seats. Theatre (in Yiddish) was to the Jewish immigrants what Shakespeare and Marlowe had been to the groundlings in Elizabethan England. Tickets were cheap—twenty-five cents to one dollar—and theatregoing was universal. It was a raucous, robust, and communal experience. Mothers brought their babies (except in some of the "swellest" theatres, which forbade it), and peddlers hawked their wares between the acts. There were theatre parties for trade unions and *landsmanschaften* (societies of fellow townsmen), and the audience milled around and renewed old friendships or argued the merits of the play. The stage curtain had bold advertisements of stores or blown-up portraits of stars.

There was an intense cult of personality in the Yiddish theatre and a system of claques not unlike that which exists in grand opera today. The undisputed monarch was Boris Thomashefsky, and a theatre program of his day offered this panegyric:

Thomashefsky! Artist great!
No praise is good enough for you!
Of all the stars you remain the king
You seek no tricks, no false quibbles;
One sees truth itself playing.
Your appearance is godly to us
Every movement is full of grace
Pleasing is your every gesture
Sugar sweet your every turn
You remain the king of the stage
Everything falls to your feet.

Many of the plays were sentimental trash—heroic "operas" on historical themes, "greenhorn" melodramas full of cruel abandonments and tearful re-unions, romantic musicals, and even topical dramas dealing with such immediate events as the Homestead Strike, the Johnstown Flood, and the Kishinev Pogrom of 1903. Adaptability and a talent for facile plagiarism were the essence of the play-wright's art in those days, and "Professor" Moses Horwitz wrote 167 plays, most of them adaptations of old operas and melodramas. The plays were so predictable that an actor once admitted he didn't even have to learn his lines; he merely had to have a sense of the general situation and then adapt lines from other plays.

There was, of course, a serious Yiddish drama, introduced principally by Jacob Gordin, who adapted classical and modernist drama to the Yiddish stage. Jewish in-tellectuals were jubilant at this development. But the process of acculturation had its amusing and grotesque aspects. Shakespeare was a great favorite but *"verbessert and vergrossert"* (improved and enlarged). There was the Jewish *King Lear* in which Cordelia becomes Goldele. (The theme of filial ingratitude was a "natural" on the Lower East Side, where parents constantly made heroic sacrifices.) *Hamlet* was also given a Jewish coloration, the prince becoming a rabbinical student who returns from the seminary to discover treachery at home. And *A Doll's House* by Ibsen was transformed into *Minna,* in which a sensitive and intelligent young woman, mar-ried to an ignorant laborer, falls in love with her boarder and ultimately commits suicide.

Related to the Jewish love of theatre was the immigrant's adoration of the can-tor, a profession which evoked as much flamboyance and egotistical preening as acting did. (In fact, actors would sometimes grow beards before the high holy-days and find jobs as cantors.) Synagogues vied with each other for celebrated cantors, sometimes as a way of getting out of debt, since tickets were sold for the high-holy-day services.

The Lower East Side was a vibrant community, full of color and gusto, in which the Jewish immigrant felt marvelously at home, safe from the terrors of the alien city. But it was a setting too for fierce conflict and enervating strain. There were three major influences at work, each pulling in a separate direction: Jewish Orthodoxy, assimilationism, and the new socialist gospel. The immigrants were Orthodox, but their children tended to break away. *Cheders* (Hebrew schools) were everywhere, in basements and stores and tenements, and the old custom of giving a child a taste of honey when he was beginning to learn to read—as symbolic of the sweetness of study—persisted. But the young, eager to be accepted into American society, despised the old ways and their "greenhorn" teachers. Fathers began to view their sons as "freethinkers," a term that was anathema to them. Observance of the Law declined, and the Saturday Sabbath was ignored by many Jews. A virulent antireligious tendency developed among many "enlightened" Jews, who would hold profane balls on the most sacred evening of the year—Yom Kippur—at which they would dance and eat nonkosher food. (Yom Kippur is a fast day.) And the trade-union movement also generated uneasiness among the pious elders of the Lower East Side. "Do you want us to bow down to your archaic God?" a radical newspaper asked. "Each era has its new Torah. Ours is one of freedom and justice."

But for many immigrants the basic discontent was with their American experience itself. The golden province turned out to be a place of tenements and sweatshops. A familiar cry was "*a klug af Columbus!*" ("a curse on Columbus") or, "Who ever asked him, Columbus, to discover America?" Ellis Island was called *Trernindzl* (Island of Tears), and Abraham Cahan, in his initial reaction to the horrors of immigration, thundered: "Be cursed, immigration! Cursed by those conditions which have brought you into being. How many souls have you broken, how many courageous and mighty souls have you shattered." The fact remains that most Jewish immigrants, in the long run, made a happy adjustment to their new land.

After 1910, the Lower East Side went into a decline. Its strange glory was over. New areas of Jewish settlement opened up in Brooklyn, the Bronx, and in upper Manhattan. By the mid-twenties, less than 10 percent of New York's Jews lived on the Lower East Side, although it still remained the heartland to which one returned to shop, to see Yiddish theatre, and to renew old ties. By 1924 Jewish immigration into the United States was severely reduced by new immigration laws, and the saga of mass immigration was done. But the intensities of the Jewish immigrant experience had already made an indelible mark on American culture and history that would endure for many years.

Reluctant Conquerors: American Army Officers and the Plains Indians

Thomas C. Leonard

The post–Civil War decades saw the tragic completion of the destruction of the cultures of the American Indian that began when Columbus first set foot in the New World. Previously, at least some of the tribes that inhabited what was to become the United States had been able to maintain their cultural integrity more or less intact by falling back before the white juggernaut into the western wilderness. After 1865 further retreat became impossible, and in a few years the free Indians were crushed and the survivors compelled to settle on reservations, where their conquerors expected them to become "civilized Americans."

The role of the Army in the destruction of the Indians has frequently been described. What is unique about Thomas C. Leonard's treatment of the subject is its focus on the thoughts and feelings of the soldiers rather than on their deeds—on their appreciation of the Indians, not on their efforts to exterminate them. That professional soldiers should respect a foe so clever, so steadfast, so courageous, so dignified in defeat is not difficult to understand. Yet Leonard does not oversimplify or romanticize the American military reactions to the Indians and their way of life. His essay presents a complex and fascinating picture of a part of American history usually depicted in grossly oversimplified terms. Professor Leonard, who teaches at the University of California at Berkeley, is the author of *Above the Battle: War-Making in America from Appomattox to Versailles.*

The white man's peace at Appomattox in 1865 meant war for the Plains Indians. In the next quarter century six and a half million settlers moved west of the Missouri River, upsetting a precarious balance that had existed between two million earlier pioneers and their hundred thousand "hostile" red neighbors. The industrial energy that had flowed into the Civil War now pushed rail lines across traditional hunting grounds. Some twenty-five thousand soldiers were sent west to meet insistent demands for protection coming from stockmen and miners spread out between the Staked Plains of Texas and the Montana lands watered by the Powder, Bighorn, and Yellowstone rivers.

It is ironic that the men who carried the wounds of the struggle to maintain the union of their own society now were ordered to dismember the culture of the native Americans. These Indian fighters today have been knocked out of that false gallery of heroes created by western novels and movies. On the centennial of the Battle of the Little Bighorn a granite mountain outside of Custer, South Dakota, is being carved into the shape of the Sioux warrior leader Crazy Horse. Times have changed, and a second look at the Army's Indian fighters is in order. They have a complex story to tell, one filled with an ambivalence about their enemy as well as about the civilians who sent them to fight.

The officer corps did not relish their double assignment of pushing Indians back from lands claimed by whites and, for good measure, "redeeming" native Americans from "barbarism"—for Christian civilization. In the letter books and official reports that these men kept so meticulously on the frontier there is a continual lament: civilian officials and opinion makers only cut budgets and issued contradictory directions. The rules of war demanded restraint and a fine regard for the enemy's rights, but it seemed as if the same civilians who interpreted these rules wanted quick work on the battlefield. The United States government itself broke the treaties that promised the Indians land, yet expected the Army to keep the peace through mutual trust.

At the same time that western settlers were clamoring for protection, their land grabs were provoking Indian retaliation. Not incidentally, army officers endured the torture of the annual congressional debate over how much their pay should be cut and seethed as western bankers charged 12 to 40 percent to convert their government paper into the coin they needed on the frontier. "Friends" of the Indian—with their talk of a "conquest by kindness"—were a special annoyance. Eastern philanthropists like Edward A. Lawrence damned the officers when blood was shed and were among those who chillingly approved the "swift retribution" meted out to General Custer by the Sioux. Frontier forts rarely had the long-timbered stockades beloved by Hollywood set designers—but perhaps many officers longed for a massive wall, high enough to repel civilians as well as Indians.

By 1870 General William T. Sherman doubted he could fight with honor on the plains; from the west and the east, he wrote, "we are placed between two fires." But Sherman may have been envied by another proud Civil War hero, General Philip H. Sheridan, who mused upon a shattered reputation as he watched whole frontier towns—wanting the extermination of Indians—turn out to hang him in effigy.

To officers so provoked, action seemed the thing to sweep away the complications of the Indian problem; to strike at the red man again and again appeared not only the quickest way to dry up civilian complaints but the just way to punish an incomprehensibly wild enemy. Sheridan pleaded with Sherman for authority to act upon the appalling reports that crossed his desk each week:

> Since 1862 at least 800 men, women, and children have been murdered within the limits of my present command, in the most fiendish manner; the men usually scalped and mutilated, their [he omits the word] cut off and placed in their mouth; women ravished sometimes fifty and sixty times in succession, then killed and scalped, sticks stuck in their persons, before and after death.

Sheridan said it was now a question of who was to remain alive in his district, red or white. As for himself: "I have made my choice." It was, in fact, Sheridan who first enunciated the judgment that would become the epitaph of so many native Americans: "The only good Indians I ever saw were dead."

Sheridan's choice, made in passion, proved extraordinarily complicated to carry out, for the fact is that the Indian fighters were troubled by various kinds of

Starting in 1867, Phillip Henry Sheridan, pictured here, was responsible for Indian campaigns in the West. In 1883, he succeeded William T. Sherman as Army commander in chief.

respect for their enemy. In the first place, no commander in the West could conceal his admiration for the red man's fighting skill. "Experience of late years," one reported to his colleagues, "has most conclusively shown that our cavalry cannot cope with the Indian man for man." Though these seasoned veterans and heroes reported a very favorable official casualty ratio, in more candid moments they pronounced that Indian fighting was the most difficult combat American soldiers had ever faced.

It followed that so high an estimate of the enemy's ability undermined the Army's pride in its own competence. Sheridan berated the inefficiency that made campaigns in the West "a series of forlorn hopes," and Sherman wrote in so many words to the Secretary of War what had silently haunted his fellow officers: ". . . it seems to be impossible to force Indians to fight at a disadvantage in their own country. Their sagacity and skill surpasses that of the white race." It further followed that victory against such valiant opponents was bittersweet. Both Sheridan and Sherman confessed to pity and compassion for the native Americans they had set out to destroy. As Sheridan wrote:

We took away their country and their means of support, broke up their mode of living, their habits of life, introduced disease and decay among them and it was for this and against this they made war. Could anyone expect less?

Few officers escaped a sort of wistful appreciation of their primitive enemy in what they took to be his insatiable appetite for war—and not a few admired precisely this unrestrained aggressiveness. Indeed, peaceful assimilation seemed not good enough for the Indians. One of Sheridan's favorite generals sought a large audience to explain the temptations of the Indian culture:

> To me, Indian life, with its attendant ceremonies, mysteries, and forms, is a book of unceasing interest. Grant that some of its pages are frightful, and, if possible, to be avoided, yet the attraction is none the weaker. Study him, fight him, civilize him if you can, he remains still the object of your curiosity, a type of man peculiar and undefined, subjecting himself to no known law of civilization, contending determinedly against all efforts to win him from his chosen mode of life.
>
> If I were an Indian, I often think I would greatly prefer to cast my lot among those of my people who adhered to the free open plains rather than submit to the confined limits of a reservation, there to be the recipient of the blessed benefits of civilization, with its vices thrown in without stint or measure.

Two years after he published this gratuitous advice, General George A. Custer met the object of his interest for the last time at the Little Bighorn.

General Nelson A. Miles, one of the officers who chased the Sioux after Custer's fall, had a personal reason for revenge: an Indian had taken a pointblank shot at him during an awkward moment in a peace parley. But Miles's reflections show the remarkable extent to which men like him overcame their anger with the enemy. The general spoke of the Indian's "courage, skill, sagacity, endurance, fortitude, and self-sacrifice of a high order" and of "the dignity, hospitality, and gentleness of his demeanor toward strangers and toward his fellow savages." Miles was inclined to think that lapses from this standard meant only that Indians had "degenerated through contact with the white man." Writing on this subject, he did not show the personal arrogance and pride that was the despair of his military superiors. Miles viewed Custer's fall in 1876 as a chastising message for the nation's centennial. He quoted Longfellow: ". . . say that our broken faith / wrought all this ruin and scathe, / In the Year of a Hundred Years."

Miles was not an eccentric in the sympathies he expressed. Colonel John Gibbon, for example, the man who discovered the mutilated bodies of the soldiers who had fallen with Custer at the Little Bighorn, seemed, during his subsequent chase of the Sioux, more angry at the "human ghouls" in the Army who had disturbed some Sioux graves than at the warriors who had killed his colleagues. Such desecrations, he thundered, "impress one with the conviction that in war barbarism stands upon a level only a little lower than our boasted civilization." By Gibbon's lights, the record of white hostility and treachery would force any man to fight: "Thus would the savage in us come to the surface under the oppression which we know the Indian suffers." Like so many Indian fighters who addressed the perennial "Indian question," Gibbon raised more questions about his own culture than he answered about his enemy's.

To these soldiers the courage and bearing of the red man suggested a purer way of life before the coming of the white man, and the military frequently searched for Greek and Roman analogies to suggest the virtues of its enemies. Heathens though they were, they had nobility. Even the Indians' faults might be excused by their manifestly lower stage of cultural evolution.

General George Crook was in a good position to speak of the red men's virtues, for as a fighting man he resembled them. In the field he dispensed with the army uniform and seemed only at ease when he was free of all cumbersome marks of civilization. Crook left one post, he tells us, "with one change of underclothes, toothbrush, etc., and went to investigate matters, intending to be gone a week. But I got interested after the Indians and did not return there again for over two years."

In the harsh campaigns in the Southwest, Crook taught his men to move over the land like Apaches, and when white men failed him, he was adept in recruiting Indians for army service. Frederic Remington observed Crook's methods and saw they made officers less "Indian fighters" than "Indian thinkers." "He's more of an Indian than I am," marveled one Apache. Crook repaid such compliments; back at West Point to deliver a graduation address, he may have shocked many with this observation:

> With all his faults, and he has many, the American Indian is not half so black as he has been painted. He is cruel in war, treacherous at times, and not over cleanly. But so were our forefathers. His nature, however, is responsive to treatment which assures him that it is based upon justice, truth, honesty, and common sense. . . .

Crook hesitated to condemn even the most ferocious Apaches, because he respected their spirit and believed that "we are too culpable as a nation, for the existing condition of affairs."

In the view of many officers the weaknesses of their own culture were more glaring than the faults of their enemy. "Barbarism torments the body; civilization torments the soul," one colonel concluded. "The savage remorselessly takes your scalp, your civilized friend as remorselessly swindles you out of your property." Indeed, many of the officers who led the fight for civilization seemed to accept Indian culture on its own terms. Colonel Henry B. Carrington—one of the field officers who supplied Sheridan with maddening accounts of Indian outrages—was an interesting case study. Carrington's official report of the eighty fallen soldiers under his command in the Fetterman fight in Wyoming in 1866 provided grisly reading:

> Eyes torn out and laid on the rocks; teeth chopped out; joints of fingers cut off; brains taken out and placed on rocks, with members of the body; entrails taken out and exposed; hands and feet cut off; arms taken out from sockets; eyes, ears, mouth, and arms penetrated with spearheads, sticks, and arrows; punctures upon

every sensitive part of the body, even to the soles of the feet and the palms of the hand.

Yet Carrington's own response to this carnage was not vengeful but reflective, even scholarly. A year later Margaret Carrington, the colonel's wife, published *Ab-sa-ra-ka,* a study of the region the Army had fought to control. In her book she treated this Indian act of warfare with impressive open-mindedness, never directly condemning it. She did note that "the noblest traits of the soldiers were touchingly developed as they carefully handled the mutilated fragments" from the battle-field—but she also praised the Indian: "In ambush and decoy, *splendid.*" Close observers, she wrote, overcame anger to become reconciled, even sympathetic, to "the bold warrior in his great struggle."

As he took charge of enlarged sections of *Ab-sa-ra-ka* in the 1870s Colonel Carrington expanded on this theme of noble resistance. To him the barbarities of the *whites,* in their "irresponsible speculative emigration," overshadowed the red "massacre" of Fetterman's men. Carrington confessed, like Custer, "if I had been a red man as I was a white man, I should have fought as bitterly, if not as brutally, as the Indian fought." And standing before the American Association for the Advancement of Science in 1880 to read his official report of the Fetterman mutilations again, Carrington explained to the scientists that the Indian's disposition of enemies was intended to disable his foe in the afterlife, and so was quite understandable. Nor did he disparage the red man's values, but rather closed his address by suggesting some inadequacies on the other—his own—side: "From 1865 until the present time, there has not been a border campaign which did not have its impulse in the aggressions of a white man."

Few men in the West raised more unusual questions about both cultures than Captain John Bourke. He entered the campaigns, he wrote later, "with the sincere conviction that the only good Indian was a dead Indian, and that the only use to make of him was that of a fertilizer." But the notebooks of this odd, inquiring soul reveal a man haunted by the details of the enemy's life. Mastering several Indian languages, Bourke produced an impressive series of monographs on native religious ceremonies, and in 1895 he became president of the American Folklore Society. Learning proved corrosive to his early cultural pride, and at the end of his army service he was willing to admit that "the American aborigine is not indebted to his pale-faced brother, no matter what nation or race he may be, for lessons in tenderness and humanity."

Admittedly, Captain Bourke's appreciation of native culture was more complex than the respect paid by other Indian fighters. Acknowledging the red man's fighting prowess and noble character, Bourke was more deeply interested in Indian snake ceremonies and scatological rites—mysteries thoroughly repulsive to most white sensibilities. Indeed, his interest in these ceremonies was as intense and sustained as were his protestations of "horror" during each "filthy" and "disgusting" rite. He put all this scholarship and his rather prurient curiosity to work in *Scatologic Rites of All Nations,* where he observed such "orgies" throughout the development of Western civilization, even surviving in nations of what he called "high enlightenment." Here was no sentimental accommodation with Indian culture but a panoramic reminder to the white race of its own barbaric past. Thus the Indians' vices, no less than their virtues, set up a mirror before the advancing Christian whites.

It did not, of course, deter the whites. However noble their image of the savage may have been, it is important to recognize in all of these Indian fighters a fundamental conviction that the price of civilization was not too high. Aware as they were of the ambiguities of their mission, their sympathies and remorse never swayed them from their duty, and no officer of tender conscience was provoked to resign his commission.

How were such mixed emotions sustained? In point of fact, the military's apologia for the red man answered certain professional and psychological needs of the workaday Army. The Army, for both noble and ignoble reasons, wanted to assume control of the administration of Indian affairs that had been held by civilians—a few good words for the long-suffering red man smoothed the way to this goal. Further, by praising the Plains Indians as relentless and efficient warriors the military justified its own ruthless strategy—and setbacks. Nor was frontier ethnology exactly disinterested; close study of the Indians often yielded military advantage for white men. And while empathy for the enemy clearly made the assignment to "redeem" the Indian more painful, there were some emotional satisfactions to be derived from even the most generous attitudes toward the Indians' way of life.

In some instances an officer's respect for the primitive's unfettered aggressiveness happily loosened his own. Thus General George Schofield, commander of the Department of the Missouri, could confess that "civilized man . . . never feels so happy as when he throws off a large part of his civilization and reverts to the life of a semi-savage." When Schofield acted on his own advice on a long hunting trip, he returned invigorated, recording that "I wanted no other occupation in life than to ward off the savage and kill off his food until there should no longer be an Indian frontier in our beautiful country." One of Sherman's aides reached a similar ominous conclusion after saluting the red man's way of life. This officer was deeply impressed by his colleagues' glowing reports of the nobility of Indian religion, and, he mused,

> There is no doubt the Indians have, at times, been shamefully treated. . . . And there is no doubt a man of spirit would rebel. . . . However, it is useless to moralize about the Indians. Their fate is fixed, and we are so near their end, it is easy to see what that fate is to be. That the Indian might be collected, and put out of misery by being shot deliberately, (as it would be done to a disabled animal), would seem shocking, but something could be said in favor of such procedure.

This puzzling mixture of aggression and regret is less surprising if we take into account the ways, according to contemporary psychologists, that anger and frustration can give rise to these contrasting emotions. The officer corps was enraged by much of what it saw happening to America. The Indians' tactics seemed horrible yet ingenious. Their culture was repellent, but also alluring for its integrity. At the same time, evident in the reports and memoirs of these officers is a disturbing sense of having been abandoned by their own unworthy civilization. Army training and experience prevented these men from acting out their anger, and some anger was instead internalized and expressed in the mourning and guilt they exhibited so frequently. Their appreciation of the native Americans for what they had been was combined with a determination to punish a society for what it refused to become. Their fight for civilized settlement as it should be was troubled by their anger that some virtues, retained by the Indians, were slipping away from the white man.

If we appreciate the military's doubts—of its mandate, of its justice, of its ability, as well as of its commitments to civilization, duty, and progress—the tragedy of the West does not go away. It deepens. Was there an escape from the emotional trap in which the Army found itself? To refuse to win the West would have required a conversion to primitivism hard to imagine inside the ranks of army life and scarcely imaginable in ordinary men living ordinary lives outside of the Army. But the career of one lieutenant in the Nez Perce war illustrates that such a transformation was possible.

Charles Erskine Scott Wood (1852–1944) served on General O. O. Howard's staff, and it was he who took down the very moving speech of the defeated Chief Joseph. Wood's reflections on the Nez Perce campaign, published in the early 1880s, struck the conventional balance between remorse and pride. Surveying the shameful record of white treaty violations, he warned his army colleagues that retribution might follow. Yet there seemed to be no other possible outcome—"forces" were "silently at work, beyond all human control," against the red man's survival. Wood, a gifted literary man, proceeded to join the somewhat crowded celebration of the culture he had worked to destroy, hymning the vividness and nobility of the Indian, qualities that seemed poignant by their passing. But in all this he declined to attack directly the civilization that had corrupted and supplanted the Indians', and his fashionable sympathy sounded much like General Custer's.

But Wood was, in time, to change greatly. He quit the Army, entered the Columbia Law School, and began to cause trouble. Not satisfied with the state of letters or the law in his time, Wood allied himself with the radical Industrial Workers of the World and searched for a literary form to express his increasingly anarchistic temperament. The fruit of this veteran's singular rehabilitation was a long experimental poem, *The Poet in the Desert,* an affecting personal renunciation of "civilization" and a call for the revolt of the masses against privilege. Wood, with booming voice and flowing white beard, was in the twentieth century rather like Father Time—reminding Americans of sins against the Indians. He knew:

> *I have lain out with the brown men*
> *And know they are favored.*
> *Nature whispered to them her secrets,*
> *But passed me by.*
> *I sprawled flat in the bunch-grass, a target*
> *For the just bullets of my brown brothers betrayed.*
> *I was a soldier, and, at command,*
> *Had gone out to kill and be killed.*
> *We swept like fire over the smoke-browned tee-pees;*
> *Their conical tops peering above the willows.*

We frightened the air with crackle of rifles,
Women's shrieks, children's screams,
Shrill yells of savages;
Curses of Christians.
The rifles chuckled continually.
A poor people who asked nothing but freedom,
Butchered in the dark.

Wood's polemic is more straightforward than many that are asserted today on behalf of the native Americans. He learned—and his colleagues in the Army demonstrated—that respect and compassion for another culture are very unsure checks on violence. And Wood's life points out one of the costs of war that Americans have generally been spared: in a prolonged campaign the victor can emerge attracted to his enemy's faith. Our frontier officers had put a civil war behind them and were not ready to turn against their society to save the red man. But their thoughtfully expressed ambivalence toward their task of winning the West throws a revealing light on a history that is still too often falsified with glib stereotypes.

3 Age of Reform

Unemployed white and black workers parade in New York City in 1909 to protest discriminatory hiring practices.

Jane Addams: Urban Crusader

Anne Firor Scott

As the reputations of Progressive political leaders have declined, those of some of the social reformers of the era have risen. This is particularly true of social workers such as Jane Addams and other founders of the settlement house movement, who in modern eyes seem to have had a more profound grasp of the true character of the problems of their age and to have worked more effectively and with greater dedication in trying to solve those problems than did any of the politicians.

These social workers were quite different from those of today—they were more personally involved and far less professionally oriented. Many were also, it is true, somewhat patronizing in their approach to those they sought to help, and they took a rather romantic and thus unrealistic view of the potentialities both of the poor and of their own capacity to help the poor. This essay by Professor Anne Firor Scott of Duke University makes clear, however, that Jane Addams of Chicago's Hull-House was neither patronizing nor a romantic. Professor Scott is the author of *The Southern Lady: From Pedestal to Politics* and *The American Woman: Who Was She?*

If Alderman Johnny Powers of Chicago's teeming nineteenth ward had only been prescient, he might have foreseen trouble when two young ladies not very long out of a female seminary in Rockford, Illinois, moved into a dilapidated old house on Halsted Street in September, 1889, and announced themselves "at home" to the neighbors. The ladies, however, were not very noisy about it, and it is doubtful if Powers was aware of their existence. The nineteenth ward was well supplied with people already—growing numbers of Italians, Poles, Russians, Irish, and other immigrants—and two more would hardly be noticed.

Johnny Powers was the prototype of the ward boss who was coming to be an increasingly decisive figure on the American political scene. In the first place, he was Irish. In the second, he was, in the parlance of the time, a "boodler": his vote and influence in the Chicago Common Council were far from being beyond price. As chairman of the council's finance committee and boss of the Cook County Democratic party he occupied a strategic position. Those who understood the inner workings of Chicago politics thought that Powers had some hand in nearly every corrupt ordinance passed by the council during his years in office. In a single year, 1895, he was to help to sell six important city franchises. When the mayor vetoed Powers' measures, a silent but significant two-thirds vote appeared to override the veto.

Ray Stannard Baker, who chanced to observe Powers in the late nineties, recorded that he was shrewd and silent, letting other men make the speeches and bring upon their heads the abuse of the public. Powers was a short, stocky man, Baker said, "with a flaring gray pompadour, a smooth-shaven face [*sic*], rather heavy features, and a restless eye." One observer remarked that "the shadow of sympathetic gloom is always about him. He never jokes; he has forgotten how to smile. . . ." Starting life as a grocery clerk, Powers had run for the city council in 1888 and joined the boodle ring headed by Alderman Billy Whalen. When Whalen died in an accident two years later, Powers moved swiftly to establish himself as successor. A few weeks before his death Whalen had collected some thirty thousand dollars—derived from the sale of a city franchise—to be divided among the party faithful. Powers alone knew that the money was in a safe in Whalen's saloon, so he promptly offered a high price for the furnishings of the saloon, retrieved the money, and divided it among the gang—at one stroke establishing himself as a shrewd operator and as one who would play the racket fairly.

From this point on he was the acknowledged head of the gang. Charles Yerkes, the Chicago traction tycoon, found in Powers an ideal tool for the purchase of city franchises. On his aldermanic salary of three dollars a week, Powers managed to acquire two large saloons of his own, a gambling establishment, a fine house, and a conspicuous collection of diamonds. When he was indicted along with two other corrupt aldermen for running a slot machine and keeping a "common gambling house," Powers was unperturbed. The three appeared before a police judge, paid each other's bonds, and that was the end of that. Proof of their guilt was positive, but convictions were never obtained.

On the same day the Municipal Voters League published a report for the voters on the records of the members of the city council. John Powers was described as "recognized leader of the worst element in the council . . . [who] has voted uniformly for bad ordinances." The League report went on to say that he had always opposed securing any return to the city for valuable franchises, and proceeded to document the charge in detail.

To his constituents in the nineteenth ward, most of whom were getting their first initiation into American politics, Powers turned a different face. To them, he was first and last a friend. When there were celebrations, he always showed up: if the celebration happened to be a bazaar, he bought freely, murmuring piously that it would all go to the poor. In times of tragedy he was literally Johnny on the spot. If the family was too poor to provide the necessary carriage for a respectable funeral, it appeared at the doorstep—courtesy of Johnny Powers and charged to his standing account with the local undertaker. If the need was not so drastic, Powers made his presence felt with an imposing bouquet or wreath. "He has," said the Chicago *Times-Herald*, "bowed with aldermanic grief at thousands of biers."

Christmas meant literally tons of turkeys, geese, and ducks—each one handed out personally by a member of the Powers family, with good wishes and no questions asked. Johnny provided more fundamental aid, too, when a breadwinner was out of work. At one time he is said to have boasted that 2,600 men from his ward (about one third of the registered voters) were working in one way or another for the city of Chicago. This did not take into account those for whom the grateful holders of traction franchises had found a place. When election day rolled around, the returns reflected the appreciation of job-holders and their relatives.

The two young ladies on Halsted Street, Jane Addams and Ellen Starr, were prototypes too, but of a very different kind of figure: they were the pioneers of the social settlement, the original "social workers." They opposed everything Johnny Powers stood for.

Jane Addams' own background could hardly have been more different from that of John Powers. The treasured daughter of a well-to-do small-town businessman from Illinois, she had been raised in an atmosphere of sturdy Christian principles.

From an early age she had been an introspective child concerned with justifying her existence. Once in a childhood nightmare she had dreamed of being the only remaining person in a world desolated by some disaster, facing the responsibility for rediscovering the principle of the wheel! At Rockford she shared with some of her classmates a determination to live to "high purpose," and decided that she would become a doctor in order to "help the poor."

After graduation she went to the Woman's Medical College of Philadelphia, but her health failed and she embarked on the grand tour of Europe customary among the wealthy. During a subsequent trip to Europe in 1888, in the unlikely setting of a Spanish bull ring, an idea that had long been growing in her mind suddenly crystallized: she would rent a house "in a part of the city where many primitive and actual needs are found, in which young women who had been given over too exclusively to study, might restore a balance of activity along traditional lines and learn something of life from life itself. . . ." So the American settlement-house idea was born. She and Ellen Starr, a former classmate at the Rockford seminary who had been with her in Europe, went back to Chicago to find a house among the victims of the nineteenth century's fast-growing industrial society.

The young women—Jane was twenty-nine and Ellen thirty in 1889—had no blueprint to guide them when they decided to take up residence in Mr. Hull's decayed mansion and begin helping "the neighbors" to help themselves. No school of social work had trained them for this enterprise: Latin and Greek, art, music, and "moral philosophy" at the seminary constituted their academic preparation. Toynbee Hall in England—the world's first settlement house, founded in 1884 by Samuel A. Barnett—had inspired them. Having found the Hull house at the corner of Polk and Halsted—in what was by common consent one of Chicago's worst wards—they leased it, moved in, and began doing what came naturally.

Miss Starr, who had taught in an exclusive girls' preparatory school, inaugurated a reading party for young Italian women with George Eliot's *Romola* as the first book. Miss Addams, becoming aware of the desperate problem of working mothers, began at once to organize a kindergarten. They tried Russian parties for the Russian neighbors, organized boys' clubs for the gangs on the street, and offered to bathe all babies. The neighbors were baffled, but impressed. Very soon children and grownups of all sorts and conditions were finding their way to Hull-House—to read Shakespeare or to ask for a volunteer midwife; to learn sewing or discuss socialism; to study art or to fill an empty stomach. There were few formalities and no red tape, and the young ladies found themselves every day called upon to deal with some of the multitude of personal tragedies against which the conditions of life in the nineteenth ward offered so thin a cushion.

Before long, other young people feeling twinges of social conscience and seeking a tangible way to make their convictions count in the world of the 1890s came to live at Hull-House. These "residents," as they were called, became increasingly

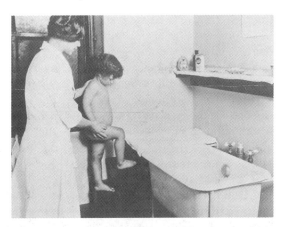

Children were Hull-House's first concern. Infants were bathed (right) and moppets put into nursery school (below).

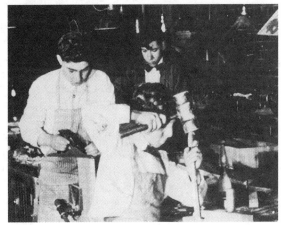

Older boys (right) took shop lessons to prepare them to become successful artisans.

interested in the personal histories of the endless stream of neighbors who came to the House each week. They began to find out about the little children sewing all day long in the "sweated" garment trade, and about others who worked long hours in a candy factory. They began to ask why there were three thousand more children in the ward than there were seats in its schoolrooms, and why the death rate was higher there than in almost any other part of Chicago. They worried about young-sters whose only playground was a garbage-spattered alley that threatened the whole population with disease. (Once they traced a typhoid epidemic to its source and found the sewer line merging with the water line.) In the early days Hull-House offered bathtubs and showers, which proved so popular a form of hospitality that the residents became relentless lobbyists for municipal baths.

Hull-House was not the only American settlement house—indeed, Jane Ad-dams liked to emphasize the validity of the idea by pointing out that it had devel-oped simultaneously in several different places. But Hull-House set the pace, and in an astonishingly short time its founder began to acquire a national reputation. As early as 1893 Jane Addams wrote to a friend: "I find I am considered the grand-mother of social settlements." She was being asked to speak to gatherings of learned gentlemen, sociologists and philosophers, on such subjects as "The Subjec-tive Necessity for Social Settlements." When the Columbian Exposition attracted thousands of visitors to Chicago in 1893, Hull-House became—along with the lake front and the stockyards—one of the things a guest was advised not to miss. By the mid-nineties, distinguished Europeans were turning up regularly to visit the House and examine its workings. W. T. Stead, editor of the English *Review of Reviews,* spent much time there while he gathered material for his sensational book, *If Christ Came to Chicago.* By that time two thousand people a week were coming to Hull-House to participate in some of its multifarious activities, which ranged from philosophy classes to the Nineteenth Ward Improvement Association.

Neither her growing reputation nor the increasing demand for speeches and articles, however, distracted Jane Addams from what was to be for forty years the main focus of a many-sided life: Hull-House and the nineteenth ward. Much of her early writing was an attempt to portray the real inner lives of America's proliferat-ing immigrants, and much of her early activity, an effort to give them a voice to speak out against injustice.

The Hull-House residents were becoming pioneers in many ways, not least in the techniques of social research. In the *Hull-House Maps and Papers,* published in 1895, they prepared some of the first careful studies of life in an urban slum, exam-ining the details of the "homework" system of garment making and describing tum-ble-down houses, overtaxed schools, rising crime rates, and other sociological prob-lems. The book remains today an indispensable source for the social historian of Chicago in the nineties.

Jane Addams' own interest in these matters was far from academic. Her con-cern for the uncollected garbage led her to apply for—and receive—an appoint-ment as garbage inspector. She rose at six every morning and in a horse-drawn buggy followed the infuriated garbage contractor on his appointed rounds, making sure that every receptacle was emptied. Such badgering incensed Alderman Pow-ers, in whose hierarchy of values cleanliness, though next to godliness, was a good bit below patronage—and he looked upon garbage inspection as a job for one of his henchmen. By now John Powers was becoming aware of his new neighbors; they were increasingly inquisitive about things close to Johnny Powers' source of power. By implication they were raising a troublesome question: Was Johnny Powers really "taking care of the poor"?

For a while, as one resident noted, the inhabitants of the House were "passive though interested observers of their representative, declining his offers of help and co-operation, refusing politely to distribute his Christmas turkeys, but feeling too keenly the smallness of their numbers to work against him." They were learning, though, and the time for passivity would end.

In company with many other American cities, Chicago after 1895 was taking a critical look at its political life and at the close connections that had grown up between politics and big business during the explosive era of industrial expansion following the Civil War. "The sovereign people may govern Chicago in theory," Stead wrote; "as a matter of fact King Boodle is monarch of all he surveys. His domination is practically undisputed."

The Municipal Voters League, a reform organization that included many of Jane Addams' close friends, was founded in 1896 in an effort to clean up the Common Council, of whose sixty-eight aldermen fifty-eight were estimated to be corrupt. The League aimed to replace as many of the fifty-eight as possible with honest men. But it was not easy: in 1896, as part of this campaign, a member of the Hull-House Men's Club ran for the second aldermanic position in the ward and against all expectations was elected. Too late, his idealistic backers found that their hero had his price: Johnny Powers promptly bought him out.

Jane Addams was chagrined but undiscouraged. By the time Powers came up for re-election in 1898, she had had time to observe him more closely and plan her attack. Her opening gun was a speech—delivered, improbably enough, to the Society for Ethical Culture—with the ponderous and apparently harmless title, "Some Ethical Survivals in Municipal Corruption." But appearances were deceptive: once under way, she took the hide off Powers and was scarcely easier on his opponents among the so-called "better elements."

She began by pointing out that for the immigrants, who were getting their first initiation in self-government, ethics was largely a matter of example: the office-holder was apt to set the standard and exercise a permanent influence upon their views. An engaging politician whose standards were low and "impressed by the cynical stamp of the corporations" could debauch the political ideals of ignorant men and women, with consequences that might, she felt, take years to erase.

Ethical issues were further complicated, she said, by habits of thought brought to the New World from the Old. Many Italians and Germans had left their respective fatherlands to escape military service; the Polish and Russian Jews, to escape government persecution. In all these cases, the government had been cast in the role of oppressor. The Irish, in particular, had been conditioned by years of resentment over English rule to regard any successful effort to feed at the public crib as entirely legitimate, because it represented getting the better of their bitterest enemies.

On the other hand, Miss Addams continued, there was nothing the immigrants admired more than simple goodness. They were accustomed to helping each other out in times of trouble, sharing from their own meager store with neighbors who were even more destitute. When Alderman Powers performed on a large scale the same good deeds which they themselves were able to do only on a small scale, was it any wonder that they admired him?

Given this admiration, and their Old World resentments toward government, the immigrants' developing standards of political morality suffered when Powers made it clear that he could "fix" courts or find jobs for his friends on the city payroll. It cheapened their image of American politics when they began to suspect that the source of their benefactor's largess might be a corrupt bargain with a traction tycoon, or with others who wanted something from the city of Chicago and were willing to pay for it.

Hull-House residents, Miss Addams said, very early found evidence of the influence of the boss's standards. When the news spread around the neighborhood that the House was a source of help in time of trouble, more and more neighbors came to appeal for aid when a boy was sent to jail or reform school, and it was impossible to explain to them why Hull-House, so ready to help in other ways, was not willing to get around the law as the Alderman did.

Removing Alderman Powers from office, Jane Addams told the sober gentlemen of the Society for Ethical Culture, would be no simple task. It would require a fundamental change in the ethical standards of the community, as well as the development of a deeper insight on the part of the reformers. These latter, she pointed out, with all their zeal for well-ordered, honest politics, were not eager to undertake the responsibilities of self-government 365 days a year. They were quite willing to come into the nineteenth ward at election time to exhort the citizenry, but were they willing to make a real effort to achieve personal relationships of the kind that stood Johnny Powers in such good stead?

On this last point, Hull-House itself had some experience. As Florence Kelley—a Hull-House resident who was to become a pioneer in the Illinois social reform movement—subsequently wrote:

> The question is often asked whether all that the House undertakes could not be accomplished without the wear and tear of living on the spot. The answer, that it could not, grows more assured as time goes on. You must suffer from the dirty streets, the universal ugliness, the lack of oxygen in the air you daily breathe, the endless struggle with soot and dust and insufficient water supply, the hanging from a strap of the overcrowded street car at the end of your day's work; you must send your children to the nearest wretchedly crowded school, and see them suffer the consequences, if you are to speak as one having authority and not as the scribes . . .

By 1898, after nine years of working with their neighbors, the Hull-House residents were ready to pit their influence against that of Powers. Jane Addams' philosophical address to the Ethical Culture society was followed by others in which she explained more concretely the relationships between Yerkes, Chicago's traction czar, and the city council, relationships in which Johnny Powers played a key role. With several important deals in the making, 1898 would be a bad year for Yerkes to lose his key man in the seats of power.

The election was scheduled for April. The reformers—led by Hull-House and supported by independent Democrats, the Cook County Republicans, and the Municipal Voters League—put up a candidate of their own, Simeon Armstrong, to oppose Powers, and undertook to organize and underwrite Armstrong's campaign. By the end of January, the usually imperturbable Powers suddenly began paying attention to his political fences. The newspapers noted with some surprise that it was the first time he had felt it necessary to lift a finger more than two weeks in advance of election day.

His first move was an attack on Amanda Johnson, a Hull-House resident who had succeeded Miss Addams as garbage inspector. A graduate of the University of Wisconsin and described by the papers as blond, blue-eyed, and beautiful, she had taken the civil service examination and duly qualified for the position. Alderman Powers announced to the world that Miss Johnson, shielded by her civil service status, was telling his constituents not to vote for him. The Chicago *Record* dropped a crocodile tear at the sad picture of the martyred alderman:

> General sympathy should go out to Mr. Powers in this, his latest affliction. Heretofore he has been persecuted often by people opposed to bad franchise ordinances. He has been hounded by the upholders of civil service reform. He has suffered the shafts of criticism directed at his career by disinterested citizens. A grand jury has been cruel to him. Invidious comments have been made in his hearing as to the ethical impropriety of gambling institutions. . . . It is even believed that Miss Johnson in her relentless cruelty may go so far as to insinuate that Mr. Powers' electioneering methods are no better than those attributed to her—that, indeed, when he has votes to win, the distinctions of the civil service law do not deter him from going after those votes in many ways.

Powers' next move was to attempt a redistricting that would cut off the eastern, or Italian, end of his ward, which he took to be most seriously under Hull-House influence. It was reported that he also felt this area had been a "large source of expense to him through the necessity of assisting the poor that are crowded into that district." "These people," the Chicago *Record* reported, "formerly tied to him by his charities are said to be turning toward Hull-House and will vote solidly against him next spring."

Neither of Powers' first efforts was notably successful. A few days after his attack on Miss Johnson the *Tribune* reported:

> Trouble sizzled and boiled for Alderman John Powers in his own bailiwick last night. The Nineteenth Ward Independent club raked over the Alderman's sins . . . and . . . much indignation was occasioned by Alderman Powers' opposition to Miss Amanda Johnson. One Irish speaker says Johnny is a disgrace to the Irish race now that he has descended to fighting "poor working girls."

Meantime, Powers' colleagues on the council redistricting committee had no intention of saving his skin at the expense of their own, and stood solidly against his gerrymandering effort. Now the shaken boss began to show signs of losing his temper. He told reporters that if Miss Addams didn't like the nineteenth ward she should move out. Later, still more infuriated, he announced that Hull-House should be driven out. "A year from now there will be no such institution," he said flatly, adding that the women at Hull-House were obviously jealous of his charities. The *Record* published a cartoon showing Powers pushing vainly against the wall of a very substantial house.

The news of the campaign soon spread beyond the bounds of Chicago. The New York *Tribune* commented that Powers

> wouldn't mind Miss Addams saying all those things about him if he didn't begin to fear that she may succeed in making some of his well-meaning but misled constituents believe them. She is a very practical person, and has behind her a large volunteer staff of other practical persons who do not confine their efforts to "gassin' in the parlors," but are going about to prove to the plain people of the nineteenth ward that a corrupt and dishonest man does not necessarily become a saint by giving a moiety of his ill-gotten gains to the poor.

By March the campaign was waxing warm, and Powers resorted to an attempt to stir up the Catholic clergy against Miss Addams and the reform candidate. One of the Hull-House residents, a deputy factory inspector and a Catholic herself, went directly to the priests to find out why they were supporting Powers. When she reported, Jane Addams wrote to a friend:

> As nearly as I can make out, the opposition comes from the Jesuits, headed by Father Lambert, and the parish priests are not in it, and do not like it. Mary talked for a long time to Father Lambert and is sure it is jealousy of Hull-House and money obligations to Powers, that he does not believe the charges himself. She cried when she came back.

In another letter written about the same time, Miss Addams said that Powers had given a thousand dollars to the Jesuit "temperance cadets," who had returned the favor with a fine procession supporting Powers' candidacy. "There was a picture of your humble servant on a transparency and others such as 'No petticoat government for us. . . .' We all went out on the corner to see it, Mr. Hinsdale carefully shielding me from the public view."

By now the battle between Hull-House and Johnny Powers was sharing headlines in Chicago newspapers with the blowing up of the *Maine* in Havana's harbor and the approach of the war with Spain. "Throughout the nineteenth ward," said the *Tribune,* "the one absorbing topic of conversation wherever men are gathered is the fight being made against Alderman Powers." It was rumored that Powers had offered a year's free rent to one of the opposition leaders if he would move out of the ward before election day, and the Hull-House group let it be known that the Alderman was spending money freely in the ward, giving his lieutenants far more cash to spread around than was his custom. "Where does the money come from?" Jane Addams asked, and answered her own question: "From Mr. Yerkes." Powers was stung, and challenged her to prove that he had ever received one dollar from any corporation.

"Driven to desperation," said the *Tribune*, "Ald. Powers has at last called to his aid the wives and daughters of his political allies." Determined to fight fire with fire, he dropped his opposition to "petticoat politicians" and gave his blessing to a Ladies Auxiliary which was instructed to counteract the work of the women of Hull-House. An enterprising reporter discovered that few of the ladies had ever seen Miss Addams or been to Hull-House, but all were obediently repeating the charge that she had "blackened and maligned the whole ward" by saying that its people were ignorant, criminal, and poor.

As the campaign became more intense, Jane Addams received numbers of violent letters, nearly all of them anonymous, from Powers' partisans, as well as various communications from lodginghouse keepers quoting prices for votes they were ready to deliver! When the Hull-House residents discovered evidence of ties between banking, ecclesiastical, and journalistic interests, with Powers at the center, they proceeded to publicize all they knew. This brought upon their heads a violent attack by the Chicago *Chronicle,* the organ of the Democratic ring.

Suddenly a number of nineteenth-ward businessmen who had signed petitions for the reform candidate came out for Powers. They were poor and in debt; Powers gave the word to a landlord here, a coal dealer there, and they were beaten. The small peddlers and fruit dealers were subjected to similar pressure, for each needed a license to ply his trade, and the mere hint of a revocation was enough to create another Powers man.

When Alderman John M. Harlan, one of the stalwarts of the Municipal Voters League, came into the ward to speak, Powers supplied a few toughs to stir up a riot. Fortunately Harlan was a sturdy character, and offered so forcefully to take on all comers in fisticuffs that no volunteers appeared. Allowed to proceed, he posed some embarrassing questions: Why did nineteenth-ward residents have to pay ten-cent trolley fares when most of the city paid five? Why, when Powers was head of the city council's free-spending committee on street paving, were the streets of the ward in execrable condition? Why were the public schools so crowded, and why had Powers suppressed a petition, circulated by Hull-House, to build more of them?

Freely admitting Powers' reputation for charity, Harlan made the interesting suggestion that the councilman's motives be put to the test: Would he be so generous as a private citizen? "Let us retire him to private life and see."

Powers was pictured by the papers as being nearly apoplectic at this attack from Miss Addams' friend. He announced that he would not be responsible for Harlan's safety if he returned to the nineteenth ward. (Since no one had asked him to assume any such responsibility, this was presumed to be an open threat.) Harlan returned at once, telling a crowd well-laced with Powers supporters that he would "rather die in my tracks than acknowledge the right of John Powers to say who should and who should not talk in this ward." Summoning up the memory of Garibaldi, he urged the Italians to live up to their tradition of freedom and not allow their votes to be "delivered."

In a quieter vein, Miss Addams too spoke at a public meeting of Italians, where, it was reported, she received profound and respectful attention. "Show that you do not intend to be governed by a boss," she told them. "It is important not only for yourselves but for your children. These things must be made plain to them."

As the campaign progressed, the reformers began to feel they had a real chance of defeating Powers. Jane Addams was persuaded to go in search of funds with which to carry out the grand finale. "I sallied forth today and got $100," she wrote, and "will have to keep it up all week; charming prospect, isn't it?" But on about the twentieth of March she began to have serious hopes, too, and redoubled her efforts.

As election day, April 6, approached, the Chicago *Tribune* and the Chicago *Record* covered the campaign daily, freely predicting a victory for the reformers. Alas for all predictions. When election day came, Powers' assets, which Jane Addams had so cogently analyzed in that faraway speech to the Society for Ethical Culture, paid off handsomely. It was a rough day in the nineteenth ward, with ten saloons open, one man arrested for drawing a gun, and everything, as Miss Addams wrote despondently when the count began to come in, "as bad as bad can be." Too many election judges were under Powers' thumb. The reform candidate was roundly defeated. Hull-House went to court to challenge the conduct of the election, but in the halls of justice Powers also had friends. It was no use.

Even in victory, however, Powers was a bit shaken. Hull-House had forced him, for the first time, to put out a great effort for re-election. It was obviously *not* going to move out of the nineteenth ward; indeed, if the past was any portent, its influence with his constituents would increase.

Powers decided to follow an ancient maxim, "If you can't lick 'em, join 'em." Early in the 1900 aldermanic campaign, several Chicago papers carried a straight news story to the effect that Hull-House and Johnny Powers had signed a truce, and quoted various paternally benevolent statements on the Alderman's part. In the *Chronicle*, for example, he was reported to have said: "I am not an Indian when it comes to hate . . . let bygones be bygones." A day or two later another rash of stories detailed a number of favors the Alderman was supposed to have done for Hull-House.

Jane Addams was furious, and after considerable deliberation she decided to reply. It was one of the few times in her long public career when she bothered to answer anything the newspapers said about her. She knew that with his eye on the campaign, the master politician was trying to give the appearance of having taken his most vigorous enemy into camp. She had been observing him too long not to realize what he was up to, and she could not possibly let him get away with it.

On February 20, 1900, a vigorous letter from Miss Addams appeared in nearly all the Chicago papers, reaffirming the attitude of Hull-House toward Mr. Powers. "It is needless to state," she concluded, "that the protest of Hull-House against a man who continually disregards the most fundamental rights of his constituents must be permanent."

Permanent protest, yes, but as a practical matter there was no use waging another opposition campaign. Powers held too many of the cards. When all was said and done, he had proved too tough a nut to crack, though Hull-House could—and did—continue to harass him. An observer of the Municipal Voters League, celebrating its success in the *Outlook* in June, 1902, described the vast improvement in the Common Council, but was forced to admit that a few wards were "well-nigh hopeless." He cited three: those of "Blind Billy" Kent, "Bathhouse John" Coughlin, and Johnny Powers.

From a larger standpoint, however, the battle between "Saint Jane" (as the neighbors called Jane Addams when she was not around) and the Ward Boss was not without significance. It was one of numerous similar battles that would characterize the progressive era the country over, and many of them the reformers would win. Because of her firsthand experience, because she lived *with* the immigrants instead of coming into their neighborhood occasionally to tell them what to do, Jane Addams was perhaps the first of the urban reformers to grasp the real pattern of bossism, its logic, the functions it performed, and the reason it was so hard to dislodge. Years later political scientists, beginning to analyze the pattern, would add almost nothing to her speech of 1898. If copies of *The Last Hurrah* have reached the Elysian fields, Jane Addams has spent an amused evening seeing her ideas developed so well in fictional form.

The campaign of 1898 throws considerable light on Jane Addams' intensely practical approach to politics, and upon a little-known aspect of the settlement-house movement. If anyone had told her and Ellen Starr in 1889 that the logic of what they were trying to do would inevitably force them into politics, they would have hooted. But in due time politics, in many forms, became central to Hull-House activity. For Jane Addams herself, the campaign against Powers was the first in a long series of political forays, all essentially based on the same desire—to see that government met the needs of the "other half."

The regulation of child labor, for example, was one political issue in which Hull-House residents became involved because of their knowledge of the lives of the neighbors. The first juvenile court in Chicago was set up as a result of their efforts; it was a direct response to the anxious mothers who could not understand why Hull-House would not help get their boys out of jail. The first factory inspection law in Illinois was also credited to Hull-House, and Florence Kelley became the first inspector. Another Hull-House resident—Dr. Alice Hamilton—pioneered in the field of industrial medicine. Because of their intimate acquaintance with the human cost of industrialization, settlement workers became vigorous advocates of promoting social justice through law.

It was a long jump but not an illogical one from the campaign against Powers to the stage of the Chicago Coliseum in August, 1912, when Jane Addams arose to second the nomination of Teddy Roosevelt by the Progressive party on a platform of social welfare. More remarkable than the ovation—larger than that given to any other seconder—was the fact that the huge audience seemed to listen carefully to what she had to say.

Some newspapers grandly estimated her value to T.R. at a million votes. "Like the report of Mark Twain's death," she commented, "the report is greatly exaggerated." But she campaigned vigorously, in the face of criticism that this was not a proper role for a woman, and when the Bull Moose cause failed, she did not believe it had been a waste of time. It had brought about, she wrote Roosevelt, more discussion of social reform than she had dared to hope for in her lifetime. Alderman Powers was still in office—as were many like him—but the sources of his power were being attacked at the roots.

When the 1916 campaign came around, Democrats and Republicans alike made bids for Jane Addams' support. The outbreak of war in Europe had turned her attention, however, in a different direction. As early as 1907, in a book called *Newer Ideals of Peace,* she had begun to elaborate William James's notion of a "moral equivalent of war," and had suggested that the experience of polyglot immigrant populations in learning to live together might be laying the foundations for a true international order. Like her ideals of social justice, those that she conceived on international peace had their beginning in the nineteenth ward.

To her, as to so many idealistic progressives, world war came as a profound shock. Her response was a vigorous effort to bring together American women and women from all the European countries to urge upon their governments a negotiated peace. In Europe, where she went in 1915 for a meeting of the Women's International Peace Conference, she visited prime ministers; at the end of that year she planned to sail on Henry Ford's peace ship, but illness forced her to withdraw at the last moment. At home she appealed to President Wilson. Unshaken in her pacifism, she stood firmly against the war, even after the United States entered it.

Her popularity seemed to melt overnight. Many women's clubs and social workers, who owed so much to her vision, deserted her. An Illinois judge who thought it dangerous for her to speak in wartime was widely supported in the press. For most of 1917 and 1918 she was isolated as never before or again. But she did not waver.

When the war ended she began at once to work for means to prevent another. Through the twenties she was constantly active in searching for ways in which women could cut across national lines in their work for peace. In 1931, in her seventy-first year, she received the Nobel Peace Prize—the second American to be so recognized. She died, full of honors, in 1935.

As for Johnny Powers, he had lived to a ripe old age and died in 1930, remaining alderman almost to the end, still fighting reform mayors, still protesting that he and Miss Addams were really friends, after all. From whichever department of the hereafter he ended up in, he must have looked down—or up—in amazement at the final achievements of his old enemy, who had been so little troubled by his insistence that there should be "no petticoats in politics."

Reforming College Football

John S. Watterson

It is no coincidence that during the Progressive Era the game of football was both reformed in the sense of being cleansed of some of the dangerous and unsporting elements that had infected it in earlier years and re-formed, given new rules that made it quite a different game from the one that occurred in 1869 when Princeton and Rutgers clashed in what traditionally has been called the first intercollegiate "football" contest. Football in 1910 was of course somewhat different from the game played in the 1990s but far closer to the modern game in form and tactics than to the game played in 1870 or even in 1900. Nor is it coincidental that Theodore Roosevelt, a man famous both as a reformer in the political sense and as a believer in the importance of physical fitness and physical competition, was president of the United States at the time and in the middle of the "progressive" changes that transformed the sport.

In the following pages, John S. Watterson describes the two "reformations" that affected collegiate football during the first decade of the twentieth century and places them in context. His essay is indeed a brief and fascinating history of football from its origin in the games of rugby and soccer to the complex (and still frequently scandal-ridden) sport we know today.

During October of 1905, President Theodore Roosevelt, who had recently intervened in a national coal strike and the Russo-Japanese War, turned his formidable attention to another kind of struggle. The President, a gridiron enthusiast who avidly followed the fortunes of his alma mater, Harvard, summoned representatives of the Eastern football establishment—Harvard, Yale, and Princeton—to the White House. He wanted to discuss brutality and the lack of sportsmanship in college play.

Theodore Roosevelt believed strongly that football built character, and he believed just as strongly that roughness was a necessary—even a desirable—feature of the game. "I have no sympathy whatever," he declared, "with the over-wrought sentimentality that would keep a young man in cotton wool. I have a hearty contempt for him if he counts a broken arm or collarbone as of serious consequences when balanced against the chance of showing that he possesses hardihood, physical prowess, and courage."

But now Roosevelt was worried that the brutality of the prize ring had invaded college football and might end up destroying it.

In an article in *McClure's Magazine*, the journalist Henry Beach Needham recounted an injury in the Dartmouth-Princeton game in which the star for Dartmouth—a black man—had his collarbone broken early in the game. A prep school friend of the Princeton quarterback who had inflicted the injury, himself black and a member of the Harvard team, confronted the offender: "You put him out because he is a black man."

"We didn't put him out because he is a black man," the Princeton quarterback replied indignantly. "We're coached to pick out the most dangerous man on the opposing side and put him out in the first five minutes of play." The author was a close friend of the President, and Roosevelt no doubt read Needham's two-part series. Soon after the first article had appeared, Roosevelt criticized flagrant disregard for the rules in his June commencement address at Harvard, and on his return trip he met with Needham.

By the fall of 1905 Roosevelt had more reason than ever to pay attention to college football. His son Ted was playing for the Harvard freshmen, and Roosevelt and other grads were concerned that the school's president, Charles Eliot, an opponent of football, might use gridiron conduct to argue for the abolition of the game at Harvard.

When Roosevelt's friend Endicott Peabody of Groton School, on behalf of an association of Eastern and Midwestern headmasters, suggested a meeting with Eastern college representatives, the President immediately sprang into action. Having ended the Russo-Japanese War and dealt with several major issues, *The New York Times* commented, Roosevelt "today took up another question of vital interest to the American people. He started a campaign of reform of football."

To the inner circle of football advisers and coaches who met with Roosevelt at the White House on October 9, 1905, the President first expressed general concerns about the game. Then he made a few remarks "on what he remembered of each college's unfair play from several things that had happened in previous years." Perhaps the examples hit too close to home; not everyone at the meeting concurred. Nevertheless, Roosevelt asked his guests to frame an agreement condemning brutality and disregard for the rules. The six men dutifully drew up a statement and pledged that their teams would honor it.

Unfortunately for Roosevelt the brief campaign did little more than draw attention to the evils of college play. The White House meeting came at the beginning of an injury-ridden season that plunged football into the worst crisis in its history. Twice more in 1905 the President intervened, behind the scenes, when lack of sportsmanship appeared to violate the spirit of the White House agreement. In the Harvard-Yale game, Harvard nearly withdrew its team from the field after a Yale tackler had hurled himself into a Harvard punt receiver who was calling for a fair catch and the referees refused to assess a penalty. Even Roosevelt's son Ted was battered in the Yale-Harvard freshman game, some said by Yale players out to ambush him.

By the end of November the protest had reached a fever pitch, and the future of college football—professional football barely existed—was more clouded than ever before. Columbia University abolished football play at the end of the season, President Nicholas Murray Butler declaring it an "academic nuisance." Professor Shailer Mathews of the University of Chicago Divinity School was more emphatic: "From the President of the United States to the humblest member of a school and college faculty there arises a general protest against this boy-killing, man-mutilating, money-making, education-prostituting, gladiatorial sport."

The crisis had been building for decades, and some of the problems that inflamed it were inherent in the American version of football, which had emerged from British rugby a generation earlier.

From its earliest years American football received mixed reviews as an entertaining sport but also a rough and sometimes dangerous one. In 1876 Yale and Harvard substituted rugby for the soccer-style version of football played in the first college matches. The British game was popular because it allowed players to run with the ball; but the rules prohibited members of the team with the ball to be in front of the ballcarrier, and the characteristic scrummage by which the ball was put in play was a far cry from the modern American system of four downs to make ten yards. In the rugby "scrum" the players gathered around the ball, their arms and bodies interlocked, and then kicked the ball until it came out of the pack. Before long the Eastern teams agreed to adopt a system of yards and downs—three downs to make five yards or lose ten yards—and devised a system of numerical scoring (a field goal counted five points, and by 1884, a touchdown counted four). The rule against interference in front of the ballcarrier, although often ignored by players and referees alike, was not repealed until 1888.

As early as 1884 a committee of Harvard faculty set about investigating the new game, and the members reported savage fistfights in which players had to be separated by the judges, the referees, and even the police. The bloodlust of the spectators also shocked the committee. While one player pushed a ballcarrier out of bounds, knocked him down, stole the ball, and returned in triumph to the field, the audience shouted, "Kill him," "Slug him," and "Break his neck." The Harvard faculty decided to ban football in 1888 but reneged after a year of angry student protest.

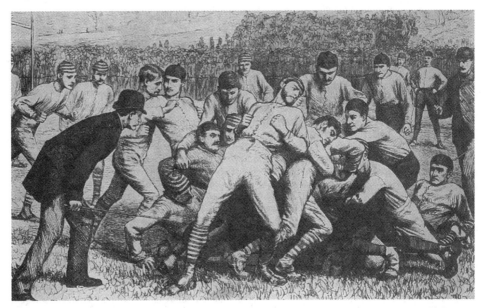

A drawing by A. B. Frost depicts one of the early struggles between Princeton and Yale, 1879.

By the early 1890s college football had overtaken college baseball in popularity, but it still was regarded with distrust by faculty, newspaper editors, and clergy; changes in the rules had ushered in an era of team violence.

In 1888 the rules committee moved to permit blocking and tackling below the waist, and the game became less individual and more team-oriented. The open-field running and kicking of rugby had given way to a regimented sport based on force and momentum. Teams concentrated their offenses near the ball rather than spread them soccer-style across the field, and now six or more men could go into motion before the ball was put into play. Working from a variety of wedge-shaped formations (the notorious flying wedge was allowed only at the start of the half or after a score, in place of today's kickoff return), players interlocked their arms—and sometimes clung to straps on the backs of fellow players' uniforms—to push, pull, or even catapult the carrier through the defense.

Violence and physical danger were not the sole complaints. President Eliot, in his 1892–93 annual report to the Harvard Corporation, denounced the training by youthful coaches, intent on winning at any cost, who, he argued, had transformed the players into "powerful animals" and thereby dulled their minds. He charged that football gave the impression that universities were little more than "places of mere physical sport and not of intellectual training" and that the sometimes hefty gate receipts from college athletics had turned amateur contests into major commercial spectacles. But Eliot's views were not yet shared by most college presidents or, for that matter, many faculty.

From the 1880s until his death in 1925, the best-known and most respected figure in college football circles was the "father of American football," Walter Camp. Camp once wrote: "Coaching a football team is the most engrossing thing in the world. It is playing chess with human pawns." He played for Yale and continued to coach there after going into business in New Haven; his teams racked up one national championship after another. As secretary of the Intercollegiate Football Rules Committee, Camp persuaded the committee to adopt the rules that converted what remained of rugby into team-oriented American football, and he kept his name before the football public by editing the annual football rules book and writing widely on the sport for newspapers and magazines. An able diplomat, Camp deftly steered football around the shoals of public criticism and intercollegiate squabbling without hampering its phenomenal growth. At the request of the Harvard Corporation, Camp assembled a committee that surveyed players and coaches, both past and present, to determine the extent of the injury problem. Most praised football and reported few problems with injuries; one player fondly recalled the "humanities dinged into me on the football field."

In 1894 the rules committee bowed to public pressure by abolishing the flying wedge and proclaiming that "no momentum mass plays shall be allowed." Such plays were defined, however, as more than three men going into motion before the ball was put in play. Ingenious coaches merely brought guards and tackles into the backfield and put their backs in motion before the ball was snapped. It seemed that no minor adjustments in the rules could contain the potential for difficulties in this crude and often violent sport. Not long after the adoption of the rules changes,

Harvard broke gridiron relations with Yale when the Yale captain, Frank Hinkey, near the end of an injury-plagued game, landed on the Harvard ballcarrier while the man was down and broke his collarbone. In a violent grudge match between Georgetown University and the Columbia Athletic Club of Washington, halfback George ("Shorty") Bahen was fatally injured, and three years later the Georgia legislature tried to ban football after the University of Georgia's Richard Von Gammon was killed in a game against the University of Virginia. Despite pleas by the dead boy's mother to save football, the Georgia legislature voted to abolish the game, and when the governor refused to sign the bill, the House of Representatives tried to pass it over his veto. Only a controversial interpretation of the legislative rules by the Speaker of the House saved football from the wrath of the legislators.

There were problems besides the violence. As football spread rapidly through the country, eligibility violations spread with it. In 1894 seven players of the University of Michigan's starting eleven were not even enrolled as students. At Ann Arbor two years later a talented halfback appeared at the season's start, never registered, attended only two courses, and dropped out after the end of the season. These "tramp" athletes became notorious for casually moving from school to school, as in the case of the Pennsylvania State College player who showed up so well in a loss to the University of Pennsylvania that he was practicing with the University of Pennsylvania team the following week. The Springfield *Republican* complained that the game had veered so far from its simple beginnings as to require an "armored eleven, twenty substitutes, a brass band, and a field telegraph."

Nevertheless, college presidents and their faculties continued to overlook many infractions because they believed football was a healthy outlet for pent-up schoolboy energies. President William H. P. Faunce of Brown University said the critics had forgotten "the old drinking and carousing of a generation ago . . . the smashing of windowpanes and destruction of property characteristic of that time." Football also provided an outlet for the faculty. Professor Woodrow Wilson's wife, Ellen, described her husband as so depressed by Princeton's first-ever loss to the University of Pennsylvania that only the election of Grover Cleveland as President that same week had relieved his gloom. "Really I think Woodrow would have had some sort of collapse if we had lost in politics, too," she wrote.

But the undercurrent of discontent evident in the 1890s continued into the early years of the new century. In the reformist tide of the Progressive Era college athletics suddenly found itself under attack along with political corruption and industrial monopolies. Taking aim at the practices in Eastern colleges, Henry Needham depicted, besides brutality, a system of laxity bordering on corruption in which prep schools such as Andover and Exeter groomed athletes for Eastern colleges and then bent the rules to allow the players to take entrance exams a year before they were eligible. "The only conclusion to be drawn," he wrote, "is that, thanks to the influence of the colleges, there is growing up a class of students tainted with commercialism."

He described the football career of an athlete named James J. Hogan, who entered Exeter in his early twenties and then went on to Yale. Though from a poor family, Hogan lived in the finest dormitory, took a free trip to Cuba with the Yale trainer Mike Murphy, and was given the lucrative franchise of representing the American Tobacco Company on campus. According to an official of the company, the player talked up the cigarettes to his friends. "They appreciate and like him; they realize that he is a poor fellow, working his way through college, and they want to help him. So they buy our cigarettes, knowing that Hogan gets a commission on every box sold in New Haven."

Even with the Needham articles and Roosevelt's concern, the public might have lost interest in the problem if the 1905 season had not brought its rash of casualties. There were twenty-three football deaths. Only a handful took place in intercollegiate play, but one in particular set in motion the movement to reform the game. In a match between Union College and New York University, Harold Moore of Union died after being kicked in the head. Chancellor Henry M. MacCracken of NYU seized the opportunity to summon a reform conference.

He invited the presidents of thirteen schools to confer in New York on December 5. Meeting less than two weeks after Columbia had dropped football, the conference came within a single vote of passing a resolution to abolish the game as then played but instead decided to hold a general convention of football-playing institutions later in the month.

The intercollegiate conference opened on December 28 with delegates from more than sixty schools attending. Some, like the representative from Columbia, wanted football done away with altogether, yet many delegates still hoped for a solution short of abolition. The pro-football forces grouped around Capt. Palmer Pierce of West Point and, according to a delegate from the University of Kansas, were the "best organized and came with a well-defined plan and a determination to save the game." The result was a proposal to appoint a rules committee to negotiate with the Intercollegiate Football Rules Committee in a final effort at joint action.

By early January the two committees were holding exploratory meetings followed by simultaneous but separate sessions at the Hotel Netherlands in New York City. Then, in a dramatic, though carefully orchestrated, move, the Harvard coach, Bill Reid, who after the White House meeting had met twice more with President Roosevelt, left the old committee to join the new group. Despite some grumbling by members of the old committee, a merger was arranged, and, symbolic of the transfer of power, Reid replaced Walter Camp as secretary of the joint rules committee. During the next months rules changes were hammered out in a series of tumultuous meetings.

As rules reform swung into motion, other complaints about football's role in college life were being hotly debated in the Midwestern "Big Nine" conference. Frederick Jackson Turner of the University of Wisconsin, best known for his essays on the American frontier, introduced a motion to suspend football for two years. An angry gathering of students marched on Turner's house. When he emerged, the students shouted, "When can we have football?" Amid hisses and shouts of "Put him in the lake!" Turner tried to reason with the students; they burned him in effigy.

In the end only Northwestern University dropped football. Many critics still wanted to give the rules committee a chance to make changes, although a few in the football world, such as Amos Alonzo Stagg, the University of Chicago coach and the only rules committee member from outside the East, feared that his fellow committee members might turn football into a "parlor game." The possibility of radical changes disturbed the old guard. Someone wrote to Walter Camp, troubled by rumors that "forward passes and other dream-like things have been brought into the realm of possibilities, even probabilities."

Already the rules committee had enacted the most sweeping changes since football had emerged from rugby a quarter-century before. In an attempt to strengthen the open-field features and to steer away from the grinding line play, a ten-yard rule was adopted. It would allow a team to have three opportunities to gain ten yards, rather than five yards as before. Walter Camp, who had proposed the change in 1904, believed that teams would have to play a more open offense to gain the extra five yards. Less palatable to older members was the "dream-like" forward pass that had been approved by the rules committee (before this change, the ball could only be lateraled).

The football world heaved a sigh of relief as all the major Eastern schools except Columbia embraced the new rules. In the 1906 season and for two years following, the verdict on the "new football" was generally favorable. In spite of fluctuations in the injury count, the number of deaths dropped to fourteen, fifteen, and ten.

Then, in the fall of 1909, the trend toward a safer game abruptly reversed itself. In a match between Harvard and West Point, the Army captain, Eugene Byrne, exhausted by continual plays to his side of the line, was fatally injured. Earl Wilson of the Naval Academy was paralyzed and later died as a result of a flying tackle. And the University of Virginia's halfback Archer Christian died after a game against Georgetown, probably from a cerebral hemorrhage suffered in a plunge through the line. "Does the public need any more proof," wrote the *Washington Post,* "that football is a brutal, savage, murderous sport? Is it necessary to kill many more promising young men before the game is revised or stopped altogether?" At both Georgetown and Virginia, football was suspended for the remainder of the season, and the District of Columbia school system banned it altogether. Even Col. John Mosby, the old Confederate raider, used Christian's death to rail against football as "murder" and said that the presence of a team doctor demonstrated that the game was tantamount to "war."

Stunned by the death of Christian, the University of Virginia's president, Eugene Alderman, who a decade earlier had declared, "I should rather see a boy of mine on the rush line fighting for his team than on the sideline smoking a cigarette," warned that the outcry was more than hysteria on the part of the press. President David Starr Jordan of Stanford referred to football as "Rugby's American pervert" and said that the "farce of football reform" that was slipped by the public in 1905 and 1906 could not be repeated. Even the presidents of the powerful triumvirate of Yale, Princeton, and Harvard, whose schools had not joined the conference of 1905, which was now known as the National Collegiate Athletic Association (NCAA), held special meetings to seek remedies.

As various sets of proposals were voted on, the forward pass loomed as the chief obstacle to settlement. By April 30, with the proceedings reaching a decisive point, opponents of the pass had collected enough votes to approve a motion to confine its reception to the area behind the line of scrimmage. While a three-man subcommittee put together a report, the Harvard coach Percy Haughton feverishly worked behind the scenes to save the apparently doomed forward pass. "To my mind," he wrote Amos Alonzo Stagg, "unless we retain the forward pass it will be the death of football."

On Friday, May 13, 1910, the committee adopted the new rules—seven men on the line of scrimmage, no pushing or pulling, no interlocking interference (arms linked or hands on belts and uniforms), and four fifteen-minute quarters—and it readopted the forward pass. Unable to invent a new formula for yards and downs, the committee stuck for the time with ten yards in three downs. Although the forward pass was narrowly saved, it still was not given a full vote of confidence; it had to be thrown at least five yards behind the line of scrimmage and was limited to twenty yards past it.

The adoption of these rules eliminated the cruder versions of nineteenth-century football and established the groundwork for a sleeker, faster, wide-open game. Two years later, in 1912, the committee added a fourth down to make ten yards, raised the value of the touchdown to six points, and reduced the field goal to three points. The twenty-yard restriction on forward passes was also eliminated, though the pass still had to be thrown from five yards behind the line of scrimmage. With the lifting of the most restrictive rules, the forward pass quickly became a potent offensive weapon, as illustrated by the brilliant performance of Knute Rockne and Gus Dorais in Notre Dame's 35–13 airborne upset of Army in 1913. In the sports-crazy 1920s the new open football proved to be entertainment as well as to have cash value, and mammoth stadiums were erected to accommodate the swelling attendance.

In the years since 1912 the size and speed of the athletes have changed the hazards of the game, but the form of football had remained much the same as it was when it emerged from the crisis of 1910. Although the upstart forward pass quickly proved itself, the rule requiring the ball to be thrown from five yards behind the line of scrimmage was not removed from college rules until 1945. Perhaps the rule change that altered the game the most was the adoption in the 1940s of free substitution, which ushered in two-platoon football. In 1954 the football solons tried to restore the old style of football, in which the same players had to play offense and defense, but this rear-guard action was abandoned in the early 1960s.

Football is safer today than in the early 1900s. Carefully engineered and tested equipment, especially headgear, has reduced the life-threatening injuries that plagued football before 1920. Early headgear, seldom worn consistently, shielded the ears and surface of the head but gave inadequate protection to the skull and brain. After World War I a sponge-rubber lining was added to the crown of the helmet, and by the late 1930s a sturdy leather helmet with an inner felt lining was being used. But it was not until 1943 that all players were required to wear headgear. The plastic helmet, which distributes shock more evenly, was introduced in the 1940s amid objections reminiscent of those that accompanied the original solely leather helmets. Some critics argued—and still do—that the hard plastic helmet, used as an offensive weapon, has as much potential for causing as for preventing serious injuries. So the game remains the subject of periodic debate requiring a battery of experts to keep it in balance between offense and defense, bodily contact and safety.

In spite of success in reforming the rules, criticism of commercial abuses of football and other sports has lingered, and the complaints of commercialism in big-time college sports are reminiscent of the criticisms in the early 1900s. Although the NCAA was in the 1940s given broader investigative and enforcement powers, problems have persisted. Professors and coaches do not love one another, and some college presidents face pressures—and quandaries—similar to those of their counterparts in the era of Charles Eliot and Frederick Jackson Turner.

Unlike turn-of-the-century crises, violence plays a comparatively minor role in today's turmoils. Rather, it is illegal payments to athletes, violations of academic standards, and drug abuse that bedevil athletic programs.

———————

Gifford Pinchot: Father of the Forests

T. H. Watkins

Gifford Pinchot is best known for his role in the so-called "Ballinger-Pinchot Controversy," a heated and in part politically motivated conflict he had as Chief Forester of the U.S. Department of Agriculture with Richard Ballinger, President William Howard Taft's Secretary of the Interior, about the disposition of certain coal-rich lands in Alaska. Actually, as T. H. Watkins explains in this essay, Pinchot was an important political leader, a three-term governor of Pennsylvania, one of the first professional foresters in America, and a lifelong supporter of conservationist causes of all types. His career in conservation is summarized and evaluated in these pages.

T. H. Watkins, editor of *Wilderness*, the magazine of the Wilderness Society, is also the author of *Righteous Pilgrim: The Life and Times of Harold L. Ickes*.

Gifford Pinchot passed through nearly six decades of American public life like a Jeremiah, the flames of certitude seeming to dance behind his dark eyes. "Gifford Pinchot is a dear," his good friend and mentor Theodore Roosevelt once said of him, "but he is a fanatic, with an element of hardness and narrowness in his temperament, and an extremist."

The complaint was legitimate, but the zealot in question also was the living expression of an idea shared by much of an entire generation (indeed, shared by Roosevelt himself): the conviction that men and women could take hold of their government and shape it to great ends, great deeds, lifting all elements of American life to new levels of probity, grace, freedom, and prosperity. The urge was not entirely selfless; the acquisition and exercise of power have gratifications to which Pinchot and his kind were by no means immune. But at the forefront was a solemn and utterly earnest desire that the lot of humanity should be bettered by the work of those who were equipped by circumstance, talent, and training to change the world. It had something to do with duty and integrity and honesty, and if it was often marred by arrogance, at its best it was just as often touched by compassion.

And the world, in fact, was changed.

"I have . . . been a Governor, every now and then, but I am a forester all the time—have been, and shall be, all my working life." Gifford Pinchot made this pronouncement in a speech not long before his death at the age of eighty-one, and repeated it in *Breaking New Ground,* his account of the early years of the conservation movement and his considerable place in it. It was true enough, but it could just as legitimately be said of him that he had been a forester every now and then but was a politician, had been and would be, all his working life.

. . . From childhood Pinchot had been active in the outdoors, fond of hiking, camping, and, especially, trout fishing. Since there was nowhere yet in the United States to study his chosen profession, after graduating from Yale he took himself back to Europe, where for more than a year he studied forest management at the French Forestry School in Nancy and put in a month of fieldwork under Forstmeister ("Chief Forester") Ulrich Meister in the city forest of Zurich, Switzerland.

Back in this country he was hired by George W. Vanderbilt in 1892 to manage the five-thousand-acre forest on his Biltmore estate in North Carolina, a ragged patchwork of abused lands purchased from numerous individual farmers. While nursing this wrecked acreage back to health, the young forester persuaded Vanderbilt to expand his holdings by an additional one hundred thousand acres of nearly untouched forest land outside the estate. This new enterprise became known as the Pisgah Forest, and it was there in 1895 that Pinchot introduced what were almost certainly the first scientific logging operations ever undertaken in this country.

By then the young man had made a secure reputation in the field; indeed, he *was* the field. In December 1893 he opened an office in Manhattan as a "consulting forester." Over the next several years, while continuing his work for Vanderbilt in North Carolina, he provided advice and research work on forest lands in Michigan, Pennsylvania, and New York State—including the six-million-acre Adirondack Park and Forest Preserve, established in 1895 as the largest state-owned park in the nation. . . .

It would be difficult to find a more convenient symbol for the dark side of American enterprise than the state of the nation's forest lands in the last quarter of the nineteenth century. Restrained only by the dictates of the marketplace, the timber industry had enjoyed a free hand for generations, and the wreckage was considerable. Most of the best forest land east of the Mississippi had long since been logged out—sometimes twice over—and while generally humid conditions had allowed some of the land to recover in second and third growth, erosion had permanently scarred many areas. Unimpeded runoff during seasonal rains had caused such ghastly floods as that leading to the destruction of Johnstown, Pennsylvania, in 1889.

The land of the Mississippi and Ohio valleys was almost entirely privately owned; west of the Mississippi most of the land belonged to the nation. It was called the public domain, its steward was the federal government, as represented by the General Land Office, and for years it had been hostage to the careless enthusiasm of a tradition that looked upon land as a commodity to be sold or an opportunity to be exploited, not a resource to be husbanded. About two hundred million acres of this federal land were forested, and much of it, too, had been systematically mutilated. In addition to legitimate timber companies that consistently misused the various land laws by clear-cutting entire claims without even bothering to remain around long enough to establish final title, many "tramp" lumbermen simply marched men, mules, oxen, and sometimes donkey engines onto an attractive (and vacant) tract of public forest land, stripped it, and moved out, knowing full well that apprehension and prosecution were simply beyond the means or interest of the understaffed, over-committed, and largely corrupt General Land Office. As early as 1866 such instances of cheerful plunder had gutted so many forests of the public domain that the surveyors general of both Washington Territory and Colorado Territory earnestly recommended to the General Land Office that the forest lands in their districts be sold immediately, while there was something left to sell.

The forests were not sold, nor did they vanish entirely, but they did remain vulnerable to regular depredation. It was not until 1891 and passage of an obscure leg-

islative rider called the Forest Reserve Clause that the slowly growing reform element in the executive branch was enabled to do anything about it. Armed with the
power of this law, President Benjamin Harrison withdrew thirteen million acres of
public forest land in the West from uses that would have been permitted by any of
the plethora of lenient land laws then on the books, and at the end of his second
term, President Grover Cleveland added another twenty-one million acres. Since
there was virtually no enforcement of the new law, however, withdrawal provided little protection from illegal use; at the same time, it specifically disallowed legitimate
use of public timber and grasslands. In response to the howl that arose in the West
and to give some semblance of protection and managed use, Congress passed the
Forest Organic Act of June 1897, which stipulated that the forest reserves were intended "to improve and protect the forest . . . for the purpose of securing favorable
conditions of water flow, and to furnish a continuous supply of timber for the use
and necessities of citizens of the United States."

Gifford Pinchot, the young "consulting forester," was the author of much of the
language of the act. In the summer of 1896 he had distinguished himself as the secretary of the National Forest Commission, a body formed by President Cleveland to
investigate conditions in the nation's public forests and to recommend action for
their proper use and protection, and it was the commission that had put forth the
need for an organic act. No one knew more about American forests than Pinchot
did, and he seemed the only logical choice to head the Department of Agriculture's Forestry Division when the position of director fell vacant in May 1898.

On the face of it, Pinchot's new post was less than prestigious. The Forestry Division was housed in two rooms of the old red-brick Agriculture Building on the
south side of the Mall in Washington, D.C. It enjoyed a total of eleven employees
and an annual appropriation of $28,500. And since the forest reserves remained
under the jurisdiction of the Interior Department, the Forestry Division had little
to do beyond advising private landowners on the proper management of their
wood lots and forests. This was anathema to an activist like Pinchot, and he was
soon honing the skills that would make him one of the most persistent and effective lobbyists who ever prowled the cloakrooms and cubbyholes of Congress.

His ambition was not a small one: He wanted nothing less than to get the forest
reserves transferred to Agriculture and placed under his care in the Forestry Division and then to build the division into the first effective agency for the management and conservation of public lands in the history of the nation. It did not hurt
his chances when he became intimate with another early American conservationist—Theodore Roosevelt. . . .

The two men combined almost immediately in an effort to get the forest reserves into Pinchot's care. The public lands committees of both the House and Senate, however, were dominated by Westerners, many of whom had vested interests in
the status quo, and it took more than three years of public campaigning and artful
cajolery, Roosevelt himself bringing the full weight of the Presidency to bear on the
point, before Pinchot was given his heart's desire: passage of the Forest Transfer
Act, on February 1, 1905. In addition to bringing over the forests—which now to-
taled more than sixty-three million acres—the new law provided for the charging of
fees for cutting timber and grazing cattle and sheep, and this was followed by the

A solitary pine tree adorns the original badge of the U.S. Forest Service, which was founded by Gifford Pinchot at the beginning of the century.

Agricultural Appropriation Act of March 3, a section of which gave federal foresters "authority to make arrests for the violation of laws and regulations relating to the forest reserves. . . ."

The government was now in the tree business with a vengeance. Shortly the name of the reserves was changed to that of national forests, the Forestry Division to that of the U.S. Forest Service, and Gifford Pinchot was solidly in place as the nation's first chief forester, a position he would hold officially only until his resignation in 1910 but would hold in his heart for the rest of his life.

With his President's blessing, Pinchot crafted the young agency into a public body whose dedication to the ideal of service to the public was nearly unique for its time (or our own, for that matter). It came directly out of Pinchot's own convictions. "It is the first duty of a public officer to obey the law," he wrote in *The Fight for Conservation,* in 1910. "But it is his second duty, and a close second, to do everything the law will let him do for the public good. . . ."

It was an elite corps that Pinchot created, built on merit and merit alone, one in which both competence and stupidity were swiftly rewarded—and little went unnoticed by the chief forester ("I found him all tangled up," Pinchot wrote to a lieutenant about one hapless employee, "and generally making an Ass of himself, with splendid success"). William R. Greeley, one of the twenty-five hundred foresters who served under Pinchot (and who later became chief forester himself), caught the spirit of Pinchot's influence precisely: "He made us . . . feel like soldiers in a patriotic cause."

The system this exemplary body of men administered was carefully structured by the chief forester. Individual forests were divided up into management units, each with its own ranger or ranger force, and administrative headquarters were established in the six districts across the West where most of the forests were grouped, from Missoula, Montana, to Portland, Oregon. Pinchot gave his district supervisors a great deal of autonomy and encouraged them to give their rangers similarly loose reins in the field—whether selecting stands of harvestable trees, supervising a timber sale, regulating the number of cows or sheep that might be allowed on a piece of grazing land, or fighting fires. . . .

. . . By the time Roosevelt left office in March 1909, the national forest system had been enlarged to 148 million acres, and the Forest Service had become one of the most respected government services in the nation—reason enough for the historian M. Nelson McGeary's encomium of 1960: "Had there been no Pinchot to build the U.S. Forest Service into an exceptionally effective agency, it would hardly have been possible to report in 1957 that 'most' of the big lumber operators had adopted forestry as a policy; or that the growth of saw timber has almost caught up with the rate of drain on forest resources from cutting, fire, and natural losses. . . ."

Nor, it is safe to say, would there have been much left of the forests themselves. The principles Pinchot put to work would inform the management of the public lands throughout most of the twentieth century and become one of the roots of the sensibility we call environmentalism. It was called conservation then, and Pinchot always claimed that he was the first to put that use upon the word. "Conservation," he wrote, "means the wise use of the earth and its resources for the lasting good of men. Conservation is the foresighted utilization, preservation, and/or renewal of forests, waters, lands, and minerals, for the greatest good of the greatest number for the longest time."

Wise use was the cornerstone, and Pinchot and his followers had little patience with the still-embryonic notion that the natural world deserved preservation quite as much for its own sake as for the sake of the men and women who used it. John Muir, a hairy wood sprite of a naturalist whom Pinchot had met and befriended as early as 1896, personified this more idealistic instinct, tracing the roots of his own inspiration back to Henry David Thoreau's declaration that "in Wildness is the preservation of the World." For a time, the two men were allies in spite of their differences, but the friendship disintegrated after 1905, when Pinchot lent his support to the efforts of the city of San Francisco to dam the Hetch Hetchy Valley in Yosemite National Park for a public water-and-power project in order to free the city from a private power monopoly.

Muir, whose writings about Yosemite had brought him a measure of fame, had founded the Sierra Club in 1892 largely as a tool to protect the glorious trench of the Yosemite Valley and other pristine areas in the Sierra Nevada. Among these was the Hetch Hetchy Valley, which these early preservationists maintained was the equal of Yosemite itself in beauty. The reservoir that would fill up behind the proposed dam on the Tuolumne River would obliterate that beauty. But this was exactly the sort of public power-and-water project that spoke most eloquently to the deepest pragmatic instincts of Pinchot and his kind, who argued that every measure of conservation as they understood it would be fulfilled by approval of the project. "Whoever dominates power," Pinchot wrote, "dominates all industry. . . ."

Pinchot's devotion to the principles of conservation went beyond the immediate question of use versus preservation. Monopoly was evil personified, and monopoly, he believed, stemmed directly from the control of the natural world. "Monopoly of resources," he wrote in *Breaking New Ground,* "which prevents, limits, or destroys equality of opportunity is one of the most effective of all ways to control and limit human rights, especially the right of self-government." With this conviction to guide him, it did not take him long to find his way from the world of conservation to the world of politics, where, like thousands of his class, he found his imagination seized by Progressive Republicanism.

The movement had been distilled from more than forty years of what the historian Howard Mumford Jones called "exuberance and wrath" following the Civil War. Its followers saw themselves and their values caught in a vise: threatened on one side by an increasingly violent and potentially revolutionary uprising on the part of the great unwashed—largely represented by the Democratic party—and on the other by a cynical plutocratic brotherhood—largely represented by the regular Republican party—which brutally twisted and subverted American institutions for purposes of personal greed and power.

Imperfectly but noisily, Theodore Roosevelt had given these people in the middle a voice and a symbol to call their own, and when he chose not to run for a third term in 1908, they felt abandoned. Prominent among them was Gifford Pinchot, and there is some evidence to suggest that he engineered his own dismissal as chief forester by President William Howard Taft, whom Roosevelt had groomed as his own chosen successor. The opportunity came in 1909, when Pinchot learned that Taft's Secretary of the Interior, Richard Ballinger, was determined to honor a number of coal-mining claims on lands in Alaska that Roosevelt had earlier withdrawn from such uses.

When Taft backed his Interior Secretary, Pinchot chose to see it as the beginning of a wholesale repudiation of all that Roosevelt had done to champion the public interest. He made no secret of his conclusions, and Taft was certain that more than bureaucratic integrity was behind Pinchot's loudly voiced concerns. . . .

Taft resisted as long as he reasonably could, but when Pinchot violated the President's direct orders to maintain silence by writing an open letter to a Senate committee investigating the Ballinger matter, he decided he had no choice. Calling the letter an example of insubordination "almost unparalleled in the history of the government," Taft fired the chief forester of the United States on January 7, 1910. . . .

But the essential legacy of this committed, driven man, this public servant, this prince of rectitude, is the national forests themselves. There are 191 million acres of them now, spreading over the mountain slopes and river valleys of the West like a great dark blanket, still the center of controversy, still threatened and mismanaged and nurtured and loved as they were when the son of a dry goods merchant first walked in an American wood and wondered what could be done to save it for the future.

4 Early Twentieth Century: Peace and War

A World War II poster depicting the many nations united in the fight against the Axis powers.

Our War with Spain Marked the First Year of the American Century

John Lukacs

In 1945 newspaper publisher Henry Luce proclaimed, prematurely but perhaps not inaccurately, the twentieth as "the American century." In this essay historian John Lukacs broadens the timespan. The "American century" began in 1898, when the United States went to war with Spain over Cuba and acquired an empire in the Pacific, thus inaugurating American overseas missions during the First and Second World Wars, the Korean War, the Vietnam War, as well as lesser operations in places such as Somalia, the Persian Gulf and, most recently, Afghanistan. In 1898 the United States shifted from being a "hemispheric power," largely uninterested in what transpired in Europe, Asia, and Africa, and became an important player in the "great game" of world affairs. What caused this shift in national orientation? Lukacs discounts the bellicose rhetoric of politicians and generals at the time. Such people had been saying similar things for decades and had been ignored. More significant, Lukacs asserts, was a convergence of ideas that acquired wide acceptance among the nation's leaders: the notion, derived from the application of Darwinian principles to human affairs, that the "fittest" nations would prevail; the conviction, based on an analysis of empires in history, that nations must control the seas to survive; the assumption that the white race, as manifestly the "fittest," had a duty to guide the lesser ones; the belief among Christians that "primitive" peoples needed the light of Christ to find their way to civilization. These ideas, or subsequent variants, helped draw Americans onto the world stage. But Lukacs hints that just as the Spanish-American war had a bitter aftermath, the same could be said of the American Century. Lukacs's most recent books include *Hitler of History* (1997), *Five Days in London: May, 1940* (1999), and *Thread of Years* (1998).

In April 1898, the American Century suddenly began. "Suddenly" because what happened then—the declaration of war against Spain—led to a rapid crystallization of a passionate nationalism. The American longing for national aggrandizement existed before 1898—indeed it was gathering momentum—but as the great French writer Stendhal wrote in his essay "On Love," passion has a way of "crystallizing" suddenly, as a reaction to external stimuli. Such a stimulus, in the history of the United States, was the Spanish-American War in 1898. When it was over, in a famous (or infamous) phrase John Hay would call it "a splendid little war." Well, as far as wars go (and many of them tend to go unexpectedly far), it *was* "a splendid little war." But its consequences were not little at all. . . .

The island of Cuba was one of the last (and the largest remaining) Spanish colonies in the Western Hemisphere. Its political class wanted independence from

Spain. It could not achieve this by itself. There was nothing very new about that. Trouble in Cuba had flared up often during the nineteenth century. But in 1895 there arose conditions resembling a civil war (or, more precisely, a guerrilla war). At first the Spanish military reacted energetically. Soon it became evident that the problem was triangular, involving not only Spain and the Cuban rebels but also the United States. For one thing, the rebels depended more and more on American support, and particularly on their abettors in Florida. (What else is new?) Perhaps more important was a surge of American public and popular opinion, which was dishonestly inflated by the novel element of the "yellow press," the national chains of Hearst and Pulitzer newspapers, proclaiming the Cuban situation to be intolerable. "Intolerable" is, of course, what people think must not be tolerated, and that was the continued presence of Spain in Cuba. In late 1897 the Spanish government showed a very considerable willingness to compromise, whereby all sensible reasons for an American intervention in Cuba could be eliminated. But passion is not governed by reason, and there were many groups of people with reasons of their own. On February 15, 1898, the U.S. battleship *Maine* blew up in Havana Harbor. There was a large loss of American lives and an immediate clamor for war. "Remember the *Maine*!" One hundred years later we do not know what caused the explosion. Possibly it was the work of Cubans, hoping to incite Americans thereby for the sake of their "liberation" from Spain. (Sixty years later a Cuban leader arose whose main purpose was to declare Cuba's "liberation" not from Spain but from the United States. Fidel Castro was not anti-Spanish but anti-American. His ancestors were Spanish-Cubans in 1898; he maintained cordial relations with Generalissimo Franco, the anti-Communist dictator of Spain, upon whose death Castro declared three days of national mourning in Cuba. Such is the irony of history—or, rather, of human nature.)

After the catastrophe, the Spanish government was willing to settle almost everything to the satisfaction of the United States, but it was too late—too late because of the inflamed state of American public opinion. President McKinley did not have the will to oppose anything like that. On April 11, 1898, he sent a message to Congress; the formal declaration of war came two weeks afterward.

One week later Commodore (soon to become Admiral) George Dewey destroyed a Spanish squadron on the other side of the world, in Manila Bay. Some of his warships now raced across the southern Pacific and around the Horn to help blast another Spanish squadron out of the warm waters of Santiago Bay. Meanwhile, American troops had landed, unopposed, in Cuba and then won battles (in reality, successful skirmishes) at El Caney and San Juan Hill. Later in July Americans, again unopposed, invaded Puerto Rico. The war was over. Spain asked for peace. An armistice was signed on August 12, and the final terms were nailed down in Paris in December. American losses were minimal: a few hundred men. The United States insisted on, and got, Cuba, Puerto Rico, the Philippines, and Guam.

And also Hawaii, whose annexation had been—unsuccessfully—urged on two Presidents by American intriguers and filibusterers. President Cleveland, and for a while McKinley, refused the annexation. But by July 1898 the nationalist tide was too much for this President and for much of the Congress: The United States annexed Hawaii.

It was thus that one hundred years ago the United States—which, during the first century of its existence, thought of itself as the prime power in the Americas, a hemispheric power—became a world power imperiously, geographically, a world power of the first rank, with incalculable consequences.

In 1898 there were no Gallup Polls; there was no such thing as public-opinion research. Still, it is possible to reconstruct the main elements of what the people of the United States thought (and perhaps felt) about these events.

That tremendous surge of national self-confidence, debouching into supernationalism (in reality, imperialism, though most Americans would shy away from such a word), must not obscure the fact that as in every war in the history of this country, Americans were divided. On one side, which turned out to be the dominant one, were the expansionists of 1898. Of their many and increasingly vocal declarations let me cite but one or two. There was Sen. H. M. Teller of Colorado, who as early as 1893 proclaimed: "I am in favor of the annexation of Hawaii. I am in favor of the annexation of Cuba. I am in favor of the annexation of the great country lying north of us." (He meant Canada.) . . . And when the war was over, Sen. Orville H. Platt of Connecticut said: "The same force that had once guided Pilgrim sails to Plymouth Rock had impressed our ships at Manila and our army at Santiago. Upon us rested the duty of extending Christian civilization, of crushing despotism, of uplifting humanity and making the rights of man prevail. Providence has put it upon us." On the other side of Congress were the opponents of the expansionists. There was Sen. George F. Hoar: "The Monroe Doctrine is gone." Or Sen. Donelson Caffery: "Sir, Christianity can not be advanced by force." What drove the expansionists was "lust of power and greed for land, veneered with the tawdriness of false humanity."

The USS Iowa *was the newest U.S. battleship in the Spanish-American War. Commissioned in 1897, the* Iowa *fired the first shot in the Battle of Santiago on July 3, 1898.*

It is at this point instructive to look at the character and the development of these divisions of American opinion. The twentieth-century terminology of "internationalists versus isolationists" does not apply. Besides the fact that "isolationism" as a category came into usage only after World War I, the expansionists of 1898 were American unilateralists, not internationalists, while their opponents were not isolationists either. What clashed were two different visions of American destiny. These were already visible well before 1898, to which I shall soon turn. More germane to the national debate of 1898 were the differing tendencies of political parties, national regions, and portions of society. With few exceptions Republicans were expansionists; Democrats were not. That was already evident earlier in the 1890s, when the Republican President Benjamin Harrison and his Secretary of State, John W. Foster (grandfather of John Foster Dulles), were in favor of the forced annexation of Hawaii, whereas the Democratic President Grover Cleveland and his Secretary of State, Walter Q. Gresham, were not. These divisions were not absolute; there were a few anti-imperialist Republicans. Yet it ought to be observed that the Republicans were the more *nationalist* party of the two, something that, by and large, remained true for most of the following century and is discernible even now. (In 1892 the Republican party platform called for "the achievement of the manifest destiny of the Republic in the broadest sense." In 1956 the Republican party platform called for "the establishment of American air and naval bases all around the world." The man who coined the term manifest destiny in the 1840s, John L. O'Sullivan, was a Democrat, who later condemned "wicked and crazy Republicanism." He died in 1895.) It is significant to note that many of the opponents of the expansionists were Southern Democrats, including such unreconstructed populists as "Pitchfork Ben" Tillman—which is interesting, since forty years earlier it was the South that had proposed the acquisition of Cuba. Many, certainly the most vocal, expansionists were Protestant churchmen; the hierarchy of American Catholics was, for the most part, not. The leaders of American finance and business (Andrew Carnegie, James J. Hill, J. P. Morgan, and most of Wall Street) opposed the war—at least for some time.

But much of this was soon swept away. Immediately after the declaration of war the businessmen's and financiers' opposition crumbled (another instance of the limitations of the economic interpretation of history, or of the flag following trade; the reverse is rather true). In the hot skillet of nationalist emotions, the opposition of most Catholics melted away fast. Two former Confederate generals, Joe Wheeler and Fitzhugh Lee, were now major-generals of the United States Army. Fifteen Democrats and Populists voted for the ratification of the peace treaty with Spain; only two Republicans voted against it. The vote was 57 to 27 in the Senate, one above the needed two-thirds majority. William Jennings Bryan, once an anti-expansionist, urged a speedy ratification. It did not do much for him; in 1900 McKinley beat him by a landslide. Less than a year later McKinley was dead, the President was now Theodore Roosevelt, and the American Century was on.

In 1898 the Spanish-American War was the culmination of a great wave of national sentiment that had begun to rise many years before. There was a change, less in the temperature of patriotism than in the national vision of the destiny of the United States, after the end of the first century of its existence. In sum, the time had come for the United States to expand not only its light and its example but its power and its institutions all around the globe. When the Chicago world's fair opened in 1893, Chauncey M. Depew gave the speech of dedication. "This day," he said, "belongs not to America but the world. . . . We celebrate the emancipation of man." No one had spoken in such tones at the Centennial in 1876 in Philadelphia. . . .

It is wrong to think that this rise of a national sentiment was nothing but emotional, fueled by war fever and declamatory rhetoric. What had begun to change the course of the mighty American ship of state was a change of mentality, including a powerful intellectual impulse. Its proponents included some of the most intelligent, and learned, Americans of a generation. The usage of the noun *intellectual* (adopted from the Russian, designating a certain kind of person) had hardly begun to appear in the American language in the 1890s, but the adjective was properly applicable to the capacities of such men as Theodore Roosevelt, Henry Cabot Lodge, Alfred Thayer Mahan, John Hay, Whitelaw Reid, and Albert J. Beveridge. Far from being provincial, they looked around the world and saw how the European powers had embarked on their imperialist expansion. For the United States to opt out from a course of spreading its influence beyond its continental boundaries would be a sickening symptom of a materialist small-mindedness.

And what were the ingredients of this philosophy—for a kind of philosophy it was. It amounted to more than a mere emulation of the other Great Powers of the present. One principal ingredient was the belief in sea power. That was the key to modern history, as Alfred Mahan wrote in his famous book *The Influence of Sea Power Upon History* in 1890, and it was more than coincidental that a Republican President and Congress embarked on a Big Navy program in the same year, the first substantial American military expenditure since the Civil War. There was a racial ingredient: the belief that the most advanced, indeed the ruling, people of the globe were of Anglo-Saxon and Teutonic stock. Besides the Roosevelt-Lodge-Mahan-Hay-Reid coterie of progressive imperialists, there were prestigious professors in the leading American universities whose eulogies of the Teutonic-Germanic races were influential as well as popular. . . . The Congregationalist minister Josiah Strong wrote as early as 1885 about the American Anglo-Saxon destined to be his brother's keeper: "If I read not amiss, this powerful race will move . . . down upon Central and South America, or upon the islands of the sea . . . and beyond. And can any one doubt that the result of this competition of races will be 'the survival of the fittest'?" Not many people know that Rudyard Kipling's "Take Up the White Man's Burden" was written for Americans; even fewer are aware that in *The Descent of Man* Charles Darwin wrote about America: "the heir of all ages, in the foremost files of time." Such a concordance of Darwinism and of racism and of Protestant Christianity sounds strange now. In the 1890s it was not. In 1894 Mahan wrote: "Comparative religion teaches that creeds which reject missionary enterprise are foredoomed to decay. May it not be so with nations?" Many of the shrill proposals for American imperialism in the name of Protestant Christianity were reconstructed later by historians, foremost among them Julius W. Pratt. Thus the editorial of the *Christian and Missionary Alliance* in April 1898: "God is stronger than either the Romish Church or the Catholic powers of Europe. We should pray not only that Cuba be free, but that these fair Eastern isles shall become scenes of gospel triumphs and the salvation of countless souls. . . ."

Such were many of the voices current in 1898. They were not necessarily what the majority of Americans thought. But such influences cannot be precisely defined. Hard and determined minorities may acquire an impact on a majority beyond numerical calculations. Still, in any event, they cannot be very influential when they represent something quite different from broader popular inclinations. The politicians knew that. So did the progressive intellects. When Captain (later Admiral) Mahan wrote that the Navy must have bases abroad, he added: "At present the positions of the Caribbean are occupied by foreign powers, nor may we, however disposed to acquisition, obtain them by means other than righteous; *but a distinct advance will have been made when public opinion is convinced.*" (The italics are mine.) In 1890 a Republican Congress voted on seven battleships and eventually authorized the building of three first-class battleships, even though the Secretary of the Navy had asked only for two. The former Republican presidential candidate James G. Blaine wrote to President Harrison in 1891 that the United States should annex Cuba and Puerto Rico and perhaps all of the West Indian islands. In June 1896 the *Washington Post* editorialized: "A new consciousness seems to have come upon us—the consciousness of strength—and with it a new appetite, the yearning to show our strength. . . . Ambition, interest, land hunger, pride, the mere joy of fighting, whatever it may be, we are animated by a new sensation. We are face to face with a strange destiny. The taste of Empire is in the mouth of the people even as the taste of blood in the jungle. It means an Imperial policy, the Republic, renascent, taking her place with the armed nations."

It was thus that in 1898 the majority of the American people took satisfaction from the pictures of the Stars and Stripes solidly planted on faraway islands and floating over the oceans, just as their ears took satisfaction from the originally somewhat odd, but soon intensely familiar, martial band music of John Philip Sousa, music with a Central European flavor, but no matter, for it was at that time that American popular music—indeed, the tuning of American ears—was changing too, from the simpler Anglo-Celtic strains to newer rhythms and melodies. It was thus that the American Dominion Over Palm and Pine came into being at the very time when Kipling in his *Recessional* warned America's British cousins that *their* dominion over palm and pine might be short-lived: "Lest we forget!"

In an article entitled "Our Blundering Foreign Policy," Henry Cabot Lodge wrote in March 1895: "Small states are of the past and have no future. . . . The great nations are rapidly absorbing for their future expansion and their present defense all the waste places of the earth. It is a movement which makes for civilization and the advancement of the race. As one of the great nations of the world, the United States must not fall out of the line of march." During the war Theodore Roosevelt wrote him: "You must get Manila and Hawaii; you must prevent any talk of peace until we get Porto Rico and the Philippines as well as secure the independence of Cuba."

Would the United States have become a world power in the early twentieth century even without the Spanish-American War and the events of 1898? Probably. But the consequences of 1898 are still with us.

Was it worth it? That was the question that American opponents of the War of 1898 were asking, among them Mark Twain. Their vision of American destiny was different, but then they were overwhelmed by the great national success of the war. However—sooner rather than later—events themselves accumulated to reveal that all was not well with this acquisition of peoples in distant parts of the world. Only a few months after the "liberation" of Manila, a rebellion in the Philippines broke out against the American occupiers. Its suppression took two years and hundreds of lives. The "liberation" of Cuba from the "tyranny" of Spain led to the rule of that island by a series of native tyrants of whom the last (and still present) one has been obsessively anti-American, in one instance not unwilling to inveigle the United States into a potential nuclear war with the distant Soviet Union. Whether the acquisition of Puerto Rico and of its people by the American Republic was a definite gain is still an open question, as is the future status of that island. . . .

There may be another consideration, on a different level. For Spain the loss of its colonies in 1898 marked the lowest point of a decline that may have begun three hundred years earlier, with the defeat of its armada by Drake. Yet that amputation in 1898 proved to be a blessing in disguise for the Spanish spirit. Reacting against antiquated institutions and mental habits of their country, a Generation of '98 arose, an intellectual revival that produced some of the leading minds not only of Spain but of the twentieth century: Miguel de Unamuno y Jugo, José Ortega y Gasset, and other great names in the arts. On the other side of the ocean, the rise of American arts and letters had nothing to do with the Spirit of '98. Years later great American writers such as Henry James and Thomas Stearns Eliot chose to abandon their American citizenship and live in England. Twenty years had to pass until American arts and letters—and popular music—began to impress the world.

And yet . . . and yet . . . all in all, and for all its strident excrescences, the rising spirit of American imperialism in 1898 was not ungenerous. Not even in the short run; if there was any popular hatred for Spain in 1898, it burned out instantly (as manifest in the words of the captain of the USS *Texas* when his men roared their approval while an ungainly Spanish war vessel sank rapidly at Santiago: "Don't cheer, boys, the poor devils are dying!"). American rule in the Philippines, in Puerto Rico, in Cuba led to a rapid and impressive improvement of living conditions, education, institutions of self-government, sanitation; under the command of the very able Brig. Gen. Leonard Wood, American Army doctors, foremost among them William Gorgas, extinguished yellow fever in Cuba within a year or two. Every foreign government expected the United States to annex Cuba. It did not do so, though an amendment proposed by Senator Platt allowed the United States to intervene there militarily, but then President Franklin D. Roosevelt abolished the Platt Amendment too. In 1946 the Philippines, one year after their American liberation from the Japanese, became fully independent. In 1959 Hawaii became the fiftieth state of the Union. Surely in the long run the record of American imperialism compares favorably with that of many other powers.

History—indeed all human thinking—depends on retrospect. And retrospect too—again, as all human thinking—has its own limitations. We may judge the past according to our standards of the present, but we ought to know that such standards are not perennial and not categorically applicable to people and events of the past. A man such as Theodore Roosevelt had his faults (who hasn't?), but his American imperialism may still have been preferable to that of the small-minded trumpeteers of Manifest Destiny, or to the cloudy evangelical populism of William Jennings Bryan, or to the imperialism of some of Roosevelt's foreign contemporaries—William II, for instance, the German kaiser. In *The Oxford History of the American People,* Samuel Eliot Morison describes William McKinley as "a kindly soul in a spineless body"—and who was our last American President with a "kindly soul"? The origins of the War of 1898—and the intentions of many of its proponents— were not simple.

And now we have to turn to its consequences to the world at large.

In the sixteenth century Spain became the greatest power in the world. In the seventeenth century it was France. In the eighteenth century France and Britain fought a series of world wars—of which the American War of Independence was but one—mainly over the inheritance of the then decaying Spanish Empire. During the nineteenth century the greatest world power was Britain. . . .

Between 1895 and 1898 there occurred a revolution in the relationship of Great Britain and the United States, a subtle and undramatic adjustment but one that had momentous consequences. In 1895 there arose a controversy between Washington and London over a boundary question in Venezuela. After a few exchanges of notes, both sides climbed down. When, less than three years later, the United States provoked a war with Spain over Cuba, the British government sided with the United States without reservation. And not only the government; in 1898 the vast majority of British public opinion and the press took our side. The global implications of this change were immense. Since 1898 there has not been a single instance when a British government opposed the United States—indeed, when a principal consideration of a British government was not the securing of American goodwill. And there was more to that. Soon after 1898 the British, for the first time in their history, were beginning to be anxious about Germany. In order to be able to respond to a German challenge, they had to secure the friendship of the United States, at almost any price. This American factor was one of the elements behind the British decision to arrive at an entente with France in 1904. Eventually this policy bore fruit: In both world wars of the twentieth century, the United States stood by Britain. This alliance brought them victory—as well as the gradual abdication of the British Empire and the continuing rise of an American one. And this went beyond and beneath governmental calculations. As early as 1898 the young Winston Churchill (he was twenty-three years old then) began to think (and write) about an ever-closer British-American alliance, perhaps even leading to an eventual confederation of the English-speaking peoples of the world. To replace the Pax Britannica with a Pax Anglo-Americana: This was the vision he pursued throughout his long life. It was not to be; but that is another story, though not unrelated to the above.

But the Spanish-American War had an immediate effect on the other European powers too. At first many of them were shocked at the sight of the aggressive newcomer bullying Spain. In December 1897 Count Goluchowski, the foreign minister of the creaking old Austrian Empire, wrote that the United States now represented "a common danger to Europe . . . the European nations must close their ranks in order successfully to defend their existence." They did nothing of the sort.

None of them did anything to help Spain. As a matter of fact the Russians kept urging the United States to take Hawaii, in order to cause trouble between the United States and Britain (as they had done during the Civil War and even after). It did not work out that way. Less than ten years after 1898, the Russians composed their differences with Britain because of Germany. A few years later Britain, France, Russia, and the United States became allies in World War I, against Germany. Had Germany won the First or the Second World War—and those were the last attempts of a European power to become the main power in the world—the twentieth century would have been a German one. It became the American Century instead.

In 1898, for the first time, the world became round—politically and not merely geographically. Until 1898 all the Great Powers were European ones. Now two other world powers arose: the United States and Japan. What was now happening in the Far East had a direct impact on the relationship of the powers in Europe and also the reverse. Thus there were seven Great Powers now, but less than fifty years later there were only two, the United States and Soviet Russia, and less than another fifty years later the United States stood alone at the end of a century that may properly be designated the American one.

Will the twenty-first century—the third century in the history of the United States—still be the American one? We may speculate on that. Yet it behooves us to recognize that the American Century began not in 1917 or in 1945 but in 1898.

Pearl Harbor: The "Day of Infamy"

Richard Ketchum

The "you are there" technique for describing dramatic events perfectly suits the problem of describing how the United States government responded to the shocking news that the Japanese had attacked the great American naval base at Pearl Harbor in the Hawaiian Islands. As used here by Richard Ketchum, a former editor of American Heritage and the author of The Borrowed Years: American on the Way to War, it demonstrates conclusively that President Roosevelt did not "trick" the Japanese into striking the first blow; it also shows how he and the top members of his administration responded to the emergency. Ketchum has captured the shock and confusion of the moment as well as the anger and determination with which all the leading actors in the drama reacted. His account takes the reader inside the White House, across the Atlantic to London, and across the Pacific to Tokyo. Generals, admirals, foreign potentates like Winston Churchill, and famous reporters speak. But so do lesser bureaucrats and secretaries unknown to the public.

For most Americans Sunday began quietly, with nothing to suggest that this was the last morning for almost four years when the nation would be at peace. It was cold and crisp, a glorious day across the eastern half of the country. The Roosevelts had company for the weekend—all old friends. The President's cousin Ellen Delano Adams and her husband, with their son and daughter-in-law, were there, as was Mrs. Charles Hamlin, known as Bertie, whom Franklin had met years before in Albany, New York, at his uncle Ted's inauguration as governor. The White House was silent when Bertie Hamlin awoke, and she dressed quietly, walked down the long hallway past the closed doors leading to the President's bedroom and study, went downstairs, and crossed Pennsylvania Avenue to St. John's Church on Lafayette Square, where the bells were pealing for morning worship. By the time she returned, a number of people were climbing the stairs from the East Entrance. The luncheon guests had arrived—some thirty-one of them, and a mixed bag they were, friends, relatives, minor officials, Army Medical Corps officers—prompting someone to observe that the First Lady's secretary was cleaning up around the edges of the invitation list.

Although they may have hoped to see the President, none of the guests much expected him to put in an appearance; he was understandably preoccupied with the tense situation in the Far East, and on top of that, Mrs. Roosevelt explained, his sinuses were acting up. He was having a relaxed lunch in his upstairs study with his friend and adviser Harry Hopkins, who recalled that they were talking about "things far removed from war." Saturday, while the White House staff took half a day off for Christmas shopping, the President had worked late, and now, after finishing the lunch on his tray, he was enjoying the undemanding company of his old-friend and his Scottie dog, Fala, while he paid a little overdue attention to his stamp collection.

At the Navy communication station the clocks read 1348 when Chief Frank Ackerson was called to the Washington–Honolulu operator's message AIR RAID ON PEARL HARBOR THIS IS NOT DRILL.

While the President and Hopkins talked, the telephone rang, and it was Frank Knox calling Roosevelt—a stunned, stricken Secretary of the Navy, reporting the staggering news from Pearl Harbor. Hopkins, hearing that Japanese planes were still attacking, thought there must be some mistake—surely Japan would not attack Hawaii—but the President thought the report was probably true. It was just the sort of surprise the Japanese *would* spring on us, he said, talking peace in the Pacific while plotting to overthrow it.

That morning the corridors of the old State, War and Navy Building had been deserted when Secretary of State Cordell Hull arrived at ten-fifteen for a meeting with Knox and Secretary of War Henry Stimson. By two o'clock they were ready to call it quits and go to the Mayflower Hotel for lunch, and they were just leaving when the Japanese envoys Kichisaburo Nomura and Saburo Kurusu arrived outside Hull's office. They had a cable for the Secretary of State, a long and insulting reply to the imperious "Ten Point Plan" that Hull had submitted to them on November 27, which demanded that the Japanese withdraw from China and Indochina.

Hull already knew the contents of the document; American cryptanalysts had broken the Japanese code in 1940, and in this particular case they had translated Japan's reply before the Japanese embassy could. In fact, the ambassadors had been so hard pressed that they were an hour late getting their translation to Hull.

When they arrived at his office, the Secretary of State was busy on the telephone. His visitors could not know it, but the President was calling to inform him of the report from Pearl Harbor, advising him to receive the ambassadors formally but under no circumstances to inform them of the attack. He was to accept the reply to his note "coolly and bow them out."

Hull let the agitated Japanese sit outside for fifteen minutes—a tense quarter of an hour that marked an end to innocence and the beginning of a new and different era in American history. When the two men were finally admitted to his office, he greeted them coldly and kept them standing, and when Nomura handed him the note, explaining that he had been instructed to deliver it at one o'clock, Hull asked why. Nomura said he did not know, but those were his instructions; the Secretary retorted sharply that he was receiving the message at two o'clock. Hull glanced perfunctorily through the document and then, according to the subsequent State Department press release, said indignantly, "In all my conversations with you during the last nine months, I have never uttered one word of untruth. This is borne out absolutely by the record.

"In all my fifty years of public service I have never seen a document that was more crowded with infamous falsehoods and distortions—infamous falsehoods and distortions on a scale so huge that I never imagined until today that any government on this planet was capable of uttering them."

If the Japanese wondered how a man could know so much about a document he had barely skimmed, they did not say, but Nomura was about to speak when Hull cut him short with a motion of his hand and gestured toward the door. The two ambassadors left without a word.

Thus the authorized version. But when Dean Acheson arrived at the department several hours later—having rushed in from his Maryland farm as soon as he heard the news on the radio—little groups of people stood in the corridor, talking in whispers, while the Secretary, still in a towering rage, remained closeted with several intimates, and the word Acheson got from those who had overheard Mr. Hull ridding himself of the two Japanese was that he had done so in "native Tennesseean," calling them "scoundrels" and "pissants" in his fury.

Secretary of War Henry Stimson was weary, and he was feeling his seventy-four years. He had hoped to get away to his Long Island place for a rest, but the news that morning got progressively worse, convincing him that something bad was going to happen, so he stayed in Washington. He was eating lunch at Woodley, his handsome Southern colonial home overlooking Rock Creek Park, when the President called and asked, in an excited voice, "Have you heard the news?"

"Well," Stimson replied, "I have heard the telegrams which have been coming in about the Japanese advances in the Gulf of Siam."

"Oh, no," Roosevelt said, "I don't mean that. They have attacked Hawaii. They are now bombing Hawaii."

That was an excitement indeed, Stimson thought, and as he prepared to leave for the White House it occurred to him that American forces in Hawaii might have won a major victory; the defense forces in the islands had been alerted and were capable of inflicting severe damage on the attackers.

At 2:28 P.M. Adm. Harold Stark, Roosevelt's chief of naval operations, phoned the White House and informed the President that the first report was true, that the attack had caused some damage to the fleet and some loss of life—no one could yet say how much. Throughout the afternoon and evening the phone at the President's side continued to ring, each time bringing an even more distressing bulletin about the extent of the devastation. Roosevelt listened calmly to each report, usually without comment, and then returned to the business at hand.

About the time of Stark's first call, Mrs. Roosevelt was bidding good-bye to her departing luncheon guests when one of the ushers told her the news. The report was so stunning, she said, that there was complete quiet, and after she had seen her guests to the door she waited until Franklin was alone, hoping to slip into his study. It took only a quick glance to make her realize that he was concentrating on what had to be done and wouldn't talk of what had happened until the first strain was over, so she went back to work—work, at that moment, consisting of going through her mail and writing letters, with one ear cocked to the voices of people going in and out of the President's study, and finding the time and strength of character to concentrate on what she would say in her weekly radio broadcast that afternoon.

Roosevelt's first move, after Stark confirmed the report, was to summon his press secretary, Stephen T. Early, and dictate a statement for immediate release, and at two-thirty Louise Hachmeister, who supervised the White House switchboard, called the three wire services, put them on a conference hookup, and asked, "All on? AP? UP? INS? Here's Mr. Early."

"This is Steve Early at the White House," the press secretary said. "At 7:55 A.M., Hawaiian time, the Japanese bombed Pearl Harbor. The attacks are continuing and . . . no I don't know how many are dead." Almost instantaneously alarm bells on teletype machines in every city across the country began to ring.

In London the CBS correspondent Robert Trout was sitting in the BBC's Studio B-2, two stories underground. He had been stationed there since early November, temporarily replacing Edward R. Murrow, who had returned to the United States with his wife, Janet, for some rest and recreation, and as Trout looked at the wall of the studio, he found himself thinking that there was a huge bomb crater on the other side and that all that stood between him and the hole was a single course of bricks.

For these nightly broadcasts, CBS leased a transatlantic telephone line for ten minutes. Even though the transmission might last for only a fraction of that, ten minutes was the minimum rental, with the result that some of the time was used in preparing for the broadcast and testing voice levels, with engineers, announcers, and others in studios on opposite sides of the ocean conversing. Trout was waiting for his cue from the CBS news department chief, Paul White, to go on the air, while next to him, as always, sat a British censor.

The procedure called for the censor to read the script that the reporter had prepared in advance, approving it or asking him to delete or alter something, but both parties knew that the censor had his hand on the control by which he could cut off Trout if he extemporized and said something that was not permitted. The regulars like Murrow and Trout had a good working relationship with the censors. It was all very informal and friendly, and in addition to his official duties the censor actually served as a technician, by cutting Trout in and out.

Trout was wearing earphones, listening to a British engineer and an American in Riverhead, Long Island, discuss the transmission. He recognized other voices from the CBS studio in New York—none of them on the air, of course, just desultory conversation between people waiting for the broadcast to begin. Paul White loved to sit in front of the complex instrument panel, surrounded by gadgets, and he would either push a lever and tell Trout to start talking or simply let his man in London listen to the broadcast and wait for the announcer to say, "And now we bring you Robert Trout in London—come in, Bob Trout."

But tonight Trout realized that his cue was being delayed for some reason, and he didn't hear White's voice. He was also aware that the door to the studio in New York had opened because he could hear the clatter of teletype machines in the hall outside, then a babble of voices, and someone saying, "Of course it means war . . . but why Pearl Harbor?," which is how he became aware of what had occurred.

Then White came on, to say he would have to tell Trout what they had just seen on the wire. "I already know," Trout told him. White didn't ask how he knew (he died before Trout ever had a chance to tell him); instead he said, "Okay then, I'm cutting you in. Give us the reaction from London."

For a horrified moment Trout couldn't believe his ears. He turned to the censor, who realized immediately the spot he was in, thought for a moment, and then nodded his approval—meaning that Trout could go ahead with the "reaction" as best he could.

"I have no idea what I said," Bob Trout recalled, "but somehow I put some words together and delivered a two-minute talk. Then I was off the air—though only for a while. I was on again any number of times that night."

A few minutes later Trout had a telephone call from Ambassador John G. Winant, who was visiting the British prime minister at Chequers and was furious. Why hadn't Trout called the embassy and told them we were at war before he began his broadcast? What did he think I should do, Trout wondered, call the American embassy and announce, "We are at war"? Until Winant asked the question, Trout hadn't realized that he had been the first person in Great Britain to learn that hostilities had begun between the United States and Japan.

Ambassador Winant had had a busy weekend. He was supposed to have gone to Anthony Eden's country house on Friday evening, to discuss the foreign secretary's forthcoming conversations with Joseph Stalin in Moscow (Eden was leaving for Russia on Sunday), but the news from the Far East intruded on the U.S. ambassador's plans. What with one thing and another, he didn't arrive at Eden's place until after midnight on Saturday, but his obliging host "found me some supper and we stayed up until the early hours of the morning discussing his mission." When Eden departed at ten o'clock, Winant left for Chequers, a hundred miles away, to see the prime minister, whom he found pacing back and forth outside the front door, the other guests having gone inside to lunch.

Churchill at once asked Winant if he thought war with Japan was imminent. When the ambassador replied yes, Churchill stated with some vehemence, "If they declare war on you, we shall declare war on them within the hour."

After lunch most of the guests departed, leaving the prime minister to work and to rest, since he had been up most of the previous night, while Winant spent a quiet afternoon with Averell Harriman, who was in England coordinating the Lend-Lease program, and his daughter. A few minutes before nine o'clock they assembled in the dining room and found Churchill sitting alone, grim and silent; as soon as they took their places, he called out to Sawyers, the butler, asking him to put a portable radio on the table so he could hear the news. Churchill switched it on, and as the sound of music faded away, it was replaced by a voice announcing that the Japanese had attacked the U.S. fleet at Pearl Harbor. As the diners looked at each other incredulously, Sawyers came back into the room to assure them, "It's quite true. We heard it ourselves outside. The Japanese have attacked the Americans."

Churchill bounded to his feet and headed for the door, exclaiming, "We shall declare war on Japan."

Winant got up and hurried after him, saying, "Good God! You can't declare war on a radio announcement! Don't you think you'd better get confirmation first?"

Churchill walked through the hall to the office, which was manned twenty-four hours a day, and told his staff to put through a call to the White House.

"Mr. President, what's this about Japan?" Churchill asked when the connection was made.

"It's quite true. They have attacked us at Pearl Harbor," Roosevelt replied. "We are all in the same boat now."

After the two leaders talked briefly (no mention was made of the serious losses that had been suffered), the prime minister and his guests returned to the table and, as Churchill said, "tried to adjust our thoughts to the supreme world event which had occurred." To the man who represented Britain's last chance, the indomitable leader whose courage and conviction had rallied his countrymen when the nation seemed doomed, the news that America would be in the war—"up to the neck and in to the death"—was a gift from the gods. "So we had won after all!" he exulted, confident now that "England would live; Britain would live; the Commonwealth of Nations and the Empire would live." After the long succession of defeats, the trials that were enough to scar men's souls—Dunkirk, the fall of France, the threat of invasion, the blitz, the U-boat war—he knew at last that there was "no more doubt about the end."

From New York, Ed and Janet Murrow had come to Washington, where they were to have dinner at the White House on Sunday, December 7. That afternoon Murrow was playing golf at the Burning Tree club when a man rushed out of the clubhouse shouting that Pearl Harbor had just been bombed. Murrow went at once to the CBS office to confirm the report and phoned Paul White in New York. Earlier in the day a friend had driven Janet Murrow to an Army airfield near Washington so that she could see the planes awaiting shipment to England. She was amazed. The field was jammed with aircraft, and until then she had had no idea that Lend-Lease was producing aid on such a scale for Britain. In the afternoon she was with their hosts, listening to the New York Philharmonic, and when the program was interrupted with a bulletin about the attack, she assumed at once that their dinner engagement would be canceled. To her surprise, when she phoned the White House, Mrs. Roosevelt told her that they were still expected.

At three o'clock the President met with the War Council—Hull, Stimson, Knox—plus the two military chiefs, Gen. George Marshall and Adm. Harold Stark, and despite the gravity of the circumstances, Harry Hopkins remarked the absence of tension. These men, for whom the imminence of war had been a constant presence, reacted as Churchill did when he heard of the attack. They had concluded long since that the ultimate enemy was Hitler; they knew the Germans could never be defeated without the force of arms; sooner or later, moreover, the United States was bound to be in the war, so it was an unexpected boon that "the crisis had come in a way which would unite all our people," as Stimson remarked.

Harry Hopkins saw things in an even more positive light. "Japan had given us an opportunity," he felt. Others looked on the day's bloody events not as opportunity but as unmitigated disaster, and Assistant Secretary of State Breckinridge Long expressed that point of view in the diary he kept for most of his life. "Sick at heart," he wrote. "I am so damned mad at the Navy for being asleep at the switch at Honolulu. It is the worst day in American history. They spent their lives in preparation for a supreme moment—and then were asleep when it came."

That state of mind was hardly unique to Long. It was the kind of reaction that was bound to surface publicly after the first shock wore off, and with the idea of controlling the damage promptly, Hopkins suggested to the President that he schedule two conferences that evening—one with the full cabinet, the other with legislative leaders. Roosevelt agreed on both counts; the cabinet would meet at eight-thirty, the congressional delegation an hour later.

Grace Tully, one of the President's private secretaries, had been resting at home that afternoon, after the grueling demands of the past few weeks, when the telephone rang. It was Louise Hachmeister, and, with a long list of people to call, she wasted no words: "The President wants you right away. There's a car on the way to pick you up. The Japs just bombed Pearl Harbor!" Twenty minutes later Tully pulled into the White House driveway, which was swarming with extra police and Secret Service men, reporters, and military brass.

In the second-floor study she found Knox, Stimson, and Hopkins, who were joined a few moments later by Marshall and Hull, whose face looked as white as his hair. Since most of the news from Pearl Harbor was coming in to Admiral Stark at the Navy Department, it was her job to answer calls from him, take down the "fragmentary and shocking reports . . . by shorthand, type them up and relay them to the Boss." At first she used a telephone in the second-floor hall, but the noise and confusion were such that she moved into the President's bedroom. Each time she put down the phone and rushed to the typewriter to transcribe her notes, a quartet of White House aides—Gen. Edwin M. Watson, Adm. Ross T. McIntire, Capt. John R. Beardall, and Marvin H. McIntyre—followed and crowded in behind her to peer over her shoulder as she typed. To all of them the news was shattering. Each time Stark called she heard the shocked disbelief in his voice; the men around the President were first incredulous, then angry; and while "the Boss maintained greater outward calm than anybody else . . . there was rage in his very calmness. With each new message he shook his head grimly and he tightened the expression of his mouth."

After talking to Churchill, the President had a long conversation with General Marshall about the disposition of troops and the Air Force, and it was evident that Marshall was increasingly edgy, impatient to get back to the War Department, where he could be in touch with commanders in the field (he had already warned Lt. Gen. Douglas MacArthur, commander of U.S. Army forces in the Far East, to take every precaution). Roosevelt impressed on Hull the necessity of keeping all the South American republics informed; he ordered protection for the Japanese embassy and consulates and had the Justice Department put Japanese citizens under surveillance; Stimson and Knox were to see to the protection of U.S. arsenals, private munitions factories, and bridges (though under no circumstances was there to be a military guard at the White House). Then the discussion turned to Roosevelt's message to Congress, which he had already decided to deliver the following day. The President dug in his heels when Hull recommended a review of the entire history of relations with Japan; no, he said, it would be a short, precise message.

For an immensely energetic man whose infirmity bound him to a chair, all this activity was a relief and a release, a means of channeling that inner rage and putting it to work, and Eleanor Roosevelt could see that at that moment "in spite of his anxiety Franklin was in a way more serene than he had appeared in a long time." Despite the confusion whirling around him, it occurred to some witnesses that the White House was the calmest place in town, with the President in his study the center of the hurricane's eye. The Under Secretary of State Sumner Welles was close by during those hectic hours and thought that of all the times he had seen the President in action he had never had such reason to admire him. Sitting calmly at his desk, receiving a continuous flow of reports on a national disaster, "he demonstrated that ultimate capacity to dominate and to control a supreme emergency which is perhaps the rarest and most valuable characteristic of any statesman." With his talent for grasping the significance of each development, by the end of the evening Roosevelt had personally handled every detail of the situation laid before him by his military advisers, had written the text of a message to Congress, and had overseen the text of the declaration of war to be submitted to that body. All the uncertainty of the recent past was over, and however daunting the future might be, it was calming to know what must be done.

The White House switchboard had an open circuit now to Gov. Joseph Poindexter in Hawaii, who confirmed the news, or as much of it as he knew. As he and the President spoke, the governor suddenly shouted into the phone, and Roosevelt turned to the group in the room to say, "My God, there's another wave of Jap planes over Hawaii right this minute!"

Reports continued to come in to what was now the nation's command headquarters, and in the meantime those present were passing on to the others their fragmentary knowledge of events. Hull, still bitterly angry, repeated "in a tone as cold as ice" his remarks to the Japanese envoys, but as Grace Tully noted, "there was nothing cold or diplomatic in the words he used." Knox and Stimson were interrogated by the President on the situation in Hawaii, on why they believed this could have happened, on what might happen next, on what could be done to repair the damage, but as the bad news continued to pour in, it became evident that the Pacific fleet had been severely crippled, that the Army and air units there were in no condition to fight off an invasion of Hawaii, and that the West Coast of the United States might even be an invasion target.

Meantime, bulletin by bulletin, a smattering of information at a time, the public at large was learning the news, struggling to comprehend and digest it and figure out how to react. Sunday afternoon still had a particular niche in the average American home; with morning church attendance behind them and the big midday dinner cooked, consumed, and cleaned up, members of the family could settle down to a few hours of quiet and rest—napping, listening to the radio, reading the Sunday paper, going for a leisurely walk. Professional football was beginning to make inroads into this domestic tranquillity, and at Washington's dingy Griffith Stadium the crowd was watching the Redskins play their last game of the season against the Philadelphia Eagles when the first bulletin hit the press box. Nearby spectators heard the news from sportswriters, the word spread from seat to seat and section to section, and soon the loudspeaker announcer began paging high-ranking Army and Navy officers, telling them to get in touch with their offices immediately; this was interspersed with summonses to editors and reporters, foreign ambassadors, and others, until individuals in every section of the grandstand seats were hurriedly leaving and running for their cars.

At the Polo Grounds in New York City, no one expected the Brooklyn Dodgers football team to be leading the Eastern champion Giants, but that was exactly what was happening, and the radio audience was as intent on the play-by-play account as those in the stands were on the game they were watching. "It's a long one down to the three-yard line," the announcer shouted; the ball was intercepted by Ward Cuff, who picked up a nice block by Alphonse Leemans before he was hit hard around the twenty-seven-yard line—at which moment another voice broke in to say, "We interrupt this broadcast to bring this important bulletin from United Press: Flash! The White House announces Japanese attack on Pearl Harbor!" Predictably, the Mutual Broadcasting System was suddenly deluged with calls from furious fans,

Wall Street crowds listen to FDR call for war.

wanting to know what was happening in the game. Mutual put the Pearl Harbor story on the air immediately; astonishingly, NBC and CBS decided not to interrupt scheduled music programs but waited until their two-thirty news broadcasts to announce the news.

At Fort Sam Houston in San Antonio, Texas, an Army officer whose exceptional performance in the Louisiana maneuvers a few months before had won him a brigadier general's star was taking a nap after lunch, having told his aide that he was tired and didn't want to be awakened under any circumstances. Under these particular circumstances, however, the aide decided that disobedience was warranted, and he called General Eisenhower. From another room, Mamie Eisenhower heard her husband saying, "Yes? When? I'll be right down," and as he ran for the door, pulling on his uniform jacket, he told her he would be at headquarters and didn't know when he would be back.

Paul Tibbets was flying a Douglas A-20 bomber from Fort Bragg, North Carolina, to Savannah, Georgia, navigating by tuning in to a Savannah station and steering by radio compass. He was listening to a Glenn Miller recording and was

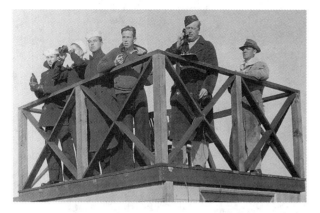

Air-raid wardens take their posts atop the Nassau County courthouse in Mineola, Long Island, New York, the day after the raid.

about twenty miles from his destination when someone interrupted the music to announce the bombing of Pearl Harbor. For Tibbets, that was the first news of the war whose end he would help bring about less than four years later, piloting a B-29 Superfortress called the *Enola Gay* over Hiroshima, Japan. (By some extraordinary turn of fate and timing, a few minutes after the atomic bomb dropped from the *Enola Gay,* Mitsuo Fuchida flew into the area. This was the same Mitsuo Fuchida who led the Japanese planes from their carriers to Pearl Harbor on December 7, 1941, bringing war to America, and as he flew past Hiroshima, he wondered what had caused the curious mushroom-shaped cloud he saw rising above the city. So the man who was present at the beginning was there at the end as well.) . . .

A few minutes before five o'clock, President Roosevelt asked Grace Tully to come to his study, and she found him alone, with two or three neat piles of notes before him on his desk containing the information he had received in the last two hours. As she came in with her notebook, he lit a cigarette, took a deep drag, and said, "Sit down, Grace. I'm going before Congress tomorrow. I'd like to dictate my message. It will be short."

With that he took another long pull on the cigarette and began to speak in a calm tone as if he were dictating a letter, but she noticed that his diction was unusually incisive and slow and that he specified each punctuation mark.

"Yesterday comma December seventh comma 1941 dash a day which will live in infamy dash the United States of America was suddenly and deliberately attacked by naval and air forces of the Empire of Japan period paragraph."

In fewer than five hundred words, spoken without hesitation or second thought, Roosevelt dictated the speech intended to lay America's case before Congress and the world. The message had none of Churchill's soaring prose, no patriotic summons, no bugle calls to action—only a simple, direct recitation of the facts, as in the conclusion: "I ask that the Congress declare that since the unprovoked and dastardly attack by Japan on Sunday comma December seventh comma a state of war has existed between the United States and the Japanese Empire period end."

FDR signs the joint congressional resolution declaring war on Japan.

When Grace Tully had transcribed her notes, the President called Hull back to the White House to go over the draft. As he anticipated, the Secretary of State had in hand a much longer message relating in explicit detail the long train of circumstances leading to war; again, Roosevelt was ready for him and would have none of it. He must have known that his wish in this grave instance was the wish of the whole American people, for he sensed that they wanted no oratory, no lawyer's brief, only the briefest summary of the facts, set forth by him in what might be described as controlled rage, so that the nation could get on with what needed to be done as quickly as possible. Except for a few minor changes of words, the only real addition he permitted was volunteered by Harry Hopkins, who suggested what appeared as the next-to-last sentence of the message: "With confidence in our armed forces—with the unbounded determination of our people—we will gain the inevitable triumph—so help us God."

Eleanor Roosevelt was carrying on gallantly downstairs, on the theory that her dinner guests had to eat somewhere and it might as well be there, but it was not a relaxed occasion for the visitors, who were acutely aware of the empty chair at the head of the table and the stream of worried-looking men scurrying through the hall to or from the study that was the focus of the nation's attention. Ed and Janet Murrow were with Mrs. Roosevelt, as were her young friends Joe Lash and Trude

Pratt, and during dinner the President sent word that Murrow was to wait, that he wanted to see him.

After the meal Janet departed to attend another party, at which the Murrows were to have been the guests of honor, while Ed went upstairs to sit on a bench outside the President's study. As he waited to be summoned, he observed the continuing procession of VIPs and overheard snatches of conversation as they passed, including a snarled rebuke to Frank Knox—"God-damnit, sir, you ought not to be in charge of a rowboat, let alone the United States Navy!" Some years later, commenting on the charges that Roosevelt and his top advisers possessed advance knowledge of the attack on Pearl Harbor, Murrow recalled the opportunity he had had that night to observe these men off guard and said, "If they were *not* surprised by the news from Pearl Harbor, then that group of elderly men were putting on a performance which would have excited the admiration of any experienced actor." . . .

By evening people were standing five and six deep on the sidewalk beyond the tall iron fence around the White House grounds, peering at the lighted windows in hopes of spotting movement inside, watching intently the arrival of each automobile to see if they could identify passengers, and by the time Secretary of the Interior Harold Ickes appeared for the cabinet meeting the moon was up, misty and indistinct. He noticed especially how quiet and serious the crowds were, and he decided their presence was an example of the human instinct to get close to the scene of action even if one could see or hear nothing. Some cabinet officers had been trying all afternoon to get back to Washington, and Ickes was pleased to see that everyone had made it. Postmaster General Frank Walker and Frances Perkins, Secretary of Labor, had flown from New York in a special plane; so had the Treasury Secretary, Henry Morgenthau.

Promptly at eight-thirty the full cabinet met, with the members forming a ring completely around the President's desk. Ickes noticed at once how solemn

The lights in the White House burned all night, and crowds waited quietly outside.

Roosevelt was: no wisecracks or jokes this evening, not even a smile, and the calmness he had displayed earlier in the afternoon was largely gone, replaced by tension and signs of enormous fatigue. The President began by telling them that this was probably the gravest crisis to confront a cabinet since 1861; then he filled them in on everything he had heard from Hawaii, making clear that what they had on their hands was the worst naval defeat in American history. Not only that: Guam had probably been captured, and it was likely that Wake was gone, while the Japanese were advancing on Manila, Singapore, Hong Kong, and other locations in the Malay States. For all anyone knew, an attack might be taking place in Hawaii at that very moment.

Even though they had heard some of this news before they arrived, the detailed catalogue of catastrophe shocked the cabinet members—that and the manner in which Roosevelt described the disaster. Frances Perkins said he actually had "physical difficulty in getting out the words that put him on record as knowing that the navy was caught unawares." It was obvious to her that he was "having a dreadful time just accepting the idea." Yet she knew him well, and she detected an evasive look, revealing the wave of relief he was reluctant to acknowledge—relief that the long period of tension, of not knowing what the Japanese would do and when they would do it, was over. The men in Tokyo, after all, had taken the decision for war or peace from the President's hands.

Throughout the meeting, according to Ickes, Hull behaved more than ever like a Christian martyr—indignant that he was the one to have been duped by the Japanese diplomats while their army and navy were plotting against us, since it was obvious that the expedition against Pearl Harbor had been in the works for months. Despite FDR's annoyance, moreover, Hull was still plumping for a long presidential message to Congress, but when Roosevelt read his own draft aloud, all but the Secretary of State agreed that he had struck exactly the right note.

Shortly after nine-thirty the congressional leaders were ushered into the study, and the cabinet members moved back to let them have the chairs surrounding the President's desk. The President reviewed the situation with them in much the same words he had used with the cabinet, informing them that "the casualties, I am sorry to say, were extremely heavy" and that "we have lost the majority of the battleships there."

Following his summary of the attack, there was dead silence until the man most visibly outraged said what most of the others were thinking. Tom Connolly of Texas, chairman of the Senate Foreign Relations Committee, asked, "How did it happen that our warships were caught like tame ducks in Pearl Harbor? I am amazed at the attack by Japan, but I am still more astounded at what happened to our navy. They were all asleep!" he exploded. "Where were our patrols? They knew these negotiations were going on." Knox was obviously deeply embarrassed by these and other questions but made no attempt to reply.

Finally, at twelve-thirty, it was Ed Murrow's turn in the study, and the President ordered beer and sandwiches. Joining them was Col. William Donovan, who was then engaged in setting up an intelligence organization that would be known as the Office of Strategic Services (OSS). Mr. Roosevelt, dead tired, his face ashen, asked Murrow a few questions about the bombing of London and the morale of the

British and then informed his visitors in detail about the losses at Pearl Harbor—the loss of life, how ships had been sunk at their moorings and planes destroyed on the airstrips—and he pounded his fist on the table and groaned, "On the ground, by God, on the ground!"

For a reporter on this night of nights, it was the chance of a lifetime, since the details that Roosevelt gave them—with no indication that what he said should be off the record—would not be made public for hours—in some cases, for months. The President mentioned that he had talked with Churchill, who told him of attacks on British bases, and he asked Donovan if he thought this might be part of an overall Axis plan. The latter had no evidence to offer but said it was certainly a reasonable assumption. Then Roosevelt asked a rather curious question, hinting at the isolationists' powerful influence on his thinking and his intense concern about public unity: Did they believe the nation would now support a declaration of war? Both men assured him that it would.

As Murrow was taking his leave after more than half an hour's conversation, the President inquired, "Did this surprise you?"

"Yes, Mr. President," he replied.

"Maybe you think it didn't surprise us!" Roosevelt responded.

In the early hours of the morning Murrow returned to the hotel and for hours paced the floor, smoking continuously, debating whether or not he could reveal the information he had heard from the President. "The biggest story of my life," he kept telling his wife, "and I can't make up my mind whether it's my duty to tell it or forget it." In the end he decided it had been told him in confidence and he should not report what Roosevelt had said.

The telephone awakened Ambassador Joseph Grew in Tokyo at 7:00 A.M. on December 8. The call was urgent, requesting that he come as quickly as possible to see Foreign Minister Shigenori Togo, and, without taking time even to shave, he threw on some clothes. When he arrived at 7:30, he found Togo grim, formal, and—as always—imperturbable. The Japanese official made a brief statement and slapped down on the table the thirteen-page memorandum that Nomura had delivered to Hull. Then he made a pretty little speech thanking Grew for his cooperation during the long negotiations and walked downstairs to see him to the door. Not a word was spoken about Pearl Harbor. Indeed, not until after he had shaved and breakfasted did Grew learn that the two countries were at war, and this was not confirmed until late morning, when a functionary appeared at the embassy and, hands trembling, read the official announcement.

Shortly thereafter the embassy gates were closed and the ambassador was told that no one could enter or leave, that no cipher messages could be sent, and that all telegrams must be submitted to the Foreign Office for approval. The British ambassador and several others from the diplomatic colony managed to get past the police outside the gates and bid farewell to the Americans, and they were followed by a group of extremely polite Japanese, who apologized profusely before confiscating all the short-wave radios in the embassy. None of the Americans knew, of course, how long it would be before they might be exchanged for Japan's diplomats in Washington, and about sixty members of the staff assembled for cocktails that evening, livened by a few brave speeches. Arrangements were made for those who

FDR's press secretary, Steve Early, briefs reporters.

lived outside the compound to move into the embassy, sharing apartments, bunking down on mattresses on the floor.

Reflecting on the way Tokyo had borrowed blitzkrieg tactics from its allies in Berlin, Grew concluded that "if the Japanese had confined themselves to the Far East and had attacked only the Philippines, there would have been pacifists and isolationists at home who would have said that we have no business in the Far East anyway, but once they attacked Hawaii it was certain that the American people would rise up in a solid unit of fury." The task ahead would not be easy, he knew, but Japan's defeat was absolutely certain, and he permitted himself a smile of satisfaction as he recalled how he had warned Washington to be ready for a step of "dangerous and dramatic suddenness"—exactly what had occurred.

Grew might be right that victory over Japan was certain, but what good was that if Britain and Russia should fall, if Hitler should triumph in Europe? Despite pressure from Stimson, in particular, who argued that Germany had pushed Japan to attack, President Roosevelt resisted the temptation to declare war on Germany and Italy, hoping that Hitler would relieve him of the necessity to act. He detected "a lingering distinction in some quarters of the public between war with Japan and war with Germany," he told the British ambassador, and although Berlin was ominously silent, he decided to wait it out to see if the Führer would resolve his dilemma.

Hitler had his hands full. Winter had closed in on Russia, and his dream of conquering that nation in a single summer campaign ended as the days grew shorter and brutal cold and blizzards descended on the land. On December 6, to the utter surprise of the German high command, the Russians seized the initiative when the temperature was thirty-five degrees below zero, launched a major assault with one hundred fresh divisions, and threw back the Wehrmacht within twelve miles of the center of Moscow. Simultaneously, Gen. Erwin Rommel's Afrika Corps began to retreat in the desert, and Hitler assumed control of all military operations. Curiously, despite the many warning signs from the Far East, the Japanese attack took him by surprise. In the spring he had urged his allies in Tokyo to move against Singapore, saying that one of the benefits would be to deter the United States from entering the war, but he had not contemplated hostilities between Japan and America. As the German foreign minister Joachim von Ribbentrop perceived, the Japanese attack "brought about what we had wanted to avoid at all costs, war between Germany and America," but Hitler himself was jubilant. Rejoicing in the news—"The turning point!" he proclaimed when he heard it—he dismissed the advice of those around him and made another monumental miscalculation: He would declare war on the United States.

Knowing virtually nothing about the United States, viewing it merely as a decadent bourgeois democracy incapable of waging or sustaining a prolonged war, he disastrously underestimated its strength (an opinion bolstered by the apparent ease of the Japanese triumph), and despite the lack of the most elementary preparations (one of his headquarters officers admitted that "we have never even considered a war against the United States") and the certainty of U.S. intervention in the European war, he left his Wolf's Lair bunker on the evening of December 8, returned to Berlin, and began to prepare a speech to the Reichstag. On December 11, after denouncing Roosevelt as "the main culprit of this war" and a creature of the Jews, he announced to deafening applause that he had arranged for the American chargé d'affaires to be handed his passport. Now the fire he had ignited with the invasion of Poland on September 1, 1939, would rage around the world.

The Holocaust

William J. vanden Heuvel

Did the United States government, and especially President Franklin D. Roosevelt, do all they might to have saved Jews from the Holocaust? In this essay William J. vanden Heuvel, formerly a U.S. representative to the United Nations and a lawyer and investment banker, defends both from charges of complicity, albeit passive complicity, in the deaths of six million Jews. Heuvel especially exonerates Roosevelt and his wife, Eleanor. Both had done much to facilitate the emigration of Jews from Nazi Germany, extending visitors' visas and goading the State Department into admitting more Jews. Immigration quotas remained a serious obstacle, but Roosevelt's refusal to call for less restrictive laws was based on his political realization that if the issue were reopened, Congress might well impose even more restrictive quotas. Roosevelt considered bombing the death camps, but such plans proved impractical; they were also opposed by many Jewish leaders. In the end, Roosevelt stopped the carnage in the only way possible: by destroying Hitler and his regime.

It was Winston Churchill's Judgment that the Holocaust "was probably the greatest and most terrible crime ever committed in the whole history of the world." The Holocaust, of course, was part of a colossal struggle in which fifty-three million people were killed, where nations were decimated, where democracy's survival was in the balance. In his campaign to exterminate the Jews of Europe, Hitler and his Nazi followers murdered six million men, women, and children for no other reason than that they were Jewish. This crime is of such profound proportions that it can never be fully understood; it must continue to be analyzed from every aspect as to how and why it happened, and its memory must unite all of us.

Nine million non-Jewish civilians were also murdered by the Nazis, as were three million Soviet prisoners of war, yet the Holocaust remains a uniquely horrible crime, and there can be no greater indictment than to allege complicity in it. Such an accusation was made against America in general and its leader, Franklin D. Roosevelt, in particular by a recent PBS documentary entitled "America and the Holocaust: Deceit and Indifference." The show drew on a substantial and growing body of scholarship that has caused many young American Jews to criticize and even condemn their grandparents and parents for being so absorbed in the effort to become assimilated in American society that they chose silence rather than voice outrage at the Nazi crimes and gave their overwhelming support to a President who was indifferent to the fate of Europe's Jews. Why did not the United States let the *St. Louis,* a German ship carrying Jewish refugees to Cuba in 1939, land at an American port when Cuba refused them admission? Also, perhaps the most frequently asked question of the last decade, why did the Allies not bomb Auschwitz and the railways that fed it? The people who pose these questions believe they know the answers. As one eminent spokesman for this viewpoint has written, "The Nazis were the murderers but we"—here he includes the American government, its President, and its people, Christians and Jews alike—"were the all too passive accomplices."

How much truth is there in these painful assertions? As we ask ourselves what more might have been done to save the innocent, we must frame our response in the context of the realities of World War II and the events and values of the years that preceded it.

Five weeks after Adolf Hitler became chancellor of Germany, in 1933, Franklin Roosevelt became President of the United States. Roosevelt's loathing for the whole Nazi regime was known the moment he took office; alone among the leaders of the world, he stood in opposition to Hitler from the very beginning. In a book published in 1937, Winston Churchill—to whom free humanity everywhere must be eternally indebted and without whose courage and strength the defeat of Nazi Germany could never have been achieved—described Hitler's treatment of the Jews, stating that "concentration camps pock-mark the German soil . . ." and concluding his essay by writing that "the world lives on hopes that the worst is over and that we may live to see Hitler a gentler figure in a happier age." Roosevelt had no such hopes. Thomas Mann, the most famous of the non-Jewish refugees from the Nazis, met with FDR at the White House in 1935 and confided that for the first time he believed the Nazis would be beaten because in Roosevelt he had met someone who truly grasped the evil of Adolf Hitler.

To comprehend the situation of European Jewry during those years, we must differentiate between the German Jews who were the immediate and constant subjects of Hitler's persecution and the Jews of Central Europe who were the principal victims of the Holocaust. The German Jews numbered about 525,000 in 1933. They were the yeast of Germany's great culture—leaders in literature, music, medicine, science, and financial and intellectual life. For the most part they wanted to be thought of as Germans. They had been a proud part of Germany's army in World War I. Anti-Semitism shadowed their lives, but they thought of Germany as *their* country and were deeply rooted in its existence. In the face of Nazi persecution, those who left Germany did so reluctantly, many seeking refuge in neighboring countries, from which they expected to return once the Hitler madness subsided. In the early years many, if not most, believed Hitler and his regime could not survive.

When, in 1933, Rabbi Stephen Wise, one of the most powerful and respected leaders of the American Jewish community during that era and a personal friend and close adviser of President Roosevelt, organized a New York rally to protest Nazi treatment of Jews, he received a message from leading German rabbis urging him to cut out such meetings and which, insultingly, indicated that American Jews were doing this for their own purposes and in the process were destroying the Germany that German Jews loved. Rabbi Wise never wavered in his belief that the only option for Jews was to leave Germany. As the Nazi persecution intensified, as the Nuremberg Laws further degraded the Jews as had nothing before, as Hitler strove to make them emigrate and confiscated their property, the prospect of escape and exile had to shadow every Jewish family. In 1933 thirty-seven thousand Jews fled Germany, but in the relative calm of the next year, sixteen thousand returned. Every

Jewish group affirmed the right of Jews to be German, to live in and love their country; they affirmed the legal right, the moral necessity, and the religious imperative of not surrendering to their persecutors. As important as any barriers to immigration in Western countries was the desire not to leave Germany until absolutely necessary. It is crucial to our understanding of these years to remember that at the time no one inside or outside Germany anticipated that the Nazi persecution would lead to the Holocaust. The actions of the German government were generally understood by both victims and bystanders as a return to the sorts of persecutions of prior centuries, not as steps on the road toward genocide.

Kristallnacht in November 1938 changed the situation dramatically. The assassination of a German diplomat in Paris by a seventeen-year-old Jewish youth whose father had been among the thousands of Polish Jews expelled from Germany and dumped across the Polish border just weeks before sparked a frenzy of arson and looting by Nazi thugs in almost every town and city. Huge, silent crowds looked on. The police did nothing to contain the violence. Many German Jews for the first time understood the hopelessness of their situation, and some looked west across the Atlantic.

The America that elected Franklin Delano Roosevelt its President in 1932 was a deeply troubled country. Twenty-five percent of its work force was unemployed—this at a time when practically every member of that work force was the principal support of a family. The economy was paralyzed, while disillusion after the sacrifices of the First World War fomented profound isolationist sentiments.

The nation's immigration laws had been established by legislation in 1921 and 1924 under Presidents Harding and Coolidge and by a Congress that had rejected the League of Nations. A formula assigned a specific quota to countries based on the population origins of Americans living in the United States in 1890. The law was aimed at Eastern Europe, particularly Russia and Poland, which were seen as seedbeds of bolshevism. Italians were targeted, and Asians practically excluded. The total number of immigrants who could be admitted annually was set at 153,774; the two countries of origin given the highest quotas were Great Britain (65,721) and Germany (25,957). The deepening Depression encouraged an unusual coalition of liberal and conservative forces, labor unions and business leaders, to oppose any enlargement of the immigration quotas. Because of the relatively large German quota, Jewish refugees from Germany had an easier time than anticommunist refugees from the Soviet Union, not to mention Chinese victims of Japan's aggression, or Armenians. The Spanish who wanted to escape a civil war that between 1936 and 1939 killed half a million people faced an annual quota of 252.

The President and Mrs. Roosevelt were leaders in the effort to help those fleeing Nazi persecution. Eleanor Roosevelt was a founder, in 1933, of the International Rescue Committee, which brought intellectuals, labor leaders, and political figures to sanctuary in the United States. President Roosevelt made a public point of inviting many of them to the White House. In 1936, in response to the Nazi confiscation of personal assets as a precondition to Jewish emigration, Roosevelt greatly modified President Hoover's strict interpretation of the refugee laws, thereby allowing a greater number of visas to be issued. As a result the United

Rabbi Stephen Wise, one of the leading spokesmen against Nazism in the 1930s, addresses the crowd at a rally he organized in 1933 to protest German anti-Semitism.

States accepted twice as many Jewish refugees as did all other countries put together. As the historian Gerhard L. Weinberg has shown, Roosevelt acted in the face of strong and politically damaging criticism for what was generally considered a pro-Jewish attitude.

When, in March 1938, the Anschluss put Austria's 185,000 Jews in jeopardy, Roosevelt called for an international conference "to facilitate the emigration from Germany and Austria of political refugees." There was no political advantage to FDR in this; no other major leader in any country matched his concern and involvement. The conference, which met in Evian, France, tried to open new doors in the Western Hemisphere. At first things went well; the Dominican Republic, for example, offered to give sanctuary to 100,000 refugees. Then came a devastating blow: The Polish and Romanian governments announced that they expected the same right as the Germans to expel their Jewish populations. There were fewer than 475,000 Jews left in Germany and Austria at this point—a number manageable in an emigration plan that the twenty-nine participating nations could prepare—but with the possibility of 3.5 million more from Eastern Europe, the concern now was that any offer of help would only encourage authoritarian governments to brutalize any unwanted portion of their populations, expecting their criminal acts against their own citizens to force the democracies to give them haven. National attitudes then were not very different from today's; no country allows any and every refugee to enter without limitations. Quotas are thought even now to deter unscrupulous and impoverished regimes from forcing their unwanted people on other countries.

The Evian Conference failed to accomplish anything except organization of the Inter-Governmental Committee (IGC), which was to pressure the Germans to allow Jewish refugees to leave with enough resources to begin their new lives. It led to direct negotiations between Hjalmar Schacht, head of the Reichsbank, and George Rublee, a distinguished Washington lawyer personally designated by FDR. Schacht proposed that 150,000 Jews be allowed to emigrate, taking 25 percent of their assets with them, the rest to be impounded in a trust fund that would serve as collateral on bonds to be issued by the German state. Schacht was trying to resolve Germany's foreign exchange crisis, but Hitler ordered an end to the discussions. The negotiations, like all barter negotiations in the years ahead, failed because the Führer never allowed them to succeed.

America's reaction to *Kristallnacht* was stronger than that of any of the other democracies. Roosevelt recalled his ambassador from Germany and at his next press conference said, "I myself can scarcely believe that such things could occur in a twentieth-century civilization." He extended the visitors' visas of twenty thousand Germans and Austrians in the United States so they would not have to return. Americans in opinion polls showed anger and disgust with the Nazis and sympathy for the Jews; nevertheless, Roosevelt remained the target of the hard-core anti-Semites in America. He fought them shrewdly and effectively, managing to isolate them from mainstream America and essentially equating their anti-Semitism with treason destructive to both the national interest and national defense. Recognizing the inertia at the State Department, he entrusted Sumner Welles, the Undersecretary of State and a man wholly sympathetic to Jewish needs, to be his instrument of action.

Immigration procedures were complicated and sometimes harshly administered. The laws and quotas were jealously guarded by Congress, supported by a strong, broad cross section of Americans who were against all immigrants, not just Jews. Of course, there were racists and anti-Semites in the Congress and in the country, as there are today, only now they dare not speak their true attitudes. The State Department, deeply protective of its administrative authority in the granting of visas, was frequently more concerned with congressional attitudes and criticisms than with reflecting American decency and generosity in helping people in despair and panic. Roosevelt undoubtedly made a mistake in appointing as Assistant Secretary of State Breckenridge Long, who many allege was an anti-Semite. His presence at State was an assurance to Congress that the immigration laws would be strictly enforced. On the other hand there were countless Foreign Service officers who did everything possible to help persecuted, innocent people, just as they would today. There was an attitude that many sanctuaries besides the United States existed in the world, so the department, controlled by a career elite, conservative and in large part anti–New Deal and anti-FDR, was quite prepared to make congressional attitudes rather than those of the White House the guide for their administration of immigration procedures. Yet, between 1933 and 1941, 35 percent of all immigrants to America under quota guidelines were Jewish. After *Kristallnacht*, Jewish immigrants were more than half of all immigrants admitted to the United States.

Of course there were other countries of refuge; public opinion in democracies everywhere indicated that people had been repelled by the Nazi persecution. Great

Britain, for example, after *Kristallnacht* granted immigration visas essentially without limit. In the first six months of 1939, there were 91,780 German and Austrian Jews admitted to England, often as a temporary port en route to the dominions or other parts of the Commonwealth.

For his part, Roosevelt, knowing that he did not have the power to change the quota system of his own country, was constantly seeking havens for the refugees in other countries. His critics severely underestimate limitations on presidential power; clearly, the President could not unilaterally command an increase in quotas. In fact, the Democratic congressional leaders, including Rep. Samuel Dickstein, who chaired the House subcommittee on immigration, warned him that reactionary forces in Congress might well use any attempt to increase the quotas as an opportunity to reduce them. In 1939 Congressman Emanuel Celler of Brooklyn, an outspoken defender of Jewish interests, gave a speech in which he warned that "it would be dangerous at this time because of public opinion in the South and West to press for the passage in Congress of [his own] bills to give asylum in the United States to refugees and to reallot for refugees the unused quotas of various countries." Congressman Celler said he had been warned by representatives from other parts of the country that if he pressed his proposals, other bills "to cut the quotas in half or to stop all immigration would be introduced and probably passed." Nor were the Jews the only refugees Congress was determined to bar. A few days later the Reverend Joseph Ostermann, executive director of the Committee for Catholic Refugees from Germany, said that there were five hundred thousand actual or potential Catholic refugees whom "Goebbels and Rosenberg in Germany have attempted to identify with communism."

By the time the war made further emigration impossible, 72 percent of all German Jews had left the country . . .

Given the reality of the Holocaust all of us in every country—and certainly in America—can only wish that we had done more, that our immigration barriers had been lower, that our Congress had had a broader world view, that every public servant had shared the beliefs of Franklin and Eleanor Roosevelt. If anyone had foreseen the Holocaust, perhaps, possibly, maybe . . . but no one did. Nevertheless, the United States, a nation remote from Europe in a way our children can hardly understand, took in double the number of Jewish refugees accepted by the rest of the world.

Among the anguishing events we read about is the fate of the ship *St. Louis* of the Hamburg-America Line, which left Germany and arrived in Cuba with 936 passengers, all but 6 of them Jewish refugees, on May 27, 1939. This was three months before the outbreak of the war and three years before the establishment of the death camps. Other ships had made the same journey, and their passengers had disembarked successfully, but on May 5 the Cuban government had issued a decree curtailing the power of the corrupt director general of immigration to issue landing certificates. New regulations requiring five-hundred-dollar bonds from each approved immigrant had been transmitted to the shipping line, but only 22 passengers of the *St. Louis* had fulfilled the requirements before leaving Hamburg on May 13. Those 22 were allowed to land; intense negotiations with the Cuban government regarding the other passengers—negotiations in which American Jewish agencies participated—broke down despite pressure from our government. It was not an unreported event. Tremendous international attention focused on the *St. Louis,* later made famous as the "Voyage of the Damned." Secretary of State Cordell Hull, Secretary of the Treasury Henry Morgenthau, Jr., and others, including Eleanor Roosevelt, worked to evade the immigration laws—for example, by attempting to land the passengers as "tourists" in the Virgin Islands. One survivor of the *St. Louis* whom I interviewed—a retired professor of human genetics at the University of Washington in Seattle—described its commander, Capt. Gustav Schroeder, as a compassionate man who ordered decent treatment for his Jewish passengers and who told them that he would run his ship aground off England rather than return them to Germany if Cuba refused admission. In the end, despite the legal inability of the United States to accept the passengers as immigrants, our diplomats were significantly helpful in resettling them. Not one was returned to Nazi Germany. They all went to democratic countries—288 in the United Kingdom, the rest in France, the Netherlands, Belgium, and Denmark. And who, in that spring of 1939, was prescient enough to foretell that in little more than a year all but one of those countries would be held by Nazi troops?

What were FDR's own attitudes toward Hitler and the Jews? Did he reflect the social anti-Semitism that was endemic in the America of that era? Contemporary Jews certainly didn't think so. Roosevelt opened the offices of government as never before to Jews. Henry Morgenthau, Jr., Samuel Rosenman, Felix Frankfurter, Benjamin Cohen, David Niles, Anna Rosenberg, Sidney Hillman, and David Dubinsky were among his closest advisers in politics and government. Rabbi Stephen Wise, the pre-eminent spokesman for American Zionism, said, "No one was more genuinely free from religious prejudice and racial bigotry."

Nazi policy changed radically after the outbreak of war. The Holocaust took place between 1941 and 1945. Hitler's conquest of the European continent let loose the full force of his psychopathic obsession about Jews. With the start of the war, on September 1, 1939, emigration from Germany was prohibited. Nevertheless, hundreds, perhaps thousands, of German Jews managed to escape across borders into Holland, Belgium, and Switzerland. But by June 1940, with the fall of France, Europe became a prison for Jews. Unoccupied France still offered an escape route, and despite intense criticism from the political left, FDR maintained diplomatic relations with Vichy, France, allowing that route to remain open. The International Rescue Committee, a group of which Eleanor Roosevelt remained very supportive, . . . helped countless refugees find sanctuary in Spain and Portugal. But the vise was tightening. The invasion of Russia in June 1941 put the lock on the most terrible dungeon in history. Special squads of the German SS—the *Einsatzgruppen*—began the slaughter of 1.5 million Jews behind the German lines in Russia. The Wannsee Conference, which structured the "Final Solution," was held in a Berlin suburb in January 1942.

The Jews of Central Europe, the Jews from the occupied nations of Western Europe, the Jews of the Soviet Union—the principal victims of the Holocaust—were not refugees; they were prisoners in a vast prison from which there was no escape and no possible rescue. They had not been subject to Nazi rule or persecution prior to the war and few had imagined that they ever would be. Zionism was not a dominant force in their communities. In 1936, in the Jewish community elections in Poland, the most highly organized Jewish community in Europe, the Social Democratic Bund won a sweeping victory on a pledge of "unyielding hostility to Zionism." Their leaders wanted Polish Jews to remain in Poland. In the Netherlands, a country whose Jewish population suffered a greater percentage loss in the extermination camps than any other in Western Europe, not more than 679 individuals, Jews and Gentiles, had migrated in any one year before 1940, far less than the Dutch quota would have allowed. The assumption was that Hitler would respect Dutch neutrality just as the kaiser had in the First World War. Once Hitler's armies marched, the Jews of Nazi-occupied Europe no longer had the possibility of being refugees.

The doors had been closed not by the United States or its allies but by Hitler. On January 30, 1942, Hitler, speaking to the Reichstag, said, "This war can end in two ways—either the extermination of the Aryan peoples or the disappearance of Jewry from Europe." Since the mid-1920s Hitler had never voluntarily spoken to a Jew. He was the most determined ideologue of racial superiority and racial conflict who ever led a country. Nothing diminished his mission—not the defeat of his armies, not the destruction of his country. . . .

Some critics of American policy during these years maintain that the news of the annihilation of Europe's Jews was deliberately kept secret so that our people would not know about it and that if Americans had been aware of the Final Solution, they would have insisted on doing more than was done. The facts are otherwise. President Roosevelt, Winston Churchill, General Eisenhower, General Marshall, the intelligence services of the Allied nations, every Jewish leader, the Jewish communities in America, in Britain, in Palestine, and yes, anyone who had a radio or newspaper in 1942 knew that Jews in colossal numbers were being murdered. They may have received the news with disbelief; there was, after all, no precedent for it in human history. But the general information of the genocide was broadly available to anyone who would read or listen. The famous telegram from Gerhart Riegner, a representative of the World Jewish Congress, in Switzerland in August 1942, was not even the first knowledge of a death camp later to become known as Auschwitz when its gas chambers and crematoria had been built. Auschwitz, like every extermination camp, was treated as a top-secret project by the Nazis. The details and even the name of Auschwitz were not confirmed until the escape of two prisoners in April 1944, two years after its murderous processes had begun. But though the names, locations, and procedures of the death camps may not have been known—some not until the end of the war—the fact of the genocide and the Nazi determination to carry it out were not in doubt.

When Rabbi Wise was given the Riegner telegram, Sumner Welles asked him not to publicize it until its information could be confirmed by sources available to the Czech and Polish governments-in-exile. There was no video of this original version of "ethnic cleansing" such as we had available to us in Bosnia; there were no enterprising reporters who could photograph the Nazi butchery as there were in Rwanda. The experience of the First World War, in which atrocities attributed to the Germans turned out to be grossly inflated or Allied propaganda, caused many to wonder if the incredible reports coming from the continent of Europe would ultimately prove false as well.

When Sumner Welles confirmed the truth of the Riegner telegram to Rabbi Wise, the rabbi wept, as countless Jews and non-Jews would do in those terrible years when the Nazis lay beyond the reach of the armies that would defeat them. Encouraged by Welles to hold a press conference to announce the news, Rabbi Wise did so, on November 28, 1942. Then he and his colleagues met with FDR and asked the President to warn Hitler and the Germans that they would be held individually responsible for what they were doing to the Jews. Roosevelt agreed immediately. An announcement to that effect in the name of the United Nations was made in Congress and in Britain's Parliament on December 17, 1942. It was repeated many times throughout the war. Parliament stood in silence for the first time in its history to mourn what was happening to the Jews and to pray for the strength needed to destroy their persecutors. In America the labor unions led the nation in a ten-minute period of mourning for the Jews of Europe. It is difficult to argue that there was a conspiracy of silence regarding the fate of Europe's Jews when the American broadcaster Edward R. Murrow, listened to throughout the nation, reported on December 13, 1942: "Millions of human beings, most of them Jews, are being gathered up with ruthless efficiency and murdered. . . . It is a picture of mass murder and moral depravity unequaled in the history of the world. It is a horror beyond what imagination can grasp. . . . There are no longer 'concentration camps'—we must speak now only of 'extermination camps.'"

American Jewry was no passive observer of these events. Despite issues that bitterly divided them, primarily relating to Palestine, the Jewish community in America spoke the same words in pleading to do whatever was possible for Europe's Jews. Jewish leaders lobbied Congress. Mass rallies were held across the country with overflow crowds throughout those years, praying, pleading for action to stop the genocide. The unremitting massacre continued because no one, no nation, no alliance of nations could do anything to close down the death camps—save, as Roosevelt said over and over again, by winning the war. . . .

The proposal to bomb Auschwitz in 1944 has become the symbol for those who argue American indifference and complicity in the Holocaust. Some would have us believe that many American Jewish groups petitioned our government to bomb Auschwitz; in fact, there was considerable Jewish opposition in both the United States and Palestine. . . .

Mainstream Jewish opinion was against the whole idea. The very thought of the Allied forces' deliberately killing Jews—to open the gates of Auschwitz so the survivors could run where?—was as abhorrent then as it is now. The Rescue Committee of the Jewish Agency in Jerusalem voted, at a meeting with the future Israeli prime minister David Ben-Gurion presiding, against even making the bombing request. Although only President Roosevelt or General Eisenhower could have ordered the bombing of Auschwitz, there is no record of any kind that indicates that either one ever heard of the proposal—even though Jewish leaders of all persuasions had clear access to both men.

A seemingly more reasonable proposal to bomb the railways to Auschwitz was made to Anthony Eden, the foreign minister of Great Britain, on July 6, 1944. Eden, with Churchill's immediate support, asked the RAF to examine the feasibility of doing so. The secretary of state for air, Sir Archibald Sinclair, replied several days later: "I entirely agree that it is our duty to consider every possible plan [to stop the murder of the Jews] but I am advised that interrupting the railways is out of our power. It is only by an enormous concentration of bomber forces that we have been able to interrupt communications in Normandy; the distance of Silesia from our bases entirely rules out doing anything of the kind." John McCloy had replied to a similar suggestion weeks earlier: "The War Department is of the opinion that the suggested air operation is impracticable for the reason that it could be executed only with the diversion of considerable air support essential to the success of our forces now engaged in decisive operations." Even the severest critics of America's response to the Nazi murder of the Jews acknowledge that successful interruption of railways required close observation of the severed lines and frequent rebombing, since repairs would take only a few days. Even bridges, which were costly to hit, were often back in operation in three or four days. Postwar studies of railway bombing totally vindicated the conclusion of the military authorities. Professor Istvan Deak of Columbia University asks in a recent article: "And if the rail lines had been bombed? The inmates of the cattle cars and those at the departure points would have been allowed to die of thirst, or of the heat, or of the cold, while the lines were being repaired."

It is often noted that American bombers were carrying out raids in the summer of 1944 on industrial targets only a few miles away from Auschwitz, suggesting how easy it would have been to bomb the gas chambers. They do not mention that preparation for the D-day invasion left only 12 percent of the U.S. Army Air Force available for the destruction of German fuel supplies, the primary mission as defined by Gen. Carl Spaatz. . . .

And what of those who managed to escape the Nazis once the war had started? President Roosevelt created the War Refugee Board in January 1944, immediately upon Henry Morgenthau's presenting the case for doing so. There were thousands of refugees stranded on the outer peripheries of Nazi Europe. With the invasion of Italy in 1943, thousands more had sought safety in camps in the south. Tito's success in Yugoslavia had enabled many to escape from Croat fascism and Serb hatred. But those were refugees who were already saved. They were not escapees from the death camps. Under pressure from Roosevelt and Churchill, Spain kept open its frontiers, stating as its policy that "all refugees without exception would be allowed to enter and remain." Probably more than forty thousand, many of them Jewish, found safe sanctuary in Spain. Makeshift transit camps there and in Portugal, Italy, and North Africa housed them in abysmal conditions. Those who fought for these people to come to America were right to do so; then, as now, refugees are generally powerless and voiceless. Governments have to be reminded constantly of their humanitarian responsibilities. But perhaps the Allied nations can be forgiven, in the midst of a war for survival, for not doing more for refugees whose lives had already been saved. Perhaps not. In remembering what we did not do, maybe we can measure our response to today's tragedies and ask whether we—now the richest, most powerful nation in history—have responded adequately to the "ethnic cleansing" of Bosnia, to the genocide in Rwanda, to the Killing Fields of Cambodia. We might question the adequacy of our response to the catalogue of horrors visible to all of us in Sierra Leone, where thousands of children as young as seven years old are forced to become soldiers, human shields, sex slaves, and instruments of torture and killing, having already witnessed the slaughter of their parents and the hacking off of the hands and feet of countless innocent civilians.

Roosevelt's intervention with the government of Hungary, which by then understood that Nazi defeat was inevitable; the actions of the War Refugee Board, such as retaining the heroic Raoul Wallenberg; the bombing of the Budapest area—all played a role in the rescue of half the Jewish community in Hungary. President Roosevelt was deeply and personally involved in this effort. Here is his statement to the nation on March 24, 1944: "In one of the blackest crimes of all history—begun by the Nazis in the day of peace and multiplied by them a hundred times in time of war—the wholesale systematic murder of the Jews of Europe goes on unabated every hour. As a result of the events of the last few days hundreds of thousands of Jews who, while living under persecution, have at least found a haven from death in Hungary and the Balkans, are now threatened with annihilation as Hitler's forces descend more heavily upon these lands. That these innocent people, who have already survived a decade of Hitler's fury, should perish on the very eve of triumph over the barbarism which their persecution symbolizes, would be a major tragedy. It is therefore fitting that we should again proclaim our determination that none who participate in these acts of savagery shall go unpunished. The United Nations have made it clear that they will pursue the guilty and deliver them up in order that justice be done. . . ."

On April 12, 1945, General Eisenhower visited Ohrdruf Nord, the first concentration camp liberated by the American Army. "The things I saw beggar description," he wrote General Marshall. According to his biographer Stephen Ambrose, "Eisenhower had heard ominous rumors about the camps, of course, but never in his worst nightmares had he dreamed they could be so bad." He sent immediately for a delegation of congressional leaders and newspaper editors; he wanted to make sure Americans would never forget this. Five months later he dismissed his close friend and brilliant army commander Gen. George Patton for using former Nazi officials in his occupation structure and publicly likening "the Nazi thing" to differences between the Republicans and Democrats. (Patton had visited the Ohrdruf camp with Eisenhower and become physically ill from what he saw.)

Eisenhower got his first glimpse into the worst horrors at the heart of the Third Reich on the day death claimed the American who had done more than any other to bring them to an end. How ironic that Franklin Roosevelt—the man Hitler hated most, the leader constantly attacked by the isolationist press and derided by the anti-Semites, vilified by Goebbels as a "mentally ill cripple" and as "that Jew Rosenfeld"—should be faulted for being indifferent to the genocide. For all of us the shadow of doubt that enough was not done will always remain, even if there was little more that could have been done. But to say that "we are all guilty" allows the truly guilty to avoid that responsibility. It was Hitler who imagined the Holocaust and the Nazis who carried it out. We were not their accomplices. We destroyed them.

The Internment of the Japanese

William H. Rehnquist

On February 19, 1942, President Franklin D. Roosevelt signed Executive Order 9066, which authorized the removal of ethnic Japanese, including those who were American citizens, from the West Coast. Subsequent laws broadened the restrictions and imposed penalties for violating them. In several cases, the Supreme Court upheld the constitutionality of these actions; these decisions are among the most controversial in the history of the Court. In this essay William H. Rehnquist, Chief Justice of the United States, revisits the decision of his predecessors. He focuses on the legal difference between the *nisei*, American citizens of Japanese extraction, and the *issei*, Japanese aliens. Nowadays, there is no legal basis for distinguishing between American citizens whatever their ethnic origin. But a generation ago legal rights were different and the nation was at war. People must be judged, Rehnquist suggests, according to the standards—including the legal standards—of their own time. The Court's decisions during the Second World War reflected as well the Latin maxim *Inter arma silent leges*: In time of war the laws are silent.

The entire nation was stunned by the Japanese attack on Pearl Harbor on December 7, 1941, but it seemed much closer to home on the West Coast than elsewhere on the mainland.

Residents became fearful of ethnic Japanese among them. Japanese immigrants had begun to settle on the West Coast shortly before the turn of the century and had not been assimilated into the rest of the population. Under the Naturalization Act of 1790, those who had emigrated from Japan were not able to become citizens; they were prohibited by law from owning land and were socially segregated in many ways. The first generation of Japanese immigrants, the issei, therefore remained aliens. But their children, the nisei, having been born in the United States, were citizens from birth. Californians particularly, including public officials—Gov. Culbert Olson, State Attorney General Earl Warren, and the mayor of Los Angeles, Fletcher Bowron—began to call for "relocation" to the interior of the country of persons of Japanese ancestry.

At the outbreak of the war the military established the Western Defense Command, which included the coastal portions of California, Oregon, and Washington. Gen. John DeWitt, its senior officer, at first resisted the clamor to remove the Japanese. But state and local public officials were adamant, and they were supported by their states' congressional delegations. The chorus became more insistent when the Roberts Commission released its report in late January 1942.

On December 18, 1941, President Roosevelt had appointed a body chaired by Owen J. Roberts, an Associate Justice of the Supreme Court, "to ascertain and report the facts relating to the attack. . . . The commission found that there had been highly organized espionage in Hawaii: "It has been discovered that the Japanese consul sent to and received from Tokyo in his own and other names many messages on commercial radio circuits. This activity greatly increased towards December 7, 1941. . . . [The Japanese] knew from maps which they had obtained, the exact location of vital air fields, hangars, and other structures. They also knew accurately where certain important naval vessels would be berthed. Their fliers had the most detailed maps, courses, and bearings, so that each could attack a given vessel or field. Each seems to have been given a specified mission."

In February 1942 a Japanese submarine shelled oil installations near Santa Barbara. The pressure built for forced evacuation. Attorney General Francis Biddle, Secretary of War Henry L. Stimson, and Assistant Secretary of War John J. McCloy were the decision-makers for the two concerned departments. None of them favored relocation at first, but eventually Stimson and McCloy changed their minds in the course of often heated discussions among themselves and their subordinates. Final approval of course rested with the President. On February 11, 1942, McCloy asked Stimson to find out if Roosevelt was willing to authorize the removal of the nisei as well as the issei. Stimson asked to see the President but was told FDR was too busy; a phone call would have to do. "I took up with him the West Coast matter first," Stimson wrote in his diary, "and told him the situation and fortunately found he was very vigorous about it and told me to go ahead on the line that I had myself thought the best."

Then, Stimson wrote in his 1947 memoirs, "mindful of its duty to be prepared for any emergency, the War Department ordered the evacuation of more than a hundred thousand persons of Japanese origin from strategic areas on the west coast. This decision was widely criticized as an unconstitutional invasion of the rights of individuals many of whom were American citizens, but it was eventually approved by the Supreme Court as a legitimate exercise of the war powers of the President. What critics ignored was the situation that led to the evacuation. Japanese raids on the west coast seemed not only possible but probable in the first months of the war, and it was quite impossible to be sure that the raiders would not receive important help from individuals of Japanese origin." . . .

Executive Order 9066, authorizing the removal of the ethnic Japanese from the West Coast, was signed by Roosevelt on February 19. Several weeks later Congress passed a law imposing criminal penalties for violations of the order or regulations that might be issued to implement it. First a curfew was imposed on the ethnic Japanese, then they were required to report to relocation centers, and finally they were taken to camps in the interior of California and in the mountain states. There was no physical brutality, but there were certainly severe hardships: removal from the place where one lived, often the forced sale of houses and businesses, and harsh living conditions in the Spartan quarters of the internment centers. As the war progressed, some restrictions were relaxed. Nisei volunteers made up the 442d Combat Team, which fought bravely in Italy against the Germans. Other internees were issued work permits that allowed them to leave the camp. Finally, most of those who were still interned were released by the beginning of 1945, as a result of the third Supreme Court decision in which the relocation policy was challenged.

Gordon Hirabayashi was born near Seattle to issei parents in 1918, and by 1942 he was a senior at the University of Washington. In May 1942 he disobeyed the curfew requirement imposed by military authorities pursuant to the President's Executive Order, and seven days later he failed to report to register for evacuation. He was indicted and convicted in a federal court in Seattle on two counts of misdemeanor and sentenced to imprisonment for three months on each. He contended that the orders he was charged with violating were unconstitutional, but the federal judge in Seattle ruled against him.

Fred Korematsu, born in the United States to issei parents, was convicted of remaining in San Leandro, California, in violation of a military exclusion order applicable to him. The federal court in San Francisco overruled his claim that the order in question was unconstitutional, suspended his sentence, and placed him on probation for five years.

The cases were argued together before the U.S. Court of Appeals for the Ninth Circuit in San Francisco. . . . The case of *Hirabayashi* was sent directly there by the court of appeals and was argued in May 1943. . . .

The Japanese-Americans were represented in the Supreme Court by able counsel . . . Their basic contention was that the President's Executive Order was unconstitutional because it proceeded on the basis that an entire racial group was disloyal, rather than being based on any individual determinations of disloyalty. Briefs supporting these petitioners were filed by the American Civil Liberties Union, the Northern California branch of the American Civil Liberties Union, and the Japanese-American Citizens League.

The government in its brief recited in great detail the calamitous military events of the early days of the war—these ranged from the Pearl Harbor raid to the fall of the British stronghold of Singapore—which it thought justified the orders now being challenged, and went on to catalogue the "concentration of war facilities and installations on the West Coast [that] made it an area of special military concern at any time and especially after the sensational Japanese successes."

The attorneys general of Washington, Oregon, and California filed a brief in support of the government that pointed out that "for the first seven months little occurred to reduce the fear of attack. . . . On June 3, 1942, Dutch Harbor, Alaska, was attacked by carrier-based planes. On June 7, 1942, the Japanese invaded continental North America by occupying the Islands of Attu and Kiska in the Aleutian group. There was an increasing indication that the enemy had knowledge of our patrols and naval dispositions, for ships leaving west coast ports were being intercepted and attacked regularly by enemy submarines." Following the oral argument and conference in the *Hirabayashi* case, Chief Justice Stone assigned the task of writing the Court's opinion to himself. He first greatly narrowed the scope of the opinion by deciding that the Court need pass only on the validity of the curfew requirement and not on the requirement that Hirabayashi report to a relocation center. Hirabayashi had been convicted of both offenses, but his sentences were to run "concurrently"—that is, he would serve only three months in prison even though he had been sentenced to serve three months on each of two different charges. Under established law at that time, if the conviction on one count was upheld, the Court would disregard the conviction on the second count, since it essentially

Japanese Americans of all ages, tagged like pieces of luggage, await their relocation to one of ten detention camps in seven states. This family was from Hayward, California.

made no difference in the amount of time the defendant would spend in prison. In this case it meant that the Court had to tackle only the easier question of whether a curfew might be imposed, rather than the more difficult one of whether Hirabayashi could be sent to an internment camp.

Stone's task in writing the opinion was not an easy one, because several of his colleagues insisted that there be little or no opportunity to challenge the order later, while Justices Douglas, Murphy, and Rutledge wanted explicitly to leave open that possibility. Indeed, Murphy circulated a draft of a caustic dissent that chastised the Court for approving a program that "utterly subverts" individual rights in war. Douglas circulated a concurrence in which he indicated his view that at some point a person interned under the program should have an opportunity to prove his loyalty. Murphy finally turned his draft dissent into a concurrence but said in it that he thought the program "goes to the very brink of constitutional power." Rutledge also filed a brief concurrence.

Stone's opinion for the Court borrowed a definition of the government's war power from a statement made by Charles Evans Hughes—not while he was a member of the Court but in an article in the *American Bar Association Journal:* The war power of the national government is "the power to wage war successfully," and it was "not for any court to sit in review of the wisdom of their [the Executive's or Congress's] actions, or to substitute its judgment for theirs." If the Court could say there was a rational basis for the military decision, it would be sustained.

Stone's opinion then adduced the facts—most of which had been set forth in the government's brief—that showed the threat by the Japanese Navy to the Pacific Coast immediately after the Pearl Harbor bombing. It went on to say: "Whatever views we may entertain regarding the loyalty to this country of the citizens of Japanese ancestry, we cannot reject as unfounded the judgment of the military authorities and of Congress that there were disloyal members of that population, whose number and strength could not be precisely and quickly ascertained. We cannot say that the war-making branches of the Government did not have ground for believing that in a critical hour such persons could not readily be isolated and separately dealt with, and constituted a menace to the national defense and safety, which demanded that prompt and adequate measures be taken to guard against it."

The Court, of course, had to respond to the charge that distinctions based on race alone were not permitted under the Constitution: "Distinctions between citizens solely because of their ancestry are by their very nature odious to a free people whose institutions are founded upon the doctrine of equality. . . . We may assume that these considerations would be controlling here were it not for the fact that the danger of espionage and sabotage, in time of war and of threatened invasion, calls upon the military authorities to scrutinize every relevant fact bearing on the loyalty of populations in the danger areas. . . . The fact alone that the attack on our shores was threatened by Japan rather than another enemy power set these citizens apart from others who have no particular associations with Japan." . . .

Korematsu's case did not come on for argument until October 1944. Here the Court was required to confront not merely the curfew but the far more draconian relocation requirement. The Court upheld relocation, in an opinion by Justice Black, basing its reasoning largely on the earlier decision. This time, however, there were separate dissents by Justices Roberts, Murphy, and Jackson.

The flavor of Black's opinion is caught in its concluding passage: "To cast this case into outlines of racial prejudice, without reference to the real military dangers which were presented, merely confuses the issue. Korematsu was not excluded from the Military Area because of hostility to him or his race. He *was* excluded because we are at war with the Japanese Empire, because the properly constituted military authorities feared an invasion of our West Coast and felt constrained to take proper security measures, because they decided that the military urgency of the situation demanded that all citizens of Japanese ancestry be segregated from the West Coast temporarily. . . . There was evidence of disloyalty on the part of some, the military authorities considered that the need for action was great, and time was short. We cannot—by availing ourselves of the calm perspective of hindsight—now say that at that time these actions were unjustified."

Murphy criticized the military for lumping together with a disloyal few of Japanese ancestry all the others against whom there had been no such showing. Jackson said that the Court was simply in no position to evaluate the government's claim of military necessity: "In the very nature of things, military decisions are not susceptible of intelligent judicial appraisal. They do not pretend to rest on evidence, but are made on information that often would not be admissible and on assumptions that could not be proved. . . . Hence courts can never have any real alternative to accepting the mere declaration of the authority that issued the order that it was reasonably necessary from a military viewpoint."

But in the case of *Endo*, argued and decided at the same time as *Korematsu*, the Court reached quite a different result. Mitsuye Endo had submitted to an evacuation order and been removed first to the Tule Lake Relocation Center in the Cascade Mountains just south of the California-Oregon border and then to another relocation center in Utah. She sued out a writ of habeas corpus, claiming that she was a loyal citizen against whom no charge had been made and that she was therefore entitled to her relief. The government agreed that she was a loyal citizen and not charged with any offense. The Court decided that under these circumstances Endo was entitled to be released from confinement. The presidential order and the act of Congress confirming it spoke of evacuation from a military zone but said nothing of detention after the evacuation. While the initial evacuation had been justified in terms of the defense facilities on the West Coast, the detention of a loyal person of Japanese ancestry after the evacuation had taken place was not reasonably necessary to prevent sabotage or espionage. Two members of the Court wrote separately, but all agreed with the result.

Although the Court based its reasoning in *Endo* on the provisions of the act of Congress and the Executive Order, and therefore Congress and the President would have been free to change those to provide for detention, the Court's opinion strongly hinted at constitutional difficulties if that were to be done. And, it should be noted, the military position of the United States was much more favorable in the fall of 1944 than it had been in the spring of 1942. In the Pacific the U.S. Navy won the Battle of Leyte Gulf in October, and American forces were moving steadily closer to the Japanese homeland. There was neither a military need nor a public demand for further restrictions on Americans of Japanese descent, and the entire program was promptly terminated only two weeks after the decision in the *Endo* case.

There is a certain disingenuousness in this sequence of three opinions—*Hirabayashi, Korematsu,* and *Endo.* There was no reason to think that Gordon Hirabayashi and Fred Korematsu were any less loyal to the United States than was Mitsuye Endo. Presumably they would have been entitled to relief from detention upon the same showings as that made by Endo. But even had Hirabayashi tried to raise that question in his case, he would have failed, for the Court chose to confine itself to the curfew issue. It was not until we were clearly winning the war that the Court came around to this view in *Endo.* The process illustrates in a rough way the Latin maxim *Inter arma silent leges* (in time of war the laws are silent).

Postwar public opinion very quickly came to see the forced relocation and detention of people of Japanese ancestry as a grave injustice. Writing in 1945, Eugene Rostow, then a professor at Yale Law School and later its dean, declared the program "a disaster" that both represented an abandonment of our traditional subordination of military to civil authority and sanctioned racially based discrimination. Edward Ennis, who as a lawyer in the Justice Department had opposed the program, reappeared nearly forty years later on behalf of the ACLU to testify before the congressionally created Commission on Wartime Relocation and Internment of Civilians. He characterized the program as "the worst blow to civil liberty in our history." In the view of this author, some of this criticism is well justified, and some not; its principal fault is that it lumps together the cases of the issei and the nisei.

The cases before the Supreme Court—*Hirabayashi, Korematsu,* and *Endo*—all involved nisei, children of immigrants, who were born in the United States and thus were American. The basis on which the Court upheld the plan were military representations as to the necessity for evacuation. These representations were undoubtedly exaggerated, and they were based in part on the view that not only the issei but their children were different from other West Coast residents.

In defense of the military it should be pointed out that these officials were not entrusted with the protection of anyone's civil liberty; their job was making sure that vital areas were as secure as possible from espionage or sabotage. The role of General DeWitt was not one to encourage a nice calculation of the costs in civil liberty as opposed to the benefits to national security. Gen. Walter Short, the Army commander in Hawaii, and Adm. Husband E. Kimmel, the Navy commander there, both were summarily removed from their commands ten days after Pearl Harbor because of their failure to anticipate the Japanese surprise attack. The head of the Western Defense command was surely going to err on the side of preparedness.

Moreover, it was not DeWitt and his associates who had first recommended evacuation of the issei and nisei; as we have seen, the principal early proponents of that idea were Governor Olson, Attorney General Warren, Los Angeles Mayor Bowron, and the congressional delegations of the three West Coast states. Public opinion should not be the determining factor in making a military appraisal, but it is bound to occur to those engaged in that task how they will be regarded if they reject a widely popular security measure that in retrospect turns out to have been necessary.

The United States prides itself on having a system in which the civilian heads of the service departments are supreme over the military chiefs, so one might expect that Henry Stimson and John McCloy would have made a more careful evaluation of the evacuation proposal than they appear to have done. Far from the Pacific Coast, they would be expected to have a more detached view than the commander on the scene. But here too there seems to have been a tendency to feel that concern for civil liberty was not their responsibility. There is even more of this feeling in Roosevelt's perfunctory approval of the plan in response to a phone call from Stimson. Biddle's protests proved futile even at the highest levels of government, in part because no significant element of public opinion opposed the relocation.

Once the relocation plan was in place, it could be challenged only in the courts. Was the Supreme Court at fault in upholding first the curfew, in *Hirabayashi,* and then the relocation, in *Korematsu?* In *Hirabayashi* the Court could have decided both the validity of the relocation requirement and the curfew requirement, for the "concurrent sentence" doctrine under which it declined to do so is discretionary. But counseling against any broader decision was the well-established rule that the Court should avoid deciding constitutional questions if at all possible, and so the *Hirabayashi* decision left the far more difficult question for another day.

When that day came, in *Korematsu,* a majority of the Court upheld the relocation program. Justice Black's opinion for the Court in *Korematsu* followed the same line of reasoning as had Chief Justice Stone's in *Hirabayashi.* But this time there were three dissenters, who had voted to uphold the curfew but wanted to strike down the relocation program.

Over the years, several criticisms have been made of the Court's opinions in these cases. The most general is of its extremely deferential treatment given to the

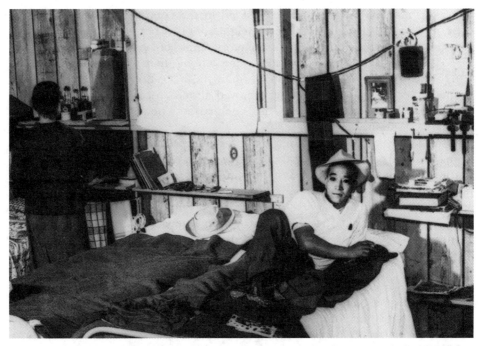

Government propaganda claimed that these evacuees were enjoying "a moment of relaxation." In reality, whole families of interned Japanese-Americans lived in a single room furnished with little more than a few cots, some blankets, and a single light bulb.

government's argument that the curfew and relocation were necessitated by military considerations. Here one can only echo Justice Jackson's observation that "in the very nature of things, military decisions are not susceptible of intelligent judicial appraisal." But it surely does not follow from this that a court must therefore invalidate measures based on military judgments. Eugene Rostow suggested holding a judicial inquiry into the entire question of military necessity, but this seems an extraordinarily dubious proposition. Judicial inquiry, with its restrictive rules of evidence, orientation toward resolution of factual disputes in individual cases, and long delays, is ill suited to determine an urgent issue. The necessity for prompt action was cogently stated by the Court in its *Hirabayashi* opinion: "Although the results of the attack on Pearl Harbor were not fully disclosed until much later, it was known that the damage was extensive, and that the Japanese by their successes had gained a naval superiority over our forces in the Pacific which might enable them to seize Pearl Harbor, our largest naval base and the last stronghold of defense lying between Japan and the west coast. That reasonably prudent men charged with the responsibility of our national defense had ample ground for concluding that they must face the danger of invasion, take measures against it, and in making the choice of measures consider our internal situation, cannot be doubted."

A second criticism is that the decisions in these cases upheld a program that, at bottom, was based on racial distinctions. There are several levels at which this criticism can be made. The broadest is that the nisei were relocated simply because the

Caucasian majority on the West Coast (and in the country as a whole) disliked them and wished to remove them as neighbors or as business competitors. The Court's answer to this attack seems satisfactory: Those of Japanese descent were displaced because of fear that disloyal elements among them would aid Japan in the war. Though there were undoubtedly nativists in California who welcomed a chance to see the issei and the nisei removed, it does not follow that this point of view was attributable to the military decision-makers. They, after all, did not at first propose relocation.

But a narrower criticism along the same line has more force to it: The nisei were evacuated notwithstanding the fact that they were American citizens. Even in wartime citizens may not be rounded up and required to prove their loyalty. They may be excluded from sensitive military areas in the absence of a security clearance and otherwise be denied access to any classified information, but it pushes these propositions to an extreme to say that a sizable geographic area, including the homes of many citizens, may be declared off-limits and the residents forced to move. It pushes it to an even greater extreme to say that such persons may be required not only to leave their homes but to report to and remain in a distant relocation center.

The Supreme Court in its *Hirabayashi* opinion pointed to several facts thought to justify this treatment of the nisei. Both federal and state restrictions on the rights of Japanese emigrants had prevented their assimilation into the Caucasian population and had intensified their insularity and solidarity. Japanese parents sent their children to Japanese-language schools, and there was some evidence that these were a source of Japanese nationalistic propaganda. As many as ten thousand American-born children of Japanese parentage went to Japan for all or a part of their education. Thus, as Stone put it in his opinion, "we cannot say that the war-making branches of the Government did not have ground for believing that in a critical hour such persons . . . constituted a menace to the national defense and safety . . ."

There is considerable irony, of course, in relying on previously existing laws discriminating against Japanese immigrants to conclude that still further disabilities should be imposed upon them because they had not been assimilated into the Caucasian majority. But in time of war a nation may be required to respond to a condition without making a careful inquiry into how that condition came about.

Were the condition or conditions described by the Court sufficient to justify treating the nisei differently from all other citizens on the West Coast? Under today's constitutional law, certainly not. Any sort of "racial" classification by government is viewed as suspect, and an extraordinarily strong reason is required to justify it.

But the law was by no means so clear when these cases were decided. A decade later the Court decided the watershed case of *Brown* v. *Board of Education,* holding that the Kansas legislature had violated the Equal Protection Clause of the Fourteenth Amendment by permitting public schools to segregate students by race. And with *Brown* there was argued a companion case, *Bolling* v. *Sharpe,* challenging similarly imposed segregation in public schools in the District of Columbia. This requirement had been imposed not by a state government but by Congress. The Court in *Bolling,* in a brief opinion not notable for clarity of reasoning, held that the Due Process Clause of the Fifth Amendment imposes on the federal government a limitation similar to that imposed on the states by the Equal Protection Clause of the Fourteenth Amendment. Had this doctrine been the law ten years earlier, the Supreme Court might have found it easier to reach a different result in *Hirabayashi* and *Korematsu*.

The discrimination against the nisei lay in the fact that any other citizen could remain in his home unless actually tried and convicted of espionage or sabotage while the nisei were removed from their homes without any individualized findings at all. The proffered justification—that an attack on the West Coast by Japan was reasonably feared and that American citizens of Japanese descent were more likely than the populace as a whole to include potential spies or saboteurs—was not wholly groundless. A May 1941 "Magic intercept," resulting from the Americans' having broken the Japanese code, contained a message from the Japanese consulate in Los Angeles that "we also have connections with our second generations working in airplane plants for intelligence purposes." But although such information might well have justified exclusion of nisei, as opposed to other citizens, from work in aircraft factories without strict security clearance, it falls considerably short of justifying the dislodging of thousands of citizens from their homes on the basis of ancestry.

The issei, however, who were not citizens, were both by tradition and by law in a quite different category. The legal difference dates back to the Alien Enemies Law enacted in 1798 during the administration of President John Adams. The Alien Law is often bracketed together with the Sedition Act passed at the same time, and there is a tendency to think that both were repealed as soon as Thomas Jefferson and his Jeffersonian Republicans came to power in 1801. But only the Sedition Act was repealed; the Alien Enemies Act, with minor amendments, remained on the books at the time of World War II. It provided: "Whenever there shall be a declared war between the United States and any foreign nation or government . . . all natives, citizens, denizens, or subjects of the hostile nation or government, being of the age of fourteen years and upward, who shall be within the United States and not actually naturalized, shall be liable to be apprehended, restrained, secured, and removed as alien enemies."

In a case decided shortly after the end of World War II, the Supreme Court, referring to the Alien Law, said: "Executive power over enemy aliens, undelayed and unhampered by litigation, has been deemed, throughout our history, essential to war-time security. This is in keeping with the practice of the most enlightened of nations and has resulted in treatment of alien enemies more considerate than that which has prevailed among any of our enemies and some of our allies. This statute was enacted or suffered to continue by men who helped found the Republic and formulate the Bill of Rights, and although it obviously denies enemy aliens the constitutional immunities of citizens, it seems not then to have been supposed that a nation's obligations to its foes could ever be put on a parity with those to its defenders. The resident enemy alien is constitutionally subject to summary arrest, internment and deportation whenever a 'declared war' exists." Thus distinctions that might not be permissible between classes of citizens must be viewed otherwise when drawn between classes of aliens.

The most frequently made charge on behalf of the issei is that the government treated Japanese enemy aliens differently from enemy aliens of German or Italian citizenship when we were at war with all three countries. It appears that there was some removal of Italian enemy aliens for a brief period, but there seems little doubt that the West Coast issei were treated differently from the majority of German or Italian nationals residing in this country. It should be pointed out, however, that there does not appear to have been the same concentration of German or Italian nationals along the West Coast in areas near major defense plants. Japanese emigration to the United States had occurred only within the preceding half-century, and the emigrants resided almost entirely on the West Coast, where U.S. aircraft production was highly concentrated and where attack and possibly invasion were at first feared. Italian emigration had taken place over a considerably longer period; and German since colonial days, and people of German and Italian ancestry were far more spread out in the population in general than were the issei.

These distinctions seem insufficient to justify such a sharp difference of treatment between Japanese and German and Italian aliens in peacetime. But they do seem legally adequate to support the difference in treatment between the two classes of enemy aliens in time of war.

An entirely separate and important philosophical question is whether occasional presidential excesses and judicial restraint in wartime are desirable or undesirable. In one sense this question is very largely academic. There is no reason to think that future wartime Presidents will act differently from Roosevelt or that future Justices of the Supreme Court will decide questions differently from their predecessors. But even though this be so, there is every reason to believe that the historic trend against the least justified of the curtailments of civil liberty in wartime will continue in the future. It is neither desirable nor remotely likely that civil liberty will occupy as favored a position in wartime as it does in peacetime. But it is both desirable and likely that the courts will pay more careful attention to the basis for the government's claims of necessity as a reason for curtailing civil liberty. The laws will thus not be silent in time of war, even though they will speak with a somewhat different voice.

Why We Had to Drop the Atomic Bomb

Robert James Maddox

That the American decision to use the atom bomb against Japan ended World War II is beyond dispute. But whether the atom bomb was the best way to accomplish that objective is still a subject of controversy among historians who have studied the question carefully.

No one argues that Japan could have escaped defeat if Hiroshima and Nagasaki had not been leveled. But at what cost in human lives, Japanese and Allied alike? In this essay, Professor Robert James Maddox discusses whether or not the killing of so many thousands of Japanese civilians was morally justified. He makes a powerful case that it was. As editor, I agree. But many readers may not. Like so many crucial events, the truth is a matter of opinion, a fact which makes history endlessly fascinating.

On the morning of August 6, 1945, the American B-29 *Enola Gay* dropped an atomic bomb on the Japanese city of Hiroshima. Three days later another B-29, *Bock's Car*, released one over Nagasaki. Both caused enormous casualties and physical destruction. These two cataclysmic events have preyed upon the American consciousness ever since. . . . Harry S Truman and other officials claimed that the bombs caused Japan to surrender, thereby avoiding a bloody invasion. Critics have accused them of at best failing to explore alternatives, at worst of using the bombs to make the Soviet Union "more manageable" rather than to defeat a Japan that they already knew was on the verge of capitulation.

By any rational calculation Japan was a beaten nation by the summer of 1945. Conventional bombing had reduced many of its cities to rubble, blockade had strangled its importation of vitally needed materials, and its navy had sustained such heavy losses as to be powerless to interfere with the invasion everyone knew was coming. By late June advancing American forces had completed the conquest of Okinawa, which lay only 350 miles from the southernmost Japanese home island of Kyushu. They now stood poised for the final onslaught.

Rational calculations did not determine Japan's position. Although a peace faction within the government wished to end the war—provided certain conditions were met—militants were prepared to fight on regardless of consequences. They claimed to welcome an invasion of the home islands, promising to inflict such hideous casualties that the United States would retreat from its announced policy of unconditional surrender. The militarists held effective power over the government and were capable of defying the emperor, as they had in the past, on the ground that his civilian advisors were misleading him.

Okinawa provided a preview of what invasion of the home islands would entail. Since April 1 the Japanese had fought with a ferocity that mocked any notion that their will to resist was eroding. They had inflicted nearly 50,000 casualties on the invaders, many resulting from the first large-scale use of kamikazes. They also had dispatched the superbattleship *Yamato* on a suicide mission to Okinawa where, after attacking American ships offshore, it was to plunge ashore to become a huge, doomed fortress. *Yamato* was sunk shortly after leaving port, but its mission symbolized Japan's willingness to sacrifice everything in an apparently hopeless cause.

The Japanese could be expected to defend their sacred homeland with even greater fervor, and kamikazes flying at short range promised to be even more devastating than at Okinawa. The Japanese had more than 2,000,000 troops in the home islands, were training millions of irregulars, and for some time had been conserving aircraft that might have been used to protect Japanese cities against American bombers. Reports from Tokyo indicated that Japan meant to fight the war to a finish. On June 8 an imperial conference adopted "The Fundamental Policy to Be Followed Henceforth in the Conduct of the War," which pledged to "prosecute the war to the bitter end in order to uphold the national polity, protect the imperial land, and accomplish the objectives for which we went to war." Truman had no reason to believe that the proclamation meant anything other than what it said.

Against this background, while fighting on Okinawa still continued, the President had his naval chief of staff, Adm. William D. Leahy, notify the Joint Chiefs of Staff (JCS) and the Secretaries of War and Navy that a meeting would be held at the White House on June 18. The night before the conference Truman wrote in his diary that "I have to decide Japanese strategy—shall we invade Japan proper or shall we bomb and blockade? That is my hardest decision to date. But I'll make it when I have all the facts."

Truman met with the chiefs at three-thirty in the afternoon. Present were Army Chief of Staff Gen. George C. Marshall, Army Air Force's Gen. Ira C. Eaker (sitting in for the Army Air Force's chief of staff, Henry H. Arnold, who was on an inspection tour of installations in the Pacific), Navy Chief of Staff Adm. Ernest J. King, Leahy (also a member of the JCS), Secretary of the Navy James Forrestal, Secretary of War Henry L. Stimson, and Assistant Secretary of War John J. McCloy. Truman opened the meeting, then asked Marshall for his views. Marshall was the dominant figure on the JCS. He was Truman's most trusted military adviser, as he had been Roosevelt's.

Marshall reported that the chiefs, supported by the Pacific commanders Gen. Douglas MacArthur and Adm. Chester W. Nimitz, agreed that an invasion of Kyushu "appears to be the least costly worthwhile operation following Okinawa." Lodgment in Kyushu, he said, was necessary to make blockade and bombardment more effective and to serve as a staging area for the invasion of Japan's main island of Honshu. The chiefs recommended a target date of November 1 for the first phase, code name Olympic, because delay would give the Japanese more time to prepare and because bad weather might postpone the invasion "and hence the end of the war" for up to six months. Marshall said that in his opinion, Olympic was "the only course to pursue." The chiefs also proposed that Operation Cornet be launched against Honshu on March 4, 1946.

Leahy's memorandum calling the meeting had asked for the casualty projections which that invasion might produce. Marshall stated that campaigns in the

Pacific had been so diverse "it is considered wrong" to make total estimates. All he would say was that casualties during the first thirty days on Kyushu should not exceed those sustained in taking Luzon in the Philippines—31,000 men killed, wounded, or missing in action. "It is a grim fact," Marshall said, "that there is not an easy, bloodless way to victory in war." Leahy estimated a higher casualty rate similar to Okinawa, and King guessed somewhere in between.

King and Eaker, speaking for the Navy and the Army Air Forces respectively, endorsed Marshall's proposals. King said that he had become convinced that Kyushu was "the key to the success of any siege operations." He recommended that "we should do Kyushu now" and begin preparations for invading Honshu. Eaker "agreed completely" with Marshall. He said he had just received a message from Arnold also expressing "complete agreement." Air Force plans called for the use of forty groups of heavy bombers, which could not be deployed without the use of airfields on Kyushu. Stimson and Forrestal concurred.

Truman summed up. He considered "the Kyushu plan all right from the military standpoint" and directed the chiefs to "go ahead with it." He said he "had hoped that there was a possibility of preventing an Okinawa from one end of Japan to the other," but "he was clear on the situation now" and was "quite sure" the chiefs should proceed with the plan. Just before the meeting adjourned, McCloy raised the possibility of avoiding an invasion by warning the Japanese that the United States would employ atomic weapons if there were no surrender. The ensuing discussion was inconclusive because the first test was a month away and no one could be sure the weapons would work.

In his memoirs Truman claimed that using atomic bombs prevented an invasion that would have cost 500,000 American lives. Other officials mentioned the same or even higher figures. Critics have assailed such statements as gross exaggerations designed to forestall scrutiny of Truman's real motives. They have given wide publicity to a report prepared by the Joint War Plans Committee (JWPC) for the chiefs' meeting with Truman. The committee estimated that the invasion of Kyushu, followed by that of Honshu, as the chiefs proposed, would cost approximately 40,000 dead, 150,000 wounded, and 3,500 missing in action for a total of 193,500 casualties.

That those responsible for a decision should exaggerate the consequences is commonplace. Some who cite the JWPC report profess to see more sinister motives, insisting that such "low" casualty projections call into question the very idea that atomic bombs were used to avoid heavy losses. By discrediting that justification as a cover-up, they seek to bolster their contention that the bombs were really used to permit the employment of "atomic diplomacy" against the Soviet Union.

The notion that 193,500 anticipated casualties were too insignificant to have caused Truman to resort to atomic bombs might seem bizarre to anyone other than an academic, but let it pass. Those who have cited the JWCP report in countless op-ed pieces in newspapers and in magazine articles have created a myth by omitting key considerations: First, the report itself is studded with qualifications that casualties "are not subject to accurate estimate" and that the projection "is admittedly only an educated guess." Second, the figures never were conveyed to Truman. They were excised at high military echelons, which is why Marshall cited only estimates for the first thirty days on Kyushu. And indeed, subsequent Japanese troop buildups on Kyushu rendered the JWPC estimates totally irrelevant by the time the first atomic bomb was dropped.

Another myth that has attained wide attention is that at least several of Truman's top military advisers later informed him that using atomic bombs against Japan would be militarily unnecessary or immoral, or both. There is no persuasive evidence that any of them did so. None of the Joint Chiefs ever made such a claim, although one inventive author has tried to make it appear that Leahy did by braiding together several unrelated passages from the admiral's memoirs. Actually, two days after Hiroshima, Truman told aides that Leahy had "said up to the last that it wouldn't go off."

Neither MacArthur nor Nimitz ever communicated to Truman any change of mind about the need for invasion or expressed reservations about using the bombs. When first informed about their imminent use only days before Hiroshima, MacArthur responded with a lecture on the future of atomic warfare and even after Hiroshima strongly recommended that the invasion go forward. Nimitz, from whose jurisdiction the atomic strikes would be launched, was notified in early 1945. "This sounds fine," he told the courier, "but this is only February. Can't we get one earlier?" Nimitz later would join Air Force generals Carl D. Spaatz, Nathan Twining, and Curtis LeMay in recommending that a third bomb be dropped on Tokyo.

Only Dwight D. Eisenhower later claimed to have remonstrated against the use of the bomb. In his *Crusade in Europe,* published in 1948, he wrote that when Secretary Stimson informed him during the Potsdam Conference of plans to use the bomb, he replied that he hoped "we would never have to use such a thing against any enemy," because he did not want the United States to be the first to use such a weapon. He added, "My views were merely personal and immediate reactions; they were not based on any analysis of the subject."

Eisenhower's recollections grew more colorful as the years went on. A later account with Stimson had it taking place at Ike's headquarters in Frankfurt on the very day news arrived of the successful test in New Mexico. "We'd had a nice evening at headquarters in Germany," he remembered. Then, after dinner, "Stimson got this cable saying that the bomb had been perfected and and was ready to be dropped. The cable was in code . . . 'the lamb is born' or some damn thing like that." In this version Eisenhower claimed to have protested vehemently that "the Japanese were ready to surrender and it wasn't necessary to hit them with that awful thing." "Well," Eisenhower concluded, "the old gentleman got furious."

The best that can be said about Eisenhower's memory is that it had become flawed by the passage of time. Stimson was in Potsdam and Eisenhower in Frankfurt on July 16, when word came of the successful test. Aside from a brief conversation at a flag-raising ceremony in Berlin on July 20, the only other time they met was at Ike's headquarters on July 27. By then orders already had been sent to the Pacific to use the bombs if Japan had not yet surrendered. Notes made by one of Stimson's aides indicate that there was a discussion of atomic bombs, but there is no mention of any protest on Eisenhower's part. Even if there had been, two factors must be kept in mind. Eisenhower had commanded Allied forces in Europe, and his opin-

This 1984 display in an Osaka department store recalls the destruction wrought by the atomic bombs dropped on Japan in 1945.

ion on how close Japan was to surrender would have carried no special weight. More important, Stimson left for home immediately after the meeting and could not have personally conveyed Ike's sentiments to the President, who did not return to Washington until after Hiroshima.

On July 8 the Combined Intelligence Committee submitted to the American and British Combined Chiefs of Staff a report entitled "Estimate of the Enemy Situation." The committee predicted that as Japan's position continued to deteriorate, it might "make a serious effort to use the USSR [then a neutral] as a mediator in ending the war." Tokyo also would put out "intermittent peace feelers" to "weaken the determination of the United Nations to fight to the bitter end, or to create inter-allied dissension." While the Japanese people would be willing to make large concessions to end the war, "For a surrender to be acceptable to the Japanese army, it would be necessary for the military leaders to believe that it would not entail discrediting warrior tradition and that it would permit the ultimate resurgence of a military Japan."

Small wonder that American officials remained unimpressed when Japan proceeded to do exactly what the committee predicted. On July 12 Japanese Foreign Minister Shigenori Togo instructed Ambassador Naotaki Sato in Moscow to inform the Soviets that the emperor wished to send a personal envoy, Prince Fuminaro Konoye, in an attempt "to restore peace with all possible speed." Although he realized Konoye could not reach Moscow before the Soviet leader Joseph Stalin and Foreign Minister V. M. Molotov left to attend a Big Three meeting scheduled to begin in Potsdam on the fifteenth, Togo sought to have negotiations begin as soon as they returned.

American officials had long since been able to read Japanese diplomatic traffic through a process known as the MAGIC intercepts. Army intelligence (G-2) prepared for General Marshall its interpretation of Togo's message the next day. The report listed several possible constructions, the most probable being that the Japanese "governing clique" was making a coordinated effort to "stave off defeat" through Soviet intervention and an "appeal to war weariness in the United States." The report added that Undersecretary of State Joseph C. Crew, who had spent ten years in Japan as ambassador, "agrees with these conclusions."

Some have claimed that Togo's overture to the Soviet Union, together with attempts by some minor Japanese officials in Switzerland and other neutral countries to get peace talks started through the Office of Strategic Services (OSS), constituted clear evidence that the Japanese were near surrender. Their sole prerequisite was retention of their sacred emperor, whose unique cultural/religious status within the Japanese polity they would not compromise. If only the United States had extended assurances about the emperor, according to this view, much bloodshed and the atomic bombs would have been unnecessary.

A careful reading of the MAGIC intercepts of subsequent exchanges between Togo and Sato provides no evidence that retention of the emperor was the sole obstacle to peace. What they show instead is that the Japanese Foreign Office was trying to cut a deal through the Soviet Union that would have permitted Japan to retain its political system and its prewar empire intact. Even the most lenient of American officials could not have countenanced such a settlement.

Togo on July 17 informed Sato that "we are not asking the Russians' mediation in *anything like unconditional surrender* [emphasis added]." During the following weeks Sato pleaded with his superiors to abandon hope of Soviet intercession and to approach the United States directly to find out what peace terms would be offered. "There is . . . no alternative but immediate unconditional surrender," he cabled on July 31, and he bluntly informed Togo that "your way of looking at things and the actual situation in the Eastern area may be seen to be absolutely contradictory." The Foreign Ministry ignored his pleas and continued to seek Soviet help even after Hiroshima.

"Peace feelers" by Japanese officials abroad seemed no more promising from the American point of view. Although several of the consular personnel and military attachés engaged in these activities claimed important connections at home, none produced verification. Had the Japanese government sought only an assurance about the emperor, all it had to do was grant one of these men authority to begin talks through the OSS. Its failure to do so led American officials to assume that those involved were either well-meaning individuals acting alone or that they were being orchestrated by Tokyo. Grew characterized such "peace feelers" as "familiar weapons of psychological warfare" designed to "divide the Allies."

Some American officials, such as Stimson and Grew, nonetheless wanted to signal to the Japanese that they might retain the emperorship in the form of a constitutional monarchy. Such an assurance might remove the last stumbling block to surrender, if not when it was issued, then later. Only an imperial rescript would bring about an orderly surrender, they argued, without which Japanese forces would fight to the last man regardless of what the government in Tokyo did. Besides, the emperor could serve as a stabilizing factor during the transition to peacetime.

There were many arguments against an American initiative. Some opposed retaining such an undemocratic institution on principle and because they feared it might later serve as a rallying point for future militarism. Should that happen, as one assistant Secretary of State put it, "those lives already spent will have been sacrificed in vain, and lives will be lost again in the future." Japanese hard-liners were certain to exploit an overture as evidence that losses sustained at Okinawa had weakened American resolve and to argue that continued resistance would bring further concessions. Stalin, who earlier had told an American envoy that he favored abolishing the emperorship because the ineffectual Hirohito might be succeeded by "an energetic and vigorous figure who could cause trouble," was just as certain to interpret it as a treacherous effort to end the war before the Soviets could share in the spoils.

There were domestic considerations as well. Roosevelt had announced the unconditional surrender policy in early 1943, and it since had become a slogan of the war. He also had advocated that peoples everywhere should have the right to choose their own form of government, and Truman had publicly pledged to carry out his predecessor's legacies. For him to have formally guaranteed continuance of the emperorship, as opposed to merely accepting it on American terms pending free elections, as he later did, would have constituted a blatant repudiation of his own promises.

Nor was that all. Regardless of the emperor's actual role in Japanese aggression, which is still debated, much wartime propaganda had encouraged Americans to regard Hirohito as no less a war criminal than Adolf Hitler or Benito Mussolini. Although Truman said on several occasions that he had no objection to retaining the emperor, he understandably refused to make the first move. The ultimatum he issued from Potsdam on July 26 did not refer specifically to the emperorship. All it said was that occupation forces would be removed after a "peaceful and responsible" government had been established according to the "freely expressed will of the Japanese people." When the Japanese rejected the ultimatum rather than at last inquire whether they might retain the emperor, Truman permitted the plans for using the bombs to go forward.

Reliance on MAGIC intercepts and the "peace feelers" to gauge how near Japan was to surrender is misleading in any case. The army, not the Foreign Office, controlled the situation. Intercepts of Japanese military communications, designated ULTRA, provided no reason to believe the army was even considering surrender. Japanese Imperial Headquarters had correctly guessed that the next operation after Okinawa would be Kyushu and was making every effort to bolster its defenses there.

General Marshall reported on July 24 that there were "approximately 500,000 troops in Kyushu" and that more were on their way. ULTRA identified new units arriving almost daily. MacArthur's G-2 reported on July 29 that "this threatening development, if not checked, may grow to a point where we attack on a ratio of one (1) to one (1) which is not the recipe for victory." By the time the first atomic bomb fell, ULTRA indicated there were 560,000 troops in southern Kyushu (the actual figure was closer to 900,000), and projections for November 1 placed the number at 680,000. A report, for medical purposes, of July 31 estimated that total battle and non-battle casualties might run as high as 394,859 *for the Kyushu operation alone.* This figure did not include those men expected to be killed outright, for obviously they would need no medical attention. Marshall regarded Japanese defenses as so formidable that even after Hiroshima he asked MacArthur to consider alternate landing sites and began contemplating the use of atomic bombs as tactical weapons to support the invasion.

The thirty-day casualty projection of 31,000 Marshall had given Truman at the June 18 strategy meeting had become meaningless. It had been based in the assumption that the Japanese had about 350,000 defenders in Kyushu and that naval and air interdiction would provide reinforcement. But the Japanese buildup since that time meant that the defenders would have nearly twice the number of troops available by "X-day" than earlier assumed. The assertion that apprehensions about casualties are insufficient to explain Truman's use of the bombs, therefore, cannot be taken seriously. On the contrary, as Winston Churchill wrote after a conversation with him at Potsdam, Truman was tormented by "the terrible responsibilities that rested upon him in regard to the unlimited effusions of American blood."

Some historians have argued that while the first bomb might have been required to achieve Japanese surrender, dropping the second constituted a needless barbarism. The record shows otherwise. American officials believed more than one bomb would be necessary because they assumed Japanese hard-liners would minimize the first explosion or attempt to explain it away as some sort of natural catastrophe, precisely what they did. The Japanese minister of war, for instance, at first refused to admit that the Hiroshima bomb was atomic. A few hours after Nagasaki he told the cabinet that "the Americans appeared to have one hundred atomic bombs . . . they could drop three per day. The next target might well be Tokyo."

Even after both bombs had fallen and Russia entered the war, Japanese militants insisted on such lenient peace terms that moderates knew there was no sense even transmitting them to the United States. Hirohito had to intervene personally on two occasions during the next few days to induce hard-liners to abandon their conditions and to accept the American stipulation that the emperor's authority "shall be subject to the Supreme Commander of the Allied Powers." That the militarists would have accepted such a settlement before the bombs is farfetched, to say the least.

Some writers have argued that the cumulative effects of battlefield defeats, conventional bombing, and naval blockade already had defeated Japan. Even without extending assurances about the emperor, all the United States had to do was wait. The most frequently cited basis for this contention is the *United States Strategic Bombing Survey*, published in 1946, which stated that Japan would have surrendered by November 1 "even if the atomic bombs had not been dropped, even if Russia had not entered the war, and even if no invasion had been planned or contemplated." Recent scholarship by the historian Robert P. Newman and others has demonstrated that the survey was "cooked" by those who prepared it to arrive at such a conclusion. No matter. This or any other document based on information available only after the war ended is irrelevant with regard to what Truman could have known at the time.

What often goes unremarked is that when the bombs were dropped, fighting was still going on in the Philippines, China, and elsewhere. Every day that the war continued thousands of prisoners of war had to live in abysmal conditions, and there were rumors that the Japanese intended to slaughter them if the homeland was invaded. Truman was Commander in Chief of the American armed forces, and he had a duty to the men under his command not shared by those sitting in moral judgment decades later. Available evidence points to the conclusion that he acted for the reason he said he did: to end the bloody war that would have been far bloodier had invasion proved necessary. One can only imagine what would have happened if tens of thousands of American boys had died or been wounded on Japanese soil and then it had become known that Truman had chosen not to use weapons that could have ended the war months sooner.

5 The Great Depression

This photograph by Dorothea Lange captures the despair of a typical migrant California family during the Great Depression.

The Big Picture of the Great Depression

John A. Garraty

The Great Depression of the 1930s was such a cataclysmic event and it produced such extraordinary changes in the political, economic, and social structure of the United States that it is understandable that American historians have tended to emphasize its uniqueness. The country has experienced other "panics" and periods of "bad times," but none, before or for that matter since, compare with it in severity or in length. To cite a single statistic, during the entire decade the unemployment rate never fell below 10 percent.

But the Great Depression was not unique to the United States. It ravaged the industrial nations of Europe and every region of the world where coal or copper or other mineral was mined or where wheat or cotton or tea or coffee or any other agricultural product was produced for export. Furthermore, the reactions of governments everywhere were quite similar. The many New Deal reform programs were "new" in the sense that they had not been tried before in America, but as I have tried to show in this article, which is based on my more detailed work, *The Great Depression*, the same kinds of policies were being applied all over the world.

Back in 1955 John Kenneth Galbraith called the Great Depression of the 1930s "the most momentous economic occurrence in the history of the United States," and thirty-odd years later that judgment, recorded in Galbraith's best seller, *The Great Crash,* still holds. Since then there have been more recessions, some quite severe, but nothing like what happened in the thirties. As dozens of economists and historians have shown, we now know, in theory, how to deal with violent cyclical downturns. We have learned what we should do to manipulate what Lester V. Chandler of Atlanta University has called "the determinants that influence the behavior of employment, output, and prices."

Yet fears of another terrible collapse persist, even among the experts. And the higher the stock market soars, the greater the underlying fear. In *The Great Crash* Galbraith spoke of "fissures" that "might open at . . . unexpected places," and Chandler warned of some sort of "political deadlock" that might prevent the government from doing the things that would revive a faltering economy.

These fears are not without foundation. The American economy is complex and influenced by forces beyond the control of economists or politicians. More and more, economists are becoming aware of what historians have always known: that they can do a good job of explaining why the economy is the way it is and how it got to be that way, but that knowing exactly what to do to make it behave in any particular way in the future is another matter entirely.

The Great Depression of the 1930s was a worldwide phenomenon, great not only in the sense of "severe," but also in the sense of "scope." While there were dif-

The Depression was not limited to the United States. This photograph of a soup kitchen was taken in the mid-1930s in Vienna, Austria.

ferences in its impact and in the way it was dealt with from one country to another, the course of events nearly everywhere ran something like this: By 1925 most countries had recovered from the economic disruptions caused by the Great War of 1914–18. There followed a few years of rapid growth, but in 1929 and 1930 the prosperity ended. Then came a precipitous plunge that lasted until early 1933. This dark period was followed by a gradual, if spotty, recovery. The revival, however, was aborted by the steep recession of 1937–38. It took a still more cataclysmic event, the outbreak of World War II, to end the Great Depression. All this is well known.

The effects of the Great Depression on the economy of the United States, and the attitudes of Americans toward both the Depression and the politics of their government, did not differ in fundamental ways from the situation elsewhere. This, too, scarcely needs saying.

However, there has been a tendency among historians of the Depression, except when dealing with specific international events, such as the London Economic Conference, and with foreign relations generally, to concentrate their attentions on developments in a single country or region. The result has been to make the policies of particular nations and particular interest groups seem both more unique and, for good or ill, more effective than they were.

It is true, to begin with, that neither President Calvin Coolidge nor President Herbert Hoover anticipated the Depression. In campaigning for the Presidency in

1928, Hoover stressed the good times, which, he assured the voters, would continue if he was handling the reins of government. After the election, in his last annual message to Congress, Coolidge remarked that "the country can regard the present with satisfaction and anticipate the future with optimism." When the bottom fell out of the American economy some months later, statements such as these came back to haunt Hoover and his party, and many historians have chortled over his discomfiture.

However, the leaders of virtually all the industrial nations were as far off the mark in their prognostications as Hoover and Coolidge were. When the German Social Democrats rode a "wave of prosperity" to power in June 1928, Hermann Müller, the new chancellor, assured the Reichstag that the Fatherland was in a "firm and unshakable" condition.

Great Britain had been plagued by high unemployment and lagging economic growth in the late 1920s, but in July 1929 Prime Minister Ramsay MacDonald scoffed at the possibility of a slump. And as late as December 1929, the French Premier, André Tardieu, announced what he described as a "politics of prosperity." Fewer than a thousand people were out of work in France, and the Treasury was full to overflowing. The government planned to spend five billion francs over the next five years on a "national retooling" of agriculture, industry, commerce, health care, and education. Statesmen of many other nations made similar comments in 1928 and 1929.

Hoover has been subject to much criticism for the way in which he tried to put the blame for the Depression on the shoulders of others. In his memoirs he offered an elaborate explanation, complete with footnote references to the work of many economists and other experts. "The Depression was not started in the United States," he insisted. The "primary cause" was the World War. In four-fifths of what he called the "economically sensitive" nations of the world, including such remote areas as Bolivia, Bulgaria, and Australia, the downturn was noticeable long before 1929, a time when the United States was enjoying a period of great prosperity.

Hoover blamed America's post-1929 troubles on an "orgy of stock speculation" resulting from the cheap-money policies adopted by the "mediocrities" who made up the majority of the Federal Reserve Board in a futile effort to support the value of the British pound and other European currencies. Hoover called Benjamin Strong, the governor of the Federal Reserve Bank of New York, a "mental annex of Europe," because the Fed had kept American interest rates low to discourage foreign investors.

According to Hoover, he had warned of the danger, but neither the Fed nor his predecessor, Calvin Coolidge (whom he detested), had taken his advice. Coolidge's announcement at the end of his term that stocks were "cheap at current prices" was, Hoover believed, particularly unfortunate, since it undermined his efforts to check the speculative mania on Wall Street after his inauguration.

But Hoover could not use this argument to explain the decline that occurred in the United States in 1930, 1931, and 1932, when he was running the country. Instead he blamed the decline on foreign countries. European statesmen "did not have the courage to meet the real issues." Their rivalries and their heavy spending on arms and "frantic public works programs to meet unemployment" led to unbalanced budgets and inflation that "tore their systems asunder." These unsound policies led to the collapse of the German banking system in 1931, which transformed what would have been no more than a minor economic downturn into the Great Depression. "The hurricane that swept our shores," wrote Hoover, was of European origin.

These squirmings to avoid taking any responsibility for the Depression do Hoover no credit. But he was certainly not alone among statesmen of the time in doing so. Prime Minister MacDonald, a socialist, blamed capitalism for the debacle. "We are not on trial," he said in 1930, "it is the system under which we live. It has broken down, not only on this little island . . . it has broken down everywhere as it was bound to break down." The Germans argued that the Depression was political in origin. The harsh terms imposed on them by the Versailles Treaty, and especially the reparations payments that, they claimed, sapped the economic vitality of their country, had caused it. One conservative German economist blamed the World War naval blockade for his country's troubles in the 1930s. In the nineteenth century "the English merchant fleet helped build up the world economy," he said. During the war "the British navy helped to destroy it."

When in its early stages the Depression appeared to be sparing France, French leaders took full credit for this happy circumstance. "France is a garden," they explained. But when the slump became serious in 1932, they accused Great Britain of causing it by going off the gold standard and adopting other irresponsible monetary policies, and the United States of "exporting unemployment" by substituting machines for workers. "Mechanization," a French economist explained in 1932, "is an essential element in the worsening of the depression."

Commentators in most countries, including the United States, tended to see the Wall Street crash of October 1929 as the cause of the Depression, placing a rather large burden of explanation on a single, local event. But in a sense the Depression was like syphilis, which before its nature was understood was referred to in England as the French pox, as the Spanish disease in France, the Italian sickness in Spain, and so on.

When the nations began to suffer the effects of the Depression, most of the steps they took in trying to deal with it were either inadequate or counterproductive. Hoover's signing of the Hawley-Smoot protective tariff further shriveled an already shrinking international trade. The measure has been universally deplored by historians, who point with evident relish to the fact that more than a thousand economists had urged the President to veto the bill. The measure was no doubt a mistake because it caused a further shrinking of economic activity, but blaming Hoover for the result ignores the policies of other countries, to say nothing of the uselessness of much of what the leading economists of the day were suggesting about how to end the Depression. Even Great Britain, a nation particularly dependent on international trade, adopted the protective imperial preference system, worked out with the dominions at Ottawa in 1932. Many Latin American countries, desperately short of foreign exchange because of the slumping prices of the raw materials they exported, tried to make do with home manufactures and protected these fledgling industries with tariffs. In Europe, country after country passed laws aimed at reducing their imports of wheat and other foreign food products.

And while the Hawley-Smoot tariff was unfortunate, if Hoover had followed all the advice of the experts who had urged him to veto it, he would surely have been pushing the American economy from the frying pan into the fire, because most of their recommendations are now seen to have been wrongheaded. Opposition to protective tariffs, almost universal among conservative economists since the time of Adam Smith and Ricardo, was no sign of prescience, then as now. In their *Monetary History of the United States,* Milton Friedman and Anna Jacobson Schwartz characterize the financial proposals of the economists of the 1930s as "hardly distinguished by the correctness or profundity of understanding of the economic forces at work." A leading French economic historian, Alfred Sauvy, compares the typical French economist of the period to a "doctor, stuffed with theories, who has never seen a sick person." An Australian historian characterizes the policies of that country as "deeply influenced by shibboleths."

The most nearly universal example of a wrongheaded policy during the Depression was the effort that nations made to balance their annual budgets. Hoover was no exception; Albert Romasco has counted no fewer than twenty-one public statements stressing the need to balance the federal budget that the President made in a four-month period. As late as February 1933, after his defeat in the 1932 election, Hoover sent a desperate handwritten letter to President-elect Roosevelt pleading with him to announce that "there will be no tampering or inflation of the currency [and] that the budget will be unquestionably balanced even if further taxation is necessary."

But Hoover had plenty of company in urging fiscal restraint. Roosevelt was unmoved by Hoover's letter, but his feelings about budget balancing were not very different. In 1928 William Trufant Foster and Waddill Catchings published a book, *The Road to Plenty,* which attracted considerable attention. Roosevelt read it. After coming across the sentence "When business begins to look rotten, more public spending," he wrote in the margin: "Too good to be true—you can't get something for nothing." One of Roosevelt's first actions as President was to call for a tax increase. According to his biographer Frank Freidel, fiscal conservatism was a "first priority" in Roosevelt's early efforts to end the Depression.

Budget balancing was an obsession with a great majority of the political leaders of the thirties, regardless of country, party, or social philosophy. In 1930 Ramsay MacDonald's new socialist government was under pressure to undertake an expensive public works program aimed at reducing Great Britain's chronic unemployment. Instead the government raised taxes by £47 million in an effort to balance the budget. The conservative Heinrich Brüning recalled in his memoirs that when he became chancellor of Germany in 1932, he promised President Hindenburg "that as long as I had his trust, I would at any price make the government finances safe."

France had fewer financial worries in the early stages of the Depression than most nations. Its 1930 budget was designed to show a small surplus. But revenues did not live up to expectations, and a deficit resulted. The same thing happened in 1931 and again in 1932, but French leaders from every point on the political spectrum remained devoted to "sound" government finance. "I love the working class," Premier Pierre Laval told the National Assembly during the debate on the 1932 budget. Hoots from the left benches greeted this remark, but Laval went on: "I have seen the ravages of unemployment. . . . The government will never refuse to go as far as the resources of the country will permit [to help]. But do not ask it to commit acts that risk to compromise the balance of the budget." In 1933, when France began to feel the full effects of the Depression, Premier Joseph Paul-Boncour, who described himself as a socialist though he did not belong to the Socialist party, called for rigid economies and a tax increase. "What good is it to talk, what good to draw up plans," he said, "if one ends with a budget deficit?"

Leaders in countries large and small, in Asia, the Americas, and Europe, echoed these sentiments. A Japanese finance minister warned in 1930 that "increased government spending" would "weaken the financial soundness of the government." Prime Minister William Lyon Mackenzie King of Canada, a man who was so parsimonious that he cut new pencils into three pieces and used them until they were tiny stubs, believed that "governments should live within their means." When King's successor, R. B. Bennett, took office in 1931, he urged spending cuts and higher taxes in order to get rid of a budget deficit of more than eighty million dollars. "When it came to . . . 'unbalancing' the budget," Bennett's biographer explains, "he was as the rock of Gibraltar."

The Brazilian dictator Getúlio Vargas is reported to have had a "high respect for a balanced budget." When a journalist asked Jaime Carner, one of a succession of like-minded Spanish finance ministers in the early 1930s, to describe his priorities, Carner replied that he had three: "a balanced budget, a balanced budget, and a balanced budget." A recent historian of Czechoslovakia reports that the statesmen of the Depression era in that country displayed an "irrational fear of the inflationary nature of a budget deficit."

These examples could be extended almost without limit. The point is not that Hoover was correct in his views of proper government finance; obviously he was not. But describing his position without considering its context distorts its significance. Furthermore, the intentions of the politicians rarely corresponded to what actually happened. Deficits were the rule through the Depression years because government revenues continually fell below expectations and unavoidable expenditures rose. Even if most budgets had been in balance, the additional sums extracted from the public probably would not have had a decisive effect on any country's economy. Government spending did not have the impact on economic activity that has been the case since World War II. The historian Mark Leff has recently reminded us, for example, that the payroll tax enacted to finance the new American Social Security system in 1935 "yielded as much each month as the notorious income tax provisions of Roosevelt's 1935 Wealth Tax did in a year."

It is equally revealing to look at other aspects of the New Deal from a broad perspective. Franklin Roosevelt's Brain Trust was novel only in that so many of these advisers were academic types. Many earlier Presidents made use of informal groups of advisers—Theodore Roosevelt's Tennis Cabinet and Andrew Jackson's Kitchen Cabinet come to mind. There is no doubt that political leaders in many nations were made acutely aware of their ignorance by the Depression, and in their bafflement they found that turning to experts was both psychologically and politically beneficial. Sometimes the experts' advice actually did some good. Sweden was blessed during the interwar era with a number of articulate, first-rate economists. The Swedish government, a recent scholar writes, was "ready to listen to the advice of [these] economists," with the result that by 1935 Sweden was deliberately practicing deficit spending, and unemployment was down nearly to pre-Depression levels.

Throughout the period British prime ministers made frequent calls on the expertise of economists such as Ralph Hawtrey, A. C. Pigou, and, of course, John Maynard Keynes. In 1930 Ramsay MacDonald, who was particularly fond of using experts to do his thinking for him, appointed a committee of five top-flight economists to investigate the causes of the Depression and "indicate the conditions of recovery." (The group came up with a number of attractive suggestions, but avoided the touchy subject of how to finance them.) The next year MacDonald charged another committee with the task of suggesting "all possible reductions of national Expenditure" in a futile effort to avoid going off the gold standard. Even in France, where political leaders tended to deny that the world depression was affecting their nation's economy and where most economists still adhered to laissez-faire principles, French premiers called from time to time on experts "to search," Sauvy explains, "for the causes of the financial difficulties of the country and propose remedies."

Many specific New Deal policies were new only in America. In 1933 the United States was far behind most industrial nations in social welfare. Unemployment insurance, a major New Deal reform when enacted in 1935, was established in Great Britain in 1911 and in Germany shortly after World War I, well before the Depression struck. The creation of the New Deal Civilian Conservation Corps and the Civil Works Administration in 1933, and later of the Works Progress Administration and Public Works Administration, only made up for the absence of a national public welfare system before 1936.

The New Deal National Recovery Administration also paralleled earlier developments. The relation of its industrywide codes of "fair" business practices to the American trade-association movement of the 1920s and to such early Depression proposals as the plan advanced by Gerard Swope of General Electric in 1931 are well known. (The Swope Plan provided that in each industry "production and consumption should be coordinated . . . preferably by the joint participation and joint administration of management and employees" under the general supervision of the Federal Trade Commission, a system quite similar to NRA, as Roosevelt himself admitted.)

That capital and labor should join together to promote efficiency and harmony, and that companies making the same products should consult in order to fix prices and allocate output and thus put a stop to cutthroat competition, all under the watchful eye of the government, were central concepts of Italian fascist corporatism in the 1920s and of the less formal but more effective German system of cartels in that period. The Nazis organized German industry along similar but more thoroughly regimented lines at about the same time as the NRA system was being set up in America. Great Britain also employed this tactic in the 1930s, albeit on a smaller scale. The British government allowed coal companies to limit and allocate production and to fix prices, and it encouraged similar practices by steel and textile manufacturers. The only major industrial power that did not adopt such a policy before the passage of the National Industrial Recovery Act was France. Later, in 1935, the Chamber of Deputies passed a measure that permitted competing companies to enter into "accords" with one another "in time of crisis." The measure would have allowed them to adjust, or put in order, the relations between production and consumption, which is essentially what NRA was supposed to make possible. This *projet Marchandeau* died in the French Senate, but some industries were encouraged to cooperate for this end by special decree.

But the area in which American historians of the Depression have been most myopic is New Deal agricultural policy. The extent to which the Agricultural Adjustment Act of 1933 evolved from the McNary-Haugen scheme of the Coolidge era and the Agricultural Marketing Act of the Hoover years has been universally conceded. Beyond these roots, however, historians have not bothered to dig. The stress on the originality of the AAA program has been close to universal. Arthur Schlesinger, Jr., put it clearly and directly when he wrote in his book *Coming of the New Deal* that "probably never in American history has so much social and legal inventiveness gone into a single legislative measure."

Schlesinger and the other historians who expressed this opinion have faithfully reflected statements made by the people most closely associated with the AAA at the time of its passage. Secretary of Agriculture Henry A. Wallace said that the law was "as new in the field of social relations as the first gasoline engine was new in the field of mechanics." President Roosevelt told Congress in submitting the bill that it was a new and untried idea.

In fact, Wallace and Roosevelt were exaggerating the originality of New Deal policy. The AAA did mark a break with the past for the United States. Paying farmers not to grow crops was unprecedented. Yet this tactic merely reflected the constitutional restrictions of the American political system; Congress did not have the power to fix prices or limit production directly. The strategy of subsidizing farmers and compelling them to reduce output in order to bring supplies down to the level of current demand for their products was far from original.

As early as 1906 Brazil had supported the prices paid its coffee growers by buying up surpluses in years of bountiful harvests and holding the coffee off the market. In the 1920s France had tried to help its beet farmers and wine makers by requiring that gasoline sold in France contain a percentage of alcohol distilled from French beets and grapes. More important in its effect on the United States, Great Britain had attempted in the 1920s to bolster the flagging fortunes of rubber planters in Britain's Asiatic colonies by restricting production and placing quotas on rubber exports. This Stevenson Plan, referred to in the American press as "the British monopoly," aroused the wrath of then Secretary of Commerce Herbert Hoover. It also caused Henry Ford and Harvey Firestone, whose factories consumed huge amounts of imported rubber, to commission their mutual friend Thomas A. Edison to find a latex-producing plant that could be grown commercially in the United States. (Edison tested more than ten thousand specimens and finally settled on goldenrod. Ford then bought a large tract in Georgia to grow the stuff, although it never became profitable to do so.)

After the Great Depression began, growers of staple crops in every corner of the globe adopted schemes designed to reduce output and raise prices. In 1930

British and Dutch tea growers in the Far East made an agreement to cut back on their production of cheaper varieties of tea. British and Dutch rubber planters declared a "tapping holiday" in that same year, and in 1931 Cuba, Java, and six other countries that exported significant amounts of cane sugar agreed to limit production and accept export quotas. Brazil began burning millions of pounds of coffee in 1931, a tactic that foreshadowed the "emergency" policy of the AAA administrators who ordered the plowing under of cotton and the "murder" (so called by critics) of baby pigs in 1933.

Far from being an innovation, the AAA was actually typical—one of many programs put into effect in countries all over the world in the depths of the Depression to deal with the desperate plight of farmers. The year 1933 saw the triumph nearly everywhere of a simple supply-and-demand kind of thinking that the French called "economic Malthusianism," the belief that the only way to raise prices was to bring output down to the level of current consumption. In February 1933, Indian, Ceylonese, and East Indian tea growers agreed to limit exports and prohibit new plantings for five years. A central committee of planters assigned and administered quotas limiting the exportation of tea. Dutch, British, French, and Siamese rubber growers adopted similar regulations for their product. In April 1933 representatives of nearly all the countries of Europe met in London with representatives of the major wheat-exporting nations, of which the United States, of course, was one of the largest. The gathering produced an International Wheat Agreement designed to cut production in hopes of causing the price of wheat to rise to a point where it would be profitable for farmers, yet still "reasonable" for consumers.

In addition to these international agreements, dozens of countries acted unilaterally in 1933 with the same goals in mind. Argentina adopted exchange controls, put a cap on imports, and regulated domestic production of wheat and cattle. The government purchased most of the 1933 wheat crop at a fixed price, then dumped the wheat abroad for whatever it could get. A Danish law of 1933 provided for government purchase and destruction of large numbers of low-quality cattle, the cost to be recovered through a slaughterhouse tax on all cattle butchered in Denmark. Declining demand caused by British restrictions on importation of Danish bacon led the Danish government to issue a specified number of "pig cards" to producers. Pigs sent to market with such cards brought one price, those without cards a lower one. The Dutch enacted similar restrictions on production of pork, beef, and dairy products.

Switzerland reduced milk production and limited the importation of feed grains in 1933, and Great Britain set up marketing boards that guaranteed dairymen a minimum price for milk. Sweden subsidized homegrown wheat and rye, and paid a bounty to exporters of butter. In 1933 France strengthened the regulations protecting growers of grapes and established a minimum price for domestic wheat. After Hitler came to power, the production, distribution, and sale of all foodstuffs was regulated. Every link from farmer to consumer was controlled.

Looking at the situation more broadly, the growers of staple crops for export were trying to push up prices by reducing supplies, ignoring the fact that higher prices were likely to reduce the demand still further. At the same time, the agricultural policies of the European industrial nations were making a bad situation worse. By reducing imports (and in some cases increasing domestic output) they were injuring the major food-producing countries and simultaneously adding to the costs of their own consumers.

It was, the British historian Sidney Pollard has written, "a world of rising tariffs, international commodity schemes, bilateral trade agreements and managed currencies." The United States was as much a part of Pollard's world as any other country.

One further example of the need to see American Depression policies in their world context is revealing. It involves the recession of 1937–38 and President Roosevelt's supposed responsibility for it. In early 1937 the American economy seemed finally to be emerging from the Depression. Unemployment remained high, but most economic indicators were improving. Industrial production had exceeded 1929 levels. A group of New Dealers who met at the home of the Federal Reserve Board chairman Marriner Eccles in October 1936 were so confident that the Depression was ending that their talk turned to how to avoid future Depressions. The general public was equally optimistic. "When Americans speak of the depression," the French novelist Jules Romains wrote after a visit to this country at that time, "they always use the past tense."

At this point Roosevelt, egged on by his conservative secretary of the treasury, Henry Morgenthau, warned the public in a radio speech that "the dangers of 1929 are again becoming possible." He ordered a steep cut in public works expenditures, and instructed the members of his cabinet to trim a total of $300 million from their departmental budgets. The President promised to balance the federal budget, and in fact brought the 1937 deficit down to a mere $358 million, as compared with a deficit of $3.6 billion in 1936. This reduction in federal spending, combined with the Federal Reserve's decision to push up interest rates and the coincidental reduction of consumer spending occasioned by the first collection of Social Security payroll taxes, brought the economic recovery to a halt and plunged the nation into a steep recession. The leading historian of the subject, K.D. Roose, called the recession a downturn "without parallel in American economic history."

Roosevelt had never been happy with deficits, and he was not much of an economist, but he was far from being alone in thinking that the time had come to apply the brakes to the economy. Economists who were far more knowledgeable than he saw the situation exactly as he did. Prices were still below 1929 levels in most countries, but they were rising rapidly. Using 1929 levels as an index, during 1937 prices jumped from 83 to 96 in Great Britain, from 80 to 93 in Italy, from 87 to 98 in Sweden, and from 80 to 86 in the United States.

These increases caused the grinding deflation of the years since 1929 to be forgotten. Fear of inflation resurfaced. The economist John Maynard Keynes had discounted the risks of inflation throughout the Depression. Inflation was a positive social good, he argued, a painless way to "disinherit" established wealth. But by January 1937 Keynes had become convinced that the British economy was beginning to overheat. He was so concerned that he published a series of articles in the *Times* of London on "How to Avoid a Slump." It might soon be necessary to "retard certain types of investment," Keynes warned. There was even a "risk of what might fairly be called inflation," he added. The next month the British government's

Committee on Economic Information issued a report suggesting a tax increase and the postponement of "road improvements, railway electrification, slum clearance," and other public works projects "which are not of an urgent character."

During this same period the Federal Reserve Board chairman Marriner Eccles, long a believer in the need to stimulate the economy, warned Roosevelt that "there is grave danger that the recovery movement will get out of hand, excessive rises in prices . . . will occur, excessive growth of profits and a boom in the stock market will arise, and the cost of living will mount rapidly. If such conditions are permitted to develop, another drastic slump will be inevitable."

It did not take much of this kind of talk to convince President Roosevelt. When Roosevelt's actions triggered the downturn, he reversed himself again, asking Congress for budget-busting increases in federal spending. The pattern elsewhere was similar. In the United States the money was spent on unemployment relief and more public works; in the major European countries the stimulus chiefly resulted from greatly increased expenditures on armaments. In 1939 World War II broke out, and the Great Depression came to a final end.

When viewed in isolation, the policies of the United States government during the periods when economic conditions were worsening seem to have been at best ineffective, at worst counterproductive. Those put into effect while conditions were getting better appear to have been at least partly responsible for the improvement. This helps to explain why the Hoover administration has looked so bad and the New Dealers, if not always good, at least less bad.

When seen in broader perspective, however, credit and blame are not so easily assigned. The heroes then appear less heroic, the villains less dastardly, the geniuses less brilliant. The Great Depression possessed some of the qualities of a hurricane; the best those in charge of the ship of state could manage was to ride it out without foundering.

Economists and politicians certainly know more about how the world economy functions than their predecessors did half a century ago. But the world economy today is far more complex and subject to many more uncontrollable forces than was then the case. A great depression like *the* Great Depression is highly unlikely. But a different great depression? Galbraith ended *The Great Crash* with this cynical pronouncement: "Now, as throughout history, financial capacity and political perspicacity are inversely correlated." That may be an overstatement. But then again, maybe not.

The Case of the Chambermaid and the "Nine Old Men"

William E. Leuchtenburg

The Supreme Court case described in this article, *West Coast Hotel Company* v. *Parrish*, is rightly described by Professor Leuchtenburg as the cause of a "constitutional revolution." It marked a great turning point in history, one in which the balance in the Court shifted from an anti–New Deal position to one supportive of New Deal reforms. Yet, like so many "landmark" constitutional cases, the litigants were not in themselves important; Elsie Parrish was a chambermaid, her employer the owners of the Cascadian Hotel in Wenatchee, Washington. The issue separating the two involved only a little more than two hundred dollars.

The case, however, resulted in a most improbable political alliance, bringing together as it did radical feminists and mossback constitutional conservatives, and it produced a deep division within the Democratic party only a few months after the Democrats had won an overwhelming victory in the 1936 elections.

Paradoxically, the decision was a tremendous victory for Franklin Roosevelt, but also a cause of the most stinging defeat of his presidency.

When, on a spring day in 1935, Elsie Parrish walked into the office of an obscure lawyer in Wenatchee, Washington, to ask him to sue the town's leading hotel for back pay, she had no idea she was linking her fate to that of exploited women in a Brooklyn laundry a whole continent away. Still less did she think that she was setting off a series of events that would deeply affect President Franklin D. Roosevelt's plans for his second term. Least of all did she perceive that she was triggering a constitutional revolution that, even today, remains the most significant chapter in the two centuries of existence of the United States Supreme Court. All that Elsie knew was that she had been bilked.

Late in the summer of 1933, Elsie Lee, a woman of about forty who would soon be Elsie Parrish, had taken a job as a chambermaid at the Cascadian Hotel in Wenatchee, entrepôt for a beautiful recreation area reaching from the Columbia valley to the Cascades, and the country's foremost apple market. "Apples made Wenatchee and apples maintain it," noted the WPA guide to Washington; "it is surrounded by a sea of orchards, covered in spring with a pink foam of blossoms, mile upon mile, filling the valleys and covering the slopes, the air of the town is sweet with the fragrance." Here, in the land of Winesaps and Jonathans, where "in summer and fall the spicy odor of apples is everywhere," Elsie worked irregularly over the next year and a half at cleaning toilets and sweeping rugs for an hourly wage of twenty-two cents, later raised to a quarter. When she was discharged in May 1935, she asked for back pay of $216.19, the difference between what she had received and what she would have gotten if she had been paid each week the $14.50 minimum wage required for her occupation under state law. The Cascadian, which was owned by the West Coast Hotel Company, offered to settle for a total of $17.00, but she would not hear of it. Instead, she, together with her husband, Ernest, brought suit for all that was due her.

Elsie and Ernest rested their case on the provisions of a statute that had been enacted by Washington State a quarter of a century before when, catching the contagion of reform from neighboring Oregon, the state legislature had taken steps to wipe out sweatshops. The 1913 act declared it "unlawful to employ women or minors . . . under conditions of labor detrimental to their health or morals; and . . . to employ women workers in any industry . . . at wages which are not adequate for their maintenance." To safeguard the welfare of female employees, the law established a commission that was authorized to call together employers, employees, and representatives of the public who would recommend a wage standard "not detrimental to health and morals, and which shall be sufficient for the decent maintenance of women." On receiving that recommendation, the commission was to issue an order stipulating the minimum wage that must be paid. For chambermaids, the weekly minimum was set at $14.50. Twice the statute had been challenged in the courts, and on both occasions the Washington Supreme Court had validated the act. Elsie Parrish appeared to have an airtight case.

Alas, any law student in the land could have told her that her case was hopeless, for, twelve years before, the United States Supreme Court had ruled, in a widely reported decision, *Adkins* v. *Children's Hospital,* that a minimum wage act for women was unconstitutional because it violated the liberty of contract that the Court claimed was guaranteed by the Constitution. Though the opinion by Justice George Sutherland commanded only five votes and elicited vigorous dissents, it reconfirmed a notion incorporated in constitutional doctrine only a generation before: that a great corporation and its employee—even someone as powerless as a chambermaid—each has an equivalent right to bargain about wages, a fantasy that Justice Oliver Wendell Holmes dismissed as "dogma" and the renowned commentator Thomas Reed Powell of Harvard Law School called "indefensible." *Adkins,* said one commentator, "makes forever impossible all other legislation along similar lines involving the regulation of wages." In principle Elsie's case was no different from *Adkins.* Any statute that deprived a person of life, liberty, or property, without due process of law, was disallowed. Though the Washington law remained on the books, it was presumed to be null and void. Hence, it startled no one when, in November 1935, after hearing Elsie's case, the presiding judge of the Superior Court of Chelan County, explaining that *Adkins* bound every court in the nation, ruled against her.

Surprisingly, the Supreme Court of the state of Washington took a different view. On April 2, 1936, it overturned the lower court's decision, thereby finding in Elsie Parrish's favor. To get around the huge obstacle of *Adkins,* the court pointed out that the U.S. Supreme Court had never struck down a *state* minimum wage law, which was true but irrelevant. The decision gave the Parrishes a moment of euphoria, but it hardly seemed likely that this opinion would, in the light of *Adkins* and the hostility of Justices such as Sutherland, survive a test in the United States Supreme Court.

Just eight weeks later the U.S. Supreme Court settled any doubt on that matter by a decision on a case that, three thousand miles from Wenatchee, had begun to wend its way through the judicial system while Elsie Parrish was still making beds in the Cascadian Hotel. It arose out of the hope of social reformers in New York, especially women active in the Consumers' League, that the Court, despite *Adkins*, might look favorably on a minimum wage law for women and minors if it was drafted to emphasize the value of the services rendered as well as the needs of women. To that end Felix Frankfurter of Harvard Law School and Benjamin Cohen, a former law clerk of Justice Brandeis, crafted a model law. New York State adopted it in 1933, during the fourth year of a great depression that had reduced some young women, paid starvation wages, to sleeping on subways. Frankfurter warned that it was "foolish beyond words" to expect the Court to reverse itself, but he hoped that the Justices might be willing to distinguish this statute, with its added feature of "value of services," from the one struck down in *Adkins*. "Every word" of the New York law, explained a prominent woman reformer, was "written with the Supreme Court of the United States in mind."

In accordance with the provisions of the model legislation, New York State obtained an indictment against Joseph Tipaldo, manager of the Spotlight Laundry in Brooklyn, who had been brutally exploiting his nine female employees, first by paying them far below the state minimum wage and then by pretending to pay the minimum but forcing the sweatshop laundresses to kick back the difference between what the state required and what he actually intended to pay. When Joe Tipaldo went to jail to stand trial on charges of disobeying the mandatory wage order and of forgery, the hotel industry (the same business that would be involved in the *Parrish* case) rushed to his side with an offer to bankroll a test of the constitutionality of the New York law. Since hotels were working their employees twelve hours a day, seven days a week, they had a high stake in the case. In fact, the state had already begun minimum wage proceedings against them. Consequently, each hotel put money in a kitty to finance Tipaldo's petition for a writ of habeas corpus to compel the warden of Brooklyn's city prison to release the laundry manager from custody. While his case was being prepared, Tipaldo, utterly shameless, renamed his firm the Bright Light Laundry and made a big investment in expanding his business. He explained, "I expect to get it back eventually on what I save in wages."

On June 1, 1936, the United States Supreme Court appeared to justify his optimism when, in a 5–4 decision, it struck down New York's minimum wage law. In a sweeping opinion by one of the most conservative Justices, the Court said that there was no meaningful difference between the New York statute and the D.C. act that had been invalidated in *Adkins*, for both violated the liberty of contract that safeguarded equally the rights of employer and employee to bargain about wages. After quoting from *Adkins* with obvious approval, the Court declared, in language that shocked champions of social reform, "The decision and the reasoning upon which it rests clearly show that the State is without power by any form of legislation to prohibit, change or nullify contracts between employers and adult women workers as to the amount of wages to be paid." Those words all but doomed Elsie Parrish's cause, and gave Joe Tipaldo the victory of a lifetime.

That victory, however, turned out to carry a very high price. "After the court decision, business looked good for a while," Joe told a reporter three months later. "I was able to undercharge my competitors a little on what I saved in labor costs." But then business started to fall off, then fell some more. "I think this fight was the cause of my trouble," he said. "My customers wouldn't give my drivers their wash." Before the summer was over, the Bright Light Laundry had folded and Joe Tipaldo was unemployed. "I'm broke now," he confessed. "I couldn't stand the gaff."

Elsie Parrish was made of sterner stuff. She was determined to carry on her struggle, though her prospects seemed bleak indeed. Given the precedent of *Adkins,* her case had never been promising. At one point the attorney for the West Coast Hotel Company asked the Washington Supreme Court judge who had written the opinion sustaining that state's minimum wage law in *Parrish* how he could possibly have done so in view of what the U.S. Supreme Court had said in *Adkins.* The judge replied, "Well, let's let the Supreme Court say it one more time." Now, in *Tipaldo,* the Court had stated unequivocally "one more time" that minimum wage laws for women were invalid. So gloomy was the outlook that, on the advice of Ben Cohen and Felix Frankfurter, the Consumers' League did not even file a brief in *Parrish.* "We are both rather pessimistic regarding its outcome," Cohen confided. Elsie Parrish had every reason to expect the worst.

The *Tipaldo* decision, though, engendered a powerful backlash, not least from some of the members of the Supreme Court. In a strongly worded dissent, Chief Justice Charles Evans Hughes upbraided the majority for failing to acknowledge either that the New York law differed from the statute in *Adkins* or that the state has "the power to protect women from being exploited by overreaching employers. . . ." Far more biting was the separate dissent filed by Justice Harlan Fiske Stone on behalf of himself and his fellow Justices Louis Brandeis and Benjamin Cardozo. In one of the most scathing criticisms ever uttered from the bench, Stone accused the Court of indulging its "own personal economic predilections," for he found "grim irony in speaking of the freedom of contract of those who, because of their economic necessities, give their services for less than is needful to keep body and soul together." In an impassioned warning to his brethren to exercise more self-restraint, Stone asserted, "The Fourteenth Amendment has no more embedded in the Constitution our preference for some particular set of economic beliefs than it has adopted, in the name of liberty, the system of theology which we may happen to approve."

Much of the nation shared Stone's sense of indignation about *Tipaldo.* Secretary of the Interior Harold Ickes noted angrily in his diary: "The sacred right of liberty of contract again—the right of an immature child or a helpless woman to drive a bargain with a great corporation. If this decision does not outrage the moral sense of the country, then nothing will." A Republican newspaper in upstate New York declared, "The law that would jail any laundry-man for having an underfed horse should jail him for having an underfed girl employee."

Only two groups applauded the decision. One was the press in a scattering of cheap-labor towns undismayed by the fact that, following the ruling, the wages of laundresses—mostly impoverished blacks and Puerto Rican and Italian migrants—were slashed in half. The other was a small faction of advanced feminists centered in Alice Paul's National Woman's Party. "It is hair-raising to consider how very close women in America came to being ruled inferior citizens," one of them wrote Justice

Sutherland. Their argument was that there should be no special privileges for women—that putting them in a protected category was discriminatory and demeaning. Most women activists, though, were horrified by that view, which they believed reflected the dogmatism of upper-class ladies who had no familiarity with the suffering of workers. They were as devoted as Alice Paul to equal rights, and they must have shuddered at the paternalism implicit in earlier opinions sustaining separate treatment for women on the grounds that they were wards of the state. But they were sure that female employees required protection, and they knew that insistence on the principle of equal rights meant no minimum wage law whatsoever, since the Court, as constituted in FDR's first term, would never sanction social legislation for men. "Thus," the historian Mary Beard wrote Justice Stone, Alice Paul "plays into the hands of the rawest capitalists."

Stone, himself, had no doubt of the implications of *Tipaldo*. "We finished the term of Court yesterday," he wrote his sister, "I think in many ways one of the most disastrous in its history. . . . Our latest exploit was a holding by a divided vote that there was no power in a state to regulate minimum wages for women. Since the Court last week said this could not be done by the national government, as the matter was local, and now it is said that it cannot be done by local governments even though it is local, we seem to have tied Uncle Sam up in a hard knot."

Tipaldo, handed down on the final day of the term, climaxed an extraordinary thirteen months in which the Court struck down more important socioeconomic legislation than at any time in history. During that brief period it destroyed the two foundation stones of Roosevelt's recovery program, the National Industrial Recovery Act and the Agricultural Adjustment Act; turned thumbs down on a number of other New Deal laws and state reforms; and cavalierly rebuked the President and his appointees. The NIRA ruling had been unanimous, but almost all the others had come in split decisions, most often with the "Four Horsemen," Pierce Butler, James McReynolds, George Sutherland, and Willis Van Devanter, a quartet of adamantly conservative judges, joined in the spring of 1935 by the youngest member of the bench, Owen Roberts. At the end of the term, a nationally syndicated columnist wrote, "After slaughtering practically every New Deal measure that has been dragged before it, the Supreme Court now begins its summer breathing spell, ending a winter's performance which leaves the stage, as in the last act of a Shakespearean tragedy, strewn with the gory dead."

Despite the enormous setbacks the New Deal had sustained, Franklin Roosevelt gave every indication that he was accepting his losses virtually without complaint. Having been drubbed in the press for stating after the NIRA was struck down that the Court was returning the nation to a "horse and buggy" conception of interstate commerce, he had said nothing for the next year. *Tipaldo* moved him to break his silence to observe that the Court had created a "no-man's-land" where no government could function. But that was all he would say. While Elsie Parrish's feeble case was advancing toward its final reckoning in the United States Supreme Court, the President gave not the slightest indication that he had any plans whatsoever to make the Justices any less refractory, for it seemed to him altogether inadvisable in the 1936 presidential campaign to hand his opponents, who were hard put to find an issue, an opportunity to stand by the Constitution. As late as the end of January

Justice George Sutherland, one of the conservative group known as the Four Horsemen.

1937, after FDR had delivered his State of the Union message and his Inaugural address, the editor of *United States Law Week* wrote that "last week it was made plain that he does not at the present time have in mind any legislation directed at the Court."

Less than two weeks later, on February 5, 1937, the President stunned the country by sending a special message to Congress that constituted the boldest attempt a Chief Executive has ever initiated to remold the judiciary. He recommended that when a federal judge who had served at least ten years waited more than six months after his seventieth birthday to resign or retire, the President could add a new judge to the bench. Since this was the most aged Court in history—they were referred to as the "nine old men"—Roosevelt would be able to add as many as six new Supreme Court Justices. He claimed he was presenting this proposal as a way of expediting litigation, but it was widely understood that what he really wanted was a more amenable tribunal. From the very first day, his program was saddled with a designation it could never shake off: the "Court-packing plan."

Though FDR's scheme provoked fierce protests, political analysts anticipated that it would be adopted. By winning in a landslide in 1936, Roosevelt had carried so many members of his party into Congress that the Republicans were left with only sixteen of the ninety-six seats in the Senate and fewer than one hundred of the more than four hundred seats in the House. So long as the Court continued to strike down New Deal reforms—and such vital legislation as the Social Security Act was still to be decided on—it was highly unlikely that enough Democrats would desert their immensely popular President to defeat the measure. The very first evidence of the attitude of the Court would come with its decision on Elsie Parrish's case, and there was every expectation that, acting not many months after *Tipaldo,* the Court would render an adverse ruling that would improve Roosevelt's already excellent chances. On the very day the *Parrish* decision was to be handed down, March 29, 1937, the president of the National Women's Republican Club declared, "I don't see how the President's bill can fail to get a majority."

March 29 came during the Easter holidays, always a gala season in Washington, D.C., and on that bright Monday morning in early spring, a host of camera-toting tourists and children carrying Easter baskets crowded the steps of the recently opened Supreme Court building and queued up in record numbers to enter the marble palace. The unusually protracted time of 103 days had elapsed since Elsie Parrish's case had been argued, and it was to be the first judgment handed down since FDR had suggested packing the Court. Some twelve thousand visitors flocked to the building in anticipation that this would be journey's end for the suit that had begun nearly two years earlier. An hour before the session was to start, at noon, four thousand visitors had already been admitted to the building, where many lined up two abreast from the courtroom doorway almost to the suite of Justice Stone in the idle hope of getting a peek at the proceedings. "There isn't room for them," said a police guard, "if they stood here all day long."

For some minutes it appeared that the spectators who were fortunate to get into the courtroom were also to be frustrated, for the proceedings began with a recital of an opinion on another case by one of the Four Horsemen that left the audience nearly numb with boredom. But when he finished, the Chief Justice leaned forward in his chair, picked up some sheets of paper, and announced, "This case presents the question of the constitutional validity of the minimum wage law of the State of Washington." This was to be Elsie Parrish's day after all, and the spectators stirred in anticipation. Hughes, fully aware of the effect he was having and surely conscious of his magnificent appearance (with his patrician features, sparkling eyes, and well-groomed beard, he was often likened to Jove), raised his voice to overcome the bustle, then paused and peered out over the crowded chamber for a moment before returning to his written opinion.

Not for some time did Hughes indicate what the Court had decided. Anxious minutes passed as he labored through a reprise of the facts in the case, and when he finally took up one of the arguments of Elsie Parrish's attorneys, he did so only to reject it disdainfully. It was "obviously futile," he said, for counsel to claim that the present case could be distinguished from *Adkins* on the grounds that Mrs. Parrish had worked for a "hotel and that the business of an innkeeper was affected with a public interest." As it happened, he noted, one of the cases *Adkins* had disposed of had dealt with a hotel employee. If the Washington State law was to survive the day, it would need a better justification than this rickety effort.

It took only a moment more for Hughes to reveal that the Court was prepared to meet *Adkins* head on. Unlike *Tipaldo*, where the U.S. Supreme Court had felt bound by the ruling of the Court of Appeals of New York that the New York minimum wage act could not be distinguished from the statute in *Adkins* and hence was invalid, *Parrish*, the Chief Justice declared, presented a quite different situation, for the highest tribunal of the state of Washington had refused to be guided by *Adkins* and had sanctioned the law in dispute. "We are of the opinion that this ruling of the state court demands on our part a reëxamination of the *Adkins* case," he continued. "The importance of the question, in which many States having similar laws are concerned, the close division by which the decision in the *Adkins* case was reached, and the economic conditions which have supervened, and in the light of which the reasonableness of the exercise of the protective power of the State must be considered, make it not only appropriate, but we think imperative, that in deciding the present case the subject should receive fresh consideration." To do so properly, he observed, required careful examination of the doctrine of freedom of contract that had bulked so large in *Adkins*.

"What is this freedom?" Hughes inquired, his voice rising. "The Constitution does not speak of freedom of contract." Instead, the Constitution spoke of liberty and forbade denial of liberty without due process of law. The Constitution did not recognize absolute liberty, however. "The liberty safeguarded is liberty in a social organization," he declared. "Liberty under the Constitution is thus necessarily subject to the restraints of due process, and regulation which is reasonable in relation to its subject and is adopted in the interests of the community is due process." As the Chief Justice spoke, members of the bar in the choice seats near the bench followed his every word as though transfixed, and Hughes's delivery of the opinion in "a clear, resonant voice," noted one correspondent, "electrified and held spellbound the spectators who crowded every corner of the majestic Supreme Court chamber."

The Court had long since established that the State had especial authority to circumscribe the freedom of contract of women, the Chief Justice continued. In *Muller* v. *Oregon* (1908), he pointed out, the Court had fully elaborated the reasons for accepting a special sphere of State regulation of female labor. In that landmark case the Court had emphasized, in the words of Justice David Brewer, that because a woman performs "maternal functions" her health "becomes an object of public interest and care in order to preserve the strength and vigor of the race." Hence, Brewer had gone on, a woman was "properly placed in a class by herself, and legislation designed for her protection may be sustained even when like legislation is not necessary for men and could not be sustained." The State could restrict her freedom of contract, the Court had determined, not merely "for her benefit, but also largely for the benefit of all."

The precedents established by *Muller* and several later rulings had led the dissenters in *Adkins* to believe that the D.C. minimum wage law should have been sustained, and with good reason, Hughes asserted. The dissenting Justices had challenged the distinction the majority in *Adkins* had drawn between maximum hours legislation (valid) and minimum wage statutes (invalid), and that challenge remained "without any satisfactory answer." The Washington State law was essentially the same as the D.C. act that had been struck down in *Adkins,* he acknowledged, "but we are unable to conclude that in its minimum wage requirement the State has passed beyond the boundary of its broad protective power." In that sentence, however convoluted, Hughes had said what for some minutes past it had been clear he was going to say: the Supreme Court was sustaining Washington's minimum wage law. Against all odds, Elsie Parrish had won.

Lest anyone miss the implication of the Court's reasoning, the Chief Justice spelled it out: "The *Adkins* case was a departure from the true application of the principles governing the regulation by the State of the relation of employer and employed." In short, *Adkins,* written by Sutherland and carrying the votes of a number of Hughes's other brethren, was being put to death in its fifteenth year. One could not possibly reconcile *Adkins,* Hughes maintained, with "well-considered" rulings such as *Muller.* "What can be closer to the public interest than the health of women and their protection from unscrupulous and overreaching employers?" he asked. "And if the protection of women is a legitimate end of the exercise of state power, how can it be said that the requirement of the payment of a minimum wage fairly fixed in order to meet the very necessities of existence is not an admissible means to that end?"

With an eloquence, even passion, few thought him capable of, the Chief Justice added: "The legislature of the State was clearly entitled to consider the situation of women in employment, the fact that they are in the class receiving the least pay, that their bargaining power is relatively weak, and that they are the ready victims of those who would take advantage of their necessitous circumstances. The legislature was entitled to adopt measures to reduce the evils of the 'sweating system,' the exploiting of workers at wages so low as to be insufficient to meet the bare cost of living, thus making their very helplessness the occasion of a most injurious competition."

Since many states had adopted laws of this nature to remedy the evil of sweatshop competition, the enactment of such legislation by the state of Washington could not be viewed as "arbitrary or capricious, and that is all we have to decide," Hughes said. "Even if the wisdom of the policy be regarded as debatable and its effects uncertain, still the legislature is entitled to its judgment." Delighted at what they were hearing, the New Deal lawyers in the chamber smiled broadly and nudged one another.

In his closing remarks the Chief Justice advanced an "additional and compelling" reason for sustaining the statute. The exploitation of "relatively defenceless" employees not only injured those women, he asserted, but directly burdened the community, because "what these workers lose in wages the taxpayers are called upon to pay." With respect to that reality, he said, the Court took "judicial notice of the unparalleled demands" the Great Depression had made upon localities. (That comment revealed how far he was reaching out, for the state of Washington had submitted no factual brief about any added responsibilities, and the statute in question had been enacted long before the Wall Street crash.) Hughes did not doubt that the state of Washington had undergone these tribulations, even if it had not troubled to say so, and that deduction led him to state, again with unexpected acerbity: "The community is not bound to provide what is in effect a subsidy for unconscionable employers. The community may direct its law-making power to correct the abuse which springs from their selfish disregard of the public interest." Consequently, the Chief Justice concluded, "The case of *Adkins* v. *Children's Hospital . . .* should be, and it is, overruled," and the judgment of the Supreme Court of the state of Washington on behalf of Elsie Parrish "is affirmed." Some two years after she changed sheets in the Cascadian Hotel for the last time, the Wenatchee chambermaid was to receive her $216.19 in back pay.

It would require some time for Court watchers to grasp the full implications of Hughes's opinion in *Parrish*—to write of the "Constitutional Revolution of 1937"—but George Sutherland's dissent revealed that the Four Horsemen understood at that very moment that their long reign, going all the way back to *Adkins* and even before, with only slight interruption, had abruptly ended. When, having spoken the final words, the Chief Justice nodded to Justice Sutherland seated to his left, Sutherland surveyed the chamber silently, almost diffidently, before picking up the sheaf of papers in front of him and beginning to read. Sensing his day had passed, Sutherland appeared barely able to bring himself to carry out his futile assignment. He started off speaking in a curiously toneless murmur, and even those nearby had trouble at first catching his words. In the rear of the room, all was lost.

Consequently, not a few missed altogether Sutherland's first sentence, and even those who did hear it needed a moment to take in its full import. "Mr. Justice Van Devanter, Mr. Justice McReynolds, Mr. Justice Butler and I think the judgment of the court below should be reversed," Sutherland began. A commonplace utterance, yet it signaled a historic shift in the disposition of the Supreme Court. Once again, the Justices had divided 5–4, but this time Owen Roberts had abandoned the Conservative Four to compose a new majority that, on this day, and in the days and months and years to come, would legitimate the kind of social legislation that in FDR's first term had been declared beyond the bounds of governmental authority. The loss of Roberts did not go down easily. In the course of the afternoon, noted one captious commentary, "the Four Horsemen of Reaction whom he had deserted looked glum and sour."

After no more than a cursory paragraph saying that all the contentions that had just been advanced in *Parrish* had been adequately disposed of in *Adkins* and *Tipaldo,* Sutherland delivered a dissent that for quite some time constituted less a reply to Hughes and the majority in *Parrish* than to Justice Stone's 1936 calls for judicial restraint in cases such as *Tipaldo.* Undeniably, a Justice was obliged to consider the contrary views of his associates, Sutherland acknowledged, "but in the end, the question which he must answer is not whether such views seem sound to those who entertain them, but whether they convince him that the statute is constitutional or engender in his mind a rational doubt upon that issue." He added: "The oath which he takes as a judge is not a composite oath, but an individual one. And in passing upon the validity of a statute, he discharges a duty imposed upon *him,* which cannot be consummated justly by an automatic acceptance of the views of others which have neither convinced, nor created a reasonable doubt in, his mind. If upon a question so important he thus surrender his deliberate judgment, he stands forsworn. He cannot subordinate his convictions to that extent and keep faith with his oath or retain his judicial and moral independence."

Though Sutherland had been directing most of his barbs at Stone (Hughes's opinion had been all but forgotten), these last words may well have had a different target. His remarks, one writer conjectured, must have been intended as a rebuke to Owen Roberts. Perhaps so, for the minority opinion did appear to be irritating Roberts, who, after looking toward Sutherland several times, raised a handkerchief to his mouth.

Sutherland, for his part, had hit full stride. After sipping some water, he seemed to gain strength, and his voice resounded throughout the chamber. Indeed, the Washington *Post* characterized the reading by the "usually mild-mannered Sutherland" as nothing less than "impassioned." The elderly judge, described in another account as "pale, grimlipped," even went so far as to rap his

Justice Owen Roberts. His vote shifted the balance of the Supreme Court.

knuckles on the dais as he took issue with the President, though never by name; with Justice Roberts, no longer his ally; and even more vigorously, again without mentioning him directly, with Justice Stone. In rebuttal to the Chief Justice's assertion that the case before the Court required a fresh examination, in part because of the "economic conditions which have supervened," Sutherland stated bluntly, "The meaning of the Constitution does not change with the ebb and flow of economic events."

When, having read nearly five pages of his opinion, Sutherland finally turned to the case before the Court, he said little more than that *West Coast Hotel Co.* replicated the situation in *Adkins.* In every important regard, the two statutes involved had identical "vices," Sutherland maintained, "and if the *Adkins* case was properly decided, as we who join in this opinion think it was, it necessarily follows that the Washington statute is invalid." It was beyond dispute, he asserted, that the due process clause embraced freedom of contract, and Sutherland remained convinced, too, that women stood on an equal plane with men and that legislation denying them the right to contract for low-paying jobs was discriminatory. "Certainly a suggestion that the bargaining ability of the average woman is not equal to that of the average man would lack substance," he declared. "The ability to make a fair bargain, as everyone knows, does not depend upon sex."

But anybody who thought that those last sentences had a hint of jocularity quite misperceived Sutherland's mood. The *Parrish* decision blew taps for the nineteenth-century world, and Sutherland, born in England in 1862 and reared on the Utah frontier, knew it. Having had his say, he understood that there was no point in going on any longer. Wearily, he concluded, "A more complete discussion may be found in the *Adkins* and *Tipaldo* cases cited *supra.*" His discourse at an end, he carefully laid his opinion on the dais and, stern-visaged, settled back in his chair.

When news of the momentous decision, relayed swiftly to every part of the nation over press association wires, reached Sutherland's supporters, they shared his sense of dismay. Conservatives were outraged. If FDR wanted a political court, said a disgruntled senator, he had one now, for the decision was blatantly political, a transparent effort to kill the Court-packing bill by demonstrating that the judges would no longer misbehave. Ardent feminists were no less incensed. One of them wrote Sutherland: "May I say that the minority opinion handed down in the Washington minimum wage case is, to me, what the rainbow was to Mr. Wordsworth? . . . You did my sex the honor of regarding women as persons and citizens."

Most reformers, though, women as well as men, hailed the *Parrish* ruling as a triumph for social justice and a vindication for FDR, who had been accorded an altogether unexpected victory in the most improbable quarter. One outspoken progressive, the columnist Heywood Broun, commented: "Mr. Roosevelt has been effective not only in forcing a major switch in judicial policy, but he has even imposed something of his style upon the majority voice of the court. There are whole sections in the document written and read by Chief Justice Hughes which sound as if they might have been snatched bodily from a fireside chat."

Partisans of the President jeered at the Court for its abrupt reversal of views on the validity of minimum wage legislation. Because of the "change of a judicial mind," observed the attorney general, Homer Cummings, sardonically, "the Constitution on Monday, March 29, 1937, does not mean the same thing that is meant on Monday, June 1, 1936." The head of one of the railway brotherhoods carried that thought a step further in noting, "On Easter Sunday, state minimum wage laws were unconstitutional, but about noon on Easter Monday, these laws were constitutional." That development perturbed some longtime critics of the Court ("What kind of respect do you think one can instill in law students for the process of the Court when things like this can happen?" Felix Frankfurter asked) but gave others no little satisfaction. A former United States senator from West Virginia wrote: "Suppose you have noticed that the untouchables, the infallible, sacrosanct Supreme Court judges have been forced to put upon the record that they are just a bundle of flesh and blood, and must walk upon the ground like the rest of human beings. I got quite a 'kick' out of reading that the Supreme Court said, right out loud in meeting, that it had been wrong. Like most of the wrongs done in life, there is no compensation for the great wrongs which that old court has been doing the country; but like all democrats, I am forgiving."

The performance of the Court proved especially embarrassing for the Chief Justice. Commentators, observing that Hughes had once said of a nineteenth-century decision that the "over-ruling in such a short time by one vote, of the previous decision, shook popular respect for the Court," pointed out that "now, within a period of only ten months, the Supreme Court had reversed itself on minimum wages, again by one vote." To be sure, Hughes did not admit that the Court had shifted, and years later Roberts claimed that he had voted with the Four Horsemen in *Tipaldo* only because New York had not presented the issue in the right manner. Furthermore, we now know that in *Parrish* Roberts had not been responding to the Court-packing threat since he had cast his vote before the plan was announced.

However, scholars, who have the advantage of information not generally known in 1937, find Roberts's contention that he did not switch unpersuasive.

At the time, no one doubted that the Court, and more particularly Mr. Justice Roberts, had crossed over. "Isn't everything today exciting?" wrote one of the women who led the National Consumers' League. "Just to think that silly Roberts should have the power to play politics and decide the fate of Minimum Wage legislation. But, thank God he thought it was politically expedient to be with us." In a more whimsical vein, *The New Yorker* remarked: "We are told that the Supreme Court's about-face was not due to outside clamor. It seems that the new building has a soundproof room, to which justices may retire to change their minds."

Yet despite all the ridicule directed at the Court, Hughes read the opinion in Elsie Parrish's case with an unmistakable note of exultation in his voice. For by being able to show that he had won Roberts to his side in *Parrish,* he had gone a long way toward defeating the Court-packing scheme. Once Roosevelt had a 5–4 majority for social legislation, there no longer appeared to be an urgent need for a drastic remedy. "Why," it was asked, "shoot the bridegroom after a shotgun wedding?" Not for nearly four months would FDR's proposal be finally rejected, and it would retain substantial backing almost to the very end, but never was it as formidable a proposition as it had been on the eve of Elsie Parrish's case. Within days after the decision was handed down, Washington insiders were regaling one another with a saucy sentence that encapsulated the new legislative situation: "A switch in time saved nine."

The Court's shift in *Parrish* proved to be the first of many. On the very day that *Parrish* was decided, "White Monday," the Court also upheld a revised farm mortgage law (the original one had been struck down on "Black Monday," in 1935) as well as other reform statutes. Two weeks later, once more by 5–4 with Roberts in the majority, it validated the Wagner Act (the National Labor Relations Act) and in the following month it turned aside challenges to the Social Security Act. Indeed, never again did the Supreme Court strike down a New Deal law, and from 1937 to the present it has not overturned a single piece of significant national or state legislation establishing minimal labor standards. Many commentators even believe that the Court has forever abandoned its power of judicial review in this field. Little wonder then that analysts speak of the "Constitutional Revolution of 1937."

Battle-scarred veterans of the minimum wage movement found themselves in a universe remade. The seventeen states with minimum wage statutes on their books now took steps to enforce them, and New York made plans to enact new legislation to replace the law struck down in *Tipaldo.* Even more consequential were the implications of *Parrish* for the national government. Late in 1936 President Roosevelt had told newspapermen of an experience on the streets of New Bedford when his campaign car was mobbed by enthusiastic well-wishers, twenty thousand of them crowded into a space intended to hold a thousand:

> "There was a girl six or seven feet away who was trying to pass an envelope to me and she was just too far away to reach. One of the policemen threw her back into the crowd and I said to my driver 'Get the note from that girl.' He got it and handed it to me and the note said this . . . 'Dear Mr. President: I wish you could do

something to help us girls. You are the only recourse we have got left. We have been working in a sewing factory . . . and up to a few months ago we were getting our minimum pay of $11 a week. . . . Today the 200 of us girls have been cut down to $4 and $5 and $6 a week. You are the only man that can do anything about it. Please send somebody from Washington up here to restore our minimum wages because we cannot live on $4 or $5 or $6 a week.'

"That is something that so many of us found in the Campaign, that these people think that I have the power to restore things like minimum wages and maximum hours and the elimination of child labor. . . . And, of course, I haven't any power to do it."

Now, thanks to the constitutional revolution that the Wenatchee chambermaid had detonated, Congress was able to give him that power, and when the Fair Labor Standards Act of 1938 that set minimum wages and maximum hours for both men and women was challenged in the courts, a reconstituted Supreme Court found no difficulty in validating it.

Long before then Elsie Parrish had faded into the anonymity from which she had risen, and when more than thirty-five years later Adela Rogers St. Johns, a reporter who had won renown as the "sob sister" of the Hearst press, tracked her down in Anaheim, California, Mrs. Parrish expressed surprise that anyone would pay attention to her. Surrounded by grandchildren, looking much younger than her years, "dressed in something pink and fresh-washed and ironed," she said that she had gotten little notice at the time and "none of the women running around yelling about Lib and such have paid any since." But she was quietly confident that she had accomplished something of historic significance—less for herself than for all the thousands of women scrubbing floors in hotels, toiling at laundry vats, and tending machines in factories who needed to know that, however belatedly, they could summon the law to their side.

FDR: The Man of the Century

Arthur M. Schlesinger, Jr.

That Franklin Roosevelt was the greatest American president of the twentieth century is generally accepted by Democrats and Republicans alike. Both the achievements of his New Deal in battling the Great Depression of the 1930s and his wartime leadership of the coalition that defeated Germany and Japan in World War II entitle him to that honor.

In this essay Arthur M. Schlesinger, Jr. concentrates on the latter aspect of Roosevelt's life. He traces his developing interests and experiences in foreign matters before and during the first world war. But he concentrates on his role during World War II. Schlesinger has written extensively on Roosevelt and his times. He admires Roosevelt greatly but he recognizes that many of his wartime actions remain controversial. He still judges him to be the "man of the century."

After half a century it is hard to approach Franklin D. Roosevelt except through a minefield of clichés. Theories of FDR, running the gamut from artlessness to mystification, have long paraded before our eyes. There is his famous response to the newspaperman who asked him for his philosophy: "Philosophy? I am a Christian and a Democrat—that's all"; there is Robert E. Sherwood's equally famous warning about "Roosevelt's heavily forested interior"; and we weakly conclude that both things were probably true.

FDR's Presidency has commanded the attention of eminent historians at home and abroad for fifty years or more. Yet no consensus emerges, especially in the field of foreign affairs. Scholars at one time or another have portrayed him at every point across a broad spectrum: as an isolationist, as an internationalist, as an appeaser, as a warmonger, as an impulsive decision maker, as an incorrigible vacillator, as the savior of capitalism, as a closet socialist, as a Machiavellian intriguer plotting to embroil his country in foreign wars, as a Machiavellian intriguer avoiding war in order to let other nations bear the brunt of the fighting. As a gullible dreamer who thought he could charm Stalin into postwar collaboration and ended by selling Eastern Europe down the river into slavery, as a tightfisted creditor sending Britain down the road toward bankruptcy, as a crafty imperialist serving the interests of American capitalist hegemony, as a high-minded prophet whose vision shaped the world's future. Will the real FDR please stand up?

Two relatively recent books illustrate the chronically unsettled state of FDR historiography—and the continuing vitality of the FDR debate. In *Wind Over Sand* (1988) Frederick W. Marks III finds a presidential record marked by ignorance, superficiality, random prejudice, erratic impulse, a man out of his depth, not waving but drowning, practicing a diplomacy as insubstantial and fleeting as wind blowing over sand. In *The Juggler* (1991), Warren F. Kimball finds a record marked by intelligent understanding of world forces, astute maneuver, and a remarkable consistency of purpose, a farsighted statesman facing dilemmas that defied quick or easy solutions. One-third of each book is given over to endnotes and bibliography, which suggests that each portrait is based on meticulous research. Yet the two historians arrive at diametrically opposite conclusions. . . .

I suppose we must accept that human beings are in the last analysis beyond analysis. In the case of FDR, no one can be really sure what was going on in that affable, welcoming, reserved, elusive, teasing, spontaneous, calculating, cold, warm, humorous, devious, mendacious, manipulative, petty, magnanimous, superficially casual, ultimately decent, highly camouflaged, finally impenetrable mind. Still, if we can't as historians try to make sense out of what he *was*, we surely must as historians try to make sense out of what he *did*. If his personality escapes us, his policies must have some sort of pattern. . . .

How did FDR conceive the historical life-interests of the United States? His conception emerged from his own long, if scattered, education in world affairs. It should not be forgotten that he arrived in the White House with an unusual amount of international experience. He was born into a cosmopolitan family. His father knew Europe well and as a young man had marched with Garibaldi. His elder half-brother had served in American legations in London and Vienna. His mother's family had been in the China trade; his mother herself had lived in Hong Kong as a little girl. As FDR reminded Henry Morganthau in 1934, "I have a background of a little over a century in Chinese affairs."

FDR himself made his first trip to Europe at the age of three and went there every summer from his ninth to his fourteenth year. As a child he learned French and German. As a lifelong stamp collector he knew the world's geography and politics. By the time he was elected President, he had made thirteen trips across the Atlantic and had spent almost three years of his life in Europe. "I started . . . with a good deal of interest in foreign affairs," he told a press conference in 1939, "because both branches of my family have been mixed up in foreign affairs for a good many generations, the affairs of Europe and the affairs of the Far East."

Now much of his knowledge was social and superficial. Nor is international experience in any case a guarantee of international wisdom or even of continuing international concern. The other American politician of the time who rivaled FDR in exposure to the great world was, oddly, Herbert Hoover. Hoover was a mining engineer in Australia at twenty-three, a capitalist in the Chinese Empire at twenty-five, and a promoter in the City of London at twenty-seven. In the years from his Stanford graduation to the Great War, he spent more time in the British Empire than he did in the United States. During and after the war he supervised relief activities in Belgium and in Eastern Europe. Keynes called him the only man to emerge from the Paris Peace Conference with an enhanced reputation.

Both Hoover and Roosevelt came of age when the United States was becoming a world power. Both saw more of the world than most of their American contemporaries. But international experience led them to opposite conclusions. What Hoover saw abroad soured him on foreigners. He took away from Paris an indignant conviction of an impassable gap between his virtuous homeland and the European snake pit. Nearly twenty years passed before he could bring himself to set foot on the despised continent. He loathed Europe and its nationalist passions and hatreds. . . . The less America had to do with so degenerate a place, the Quaker Hoover felt, the better.

The patrician Roosevelt was far more at home in the great world. Moreover, his political genealogy instilled in him the conviction that the United States must at last take its rightful place among the powers. In horse breeder's parlance, FDR was by Woodrow Wilson out of Theodore Roosevelt. These two remarkable Presidents taught FDR that the United States was irrevocably a world power and poured substance into his conception of America's historic life-interests.

FDR greatly admired TR, deserted the Democratic party to cast his first presidential vote for him, married his niece, and proudly succeeded in 1913 to the office TR had occupied 15 years earlier, Assistant Secretary of the Navy. From TR and from that eminent friend of both Roosevelts, Admiral Mahan, young Roosevelt learned the strategic necessities of international relations. He learned how to distinguish between vital and peripheral interests. He learned why the national interest required the maintenance of balances of power in areas that, if controlled by a single power, could threaten the United States. He learned what the defense of vital interests might require in terms of ships and arms and men and production and resources. His experience in Wilson's Navy Department during the First World War consolidated these lessons.

But he also learned new things from Wilson, among them that it was not enough to send young men to die and kill because of the thrill of battle or because of war's morally redemptive qualities or even because of the need to restore the balance of power. The awful sacrifices of modern war demanded nobler objectives. The carnage on the Western Front converted FDR to Wilson's vision of a world beyond war, beyond national interest, beyond balances of power, a world not of secret diplomacy and antagonistic military alliances but of an organized common peace, founded on democracy, self-determination, and the collective restraint of aggression.

Theodore Roosevelt had taught FDR geopolitics. Woodrow Wilson now gave him a larger international purpose in which the principles of power had a strong but secondary role. FDR's two mentors detested each other. But they joined to construct the framework within which FDR, who cherished them both, approached foreign affairs for the rest of his life.

As the Democratic vice presidential candidate in 1920, he roamed the country pleading for the League of Nations. Throughout the twenties he warned against political isolationism and economic protectionism. America would commit a grievous wrong, he said, of it were "to go backwards towards an old Chinese Wall policy of isolationism." Trade wars, he said, were "symptoms of economic insanity." But such sentiments could not overcome the disillusion and disgust with which Americans in the 1920s contemplated world troubles. As President Hoover told the Italian foreign minister in 1931, the deterioration of Europe had led to such "despair . . . on the part of the ordinary American citizen [that] now he just wanted to keep out of the whole business."

Depression intensified the isolationist withdrawal. Against the national mood, the new president brought to the White House in 1933 an international outlook based, I would judge, on four principles. One was TR's commitment to the preservation of the balance of world power. Another was Wilson's vision of concerted international action to prevent or punish aggression. The third principle argued that lasting peace required the free flow of trade among nations. The fourth was that in a democracy foreign policy must rest on popular consent. In this isolationist climate of the late 1930s, this fourth principle compromised and sometimes undermined the first three.

Diplomatic historians are occasionally tempted to overrate the amount of time Presidents spend in thinking about foreign policy. In fact, from Jackson to FDR, domestic affairs have always been, with a few fleeting exceptions—perhaps Polk, McKinley, Wilson—the presidential priority. This was powerfully the case at the start for FDR. Given the collapse of the economy and the anguish of unemployment, given the absence of obvious remedy and the consequent need for social experiment, the surprise is how much time and energy FDR did devote to foreign affairs in these early years.

He gave time to foreign policy because of his acute conviction that Germany and Japan were, or were about to be, on the rampage and that unchecked aggression would ultimately threaten vital interests of the United States. He packed the State Department and embassies abroad with unregenerate Wilsonians . . . He relished meetings with foreign leaders and found himself in advance of most of them in his forebodings about Germany and Japan. He invited his ambassadors, especially his political appointees, to write directly to him, and nearly all took advantage of the invitation.

His diplomatic style had its capricious aspects. FDR understood what admirals and generals were up to, and he understood the voice of prophetic statesmanship. But he never really appreciated the professional diplomat and looked with some disdain on the career Foreign Service as made up of tea drinkers remote from the realities of American life. His approach to foreign policy, while firmly grounded in geopolitics and soaring easily into the higher idealism, always lacked something at the middle level.

At the heart of Roosevelt's style in foreign affairs was a certain incorrigible amateurism. His off-the-cuff improvisations, his airy tendency to throw out half-baked ideas, caused others to underrate his continuity of purpose and used to drive the British especially wild, as minutes scribbled on Foreign Office dispatches make abundantly clear. This amateurism had its good points. It could be a source of boldness and creativity in a field populated by cautious and conventional people. But it also encouraged superficiality and dilettantism.

The national mood, however, remained FDR's greatest problem. Any U.S. contribution to the deterrence of aggression depended on giving the government power to distinguish between aggressors and their victims. He asked Congress for this authority, first in cooperating with the League of Nations sanctions in 1933, later in connection with American neutrality statutes. Fearing that aid to one side would eventually involve the nation in war, Congress regularly turned him down. By rejecting policies that would support victims against aggressors, Congress effectively nullified the ability of the United States to throw its weight in the scales against aggressors.

Roosevelt, regarding the New Deal as more vital for the moment than foreign policy and needing the support of isolationists for his domestic program, accepted what he could not change in Congressional roll calls. But he did hope to change public opinion and began a long labor of popular education with his annual message in January 1936 and its condemnation of "autocratic institutions that beget slavery at home and aggression abroad."

It is evident that I am not persuaded by the school of historians that sees Roosevelt as embarked until 1940 on a mission of appeasement, designed to redress German grievances and lure the Nazi regime into a constructive role in a re-ordered Europe. The evidence provided by the private conversations as well as by public pronouncements is far too consistent and too weighty to permit the theory that Roosevelt had illusions about coexistence with Hitler. Timing and maneuver were essential, and on occasion he tacked back and forth like the small boat sailor that Gaddis Smith reminds us he was. Thus, before positioning the United States for entry into war, he wanted to make absolutely sure there was no prospect of negotiated peace. . . . But his basic course seems pretty clear: one way or another to rid the world of Hitler.

I am even less persuaded by the school that sees Roosevelt as a President who rushed the nation to war because he feared German and Japanese economic competition. America "began to go to war against the Axis in the Western Hemisphere," the revisionist William Appleman Williams tells us, because Germany was invading U.S. markets in Latin America. The Open Door Cult recognizes no geopolitical concerns in Washington about German bases in the Western Hemisphere. Oddly, the revisionists accept geopolitics as an O.K. motive for the Soviet Union but deny it to the United States. In their view American foreign policy can never be aimed at strategic security but must forever be driven by the lust of American business for foreign markets.

In the United States, of course, as any student of history knows, economic growth has been based primarily on the home market, not on foreign markets, and the preferred policy of American capitalists, even after 1920, when the United States became a creditor nation, was protection of the home market, not freedom of trade. Recall Fordney-McCumber and Smoot-Hawley. The preference of American business for high tariffs was equally true in depression. When FDR proposed his reciprocal trade agreements program in 1934, the American business community, instead of welcoming reciprocal trade as a way of penetrating foreign markets, denounced the whole idea. Senator Vandenberg even called the bill "Fascist in its philosophy, Fascist in its objectives." A grand total of two Republicans voted for reciprocal trade in the House, three in the Senate.

The "corporatism" thesis provides a more sophisticated version of the economic interpretation. No doubt we have become a society of large organizations, and no doubt an associational society generates a certain momentum toward coordination. But the idea that exporters, importers, Wall Street, Main Street, trade unionists, and farmers form a consensus on foreign policy and impose that consensus on the national government is hard to sustain.

It is particularly irrelevant to the Roosevelt period. If Roosevelt was the compliant instrument of capitalist expansion, as the corporatism thesis implies, why did the leaders of American corporate capitalism oppose him so viciously? Business leaders vied with one another in their hatred of "that man in the White House." The family of J.P. Morgan used to warn visitors against mentioning Roosevelt's name lest fury raise Morgan's blood pressure to the danger point. When Averell Harriman, one of that rare breed, a pro-New Deal businessman, appeared on Wall Street, old friends cut him dead. . . .

What was at stake, as FDR saw it, was not corporate profits or Latin American markets but the security of the United States and the future of democracy. Basking as we do in the glow of democratic triumph, we forget how desperate the democratic cause appeared a half a century ago. The Great War had apparently proved that democracy could not produce peace; the Great Depression that it could not produce prosperity. By the 1930s contempt for democracy was widespread among elites and masses alike: contempt for parliamentary methods, for government by discussion, for freedoms of expression and opposition, for bourgeois individualism, for pragmatic muddling through. Discipline, order, efficiency, and all-encompassing ideology were the talismans of the day. Communism and fascism had their acute doctrinal differences, but their structural similarities—a single leader, a single body of infallible dogma, a single mass of obedient followers—meant that each in the end had more in common with each other than with democracy, as Hitler and Stalin acknowledged in August 1939.

The choice in the 1930s seemed bleak: either political democracy with economic chaos or economic planning with political tyranny. Roosevelt's distinctive contribution was to reject this either/or choice. The point of the New Deal was to chart and vindicate a middle way between laissez-faire and totalitarianism. When the biographer Emil Ludwig asked FDR to define his "political motive," Roosevelt replied, "My desire to obviate revolution . . . I work in a contrary sense to Rome and Moscow."

Accepting re-nomination in 1936, FDR spoke of people under economic stress in other lands who had sold their heritage of freedom for the illusion of a living. "Only our success," he continued, "can stir their ancient hope. They begin to know that here in America we are waging a great and successful war. It is not alone a war against want and destitution and economic demoralization. It is more than that: it is a war to save a great and precious form of government for ourselves and for the world."

Many people around the world thought it a futile fight. Let us not underestimate the readiness of Europeans, including leading politicians and intellectuals, to come to terms with a Hitler-dominated Europe. Even some Americans thought the downfall of democracy inevitable. As Nazi divisions stormed that spring across Scandinavia, the Low Countries, and France, the fainthearted saw totalitarianism, in the title of a poisonous little book published in the summer by Anne Morrow Lindbergh, a book that by December 1940 had rushed through seven American printings, as "the wave of the future." While her husband, the famous aviator, predicted Nazi victory and opposed American aid to Britain, the gentle Mrs. Lindbergh lamented "the beautiful things . . . lost in the dying of an age," saw totalitarianism as democracy's predestined successor, a "new, and perhaps even ultimately good, conception of humanity trying to come to birth," discounted the evils of Hitlerism and Stalinism as merely "scum on the wave of the future," and concluded that "the wave of the future is coming and there is no fighting it." For a while Mrs. Lindbergh seemed to be right. Fifty years ago there were only two democracies left on the planet.

Roosevelt, however, believed in fighting the wave of the future. He still labored under domestic constraints. The American people were predominantly against Hitler. But they were also, and for a while more strongly, against war. I believe that FDR himself, unlike the hawks of 1941—Stimson, Morganthau, Hopkins, Ickes, Knox—was in no hurry to enter the European conflict, He remembered what Wilson had told him when he himself had been a young hawk a quarter-century before: that a President could commit no greater mistake than to take a divided country into war. He also no doubt wanted to minimize American casualties and to avoid breaking political promises. But probably by the autumn of 1941 FDR had finally come to believe that American participation was necessary if Hitler was to be beaten. An increasing number of Americans were reaching the same conclusion. Pearl Harbor in any case united the country, and Hitler then solved another of FDR's problems by declaring war on the United States.

We accepted war in 1941, as we had done in 1917, in part because, as Theodore Roosevelt had written in 1910, if Britain ever failed to preserve the European balance of power, "the United States would be obliged to get in . . . in order to restore the balance." But restoration of the balance of power did not seem sufficient reason in 1941, any more than it had in 1917, to send young men to kill and die. In 1941 FDR provided higher and nobler aims by resurrecting the Wilsonian vision in the Four Freedoms and the Atlantic Charter and by proceeding, while the war was on, to lay the foundations for the postwar reconstruction of the world along Wilsonian lines. . . .

The war, he believed, would lead to historic transformations around the world. "Roosevelt," Harriman recalled, "enjoyed thinking aloud on the tremendous changes he saw ahead—the end of colonial empires and the rise of newly independent nations across the sweep of Africa and Asia." FDR told Churchill, "A new period has opened in the world's history, and you will have to adjust yourself to it." He tried to persuade the British to leave India and to stop the French from returning to Indochina, and he pressed the idea of UN trusteeships as the means of dismantling empires and preparing colonies for independence.

Soviet Russia, he saw, would emerge as a major power. FDR has suffered much criticism in supposedly thinking he could charm Stalin into postwar collaboration. Perhaps FDR was so naïve after all in concentrating on Stalin. The Soviet dictator was hardly the helpless prisoner of Marxist-Leninist ideology. He saw himself not as a disciple of Marx and Lenin but as their fellow prophet. Only Stalin had the power to rewrite the Soviet approach to world affairs; after all, he had already rewritten Soviet ideology and Soviet history. FDR was surely right in seeing Stalin as the only

FDR inspects General Eisenhower's troops in Sicily in 1943.

lever capable of overturning the Leninist doctrine of irrevocable hostility between capitalism and communism. As Walter Lippmann once observed, Roosevelt was too cynical to think he could charm Stalin. "He distrusted everybody. What he thought he could do was to outwit Stalin, which is quite a different thing."

Roosevelt failed to save Eastern Europe from communism, but that could not have been achieved by diplomatic methods alone. With the Red Army in control of Eastern Europe and a war still to be won against Japan, there was not much the West could do to prevent Stalin's working his will in countries adjacent to the Soviet Union. But Roosevelt at Yalta persuaded Stalin to sign American-drafted Declarations on Liberated Europe and on Poland—declarations that laid down standards by which the world subsequently measured Stalin's behavior in Eastern Europe and found it wanting. And FDR had prepared a fallback position in case things went wrong: not only tests that, if Stalin failed to meet them, would justify a change in policy but also a great army, a network of overseas bases, plans for peacetime universal military training, and the Anglo-American monopoly of the atomic bomb.

In the longer run Roosevelt anticipated that time would bring a narrowing of differences between democratic and Communist societies. He once told Sumner

Welles that marking American democracy as one hundred and Soviet Communism as zero, the American system, as it moved away from laissez-faire, might eventually reach sixty, and the Soviet system, as it moved toward democracy, might eventually reach forty. The theory of convergence provoked much derision in the Cold War years. Perhaps it looks better now.

So perhaps does his idea of making China one of the Four Policemen of the peace. Churchill, with his scorn for "the pigtails," dismissed Roosevelt's insistence on China as the "Great American Illusion." But Roosevelt was not really deluded. As he said at Tehran, he wanted China there "not because he did not realize the weakness of China at present, but he was thinking farther into the future." At Malta he told Churchill that it would take "three generations of education and training . . . before China could become a serious factor." Today, two generations later, much rests on involving China in the global web of international institutions.

As for the United States, a great concern in the war years was that the country might revert to isolationism after the war just as it had done a quarter-century before—a vivid memory for FDR's generation. Contemplating Republican gains in the midterm election, Cordell Hull told Henry Wallace that the country was "going in exactly the same steps it followed in 1918." FDR himself said privately, "Anybody who thinks that isolationism is dead in this country is crazy."

He regarded American membership in a permanent international organization, in Charles Bohlen's words, as "the only device that could keep the United States from slipping back into isolationism." And true to the Wilsonian vision, he saw such an organization even more significantly as the only device that could keep the world from slipping back into war. He proposed the Declaration of the United Nations three weeks after Pearl Harbor, and by 1944 he was grappling with the problem that had defeated Wilson: how to reconcile peace enforcement by an international organization with the American Constitution. For international peace enforcement requires armed force ready to act swiftly in the command of the organization, while the Constitution requires (or, in better days, required) the consent of Congress before American troops can be sent into combat against a sovereign state. Roosevelt probably had confidence that special agreements provided for in Article 43 of the UN Charter would strike a balance between the UN's need for prompt action and Congress's need to retain its war-making power and that the great-power veto would further protect American interests.

He moved in other ways to accustom the American people to a larger international role—and at the same time to assure American predominance in the postwar world. By the end of 1944 he had sponsored a series of international conferences designed to plan vital aspects of the future. These conferences, held mostly by American initiative and dominated mostly by American agendas, offered the postwar blueprints for international organization (Dumbarton Oaks), for world finance, trade, and development (Bretton Woods), for food and agriculture (Hot Springs), for relief and rehabilitation (Washington), for civil aviation (Chicago). In his sweeping and sometimes grandiose asides, FDR envisaged plans for regional development with environmental protection in the Middle East and elsewhere, and his Office of the Coordinator for Inter-American affairs pioneered economic and technical assistance to developing countries. Upon his death in 1945 FDR left an imaginative and comprehensive framework for American leadership in making a better world—an interesting achievement for a President who was supposed to subordinate political to military goals.

New times bring new perspectives. In the harsh light of the Cold War some of FDR's policies and expectations were condemned as naïve or absurd or otherwise misguided. The end of the cold war may cast those policies in a somewhat different light.

FDR's purpose, I take it, was to find ways to safeguard the historic life-interests of the Republic—national security at home and a democratic environment abroad—in a world undergoing vast and fundamental transformations. This requires policies based on a grasp of the currents of history and directed to the protection of U.S. interests and to the promotion of democracy elsewhere. From the vantage point of 1994, FDR met this challenge fairly well. . . .

The world we live in today is Franklin Roosevelt's world. Of the figures who, for good or for evil, bestrode the narrow world half a century ago, he would be the least surprised by the shape of things at the end of the century. Far more than the rest, he possessed what William James called a "sense of futurity." For all his manifold foibles, flaws, follies, and there was a sufficiency of all of those, FDR deserves supreme credit as the twentieth-century statesman who saw most deeply into the grand movements of history.

The Automobile

John Steele Gordon

That the automobile has changed modern life is as obvious as the gray-black asphalt beyond our doors. We all know that the automobile was responsible for the suburbs (and concomitant decline of the inner cities), for take-out food and drive-in movies, and for a staggering annual death toll (in 1972 alone, cars killed 54,898 Americans, nearly as many as died in the Vietnam war). But John Steele Gordon chronicles many of the subtler, and perhaps more consequential, ways in which the automobile transformed American life, ranging from its impact on graphic arts and advertising (to be comprehended at high speeds, signs must be large and striking, with familiar icons replacing descriptive text) to its transformation of consumption (automobiles, as the most expensive industrial consumer good, enormously expanded consumer credit mechanisms). He shows how, for good and ill, the automobile conferred upon twentieth-century America its distinctive character. Gordon's most recent book is *The Business of America* (2001).

. . . You hear the horses? In the greatest metropolis of the Western Hemisphere there are nearly as many horses as there are people, perhaps two million animals throughout the five boroughs. The thousands of vehicles plunging up and down the avenue and the nearby cross streets in the gathering rush hour are almost all pulled by one or more of them. Their iron shoes clang on the Belgian paving blocks at every step; their harnesses and bells jingle with every movement; their snorts and whinnies and occasional screams punctuate the background noise.

You take a deep breath. What do you smell?

You smell the horses. It is an odor as overwhelming and pervasive as the smell of cheese in a cheese factory. To be sure, the inhabitants of that world do not notice it. They have smelled it all their lives, and their brains, in self-defense, have long since ceased to bring it to conscious attention. But we, brief visitors from the future, are almost gagged by it.

You look about you. What do you see?

You see the horses. Far worse, you see what the horses do to the streets. Many are sweating profusely, their tongues lolling out of their foam-beslobbered mouths as they labor in the heat. All are urinating and defecating frequently. Each horse produces about two gallons of urine a day and twenty pounds of excrement. That's twenty thousand tons a day in New York City, greater than the weight of a battleship of the time. House sparrows, imported in the 1850s, ate the seeds in the droppings and help break them up to be more easily washed away. Nourished by this inexhaustible food supply, the birds breed in enormous numbers and excrete in their turn.

And horses die. The more unfortunate, which pull not the carriages of the rich but the drays of ordinary commerce, often die in harness, and their bodies are left by the sides of the streets, to be dragged off by private contractors paid by the city. Perhaps an average of twenty-five a day drop dead on the streets of Manhattan, more in the heat and stress of high summer. The bodies are cleared quickly from so busy and fashionable a corner as Forty-second and Fifth, but in the side streets and less elegant parts of town their remains can lie for days, swelling and stinking in the August sun, a mecca for flies, before they are carted off and disposed of.

In 1996, however, they all are gone, except for a few dozen carriage horses that haul tourists at extravagant prices in nice weather. Today the swish of tires over asphalt and the hum of engines provide the background music for the city's streets, rather than the clip-clop of horses. The horn blast of an angry driver has replaced the shriek of a suddenly terrified animal.

The next time you read an article on the horrors of automobile pollution, you might remember your brief visit to another time and another place, a place and time where the pollution of horses lay underfoot as thick as fallen snow and filled the air as thick as fog. Then, perhaps, you'll give a silent thank-you to Henry Ford and his brethren for freeing us from the tyranny of the horse, which, after all, was exactly what they set out to do in the first place.

Of course, those men did much more than that. It was the cheap automobile, far beyond any other invention, that transformed the daily life of the nineteenth century into that of the twentieth, especially in America, a country that loves its cars almost as much as it loves its liberty.

Let's be clear though. For all its importance the automobile was not a fundamental invention. Such an invention must be something completely new under the sun, and the automobile, when all is said and done, is still just a horseless carriage. Fundamental inventions overturn the cultures that created them and bring forth whole new ones in their place. Twelve thousand years ago agriculture doomed the hunter-gatherer way of life and, in a few millenniums, created civilization. The printing press brought the Middle Ages to a crashing halt in only a few decades. Three centuries later the steam engine ended the primacy of land as the basis of wealth and made possible the triumph of capitalism and democracy. In our own day the computer in the form of the microprocessor is, right before our eyes, remaking the world once again in ways that as yet we only dimly perceive.

But if the automobile did not overturn nineteenth-century civilization, it greatly enlarged its possibilities and strengthened numerous trends already under way—and, as we have seen, made the world a much nicer place. In doing so, it put its stamp on this country, visually, economically, and socially, even artistically, as no other invention—including that great transformer of the nineteenth century, the railroad—ever has.

First, let's look at the visual. One need only compare a nineteenth-century city, such as Chicago, with an essentially twentieth-century one, such as Houston or Los Angeles, to see how profound has been the impact of the automobile on the urban landscape. It has had an equally profound effect on the rural one.

In 1900 there were only some two hundred miles of paved roads in the entire country outside of cities. There was little need for them because only 4,000 cars were manufactured in the United States that year. A decade later, however, 187,000 cars were produced in a single year, and the demand for good roads was growing as quickly as the nation's auto fleet. The Bronx River Parkway, begun in 1907 in New

Grant Wood, Death on the Ridge Road, *1935. By the mid-1930s nearly 30 million auto-mobiles were traveling the two-lane highways that criss-crossed the nation.*

York, was the first limited-access highway, intended as much for "outings" as for ac-tually getting somewhere. By the 1920s a system of interstate highways was begin-ning to take shape, one that would be completely replaced by another, far grander, starting in the 1950s.

The commerce along these new thoroughfares was from the outset affected by the automobile. The new cars needed gasoline. At first this could be purchased at general stores, bicycle shops, or smithies trying to reverse an irreversible decline. Then in 1905 the first purpose-built gas station opened, in St. Louis, Missouri. In 1913 the big oil companies, sensing opportunity, began opening their own stations. Soon there were hundreds of thousands.

But the new gas stations faced a problem. At the speed of a horse, about six miles an hour, people had time to look ahead and see what they were approaching. At thirty and soon forty miles per hour, however, that was much more difficult. So signs grew larger, and corporate logos became important for the first time because they could be grasped in an instant. The wordy style of nineteenth-century advertis-ing started to disappear, not just from billboards but from newspapers and maga-zines, as the old sort of ad began to seem antiquated. The new punchy, visual style, of course, was perfectly preadapted to what would become the dominant advertising medium by the 1950s, television.

The new advertising style soon affected American literature as well, as did the automobile directly. For instance, the Philip Marlowe novels of Raymond Chandler—set in the already auto-besotted Los Angeles of the 1930s and 1940s—are unlike anything written in the nineteenth century.

The need to grab the attention of the passerby in an instant also led to numerous minor American art forms, such as buildings in the shape of ducks, tepees, Paul Bunyan, and heaven only knows what else. There was even a new kind of poetry. In 1925 a retired insurance salesman named Clinton Odell began manufacturing a brushless shaving cream. He sought to find a new way to bring it to the public's attention, and it was his son, Allan, who found it. He suggested using a series of small billboards, each with one line of a jingle on it and the last with the name of the product: WITHIN THIS VALE/OF TOIL/AND SIN/YOUR HEAD GROWS BALD/BUT NOT YOUR CHIN—USE/BURMA-SHAVE.

It virtually demanded the attention of the passing motorist (and, perhaps especially, any child passengers), and the result was immediate commercial success for Burma-Shave and a national craze for jingle writing. By the 1940s there were as many as seven thousand different Burma-Shave jingles lining the nation's highways, and the company paid a hundred dollars for every one sent in and accepted. Today the Burma-Shave campaign lives only in the advertising hall of fame (if there is such a thing), but perhaps an echo can be seen in a latter-day minor art form, the vanity license plate, which also commands close attention from passersby. (My favorite was on a Rolls-Royce Corniche convertible spotted on Sutton Place in Manhattan. Its license plate: "2ND CAR.")

Soon hotels were forced to evolve to satisfy the needs of motorists. Motels (the word dates to 1925) sprang up, surrounded by ample parking and with each guest's room only a few feet from his vehicle. . . .

But it was only after World War II that the automobile made its biggest impact on the American landscape by making possible the modern suburb. Suburbs were created in the first instance by the railroads. The editor Horace Greeley used to commute to New York in the summer from his farm in Chappaqua, forty miles north of the city. These suburbs were very limited, however, because once the passengers disembarked from the train, they were again reduced to the speed of a horse. (Even worse, they had to wait to be picked up at the station. A horse can't sit in a parking lot all day long.) So a demographic map of an American city in 1900 would have looked a bit like a daddy longlegs, with a dense core of population in the city center and only thin streaks of population running outward along the railroad and trolley tracks. All the rest was deep country.

The automobile allowed a completely different pattern. Today there is often a semi-void of residential population at the heart of a large city, surrounded by rings of less and less densely settled suburbs. These suburbs, primarily dependent on the automobile to function, are where the majority of the country's population lives, a fact that has transformed our politics. Every city that had a major-league baseball team in 1950, with the exception only of New York—ever the exception—has had a drastic loss in population within its city limits over the last four and a half decades, sometimes by as much as 50 percent as people have moved outward, thanks to the automobile.

In more recent years the automobile has had a similar effect on the retail commercial sectors of smaller cities and towns, as shopping malls and superstores such as the Home Depot and Wal-Mart have sucked commerce off Main Street and into the surrounding countryside.

But the automobile has had as great an effect on the country's economy as on its landscape. Nineteenth-century industry was largely dedicated to making industrial products, such as steel, products not bought by individuals. But the twentieth century's economy has been increasingly consumer-oriented. The automobile was the first great industrial consumer product and did much to generate that sector of the economy. A trivial part of the American economy in 1900, the automobile industry was by the 1920s the country's largest, as it remains to this day. For the automobile industry is not just the manufacture of automobiles. It encompasses as well the maintenance, servicing, and fueling of cars. Their garaging and parking are major industries in large cities. More, cars must be insured. Traffic must be policed. There are now magazines devoted solely to the sound systems in cars. Auto racing is no small affair. Highway building is a major component of the construction industry. Automobiles account for a very large percent of the gross domestic product.

Indirectly, the economic effect of the automobile has been equally profound. The vast growth of the petroleum, glass, and rubber industries, among others, . . . was largely fueled by the automobile. The drastic decline in the horse population resulted in vast amounts of agricultural land being switched from forage crops to human food, greatly reducing the cost of the latter as the supply increased. The twentieth-century advertising and hotel and tourism industries were built upon the automobile.

So was commercial credit. The automobile remains the most expensive major consumer product, an average-price car costing a very substantial fraction of average annual income. Banks in the early twentieth century dealt mostly with business and the very affluent, not the average worker. So automobile manufacturers set up their own credit organizations (such as the General Motors Acceptance Corporation) to help finance automobile purchases.

The idea of ordinary citizens borrowing money to buy the wherewithal of a better life was radically new in the early twentieth century, when most Americans still did not even have bank accounts or own their homes. But once it was established by the automobile, it was, inevitably, soon applied to other expensive consumer products, such as household appliances. Credit has been moving outward ever since to encompass more and more of the American economy. Today's near-universal use of credit cards to purchase even such minor items as meals is, in a very real sense, a product of the automobile. . . .

But it is socially, perhaps, that the automobile has had its greatest impact on American civilization. For much of its history America was a lonely place. Europe was rich in people, poor in land. European farmers usually lived in villages. They walked out to the surrounding fields . . . to work and back to the close proximity of their friends and neighbors at night.

But this country abounded in land, and its people were spread thinly upon it. The isolated farmhouse, set upon the family's own land, quickly became the norm here, rather than the village. Many a pioneer family came to grief when one or more of its members could not cope with the lack of society. Until the automobile, there was no solution. The railroad had made rapid long-distance movement relatively easy, but local movement remained at the speed of the horse.

So if the nearest town was a mere five miles away, a visit to it would require virtually an entire day to accomplish, an expenditure of time that few farm families could afford very often. Even a visit to a nearby farm could be a considerable undertaking. The horses had to be hitched to a wagon or buggy, a matter that took several minutes even if the horse was in a cooperative mood, which was by no means guaranteed. Then, when the family returned, the horses had to be unhitched, cooled down, and cared for. Then, as now, horses were delicate and expensive means of transportation and required very high maintenance. Unless the family was affluent enough to hire people to handle these chores for them, they often had no real choice but to stay home.

The automobile, of course, changed that. Now a trip to town might take no more than an hour, a trip to a neighbor's place for a cup of coffee only a few minutes. The stifling isolation of American farm life began to lift. So did the isolation of the individual towns and the cozy local monopolies of bank and general store. Now families could easily get to the next town if they didn't like the service or the prices available in their own.

Another aspect of social life that the automobile changed was courting. Before the automobile, courting had to be largely accomplished in front of families and the watchful eyes of chaperons and was largely confined to one's closest neighbors. Now real privacy and a far wider selection was possible. The "date," once available in large measure only to city dwellers (a minority of the population in the nineteenth century), spread rapidly through the small towns and farms of rural America.

The automobile also gave women much more mobility and freedom. The skills needed to handle horses with confidence are difficult to acquire, but driving a car is easy. Once the electric starter removed the need for physical strength (and the device was commonplace by 1916), women began to move. It was the automobile as much as the Second World War that liberated women. American society, long the most fluid and thus the most dynamic in the world, has seen a quantum leap in that fluidity in the twentieth century, thanks to the automobile. And this evolving change has by no means played itself out.

Needless to say, much of this change did not come easily. The shift in agriculture caused by the automobile resulted in the squeezing out of marginal farmers and contributed in no small way to the onset of the Great Depression. The Joad family in Steinbeck's *The Grapes of Wrath* were forced to migrate to California (in, of course, an automobile) when their drought-suffering farm could no longer sustain them.

Americans had to learn, all too often at first hand, the power of half a ton or more of metal, glass, and rubber moving at forty miles an hour. Because the number of cars in the early days was small compared with later, the number of deaths was relatively low. But the slaughter on a vehicle-mile basis was awesome; in 1921 the rate was 24 per hundred million miles of travel. It began to decline as people became better drivers (most states did not require driver's licenses until the 1930s), roads improved, and cars became more ruggedly constructed. The year 1972 proved the worst in terms of highway deaths when 54,589 people died on the nation's highways, not much lower than the number who lost their lives in the entire Vietnam War then raging.

Since then the rate has dropped more or less steadily, thanks to far better-designed cars and highways (padded bridge abutments, for instance) and a decline in alcohol consumption. In 1995 the death rate per hundred million vehicle miles was only 1.7.

The mechanics and tinkerers banging away in basements and carriage sheds at the turn of the century—men with names like Ford, Durant, Leland, Chrysler, Dodge, and Olds—weren't trying to change the world. Many looked no further than just getting their latest designs to work. Most hoped only to make a buck out of what they were doing, and many of course did so, some in huge amounts.

But unintentionally they also gave American civilization, and thus the world in this "American Century," their twentieth-century character, their very nature. That's why when people a hundred years from now imagine themselves standing at the corner of Forty-second Street and Fifth Avenue on a hot August day in the year 2000, they will have to conjure up the automobile—its sounds, its smells, its shapes—to bring the scene to life.

6 Postwar Presidents

Faced with the release of his secret tapes and impending impeachment proceedings, Richard Nixon resigned the office of president on August 9, 1974. Here he signals his farewell as he prepares to leave the White House for the last time. The Watergate scandal and Nixon's role in it undermined public trust in and respect for the presidency.

Eisenhower as President

Steve Neal

The reputations of statesmen, like the reputations of artists, writers, and composers, tend to fluctuate over time. However, at least where statesmen are concerned, no mere shift in taste or fashion accounts for the changes that occur. In the first place, the passage of time can actually alter the significance of past events and thus change historians' judgments about the actors who shaped these events. Then too, new facts and new documents continually come to light, frequently suggesting more convincing explanations of what people did and why they behaved as they did, thus causing historians to change their minds.

No better recent example of the ups and downs of a major figure's reputation exists than that provided by the case of President Dwight D. Eisenhower. In the following essay Steve Neal, the chief political correspondent of the *Chicago Sun Times*, traces the way historians have viewed the Eisenhower presidency. Neal explains why most historians took a dim view of "Ike" in the late 1950s and early 1960s, a time when the public admired him extravagantly, and why the historians' opinion of him has changed so much in recent years. Neal is the author of *The Eisenhowers*, a kind of history of the Eisenhower family, of *Dark Horse: A Biography of Wendell Willkie*, and other books.

Early in 1952, Gen. Dwight David Eisenhower confided to a friendly Republican politician why he was reluctant to seek the Presidency: "I think I pretty well hit my peak in history when I accepted the German surrender."

Emerging from World War II as the organizer of the Allied victory, Eisenhower was America's most celebrated hero. Both major political parties sought to nominate him for the Presidency. And when Ike decided to risk his historical reputation, he captured the 1952 Republican presidential nomination and ended twenty years of Democratic rule. Ronald Reagan was among the millions of Democrats who crossed party lines to support the Republican general. Afterward, the badly beaten Democratic candidate, Adlai E. Stevenson, asked his friend Alistair Cooke: "Who did I think I was, running against George Washington?"

Not only did Eisenhower win two terms by margins of historic proportions, but he maintained his popularity throughout his Presidency. He left office in 1961 still revered by two-thirds of his countrymen, and the American public never stopped liking Ike.

But until recently it seemed that Eisenhower had lost his gamble with history. Like Ulysses S. Grant and Zachary Taylor, Eisenhower was frequently portrayed by historians and political scholars as a mediocre Chief Executive. Soon after Ike left the White House, a poll of leading scholars ranked him among the nation's ten worst Presidents.

Since then, however, Eisenhower's historical image has been dramatically reha- bilitated. In 1982 a similar poll of prominent historians and political scholars rated him near the top of the list of Presidents. Eisenhower is gaining recognition as one of the large figures of the twentieth century, not just for his role as Supreme Allied Commander in World War II, but also for his eight years as President of the United States.

One of the reasons for Eisenhower's comeback is nostalgia for an enormously popular President after an era of assassinations, political scandals, military defeat, and economic turmoil. Another factor in the reassessment is Eisenhower's record of eight years of peace and prosperity, which is unique among twentieth-century Presidents.

Eisenhower, a man of war, conducted his foreign policy with restraint and mod- eration. During the most turbulent era of the Cold War, he ended the Korean War, blocked British and French efforts to crush Arab nationalism, opposed military in- tervention in Southeast Asia, opened a new dialogue with the Soviet Union, and alerted the nation to the dangers of the expanding military-industrial complex. He was criticized for being too passive by the Cold Warriors Henry Kissinger and Gen. Maxwell Taylor, and the same critics berated him for a missile gap that turned out to be nonexistent. In retirement, Eisenhower said his most notable presidential achievement was that "the United States never lost a soldier or a foot of ground in my administration. We kept the peace."

In domestic affairs, Eisenhower also strove to maintain a peaceful equilibrium in handling such explosive issues as McCarthyism and segregation. While critics charged that Ike was spineless in his refusal to openly fight Sen. Joseph McCarthy, the President worked behind the scenes to reduce McCarthy's influence. Despite private doubts about a Supreme Court decision that outlawed segregation, he sent the 101st Airborne into Little Rock, Arkansas, when the state's governor defied the law. He also pushed through the first federal civil rights law since Reconstruction and established the United States Commission on Civil Rights.

Although Eisenhower's memoir of his first term was entitled *Mandate for Change,* his most notable achievement in domestic policy was the continuance of New Deal reforms initiated under President Roosevelt. For nearly a generation, congressional Republicans had been pledging to dismantle FDR's social programs. But Eisenhower had other ideas. "Should any political party attempt to abolish So- cial Security, unemployment insurance, and eliminate labor laws and farm pro- grams, you would not hear of that party again in our political history," he wrote to his brother Edgar, an outspoken conservative. During the Eisenhower era the num- ber of Americans covered by Social Security doubled, and benefits were increased. The Department of Health, Education, and Welfare was established as a domestic Pentagon. Eisenhower also launched the largest public-works project in American history by building the federal highway system, which turned out to be almost as important as the transcontinental railroad. Barry Goldwater denounced the Eisen- hower administration as a "dime-store New Deal," and another conservative critic, William F. Buckley, Jr., characterized Eisenhower's record as "measured socialism." But the Republican President's acceptance of the Roosevelt legacy effectively ended debate over the New Deal and meant that the reforms would endure.

The prosperity of the Eisenhower years was no accident. He produced three balanced budgets; the gross national product grew by over 25 percent; and inflation averaged 1.4 percent. To hold the line on inflation, Eisenhower made the tough choice to accept three recessions. The AFL-CIO president George Meany, who often criticized Ike's policies, nonetheless said that the American worker had "never had it so good."

Although he continued Roosevelt's social programs, Eisenhower's concept of presidential leadership was very different from FDR's. Ike's style was managerial with an orderly staff system and a strong cabinet. FDR was an activist who encouraged chaos and creative tension among his hyperactive staff and cabinet. Most political scholars shared Roosevelt's philosophy of government and viewed Eisenhower as an ineffectual board chairman. There were jokes about the Eisenhower doll; you wound it up and it did nothing for eight years. A memorable Herblock cartoon showed Ike asking his cabinet, "What shall we refrain from doing now?"

The early Eisenhower literature consisted of affectionate memoirs by World War II associates and adoring biographies by war correspondents. But as Chief Executive, Ike suddenly found a more independent panel of observers judging him by new and different standards.

Many of Ike's critics were Democratic partisans. A large factor in his low rating among scholars and liberal commentators was the extraordinary popularity among intellectuals of his major political rival, Adlai Stevenson. Stevenson's admirers were bitter that Eisenhower had twice routed their champion. In *Anti-Intellectualism in American Life,* the historian Richard Hofstadter described Stevenson as a "politician of uncommon mind and style" and Eisenhower as "conventional in mind, relatively inarticulate."

Arthur Larson, the University of Pittsburgh law dean who became an Eisenhower speech writer, recalled: "It was one of the paradoxes of my position in those days that the people I was most at home with, intellectually and ideologically, were more often than not bitterly critical of Eisenhower, if not downright contemptuous of him." Eisenhower did not improve his image in the academic community by flippantly remarking that an intellectual was someone "who takes more words than are necessary to tell more than he knows." As for the syndicated columnists, he declared that "anyone who has time to listen to commentators or read columnists obviously doesn't have enough work to do."

Eisenhower's poor showing in the poll taken shortly after he left office in which Arthur M. Schlesinger, Jr., got seventy-five historians to rate Ike's Presidency should not have been surprising: the participants included two of Stevenson's speech writers, a leader of the 1952 "Draft Stevenson" movement, and other Democratic partisans. Malcolm Moos, a political scholar and former Eisenhower speech writer, declined to participate in the survey, which he believed was stacked against Ike.

In the poll, Eisenhower finished twenty-second out of thirty-one Presidents, which placed him just between the White House mediocrities Chester Alan Arthur and Andrew Johnson. John F. Kennedy reportedly chuckled over Ike's low score in the Schlesinger survey. Eisenhower's associates were concerned that the negative rating might have staying power. "I'm very distressed at this tendency of academics to look down their noses at the Eisenhower administration," the former White

House chief of staff Sherman Adams acknowledged years later. "It's a common sort of thing with the intelligentsia. It's just typical. Look at Mr. Roosevelt. He's a great favorite with the academics, and he's probably a great man. But he lost a lot of battles, didn't he? . . . Well, we may not have done as much, may not have been as spectacular in terms of our willingness to break with the past, but we didn't lose a lot of battles either. A lot of our most important accomplishments were negative—things we avoided. We maintained a peaceful front and adjudicated a lot of issues that seemed ominous and threatening at the time."

Had Eisenhower served just one term, it is unlikely that his historical stock would have dropped so much. Near the end of his first term, his reputation looked fairly secure. A respected journalist, Robert J. Donovan, had written an authoritative history of Eisenhower's first term, which in many ways remains the best study of a sitting President, and which showed Ike firmly in charge. The Pulitzer Prize-winning historian Merlo Pusey had written a friendly treatment of the Eisenhower administration and predicted that Ike would be remembered as a great President, while the political scholar Clinton Rossiter wrote in *The American Presidency* (1956) that Eisenhower "already stands above Polk and Cleveland, and he has a reasonable chance to move up to Jefferson and Theodore Roosevelt."

But like most second terms, Eisenhower's last four years were less productive than his first. The nation was jolted when the Soviet Union launched Sputnik in 1957, and it took months to rebuild American confidence. The recession of 1958 marked the worst economic slide since the Great Depression; more than five million workers were jobless before the recovery began. Ike's 1957 stroke, his third major illness in three years, reinforced doubts about his health and capability to govern. His chief aide, Sherman Adams, became entwined in a political scandal and was forced to resign in 1958.

Eisenhower's 1960 Paris summit with Soviet premier Nikita Khrushchev and leaders of the Western alliance was ruined when an American reconnaissance aircraft, the U-2, was shot down over Central Russia and the pilot, Francis Gary Powers, was captured. Khrushchev stormed out of the summit, withdrawing his invitation for the President's scheduled June visit to the Soviet Union. Had Eisenhower followed his instincts, the U-2 fiasco might have been avoided. A year earlier, he had suggested that the spy flights be halted, but he relented when his National Security Council advisers objected. Later he personally approved Powers' flight. In suggesting that Eisenhower might not have known of the secret mission over the Soviet Union, Khrushchev provided Ike with an alibi that might have salvaged the summit. Indeed, Sen. J. William Fulbright had urged Ike to disclaim responsibility. But Eisenhower told associates that denials would have been ineffectual because of the overpowering evidence. Furthermore, Eisenhower did not want to give credibility to the charge made by his detractors that he was not in control of his own administration.

In his critical 1958 portrait, *Eisenhower: Captive Hero,* the journalist Marquis Childs suggested that Ike was in the wrong job. "If his public record had ended with his military career, it seems safe to assume that a high place would be secure for him," Childs wrote. "But Eisenhower's performance in the presidency will count much more heavily in the final summing up." Childs offered the interpretation that

Eisenhower had been a weak and ineffective President, "a prisoner of his office, a captive of his own indecisiveness," another James Buchanan.

Striking a similar theme, the Harvard political scholar Richard Neustadt depicted Eisenhower as a passive, detached Chief Executive in his 1960 study, *Presidential Power*. According to Neustadt, Eisenhower became too isolated from his staff and should have been more involved in discussing policy options. "The less he was bothered," Neustadt quoted a White House observer, "the less he knew, and the less he knew, the less confidence he felt in his own judgment. He let himself grow stale."

In a revised 1960 edition of *The American Presidency*, Rossiter concluded that Eisenhower had been a disappointment. "He will be remembered, I fear, as the unadventurous president who held on one term too long in the new age of adventure." Without directly attacking Eisenhower, Kennedy suggested in his 1960 presidential campaign that the Republican incumbent was a tired old man, whose lack of leadership had weakened America's prestige in the world. Following his election, Kennedy privately acknowledged that he was struck by Eisenhower's vitality and ruddy health.

Eisenhower's own history of his Presidency was more authoritative but less provocative than those written by his critics, and it had little immediate impact on his reputation. The first volume, *Mandate for Change,* was published in late 1963, and *Waging Peace,* the second installment, came out two years later.

The former President's refusal to disclose his unvarnished opinions of political contemporaries or admit mistakes helped set a bland tone for both volumes. In *Mandate,* Eisenhower described a secret meeting at the Pentagon with a prominent Republican senator in the winter of 1951, without revealing the other man's identity. At the meeting Ike offered to renounce all political ambitions if the senator would make a public commitment to economic and military aid to Western Europe and American participation in the North Atlantic Treaty Organization. When the senator declined, Eisenhower began thinking much more seriously about running for the Presidency.

This meeting had been a turning point in modern American history because the senator Eisenhower neglected to identify in his memoirs was Robert A. Taft, the leading conservative contender for the 1952 Republican presidential nomination. Ike's memoirs would have been much more compelling reading if he had written what he told associates—that in the wake of their meeting he considered Taft a very stupid man. Had the Ohio senator accepted Eisenhower's offer at the Pentagon, it is more than likely that he would have been nominated for the Presidency and Eisenhower would have remained a soldier.

When Johns Hopkins University Press issued the first five volumes of Ike's papers in 1970, the former President's historical image received a boost almost overnight. John Kenneth Galbraith, who had been Stevenson's adviser and had once described the Eisenhower administration as "the bland leading the bland," wrote in *The Washington Post* that Ike's private writings demonstrated that he had been an "exceedingly vigorous, articulate, and clearheaded administrator, who shows himself throughout to have been also a very conscientious and sensible man."

With the opening of Eisenhower's private correspondence and other key documents of his administration to scholars in the seventies, experts were soon focusing attention on the primary source material, and a major reassessment of the Eisenhower Presidency was inevitable. Herbert S. Parmet, one of the first historians to make extensive use of newly declassified papers, made the argument in *Eisenhower and the American Crusades* (1972) that those who rated presidential greatness had overlooked Ike's importance in restoring confidence and building a national consensus in postwar America. To many erstwhile critics, Eisenhower's restrained style of leadership looked better in retrospect during the Vietnam War. At a time when thousands of Americans were dying in a long, bloody, fruitless struggle in Southeast Asia, there were new interpretations of the Eisenhower foreign policy. Murray Kempton's "The Underestimation of Dwight D. Eisenhower," which appeared in the September 1967 issue of *Esquire,* described how Ike had rejected the advice of Cold Warriors to seek military adventure in Vietnam. "He is revealed best, if only occasionally, in the vast and dreary acreage of his memoirs of the White House years," wrote Kempton. "The Eisenhower who emerges here . . . is the President most superbly equipped for truly consequential decision we may ever have had, a mind neither rash nor hesitant, free of the slightest concern for how things might look, indifferent to any sentiment, as calm when he was demonstrating the wisdom of leaving a bad situation alone as when he was moving to meet it on those occasions when he absolutely had to."

Other influential political analysts later expanded the same theme. On the left, I. F. Stone noted that Eisenhower, because of his confidence in his own military judgment, was not intimidated into rash action by the Pentagon.

Eisenhower's most enduring and prescient speech was his 1961 farewell address warning of the potential dangers of the military-industrial complex. "In the councils of government," he declared, "we must guard against the acquisition of unwarranted influence, whether sought or unsought, by the military-industrial complex. The potential for the disastrous rise of misplaced power exists and will persist."

Eisenhower's correspondence effectively demonstrates that his farewell address was an accurate reflection of his political philosophy. In an October 1951 letter to the General Motors executive Charles E. Wilson, Eisenhower wrote: "Any person who doesn't clearly understand that national security and national solvency are mutually dependent, and that permanent maintenance of a crushing weight of military power would eventually produce dictatorship, should not be entrusted with any kind of responsibility in our country." The White House press secretary James Hagerty wrote in his diary that Ike had confided, "You know, if you're in the military and you know about these terrible destructive weapons, it tends to make you more pacifistic than you normally have been."

Stephen E. Ambrose, a former editor of the Eisenhower papers and author of the most comprehensive Eisenhower biography, shows how Ike slowed the arms race and exerted firm leadership in rejecting the Gaither Commission's call for sharp increases in defense spending. "Eisenhower's calm, common-sense, deliberate response to [the Soviets launching of Sputnik] may have been his finest gift to the nation," wrote Ambrose, "if only because he was the only man who could have

Ike (second from left) conferred with Nikolai Bulganin of the Soviet Union, Edgar Faure of France, and Anthony Eden of Great Britain in Geneva in 1955. They were trying to promote détente by pushing for open exchange of military plans and aerial inspection of military bases.

given it." Because of his military background, Eisenhower spoke with more authority about the arms race than his critics. In a 1956 letter to Richard L. Simon, president of Simon & Schuster, who had written him and enclosed a column urging a crash program for nuclear missiles, Eisenhower replied, "When we get to the point, as we one day will, that both sides know that in any outbreak of general hostilities, regardless of the element of surprise, destruction will be both reciprocal and complete, possibly we will have sense enough to meet at the conference table with the understanding that the era of armaments has ended and the human race must conform its actions to this truth or die."

But while many recent historians have portrayed Eisenhower as a dove, a pioneer of détente, there are dissenters. Peter Lyon argued in his 1974 Eisenhower biography that the President's 1953 inaugural address was a "clarion" that "called to war," and that the general was a hawkish militarist. In her 1981 study *The Declassified Eisenhower,* Blanche Wiesen Cook says that Eisenhower used the CIA to launch a "thorough and ambitious anti-Communist crusade" that toppled governments on three continents.

Arthur Schlesinger, Jr., who had previously described Eisenhower as a weak, passive, and politically naïve executive, asserted in his 1973 book *The Imperial Presidency* that Ike went overboard in his use of presidential powers by introducing claims for "executive privilege" in denying government documents to Sen. Joseph McCarthy and by also approving the buildup of the CIA. Even so, Schlesinger now ranks Eisenhower with Truman and his former White House boss, John F. Kennedy, as the successful Presidents of the postwar era.

Another Eisenhower critic, William Leuchtenburg, insists that Ike was not so different from his more obviously hawkish successors. He points to Eisenhower's covert intervention in Iran and Guatemala, his threats to use nuclear weapons in Korea, and his war of words with China over the islands of Quemoy and Ma-tsu. Leuchtenburg also blames Eisenhower for neglecting major public issues, especially in the field of civil rights, "at a considerable cost." Even so, Schlesinger and Leuchtenburg both concede that Eisenhower was much more of a hands-on executive than was realized during his administration.

The records of the Eisenhower administration have ended the myth that the old soldier left foreign policy to his influential secretary of state, John Foster Dulles. A leading Eisenhower revisionist, Fred I. Greenstein, reported in his 1982 study *The Hidden-Hand Presidency* that Ike made the decisions and Dulles carried them out. Greenstein said that it was Eisenhower's international political strategy to be the champion of peace in his public statements, while his secretary of state acted as a Cold Warrior. Dulles once claimed that he, as secretary of state, had ended the Korean War by threatening the use of atomic weapons. But the diplomatic historian Robert A. Divine wrote in *Eisenhower and the Cold War* (1981) that Dulles had exaggerated his role. "It was Eisenhower, in his own characteristically quiet and effective way, who had used the threat of American nuclear power to compel China to end its intervention in the Korean conflict. . . ."

Eisenhower's decision not to intervene militarily in Vietnam is described by some revisionists as his finest hour. Nine years later Eisenhower explained in a private memorandum that he had not wanted to tarnish the image of the United States as the world's foremost anticolonial power. "It is essential to our position of leadership in a world wherein the majority of the nations have at some time or another felt the yoke of colonialism. Thus it is that the moral position of the United States was more to be guarded than the Tonkin Delta, indeed than all of Indochina."

Largely because of his White House staff structure and the authority that he delegated to ranking subordinates, Eisenhower was often characterized as a disengaged President. His chief of staff, Sherman Adams, wielded more power than any White House adviser since FDR's Harry Hopkins, and a popular joke of the fifties had the punch line: "What if Sherman Adams died and Ike became President?" But the memoirs of Adams, Richard M. Nixon, Henry Cabot Lodge, Hagerty, Emmet John Hughes, Milton and John Eisenhower have shown a President firmly in command.

Eisenhower's uneasy relationship with Nixon has also been distorted by some revisionist scholars. While Ike and Nixon were never close, some historians have demonstrated political naïveté in accepting Eisenhower's private criticism of his Vice-President at face value. If Eisenhower held such strong reservations about Nixon as they have suggested, it is unlikely that he would have retained him on the ticket in 1956 and supported him for the Presidency in 1960 and 1968. Eisenhower did not share Nixon's zest for Republican partisanship, but he considered him a loyal and capable Vice-President. Had one of Ike's personal favorites, such as his brother Milton or Treasury Secretary Robert Anderson, emerged as a potential heir, there is evidence that Eisenhower might have supported them over Nixon. But Ike definitely preferred his Vice-President over Nelson Rockefeller and Barry Goldwater.

Nothing damaged Eisenhower's standing with intellectuals more than his vague position on McCarthyism. Eisenhower historians are sharply divided over the

President's role in ending the Wisconsin senator's reign of fear. Ambrose criticizes Eisenhower's "muddled leadership" and unwillingness to publicly condemn McCarthy and his abusive tactics. But Greenstein and William Bragg Ewald have made a strong argument that Eisenhower's behind-the-scenes efforts set the stage for McCarthy's censure by the Senate and destroyed his political influence. Eisenhower loathed McCarthy but believed that a direct presidential attack on him would enhance the senator's credibility among his right-wing followers. "I just won't get into a pissing contest with that skunk," Eisenhower told his brother Milton. The President's papers indicate that he never doubted his strategy against McCarthy, and in the end he felt vindicated.

Eisenhower is also still criticized for not showing sufficient boldness in the field of civil rights. The President was not pleased with the 1954 Supreme Court decision that overturned the "separate but equal" doctrine in public education, and he privately observed that the firestorm touched off by the *Brown* v. *Board of Education* decision had set back racial progress fifteen years. Despite his misgivings, Eisenhower never considered defying the Court, as his successors Gerald Ford and Ronald Reagan would do, over the volatile issue of school desegregation. Eisenhower enforced the Court's decision in sending federal troops into Little Rock, and he went on to establish a civil rights division in the Justice Department in 1957 that committed the federal government to defend the rights of minorities and provided momentum to the civil rights movement.

As a national hero, Eisenhower's popular appeal transcended his political party. According to a 1955 Gallup Poll, 57 percent of the nation's voters considered Eisenhower a political independent, which may have been why Eisenhower was unable to transfer his enormous popularity to the Republican party. Between 1932 and 1968, he was the only Republican elected to the White House. Ironically the GOP-controlled Eightieth Congress may have shortened the Eisenhower era five years before it began by adopting the Twenty-second Amendment, prohibiting any future President from serving more than two terms. Without the constitutional limit, John Eisenhower said his father would have run for a third term in 1960. Even Truman acknowledged that Eisenhower would have been reelected in another landslide.

Eisenhower restored confidence in the Presidency as an institution and set the agenda for the economic growth of the next decade. He understood public opinion as well as Roosevelt had, and he had a keener sense of military problems than any President since George Washington. As the failings of his successors became apparent, Eisenhower's Presidency grew in historical stature. A 1982 Chicago *Tribune* survey of forty-nine scholars ranked him as the ninth best President in history, just behind Truman and ahead of James K. Polk.

With the renewed appreciation of Eisenhower's achievements, Ambrose predicts that Ike may eventually be ranked ahead of Truman and Theodore Roosevelt, and just behind Washington, Jefferson, Jackson, Lincoln, Wilson, and FDR. "I'd put Ike rather high," the historian Robert Ferrell says, "because when he came into office at the head of an only superficially united party . . . he had to organize that heterogeneous group, and get it to cooperate, which he did admirably with all those keen political instincts of his."

"Whatever his failings," Robert J. Donovan wrote of Eisenhower in 1984, "he was a sensible, outstanding American, determined to do what he believed was right. He was a dedicated peacemaker, a president beloved by millions of people . . . and, clearly, a good man to depend on in a crisis. Of his high rank on the list of presidents there can be little doubt."

Henry Steele Commager, who was among Eisenhower's most thoughtful critics during his Presidency, said recently that he would now rank him about tenth from the top. Though Commager faults Eisenhower for not showing leadership against McCarthyism and on behalf of civil rights, he gives Ike high marks in foreign policy for not intervening in Vietnam and "having the sense to say 'no' to the Joint Chiefs of Staff."

Commager says that Eisenhower's election was the decisive factor in ending the Korean War. "Only a general with enormous prestige could have made peace in Korea. An outsider couldn't have done it." Even Adlai Stevenson told a reporter that the election of Eisenhower in 1952 had been good for the country. (He did not, however, feel the same way about Ike's second term.)

William Appleman Williams, the dean of revisionist historians, says that Eisenhower was far more perceptive in international politics than his predecessor or those who followed him. "He clearly understood that crusading imperial police actions were extremely dangerous," Williams notes, and he was determined to avoid World War III.

In the final months of his Presidency, Eisenhower made this private assessment of his managerial style: "In war and in peace I've had no respect for the desk-pounder, and have despised the loud and slick talker. If my own ideas and practices in this matter have sprung from weakness, I do not know. But they were and are deliberate or, rather, natural to me. They are not accidental."

The Education of John F. Kennedy

Richard Reeves

When he ran for president in 1960, John F. Kennedy projected himself as more forward looking, imaginative, and flexible than his predecessor, Republican Dwight D. Eisenhower. He promised to "get the country moving again" and suggested that the kindly and elderly "Ike" had been too bureacratic and precedent bound, probably because of his military background.

In this essay, the journalist and historian Richard Reeves, author of *President Kennedy: Profile of Power* (1993), discusses Kennedy's method of administration during his tragically brief presidency. Although an admirer of Kennedy, Reeves points out the weaknesses of his informal way of gathering information and making decisions. Reeves concludes that Eisenhower's more organized method had much to recommend itself.

In early October of 1963, Rep. Clement Zablocki, a Wisconsin Democrat, led a House Foreign Affairs Committee fact-finding delegation to South Vietnam. Invited to the White House when he returned, Zablocki told President John F. Kennedy he thought that removing President Ngo Dinh Diem would be a big mistake, unless the United States had a successor in the wings. Remember Cuba, Zablocki said. "Batista was bad, but Castro is worse."

It was a little late for that. By then Kennedy was just about ready to sign off on the overthrow of Diem. In Saigon, Ambassador Henry Cabot Lodge and agents of the Central Intelligence Agency were aiding and encouraging the plots of various coup-minded Vietnamese generals. In Washington, schemers in the State Department, led by Averill Harriman, had persuaded the President that the fight against North Vietnamese communism was being lost because Diem was corrupt and foolish—and was not taking orders from his American sponsors and allies.

So Kennedy told Zablocki, "I hope you'll write an objective report and not put President Diem in a favorable light."

"Well, you know what the boss wants," Pierre Salinger remarked cheerfully as Zablocki left the White House.

"The boss will get what we think is right," the congressman said. "Somebody's giving the boss some bad information."

Somebody always seemed to be giving the President bad information in those days, a situation that repeated itself thirty years later in the Presidency of William Jefferson Clinton. The power at the center of American democracy is a function of what the President knows and when he knows it. And Presidents Kennedy and Clinton came to office sharing more than youth and membership in the Democratic party. Each wanted to open up the White House to new information, breaking up or dismantling the old bureaucracies and systems that they thought isolated their

predecessors—the councils and committees and boards that channeled information into the President and then implemented and followed through on his orders.

In his turn Kennedy immediately replaced the rigid and formal organization of
President Dwight Eisenhower's National Security Council with small ad hoc task
forces, their number rising and falling with the President's perception of crises.
Ideally the task forces would be unofficial, never permanent, never functioning
long enough to generate their own bureaucracies or get around the direct control
of the man at the center in the Oval Office.

Short conversations and long hours substituted for Ike's inflexible organization. The best way to reach Kennedy was to hang around the office of his secretary,
Evelyn Lincoln. Periodically he would come out to look at newspapers and talk to
whoever was standing there. Harriman, who had served, in his own way, two presidents before Kennedy, told his assistants that a man had seven seconds to make an
impression on the boss. If the President looked your way, you seized the moment or
it was lost forever.

After a couple of months in office, Kennedy invited NBC into the White House
for a prime-time television special and described his no-meetings, hands-on management of the building, the country, and the world. It seemed spontaneous and
flexible, a new management style, though some of his own men worried that there
was more style than management. He had called only two cabinet meetings, he told
NBC. "They're a waste of time." He repeated the line when he was asked why there
had been no National Security Council meetings during his first months in office.
"These general meetings are a waste of time," he said. "Formal meetings of the NSC
are not as effective, and it is much more difficult to decide matters involving high
national security if there is a wider group present."

Perhaps. On April 5, 1961, the President's national security adviser, McGeorge
Bundy, sent Kennedy a memo under the title "Crisis Commanders in Washington,"
saying, in effect, that in the most important of ongoing foreign policy crises, no one
was in charge: "Over and over since January 20th we have talked of getting 'task
forces with individual responsible leaders' here in Washington for crisis situations.
At the beginning, we thought we had task forces for Laos, the Congo, and Cuba.
We did get working groups with nobody in particular in charge, but we did not get
clearly focused responsibility. The reason was that the Department of State was not
quite ready . . . these Assistant Secretaries, although men of good will, were not really prepared to take charge of the 'military' and 'intelligence' aspects—the government was in the habit of 'coordination' and out of the habit of the acceptance
of individual executive leadership. More than once the ball has been dropped because no one person felt a continuing clear responsibility."

Two weeks after that, the ball and a lot more were dropped—on Kennedy's
head. After a series of unstructured meetings with Secretary of State Dean Rusk,
Secretary of Defense Robert McNamara, CIA Director Allen Dulles, and pretty
much whoever else happened to be around, the President signed off on a CIA plan
for an exile invasion of Fidel Castro's Cuba; fifteen hundred Cubans were landed at
Castro's favorite fishing spot, the Bay of Pigs. Of course, Kennedy did not know
about Castro's leisure habits, or much of anything else about the plan, because he
never questioned whether or not the CIA knew what it was doing, and no one on

his staff or in his cabinet or on the Joint Chiefs of Staff had any direct responsibility for the project. Kennedy himself never even saw the paperwork; at the end of each meeting he sat silently as the papers were collected by the operation's planner, the CIA's deputy director for operations, Richard Bissell, who took the only copies of the maps and such back to his office at agency headquarters in Langley, Virginia.

After the invasion, a perfect failure, Bundy wrote the President another memo, on May 16, this time dropping any pretense that the Executive problem was in the State Department.

"I hope you'll be in a good mood when you read this . . . ," he began. "Cuba was a bad mistake. But it was not a disgrace and there were reasons for it. . . . We do have a problem of management; centrally it is a problem of your use of time. What follows represents, I think, a fair consensus of what a good many people would tell you . . . We can't get you to sit still. . . ."

"The National Security Council, for example, really cannot work for you unless you authorize work schedules that do not get upset from day to day. Calling three meetings in five days is foolish—and putting them off for six weeks at a time is just as bad.

"Truman and Eisenhower did their daily dozens in foreign affairs the first thing in the morning, and a couple of weeks ago you asked me to begin to meet you on this basis. I have succeeded in catching you on three mornings, for a total of about 8 minutes, and I conclude that this is not really how you like to begin the day. Moreover, 6 of the 8 minutes were given not to what I had for you but what you had for me."

Bundy, the former dean of Harvard College, went on like that, scolding America's most important student: "Right now it is so hard to get to you with anything not urgent and immediate that about half of the papers and reports you personally ask for are never shown to you because by the time you are available you have clearly lost interest in them. . . . Above all you are entitled to feel confident that (a) there is no part of government on the national security area that is not watched over closely by someone from your own staff, and (b) there is no major problem of policy that is not out where you can see it and give a proper stimulus to those who should be attacking it."

Within a month, on June 13, the President heard the same thing again, this time in the top-secret 180-page Bay of Pigs investigation by retired Army Chief of Staff Maxwell Taylor and Attorney General Robert Kennedy. There was a single copy of the report; to prevent leaks, it could be read only in a locked room with an observer present to be sure no notes were taken. The document concluded with a dry summary of Kennedy's management: "The executive branch of the government was not organizationally prepared to cope with this kind of paramilitary operation. . . . There was no single authority short of the President capable of coordinating the actions of the CIA, State, Defense, and USIA. Top level direction was given through ad hoc meetings of senior officials without consideration of operational plans in writing and with no arrangement for recording conclusions and decisions reached."

In receiving the Bundy and Taylor memorandums, President Kennedy had also been unpleasantly surprised at home. He found out there was a revolution in his country by reading the *New York Times* on May 15, 1961. That Monday morning, under the headline, BI-RACIAL BUSES ATTACKED, RIDERS BEATEN IN ALABAMA, the paper published an Associated Press story that began: "Anniston, Ala.—A group of white persons today ambushed two buses carrying Negroes and whites who were seeking to knock down bus station racial barriers. A little later, sixty miles to the west, one of the buses ran into another angry crowd of white men at a Birmingham bus station. The interracial group took a brief but bloody beating, and fled. . . . They call themselves 'Freedom Riders.'"

The organizer of the rides, James Farmer, director of the Congress of Racial Equality, and black journalists, too, had tried without success to alert the President or Attorney General Robert Kennedy before the rides set off from the Greyhound and Trailways bus terminals a few blocks from the White House. But apparently their announcements and notes were lost somewhere in the channels President Kennedy deliberately broke up when he took office. Ignorance of the rides, however, was not as personally embarrassing as his first meeting with British Prime Minister Harold Macmillan to discuss Britain's "Grand Design" for Europe. The prime minister hoped to develop a compromise power-sharing scheme on European security matters that was halfway between the United States' inclination to make unilateral decisions and French President Charles de Gaulle's insistence that France, Britain, and the United States must be equal partners in decision making. Kennedy had not read Macmillan's ideas; in fact, he had lost the papers. It took several hours to find them—in the bedroom of Kennedy's two-year-old daughter, Caroline.

One of the men in the Kennedy administration with extensive Executive experience, Undersecretary of State Chester Bowles, the former governor of Connecticut and a founder of the advertising agency BBO&O said: "Management in Jack's mind, I think, consists largely of calling Bob on the telephone and saying 'Here are ten things I want to get done. Why don't you go ahead and get them done.'" That judgment was often confirmed by the President himself, expressing his admiration for his brother-manager this way: "With Bobby, I don't have to think about organization. I just show up."

Management, in general, does not greatly interest politicians, but it happened that it was an important part of the two long conversations between Eisenhower and Kennedy during the 1960–61 transition period. As the President-elect began asking questions, Eisenhower quickly realized what was on Kennedy's mind, and he didn't like it. The new man's questions were about the structure of decision making on matters of national security and national defense. The senator obviously thought the Eisenhower White House structure was too complicated, too bureaucratic, too formal, and too slow—with too many decisions outside the President's reach and control. Ike thought Kennedy naïve, but he was not about to say that, so he began a long explanation of how and why he had built up what amounted to a military staff apparatus to methodically collect and feed information to the Commander in Chief and, at the same time, had created separate operations to coordinate and implement his decision making.

"No easy matters will come to you as President. If they are easy, they will be settled at a lower level," Eisenhower said. And Kennedy did not much like that idea.

"I did urge him to avoid any reorganization until he himself could become well acquainted with the problem," the President dictated to his secretary after Kennedy left. But it was obvious that the President-elect was not much interested in his organization charts—or organization itself, for that matter. Ike's bent toward order was exactly the kind of passive thinking Kennedy wanted to sweep away. He had no use for the process of note making, minutes taking, and little boxes on charts showing the Planning Board and the Operations Coordinating Board. He did not think of himself as being on top of a chart; rather he wanted to be in the center, the center of all the action.

Ike, dictating for his journal, worried that the new man did not understand the complexity of the job, that Kennedy thought the Presidency was a personal thing, a question of getting the right people in a few jobs here and there.

That was just about right. Kennedy did believe that problem solving meant getting the right man into the right place at the right time—and, if things went wrong, putting in someone else. And he saw himself as the right man. Lines of power, he said, were supposed to be like the spokes of a wheel, all coming from him, all going to him. "It was instinctive at first," he said. "I had different identities, and this was a useful way of expressing each without compromising the others."

He preferred to work one-on-one—hallway meetings and telephone calls to desk officers in the State Department or to surprised professors and reporters. Anyone who had just been to countries in crisis or had written something the President had heard about was liable to be awakened by a Boston-accented voice saying: "This is Jack Kennedy. Can you tell me . . . ?" Some of them hung up on him, thinking it was a joke.

He wanted the action to be wherever he was: follow the body. At the far end-points of American policy, his policy, there would be young men like his own staff, hard-thinking patriots in chinos and work shirts, or Army berets or even native dress, ready to turn a crowd of demonstrating students or neutralize a Communist plot.

He was determined not to be trapped by establishment procedures. His bent was toward chaos; he was comfortable with a certain disorder around him; it kept his people off-balance, made them try a little harder. In dismantling Eisenhower's military-style national security bureaucracy, beginning with the Operations Control Board, a small unit responsible for systematically channeling foreign policy information to and from the President, Kennedy said, in an Executive Order: "We plan to work by maintaining direct communication with the responsible agencies, so that everyone will know what I have decided, while I in turn keep fully informed of the actions taken to carry out decisions." His use of the National Security Council itself was casual enough that when Gen. Earle Wheeler, the chief staff officer of the Joint Chiefs of Staff, was handed National Security Action Memorandum 22—the twenty-second formal national security order approved by the President—he realized he had never seen numbers 5 to 21. "The lines of control have been cut," Wheeler told his staff. "But no others have been established."

That cost Kennedy. The next time he saw Eisenhower was after the Bay of Pigs, at Camp David, named for Ike's grandson. It was the first time Kennedy had ever been to the place. The meeting of the two Presidents was part of a show of national unity after the capture of almost the entire exile brigade by Castro's waiting troops. Eisenhower supported Kennedy totally in public, but in private, as they walked the wooded paths of the Maryland mountain retreat, Ike gave Kennedy a tongue-lashing, saying, "Mr. President, before you approved this plan, did you have everybody in front of you debating the thing so you got the pros and cons yourself and then made the decision, or did you see these people one at a time?"

"Well, I didn't have a meeting. . . . I just approved a plan that had been recommended by the CIA and by the Joint Chiefs of Staff. I just took their advice."

"Mr. President, were there any changes in the plan . . . ?"

"Yes, there were. . . . We did want to call off one bombing sally."

"Why was that called off? Why did they change plans after the troops were already at sea?"

"Well," Kennedy said, "we felt it necessary that we keep our hand concealed in this affair; we thought that if it was learned that we were really doing this and not these rebels themselves, the Soviets would be very apt to cause trouble in Berlin."

"Mr. President, how could you expect the world to believe that we had nothing to do with it? Where did these people get the ships to go from Central America to Cuba? Where did they get the weapons? Where did they get all the communications and all the other things that they would need? How could you possibly have kept from the world that the United States had been involved?"

"No one knows how tough this job is until after he has been in it a few months," Kennedy said kind of ruefully.

"Mr. President," Eisenhower said, "If you will forgive me, I think I mentioned that to you three months ago."

"I certainly have learned a lot since," Kennedy said.

Certainly he did learn. A lot of that was just figuring out the right questions, as he showed only a week after the Bay of Pigs in questioning Gen. Lyman Lemnitzer, the chairman of the Joint Chiefs, about recommendations to airlift U.S. troops into Laos that spring of 1961.

"How will they get in there?"

"They can land at two airports," said the general. The places were named Savanaket and Peske. "How many can land at those airports?" Kennedy continued.

"If you have perfect conditions, you can land a thousand a day."

"How many Communist troops are in the area?"

"We would guess three thousand."

"How long will it take them to bring up four?"

"They can bring up five or six thousand, eight thousand, in four more days."

"What's going to happen," snapped the President, "if on the third day you've landed three thousand—and then they bomb the airport? And then they bring up five or six thousand more men! What's going to happen? Or if you land two thousand—and then they bomb the airport?"

Some histories of the Kennedy Presidency emphasize that kind of evidence of growth in the job, focusing on American domination of the Soviets during the Cuban missile crisis of 1962 and the Limited Nuclear Test Ban Treaty negotiated in the summer of 1963. But without gainsaying those achievements, it seems clear that after two years in office Kennedy was moving the United States into combat in

South Vietnam in a slow and drawn-out replay of the Bay of Pigs invasion. He still seemed unable to sort through bad information. He focused on political appearance rather than military reality and continued to think the key to the problem was finding the right man—which meant eliminating the wrong one, Castro or Diem.

"Looking under bushes for the Vietnamese George Washington" was the way Gen. Maxwell Taylor privately described the process after Kennedy appointed him to succeed Lemnitzer as chairman of the Joint Chiefs. Twice Kennedy dispatched Taylor to South Vietnam, in October of 1961 and in again in September of 1963—two of more than a dozen fact-finding missions the President sent there, searching almost desperately for good information.

Taylor was one of the very few military men Kennedy trusted. Another was a Marine general, Victor Krulak. The President and that general had known each other since 1943, when they were a Navy lieutenant (junior grade) and a Marine lieutenant colonel. Kennedy's boat, *PT 109,* had rescued Marines under Krulak's command in the South Pacific, and Krulak had promised him a bottle of Three Feathers whiskey when they got home. He delivered it to the White House eighteen years later, as an inaugural gift. President Kennedy appointed Krulak as the Joint Chiefs' director of counter-insurgency, a job created by Kennedy in his devotion to the ideas presented by Eugene Burdick and William Lederer in their best-selling and extraordinarily influential novel *The Ugly American.*

The book, by Burdick, a political science professor, and Lederer, a captain in the U.S. Navy, sold more than five million copies during the 1960 presidential campaign, more than a few of them to Sen. John F. Kennedy. . . .

Krulak traveled to South Vietnam with a State Department officer named Joseph Mendenhall, whom Undersecretary of State Averill Harriman slipped aboard the plane just before it took off from Andrews Air Force Base near Washington. "The Crocodile," as Harriman was called because of his infighting skills, wanted to protect his own political view that Diem had to be removed against the Pentagon's concentration on military matters.

Krulak and Mendenhall reported back to Kennedy on September 10, 1963. Predictably the general said: "The shooting war is still going ahead at an impressive pace. . . . There is a lot of war left to fight. Particularly in the Delta, where the Viet Cong remains strong. . . . The Viet Cong war will be won if the current U.S. military and sociological programs are pursued, irrespective of the grave defects of the ruling regime."

Mandenhall disagreed: "I was struck be the fear that pervades Saigon, Hue and Da Nang. These cities have been living under a reign of terror. . . ." He said the war could not be won without changing the regime.

The President looked fron Krulak to Mendenhall and back, finally asking, "Did you two gentlemen visit the same country?"

The decision-making in Kennedy's White House did, at times, lend itself to parody. . . .

Sometimes it seems this was the model for Bill Clinton, who met President Kennedy that month in the Rose Garden, when he was a seventeen-year-old delegate from Arkansas to Boys Nation, an American Legion leadership program. Thirty years later President Clinton met "Brute" Krulak—the nickname is a compli-

A young Bill Clinton greets President John F. Kennedy in Washington in 1963.

ment in his business—at a televised town meeting in San Diego. Krulak, who went on to become the president of the Copley newspaper chain, beat up on Clinton for military spending cuts, saying they would eventually produce "terrible fields of white crosses."

President Clinton took that, not having the vaguest idea who Krulak was. The same thing might have happened to Kennedy, because of another trait they shared: a reluctance to prepare and an absolute unwillingness to rehearse. They were both secure—or deluded—in the belief that they would prevail in any one-on-one encounter. That politicians' arrogance got Clinton, unprepared, into a room of hostile conservatives in San Diego led by Krulak—all on national television.

In his time it got President Kennedy into the bathroom. The first Medal of Freedom he awarded was to Paul-Henri Spaak, the retiring secretary-general of the North Atlantic Treaty Organization, in February of 1961. Kennedy, impatient as always, quickly read the proclamation, presented the medal, circled the Oval Office, shaking hands with various ambassadors, and stepped out the door. He had no idea where he was, saw another door, and went in—to the bathroom. He stayed there in solitary dignity until Spaak and the others left his office.

Lyndon B. Johnson and Vietnam

Larry L. King

President Lyndon B. Johnson was the kind of politician people tend to tell tall stories about. He always had a strong—some would say an overpowering—personality. When he was placed by fate and an assassin's bullet in a position of enormous power, he came to project a larger-than-life image, to seem a kind of elemental, irresistible force that no mere mortal could successfully resist. He swiftly pushed through economic and social reforms that had appeared to paralyze his predecessor in the White House, the popular John F. Kennedy.

Although he could certainly be devious, Johnson was not a very subtle person and when, during the Vietnam war, he decided that the national honor and the safety of what he called the free world required that the United States pursue the conflict to victory, he devoted all his energies to the task. Of course he failed. Why he failed and how he reacted to failure is the subject of this article by Larry L. King. The account is one of the most graphic and tragic portraits we have of Johnson, or for that matter of any president. King is the author of a number of novels and also of *Confessions of a White Racist*. He was active in the 1960 and 1964 presidential campaigns.

He was an old-fashioned man by the purest definition. Forget that he was enamored of twentieth-century artifacts—the telephone, television, supersonic airplanes, spacecraft—to which he adapted with a child's wondering glee. His values were the relics of an earlier time; he had been shaped by an America both rawer and more confident than it later would become; his generation may have been the last to believe that for every problem there existed a workable solution: that the ultimate answer, as in old-time mathematics texts, always reposed in the back of the book. He bought the prevailing American myths without closely inspecting the merchandise for rips or snares. He often said that Americans inherently were "can-do" people capable of accomplishing anything they willed; it was part of his creed that Americans were God's chosen: why otherwise would they have become the richest, the strongest, the freest people in the history of man? His was a God, perhaps, who was a first cousin to Darwin: Lyndon B. Johnson believed in survival of the fittest, that the strong would conquer the weak, that almost always the big 'uns ate the little 'uns.

There was a certain pragmatism in his beliefs, a touch of fatalism, even a measure of common sense. Yet, too, he could be wildly romantic. Johnson truly believed that any boy could rise to become President, though only thirty-five had. Hadn't he—a shirt-tailed kid from the dusty hard-scrabble precincts of the Texas outback—walked with kings and pharaohs while reigning over what he called, without blushing, the Free World? In his last days, though bitter and withering in retirement at his rural Elba, he astonished and puzzled a young black teen-ager by waving his arms in windmill motions and telling the youngster, during a random encounter, "Well, maybe someday all of us will be visiting *your* house in Waco, because you'll be President and your home will be a national museum just as mine is. It'll take a while, but it'll happen, you'll see. . . ." Then he turned to the black teenager's startled mother: "Now, you better get that home of yours cleaned up spick-and-span. There'll be hundreds of thousands coming through it, you know, wanting to see the bedroom and the kitchen and the living room. Now, I hope you get that dust rag of yours out the minute you get home."

Doris Kearns, the Harvard professor and latter-day L.B.J. confidante, who witnessed the performance, thought it to be a mock show: "almost a vaudeville act." Dr. Johnson peddling the same old snake oil. Perhaps. Whatever his motives that day, Lyndon Johnson chose his sermon from that text he most fervently believed throughout a lifetime; his catechism spoke to his heart of American opportunity, American responsibility, American good intentions, American superiority, American destiny, American infallibility. Despite a sly personal cynicism—a suspicion of others, the keen, cold eye of a man determined not to be victimized at the gaming tables—he was, in his institutional instincts, something of a Pollyanna. There *was* such a thing as a free lunch; there *was* a Santa Claus; there *was*, somewhere, a Good Fairy, and probably it was made up of the component parts of Franklin Roosevelt, Saint Francis, and Uncle Sam.

These thoroughly American traits—as L.B.J. saw them—comprised the foundation stone upon which he built his dream castle; he found it impossible to abandon them even as the sands shifted and bogged him in the quagmire of Vietnam. If America was so wonderful (and it *was;* he had the evidence of himself to prove it), then he had the obligation to export its goodness and greatness to the less fortunate. This he would accomplish at any cost, even if forced to "nail the coonskin to the wall." For if Lyndon B. Johnson believed in God and greatness and goodness, he also believed in guts and gunpowder.

All the history he had read, and all he had personally witnessed, convinced him that the United States of America—if determined enough, if productive enough, if patriotic enough—simply could not lose a war. As a boy his favorite stories had been of the minutemen at Lexington and Concord, of the heroic defenders of the Alamo, of rugged frontiersmen who'd at once tamed the wild land and marauding Indians. He had a special affinity for a schoolboy poem proclaiming that the most beautiful sight his eyes had beheld was "the flag of my country in a foreign land." He so admired war heroes that he claimed to have been fired on "by a Japanese ace," though no evidence supported it; he invented an ancestor he carelessly claimed had been martyred at the Alamo; at the Democratic National Convention in 1956 he had cast his state's delegate votes for the Vice-Presidential ambitions of young John F. Kennedy, "that fighting sailor who bears the scars of battle."

On a slow Saturday afternoon in the 1950s, expansive and garrulous in his posh Senate majority-leader quarters, Johnson discoursed to a half dozen young Texas staffers in the patois of their shared native place. Why—he said—you take that ragtag bunch at Valley Forge, who'd have given them a cut dog's chance? There they were, barefoot in the snow and their asses hanging out, nothing to eat but moss and dead leaves and snakes, not half enough bullets for their guns, and facing the soldiers of the most powerful king of his time. Yet they sucked it up, wouldn't quit, lived to fight another day—and won. Or you take the Civil War, now: it had been so exceptionally bloody because you had aroused Americans fighting on *both* sides; it had been something like rock against rock, or like two mean ol' pit bull-dogs going at each other with neither of them willing to be chewed up and both of 'em thinking only of taking hunks out of the other. He again invoked the Alamo: a mere handful of freedom-loving men standing against the Mexican hordes, knowing they faced certain death, but they'd carved their names in history for all time, and before they got through with ol' General Santa Anna he thought he'd stumbled into a nest of stinging scorpions or bumble-bees.

Fifteen years later Johnson would show irritation when Clark Clifford suggested that victory in Vietnam might require a sustaining commitment of twenty to thirty years. No—L.B.J. said—no, no, the thing to do was get in and out quickly, pour everything you had into the fight, land the knockout blow: hell, the North Vietnamese *had* to see the futility of facing all that American muscle. If you really poured it on 'em, you could clean up that mess within six months. We had the troops, the firepower, the bombs, the sophisticated weaponry, the oil—everything we needed to win. Did we have the resolve? Well, the Texas Rangers had a saying that you couldn't stop a man who just kept on a-coming. And that's what we'd do in Vietnam, Clark, just keep on a-coming. . . .

Always he talked of the necessity to be strong; he invoked his father's standing up to the Ku Klux Klan in the 1920s, Teddy Roosevelt's carrying that big stick, F.D.R's mobilizing the country to beat Hitler and Tojo. He liked ol' Harry Truman—tough little bastard and his own man—but, listen, Harry and Dean Acheson had lost control when they failed to properly prosecute the Korean War. They lost the public's respect, lost control of General MacArthur, lost the backing of Congress, lost the *war* or the next thing to it. Next thing you know, they got blamed for losing China and then there was Joe McCarthy accusing them of being soft on communism and everybody believed it. Well, it wouldn't happen to him, nosir. *He* hadn't started the Vietnam war—Jack Kennedy had made the first commitment of out-and-out combat troops, don't forget—but *he* wouldn't bug out no matter how much the Nervous Nellies brayed. Kennedy had proved during the Cuban missile crisis that if you stood firm then the Reds would back down. They were playground bullies, and he didn't intend to be pushed around any more than Jack Kennedy had. When a bully ragged you, you didn't go whining to the teacher but gave him some of his own medicine.

Only later, in exile, when he spoke with unusual candor of his darker parts, did it become clear how obsessed with failure Lyndon Johnson always had been. As a preschool youngster he walked a country lane to visit a grandfather, his head stuffed with answers he knew would be required ("How many head of cattle you got, Lyndon? How much do they eat? How many head can you graze to the acre?") and fearing he might forget them. If he forgot them, he got no bright-red apple but received, instead, a stern and disapproving gaze. L.B.J.'s mother, who smothered him with affection and praise should he perform to her pleasure, refused to acknowledge his presence should he somehow displease or disappoint her. His father accused him of being a sleepyhead, a slow starter, and sometimes said every boy in town had a two-hour head start on him. Had we known these things from scratch, we might not have wondered why Lyndon Johnson seemed so blind for so long to the Asian realities. His personal history simply permitted him no retreats or failures in testings.

From childhood L.B.J. experienced bad dreams. As with much else, they would stay with him to the grave. His nightmares were of being paralyzed and unable to act, of being chained inside a cage or to his desk, of being pursued by hostile forces. These and other disturbing dreams haunted his White House years; he could see himself stricken and ill on a cot, unable even to speak—like Woodrow Wilson—while, in an adjoining room, his trusted aides squabbled and quarreled in dividing his power. He translated the dreams to mean that should he for a moment show weakness, be indecisive, then history might judge him as the first American President who had failed to stand up and be counted.

These deep-rooted insecurities prompted Lyndon Johnson always to assert himself, to abuse staff members simply to prove that he held the upper hand, to test his power in small or mean ways. Sometimes, in sending Vice President Hubert Humphrey off on missions or errands with exhortations to "get going," he literally kicked him in the shins. "Hard," Humphrey later recalled, pulling up his trouser leg to exhibit the scars to columnist Robert Allen. Especially when drinking did he swagger and strut. Riding high as Senate majority leader, Johnson one night after a Texas State Society function, at the National Press Club in Washington—in the spring of 1958—repaired to a nearby bar with Texas Congressmen Homer Thornberry and Jack Brooks. "I'm a powerful sumbitch, you know that?" he repeatedly said. "You boys realize how goddamn *powerful* I am?" Yes, Lyndon, his companions uneasily chorused. Johnson pounded the table as if attempting to crack stout oak: "Do you know Ike couldn't pass the Lord's Prayer in Congress without me? You understand that? Hah?" Yes, Lyndon. "Hah? Do you? Hah?" An observer thought he never had seen a man more desperate for affirmations of himself.

Johnson always was an enthusiastic Cold Warrior. He was not made uncomfortable by John Foster Dulles' brinkmanship rhetoric about "rolling back" communism or of "unleashing" Chiang Kai-shek to free the Chinese mainland. He was, indeed, one of the original soldiers of the Cold War, a volunteer rather than a draftee, just as he had been the first member of Congress to rush to the recruiting station following Pearl Harbor. Immediately after World War II he so bedeviled House Speaker Sam Rayburn about his fears of America dismantling its military machine that Rayburn appointed him to the postwar Military Policy Committee and to the Joint Committee on Atomic Energy. L.B.J. early had a preference for military assignments in Congress; he successfully campaigned for a seat on the House Naval Affairs Committee in the 1930s and, a decade later, the Senate Armed Services Committee. He eventually chaired the Senate Preparedness Committee and the Senate Space Committee. Perhaps others saw the exploration of outer space in scientific or peaceful terms. Johnson, however, told Senate Democrats that outer space offered "the ultimate position from which total control of the earth may be exercised. Whoever gains that ultimate position gains control, total control, over the earth."

Lyndon Johnson was a nagger, a complainer, a man not always patient with those of lesser gifts or with those who somehow inconvenienced him in the moment. Sometimes he complained that the generals knew nothing but "spend and bomb"; almost always, however, he went along with bigger military spending and, in most cases, with more bombing or whatever other military action the brass proposed. This was his consistent record in Congress, and he generally affirmed it as President.

On November 12, 1951, Senator Johnson rattled his saber at the Russians:

> We are tired of fighting your stooges. We will no longer sacrifice our young men on the altar of your conspiracies. The next aggression will be the last. . . . We will strike back, not just at your satellites, but at you. We will strike back with all the dreaded might that is within our control, and it will be a crushing blow.

Even allowing for those rhetorical excesses peculiar to senatorial oratory, those were not the words of a man preoccupied with the doctrine of peaceful coexistence. Nor were they inconsistent with Johnson's mind-set when he made a public demand—at the outbreak of the Korean War, in June, 1950—that President Truman order an all-out mobilization of all military reserve troops, national guard units, draftees, and even civilian manpower and industry. In a Senate debate shortly thereafter Senator Johnson scolded colleagues questioning the Pentagon's request for new and supplementary emergency billions: "Is this the hour of our nation's twilight, the last fading hour of light before an endless night shall envelop us and all the Western world?"

His ties with Texas—with its indigenous xenophobic instincts and general proclivities toward a raw yahooism—haunted him and, in a sense, may have made him a prisoner of grim political realities during the witch-hunting McCarthy era. "I'm damn tired," he said, "of being called a Dixiecrat in Washington and a Communist in Texas"; it perfectly summed up those schizophrenic divisions uneasily compartmentalizing his national political life and the more restrictive parochial role dictated by conditions back home. He lived daily with a damned-if-I-do-and-damned-if-I-don't situation. Texas was a particularly happy hunting ground for Senator Joe McCarthy, whose self-proclaimed anticommunist crusade brought him invitation after invitation to speak there; the Texas legislature, in the 1950s controlled beyond belief by vested interests and showing the ideological instincts of the early primates, whooped through a resolution demanding that Senator McCarthy address it despite the suggestion of State Representative Maury Maverick, Jr., that the resolution be expanded to invite Mickey Mouse. Both Johnson's powerful rightist adversaries and many of his wealthy Texas benefactors were enthusiastic contributors to the McCarthy cause.

Privately Johnson groused to intimates of McCarthy's reckless showboat tactics and particularly of the Texas-directed pressures they brought down on him: why, Joe McCarthy was just a damn drunk, a blowhard, an incompetent who couldn't tie his own shoelaces, probably the biggest joke in the Senate. But—L.B.J. reminded those counseling him to attack McCarthy—people believed him, they were so afraid of the Communists they would believe anything. McCarthy was as strong as horseradish. There would come a time when the hysteria died down, and then McCarthy would be vulnerable; such a fellow was certain to hang himself in time. But right now anybody openly challenging McCarthy would come away with dirty hands and with his heart broken. "Touch pitch," he paraphrased the Bible, "and you'll be defiled." By temperament a man who coveted the limelight and never was bashful about claiming credit for popular actions, Johnson uncharacteristically remained in the background when the U.S. Senate voted to censure McCarthy in late 1954. Though he was instrumental in selecting senators he believed would be effective and creditable members in leading the censure effort, Johnson's fine hand was visible only to insiders.

Johnson believed, however—and probably more deeply than Joe McCarthy—in a worldwide, monolithic Communist conspiracy. He believed it was directed from Moscow and that it was ready to blast America, or subvert it, at the drop of a fur hat. L.B.J. never surrendered that view. In retirement he suggested that the Communists were everywhere, honeycombing the government, and he told surprised visitors that sometimes he hadn't known whether he could trust even his own staff. The Communists (it had been his first thought on hearing the gunshots in Dallas, and he never changed his mind) had killed Jack Kennedy; it had been their influence that turned people against the Vietnam war. One of L.B.J.'s former aides, having been treated to that angry lecture, came away from the Texas ranch with the sad and reluctant conclusion that "the Old Man's absolutely paranoid on the Communist thing."

In May, 1961, President Kennedy dispatched his Vice President to Asia on a "fact-finding" diplomatic trip. Johnson, who believed it his duty to be a team player, to reinforce the prevailing wisdom, bought without qualification the optimistic briefings of military brass with their charts and slides "proving" the inevitable American victory. "I was sent out here to report the *progress* of the war," he told an aide, as if daring anyone to give him anything other than good news. Carried away, he publicly endowed South Vietnam's President Ngo Dinh Diem with the qualities of Winston Churchill, George Washington, Andrew Jackson, and F.D.R. Visiting refugee camps, he grew angry at Communist aggressions "against decent people" and concluded: "There is no alternative to United States leadership in Southeast Asia. . . . We must decide whether to help to the best of our ability or throw in the towel . . . [and] . . . pull back our defenses to San Francisco and a 'Fortress America' concept." He believed then—and always would—in the "domino theory" first stated by President Eisenhower. Even after announcing his abdication, he continued to sing the tired litany: if Vietnam fell then the rest of Asia might go, and then Africa, and then the Philippines. . . .

When Lyndon Johnson suddenly ascended to the Presidency, however, he did not enter the Oval Office eager to immediately take the measure of Ho Chi Minh. Although he told Ambassador Henry Cabot Lodge that "I am not going to be the President who saw Southeast Asia go the way China went," he wanted, for the moment, to keep the war—and, indeed, all foreign entanglements—at arm's length. His preoccupation was with his domestic program; here, he was confident, he knew what he was doing. He would emulate F.D.R. in making people's lives a little brighter. To aides he eagerly talked of building schools and houses, of fighting poverty and attaining full employment, of heating the economy to record prosperity. The honeymoon with Congress—he said—couldn't last; he had seen Congress grow balky and obstinate, take its measure of many Presidents, and he had to assume it would happen again. Then he would lean forward, tapping a forefinger against someone's chest or squeezing a neighboring knee, and say: "I'm like a sweetheart to Congress right now. They love me because I'm new and courting 'em and it's kinda exciting, like that first kiss. But after a while the new will wear off. Then Congress will complain that I don't bring enough roses or candy and will accuse me of seeing other girls." The need was to push forward quickly: pass the Civil Rights bill in the name of the martyred John F. Kennedy, then hit Capitol Hill with a blizzard of domestic proposals and dazzle it before sentiment and enthusiasms cooled. Foreign affairs could wait.

Lyndon Johnson at that point had little experience in foreign affairs. Except for showcase missions accomplished as Vice President, he had not traveled outside the United States save for excursions to Mexico and his brief World War II peregrinations. He probably had little confidence in himself in foreign affairs; neither did he have an excessive interest in the field. "Foreigners are not like the folks I am used to," he sometimes said—and though it passed as a joke, his intimates felt he might be kidding on the level.

Ambassadors waiting to present their credentials to the new President were miffed by repeated delays—and then angrily astonished when L.B.J. received them in groups and clumps, seemingly paying only perfunctory attention, squirming in his chair, scowling or muttering during the traditional ceremonies. He appeared oblivious to their feelings, to their offended senses of dignity. "Why do *I* have to see them?" the President demanded. "They're Dean Rusk's clients, not mine."

Defense Secretary Robert McNamara was selected to focus on Vietnam while L.B.J. concocted his Great Society. McNamara should send South Vietnam equipment and money as needed, a few more men, issue the necessary pronouncements. But don't splash it all over the front pages, don't let it get out of hand, don't give Barry Goldwater Vietnam as an issue for the 1964 campaign. Barry, hell, he was a hip shooter; he'd fight Canada or Mexico—or, at least, give that impression—so the thing to do was sit tight, keep the lid on, keep all Vietnam options open. Above all, "Don't let it turn into a Bay of Pigs." Hunker down; don't gamble.

The trouble—Johnson said to advisers—was that foreign nations didn't understand Americans or the American way; they saw us as "fat and fifty, like the countryclub set"; they didn't think we had the steel in our souls to act when the going got rough. Well, in time they'd find out differently. They'd learn that Lyndon Johnson was not about to abandon what other Presidents had started; he wouldn't permit history to write that he'd been the only American President to cut and run; he wouldn't sponsor any damn Munichs. But for right now—cool it. Put Vietnam on the back burner and let it simmer.

But the Communists—he later would say—wouldn't permit him to cool it. There had been the Gulf of Tonkin attack on the United States destroyer *Maddox*, in August of 19-and-64, and if he hadn't convinced Congress to get on record as backing him up in Vietnam, why, then, the Reds would have interpreted it as a sign of weakness and Barry Goldwater would have cut his heart out. And in February of

19-and-65, don't forget, the Vietcong had made that attack on the American garrison at Pleiku, and how could he be expected to ignore that? There they came, thousands of 'em, barefoot and howling in their black pajamas and throwing homemade bombs: it had been a damned insult, a calculated show of contempt. L.B.J. told the National Security Council: "The worst thing we could do would be to let this [Pleiku] thing go by. It would be a big mistake. It would open the door to a major misunderstanding." Twelve hours later American aircraft—for the first time—bombed in North Vietnam; three weeks later L.B.J. ordered continuing bombing raids in the north to "force the North Vietnamese into negotiations"; only a hundred and twenty days after Pleiku, American forces were involved in a full-scale war and seeking new ways to take the offensive. Eight Americans died at Pleiku. Eight. Eventually fifty thousand plus would die in Asia.

Pleiku was the second major testing of American will within a few months, in L.B.J.'s view. Then in the spring of 1965 rebels had attacked the ruling military junta in the Dominican Republic. Lives and property of U.S. citizens were endangered, as Johnson saw it, but—more—this might be a special tactic by the Reds, a dry run for bigger mischief later on in Vietnam. The world was watching to see how America would react. "It's just like the Alamo," he lectured the National Security Council. "Hell, it's like you were down at that gate, and you were surrounded, and you damn well needed somebody. Well, by God, I'm going to *go*—and I thank the Lord that I've got men who want to go with me, from McNamara right down to the littlest private who's carrying a gun."

Somewhat to his puzzlement, and certainly to his great vexation, Lyndon Johnson would learn that not everybody approved of his rushing the Marines into the Dominican Republic, and within days building up a twenty-one-thousand-man force. Attempting to answer criticism, he would claim thousands of patriots "bleeding in the streets and with their heads cut off," paint a false picture of the United States ambassador cringing under his desk "while bullets whizzed over his head," speak of howling Red hordes descending on American citizens and American holdings, and, generally, open what later became known as the Credibility Gap.

By now he had given up on his original notion of walking easy in Vietnam until he could put the Great Society across. Even before the three major testings of Tonkin Gulf, the Dominican Republic, and Pleiku, he had said—almost idly—"Well, I guess we have to touch up those North Vietnamese a little bit." By December, 1964, he had reversed earlier priorities: "We'll beat the Communists first, then we can look around and maybe give something to the poor." Guns now ranked ahead of butter.

Not that he was happy about it. Though telling Congress "This nation is mighty enough, its society is healthy enough, its people are strong enough to pursue our goals in the rest of the world while still building a Great Society here at home," he knew, in his bones, that this was much too optimistic an outlook. He privately fretted that his domestic program would be victimized. He became touchy, irritable, impatient with those who even timorously questioned America's increasing commitment to the war. Why should *I* be blamed—he snapped—when the Communists are the aggressors, when President Eisenhower committed us in Asia in 1954, when Kennedy beefed up Ike's efforts? If he didn't prosecute the Vietnam war now, then later Congress would sour and want to hang him because he hadn't—and would gut his domestic programs in retaliation. He claimed to have "pounded President Eisenhower's desk" in opposing Ike's sending two hundred Air Force "technicians" to assist the French in Indochina (though those who were present recalled that only Senators Russell of Georgia and Stennis of Mississippi had raised major objections). Well, he'd been unable to stop Ike that time, though he *had* helped persuade him against dropping paratroopers into Dien Bien Phu to aid the doomed French garrison there. And after all that, everybody now called Vietnam Lyndon Johnson's war. It was unfair. "The only difference between the Kennedy assassination and mine is that I am alive and it [is] more torturous."

Very well; if it was his war in the public mind, then he would personally oversee its planning. "Never move up your artillery until you move up your ammunition," he told his generals—a thing he'd said as Senate majority leader when impatient liberals urged him to call for votes on issues he felt not yet ripe. Often he quizzed the military brass, sounding almost like a dove, in a way to resemble courtroom cross-examinations. He forced the admirals and generals to affirm and reaffirm their recommendations as vital to victory. Reading selected transcripts, one might make the judgment that Lyndon Johnson was a most reluctant warrior, one more cautious than not. The evidence of Johnson's deeds, however, suggests that he was being a crafty politician—making a record so that later he couldn't be made the sole scapegoat. He trusted McNamara's computers, perhaps more than he trusted men, and took satisfaction when their print-outs predicted that X amount of bombing would damage the Vietcong by Y, or that X number of troops would be required to capture Z. Planning was the key. You figured what you had to do, you did it, and eventually you'd nail the coonskin to the wall.

He devoutly believed that all problems had solutions: in his lifetime alone we'd beaten the Great Depression, won two world wars, hacked away at racial discrimination, made an industrial giant and world power of a former agrarian society, explored outer space. This belief in available solutions led him, time and again, to change tactics in Vietnam and discover fresh enthusiasm for each new move; he did not pause, apparently, to reflect upon why given tactics, themselves once heralded as practical solutions, had failed and had been abandoned. If counterinsurgency failed, you bombed. If bombing wasn't wholly effective, then you tried the enclave theory. If *that* proved disappointing, you sent your ground troops on search-and-destroy missions. If, somehow, the troops couldn't find the phantom Vietcong in large numbers (and therefore couldn't destroy them), you began pacification programs in the areas you'd newly occupied. And if *this* bogged down, you beefed up your firepower and sent in enough troops to simply outmuscle the rice-paddy ragtags: napalm 'em, bomb 'em, shoot 'em. Sure it would work. It always had. Yes, surely the answer was there somewhere in the back of the book, if only you looked long enough. . . .

He sought, and found, assurances. Maybe he had only a "cow-college" education, perhaps he'd not attended West Point, he might not have excessive experience in foreign affairs. But he was surrounded by good men, what David Halberstam later would label "the best and the brightest," and certainly these were unanimous in their supportive conclusions. "He would look around him," Tom Wicker later said, "and see in Bob McNamara that [the war] was technologically feasible, in McGeorge Bundy that it was intellectually respectable, and in Dean Rusk that it was historically necessary." It was especially easy to trust expertise when the experts in their calculations bolstered your own gut feelings—when their computers and high-minded statements and mighty hardware all boiled down to reinforce your belief in American efficiency, American responsibility, American destiny. If so many good men agreed with him, then what might be wrong with those who didn't?

He considered the sources of dissatisfaction and dissent: the liberals—the "red-hots," he'd often sneeringly called them, the "pepper pots"—who were impractical dreamers, self-winding kamikazes intent on self-destruction. He often quoted an aphorism to put such people in perspective: "Any jackass can kick down a barn, but it takes a carpenter to build one." He fancied, however, that he knew all about these queer fellows. For years, down home, Ronnie Dugger and his *Texas Observer* crowd, in L.B.J.'s opinion, had urged him to put his head in the noose by fighting impossible, profitless fights. They wanted him to take on Joe McCarthy, slap the oil powers down, kick Ike's rear end, tell everybody who wasn't a red-hot to go to hell. Well, he'd learned a long time ago that just because you told a fellow to go to hell, he didn't necessarily have to go. The liberals didn't understand the Communists. Bill Fulbright and his bunch—the striped-pants boys over at the State Department and assorted outside pepper pots—thought you could *trust* the Communists; they made the mistake of believing the Reds would deal with you honorably when—in truth— the Communists didn't respect anything but force. You had to fight fire with fire; let them know who had the biggest guns and the toughest heart.

Where once he had argued the injustice of Vietnam being viewed as "his" war, Lyndon Johnson now brought to it a proprietary attitude. This should have been among the early warnings that L.B.J. would increasingly resist less than victory, no matter his periodic bombing halts or conciliatory statements inviting peace, because once he took a thing personally, his pride and vanity and ego knew no bounds. Always a man to put his brand on everything (he wore monogrammed shirts, boots, cuff links; flew his private L.B.J. flag when in residence at the L.B.J. ranch; saw to it that the names of Lynda Bird Johnson and Luci Baines Johnson and Lady Bird Johnson—not Claudia, as she had been named—had the magic initials L.B.J.), he now personalized and internalized the war. Troops became "my" boys, those were "my" helicopters, it was "my" pilots he prayed might return from their bombing missions as he paid nocturnal calls to the White House situation room to learn the latest from the battlefields; Walt Rostow became "my" intellectual because he was hawkish on L.B.J.'s war. His machismo was mixed up in it now, his manhood. After a cabinet meeting in 1967 several staff aides and at least one cabinet member—Stewart Udall, Secretary of the Interior—remained behind for informal discussions; soon L.B.J. was waving his arms and fulminating about his war. Who the hell was Ho Chi Minh, anyway, that he thought he could push America around? Then the President did an astonishing thing: he unzipped his trousers, dangled a given appendage, and asked his shocked associates: "Has Ho Chi Minh got anything like that?"

By mid-1966 he had cooled toward many of his experts: not because they'd been wrong in their original optimistic calculations so much as that some of them had recanted and now rejected *his* war. This Lyndon Johnson could not forgive:

they'd cut and run on him. Nobody had deserted Roosevelt, he gloomed, when he'd been fighting Hitler. McGeorge Bundy, deserting to head the Ford Foundation, was no longer the brilliant statesman but merely "a smart kid, that's all." Bill Moyers, quitting to become editor of *Newsday,* and once almost a surrogate son to the President, suddenly became "a little puppy I rescued from sacking groceries"— a reference to a part-time job Moyers held while a high-school student. George Ball, too, was leaving? Well, he'd always been a chronic belleracher. When Defense Secretary McNamara doubted too openly (stories of his anguish leaked to the newspapers), he found it difficult to claim the President's time; ultimately he rudely was shuttled to the World Bank. Vice President Hubert Humphrey, privately having second thoughts, was not welcomed back to high councils until he'd muffled his dissent and shamelessly flattered L.B.J. Even then Johnson didn't wholly accept his Vice President; Hubert, he said, wasn't a real man, he cried as easily as a woman, he didn't have the weight. When Lady Bird Johnson voiced doubts about the war, her husband grumbled that *of course* she had doubts; it was *like* a woman to be uncertain. *Has Ho Chi Minh got anything like that?*

Shortly after the Tet offensive began—during which Americans would be shocked by the Vietcong temporarily capturing a wing of the American embassy in Saigon—the President, at his press conference of February 2, 1968, made such patently false statements that even his most loyal friends and supporters were troubled. The sudden Tet offensive had been traumatic, convincing many Americans that our condition was desperate, if not doomed. For years the official line ran that the Vietcong could not hang on: would shrink by the attritions of battle and an ebbing of confidence in a hopeless cause; stories were handed out that captured documents showed the enemy to be of low morale, underfed, ill-armed. The Vietcong could not survive superior American firepower; the kill ratio favored our side by 7-to-1, 8-to-1, more. These and other optimisms were repeated by the President, by General Westmoreland, by this ambassador or that fact-finding team. Now, however, it became apparent that the Vietcong had the capability to challenge even our main lair in Asia—and there to inflict serious damage as well as major embarrassments.

It was a time demanding utmost candor, and L.B.J. blew it. He took the ludicrous position that the Tet offensive (which would be felt for weeks to come) had abysmally failed. Why, we'd known about it all along—had, indeed, been in possession of Hanoi's order of battle. Incredible. To believe the President one had also to believe that American authorities had simply failed to act on this vital intelligence, had wittingly and willingly invited disaster. The President was scoffed at and ridiculed; perhaps the thoughtful got goose bumps in realizing how far Lyndon Johnson now lived from reality. If there was a beginning of the end—of Johnson, of hopes of anything remotely resembling victory, of a general public innocence, of official razzmatazz—then Tet, and that press conference, had to be it.

Even the stubborn President knew it. His Presidency was shot, his party ruined and in tatters; his credibility was gone; he could speak only at military bases, where security guaranteed his safety against the possibility of mobs pursuing him through the streets as he had often dreamed. The nightmare was real now. Street dissidents long had been chanting their cruel "Hey, Hey, L.B.J./How Many Kids Did You Kill

L.B.J. listens to a tape from his son-in-law, Marine Captain Charles Robb, describing action in Vietnam.

Today"; Senator Eugene McCarthy soon would capture almost half the vote in the New Hampshire primary against the unpopular President. There was nothing to do but what he'd always sworn he would not do: quit. On March 31, 1968, at the end of a televised speech ordering the end of attacks on North Vietnam in the hope of getting the enemy to the negotiation table, Johnson startled the nation by announcing: ". . . I do not believe that I should devote an hour or a day of my time to any personal partisan causes or to any duties other than the awesome duties of this office—the Presidency of your country. Accordingly, I shall not seek, and I will not accept, the nomination of my party for another term . . ."

"In the final months of his Presidency," former White House aide Eric Goldman wrote, "Lyndon Johnson kept shifting in mood. At times he was bitter and petulant at his repudiation by the nation; at times philosophical, almost serene, confidently awaiting the verdict of the future." The serenity always was temporary; he grew angry with Hubert Humphrey for attempting to disengage himself from the Johnson war policy and, consequently, refused to make more than a token show of support for him. He saw Richard Nixon win on a pledge of having "a secret plan" to end the war—which, it developed, he did not have.

In his final White House thrashings—and in retirement—Lyndon Johnson complained of unfinished business: he had wanted to complete Vietnam peace talks, free the crew of the *Pueblo,* begin talks with the Russians on halting the arms race, send a man to the moon. But the war—he would say in irritation—the war had ruined all that; the people hadn't rallied around him as they had around F.D.R. and Woodrow Wilson and other wartime Presidents; he had been abandoned—by Congress, by cabinet members, by old friends; no other President had tried so hard or suffered so much. He had a great capacity for self-pity and often indulged it, becoming reclusive and rarely issuing a public statement or making public appearances. Doris Kearns has said that she and others helping L.B.J. write his memoirs, *The Vantage Point,* would draft chapters and lay out the documentation— but even then Lyndon Johnson would say no, no, it wasn't like that, it was like *this;* and he would rattle on, waving his arms and attempting to justify himself, invoking the old absolutes, calling up memories of the Alamo, the Texas Rangers, the myths and the legends. He never seemed to understand where or how he had gone wrong.

Watergate

Walter Karp

In 1984, ten years after the resignation of President Richard M. Nixon, the editors of *American Heritage* asked the journalist Walter Karp and the novelist Vance Bourjaily to look back at the events that followed the "third-rate burglary" that we know of as "Watergate" and to write articles describing and explaining those events. Both produced fascinating accounts. Bourjaily's is primarily personal; Karp's is in the form of a narrative account of events and is better suited to the purposes of this volume. Karp takes a dim view of the courage and moral character not merely of the chief culprits and the other main characters in the drama he describes, but also of most of the members of Congress who, he argues, put off doing what in their hearts they knew they had to do for far too long. Whether or not one agrees with this judgment, Karp's account is both good history and eventually heartening, for it is a tale in which justice, after many trials and tribulations, finally triumphs.

Exactly ten years ago this August, the thirty-seventh President of the United States, facing imminent impeachment, resigned his high office and passed out of our lives. "The system worked," the nation exclaimed, heaving a sigh of relief. What had brought that relief was the happy extinction of the prolonged fear that the "system" might not work at all. But what was it that had inspired such fears? When I asked myself that question recently, I found I could scarcely remember. Although I had followed the Watergate crisis with minute attention, it had grown vague and formless in my mind, like a nightmare recollected in sunshine. It was not until I began working my way through back copies of the *New York Times* that I was able to remember clearly why I used to read my morning paper with forebodings for the country's future.

The Watergate crisis had begun in June 1972 as a "third-rate burglary" of the Democratic National Committee headquarters in Washington's Watergate building complex. By late March 1973 the burglary and subsequent efforts to obstruct its investigation had been laid at the door of the White House. By late June, Americans were asking themselves whether their President had or had not ordered the payment of "hush money" to silence a Watergate burglar. Investigated by a special Senate committee headed by Sam Ervin of North Carolina, the scandal continued to deepen and ramify during the summer of 1973. By March 1974 the third-rate burglary of 1972 had grown into an unprecedented constitutional crisis.

By then it was clear beyond doubt that President Richard M. Nixon stood at the center of a junto of henchmen without parallel in our history. One of Nixon's attorneys general, John Mitchell, was indicted for obstructing justice in Washington and for impeding a Securities and Exchange Commission investigation in New York. Another, Richard Kleindienst, had criminally misled the Senate Judiciary Committee in the President's interest. The acting director of the Federal Bureau of

Investigation, L. Patrick Gray, had burned incriminating White House documents at the behest of a presidential aide. Bob Haldeman, the President's chief of staff, John Ehrlichman, the President's chief domestic adviser, and Charles Colson, the President's special counsel, all had been indicted for obstructing justice in the investigation of the Watergate burglary. John Dean, the President's legal counsel and chief accuser, had already pleaded guilty to the same charge. Dwight Chapin, the President's appointments secretary, faced trial for lying to a grand jury about political sabotage carried out during the 1972 elections. Ehrlichman and two other White House aides were under indictment for conspiring to break into a psychiatrist's office and steal confidential information about one of his former patients, Daniel Ellsberg. By March 1974 some twenty-eight presidential aides or election officials had been indicted for crimes carried out in the President's interest. Never before in American history had a President so signally failed to fulfill his constitutional duty to "take care that the laws be faithfully executed."

It also had been clear for many months that the thirty-seventh President of the United States did not feel bound by his constitutional duties. He insisted that the requirements of national security, as he and he alone saw fit to define it, released him from the most fundamental legal and constitutional constraints. In the name of "national security," the President had created a secret band of private detectives, paid with private funds, to carry out political espionage at the urging of the White House. In the name of "national security," the President had approved the warrantless wiretapping of news reporters. In the name of "national security," he had approved a secret plan for massive, illegal surveillance of American citizens. He had encouraged his aides' efforts to use the Internal Revenue Service to harass political "enemies"—prominent Americans who endangered "national security" by publicly criticizing the President's Vietnam War policies.

The framers of the Constitution had provided one and only one remedy for such lawless abuse of power: impeachment in the House of Representatives and trial in the Senate for "high Crimes and Misdemeanors." There was absolutely no alternative. If Congress had not held President Nixon accountable for lawless conduct of his office, then Congress would have condoned a lawless Presidency. If Congress had not struck from the President's hands the despot's cudgel of "national security," then Congress would have condoned a despotic Presidency.

Looking through the back issues of the *New York Times,* I recollected in a flood of ten-year-old memories what it was that had filled me with such foreboding. It was the reluctance of Congress to act. I felt anew my fury when members of Congress pretended that nobody really cared about Watergate except the "media" and the "Nixon-haters." The real folks "back home," they said, cared only about inflation and the gasoline shortage. I remembered the exasperating actions of leading Democrats, such as a certain Senate leader who went around telling the country that President Nixon could not be impeached because in America a person was presumed innocent until proven guilty. Surely the senator knew that impeachment was not a verdict of guilt but a formal accusation made in the House leading to trial in the Senate. Why was he muddying the waters, I wondered, if not to protect the President?

It had taken one of the most outrageous episodes in the history of the Presidency to compel Congress to make even a pretense of action.

Back on July 16, 1973, a former White House aide named Alexander Butterfield had told the Ervin committee that President Nixon secretly tape-recorded his most intimate political conversations. On two solemn occasions that spring the President had sworn to the American people that he knew nothing of the Watergate cover-up until his counsel John Dean had told him about it on March 21, 1973. From that day forward, Nixon had said, "I began intensive new inquiries into this whole matter." Now we learned that the President had kept evidence secret that would exonerate him completely—if he were telling the truth. Worse yet, he wanted it kept secret. Before Butterfield had revealed the existence of the tapes, the President had grandly announced that "executive privilege will not be invoked as to any testimony [by my aides] concerning possible criminal conduct, in the matters under investigation. I want the public to learn the truth about Watergate. . . ." After the existence of the tapes was revealed, however, the President showed the most ferocious resistance to disclosing the "truth about Watergate." He now claimed that executive privilege—hitherto a somewhat shadowy presidential prerogative—gave a President "absolute power" to withhold any taped conversation he chose, even those urgently needed in the ongoing criminal investigation then being conducted by a special Watergate prosecutor. Nixon even claimed, through his lawyers, that the judicial branch of the federal government was "absolutely without power to reweigh that choice or to make a different resolution of it."

In the U.S. Court of Appeals the special prosecutor, a Harvard Law School professor named Archibald Cox, called the President's claim "intolerable." Millions of Americans found it infuriating. The court found it groundless. On October 12, 1973, it ordered the President to surrender nine taped conversations that Cox had been fighting to obtain for nearly three months.

Determined to evade the court order, the President on October 19 announced that he had devised a "compromise." Instead of handing over the recorded conversations to the court, he would submit only edited summaries. To verify their truthfulness, the President would allow Sen. John Stennis of Mississippi to listen to the tapes. As an independent verifier, the elderly senator was distinguished by his devotion to the President's own overblown conception of a "strong" Presidency. When Nixon had ordered the secret bombing of Cambodia, he had vouchsafed the fact to Senator Stennis, who thought that concealing the President's secret war from his fellow senators was a higher duty than preserving the Senate's constitutional role in the formation of United States foreign policy.

On Saturday afternoon, October 20, I and millions of other Americans sat by our television sets while the special prosecutor explained why he could not accept "what seems to me to be non-compliance with the court's order." Then the President flashed the dagger sheathed within his "compromise." At 8:31 P.M. television viewers across the country learned that he had fired the special prosecutor; that attorney general Elliot Richardson had resigned rather than issue that order to Cox; that the deputy attorney general, William Ruckelshaus, also had refused to do so and had been fired for refusing; that it was a third acting attorney general who had finally issued the order. With trembling voices, television newscasters reported that the President had abolished the office of special prosecutor and that the FBI was standing guard over its files. Never before in our history had a President, setting law at defiance, made our government seem so tawdry and gimcrack. "It's like living in a banana republic," a friend of mine remarked.

Now the question before the country was clear. "Whether ours shall continue to be a government of laws and not of men," the ex-special prosecutor said that evening, "is now for the Congress and ultimately the American people to decide."

Within ten days of the "Saturday night massacre," one million letters and telegrams rained down on Congress, almost every one of them demanding the President's impeachment. But congressional leaders dragged their feet. The House Judiciary Committee would begin an inquiry into *whether* to begin an inquiry into possible grounds for recommending impeachment to the House. With the obvious intent, it seemed to me, of waiting until the impeachment fervor had abated, the Democratic-controlled committee would consider whether to consider making a recommendation about making an accusation.

Republicans hoped to avoid upholding the rule of law by persuading the President to resign. This attempt to supply a lawless remedy for lawless power earned Republicans a memorable rebuke from one of the most venerated members of their party: eighty-one-year-old Sen. George Aiken of Vermont. The demand for Nixon's resignation, he said, "suggests that many prominent Americans, who ought to know better, find the task of holding a President accountable as just too difficult. . . . To ask the President now to resign and thus relieve Congress of its clear congressional duty amounts to a declaration of incompetence on the part of Congress."

The system was manifestly not working. But neither was the President's defense. On national television Nixon bitterly assailed the press for its "outrageous, vicious, distorted" reporting, but the popular outrage convinced him, nonetheless, to surrender the nine tapes to the court. Almost at once the White House tapes began their singular career of encompassing the President's ruin. On October 31 the White House disclosed that two of the taped conversations were missing, including one between the President and his campaign manager, John Mitchell, which had taken place the day after Nixon returned from a Florida vacation and three days after the Watergate break-in. Three weeks later the tapes dealt Nixon a more potent blow. There was an eighteen-and-a-half-minute gap, the White House announced, in a taped conversation between the President and Haldeman, which had also taken place the day after he returned from Florida. The White House suggested first that the President's secretary, Rose Mary Woods, had accidentally erased part of the tape while transcribing it. When the loyal Miss Woods could not demonstrate in court how she could have pressed the "erase" button unwittingly for eighteen straight minutes, the White House attributed the gap to "some sinister force." On January 15, 1974, court-appointed experts provided a more humdrum explanation. The gap had been produced by at least five manual erasures. Someone in the White House had deliberately destroyed evidence that might have proved that President Nixon knew of the Watergate cover-up from the start.

At this point the Judiciary Committee was in its third month of considering whether to consider. But by now there was scarcely an American who did not think the President guilty, and on February 6, 1974, the House voted 410 to 4 to authorize the Judiciary Committee to begin investigating possible grounds for impeaching the President of the United States. It had taken ten consecutive months of the most damning revelations of criminal misconduct, a titanic outburst of public indignation, and an unbroken record of presidential deceit, defiance, and evasion in order to compel Congress to take its first real step. That long record of immobility and feigned indifference boded ill for the future.

The White House knew how to exploit congressional reluctance. One tactic involved a highly technical but momentous question: What constituted an impeachable offense? On February 21 the staff of the Judiciary Committee had issued a report. Led by two distinguished attorneys, John Doar, a fifty-two-year-old Wisconsin Independent, and Albert Jenner, a sixty-seven-year-old Chicago Republican, the staff had taken the broad view of impeachment for which Hamilton and Madison had contended in the *Federalist* papers. Despite the constitutional phrase "high Crimes and Misdemeanors," the staff report had argued that an impeachable offense did not have to be a crime. "Some of the most grievous offenses against our Constitutional form of government may not entail violations of the criminal law."

The White House launched a powerful counterattack. At a news conference on February 25, the President contended that only proven criminal misconduct supplied grounds for impeachment. On February 28, the White House drove home his point with a tightly argued legal paper: If a President could be impeached for anything other than a crime of "a very serious nature," it would expose the Presidency to "political impeachments."

The argument was plausible. But if Congress accepted it, the Watergate crisis could only end in disaster. Men of great power do not commit crimes. They procure crimes without having to issue incriminating orders. A word to the servile suffices. "Who will free me from this turbulent priest?" asked Henry II, and four of his barons bashed in the skull of Thomas à Becket. The ease with which the powerful can arrange "deniability," to use the Watergate catchword, was one reason the criminal standard was so dangerous to liberty. Instead of having to take care that the laws be faithfully executed, a President, under that standard, would only have to take care to insulate himself from the criminal activities of his agents. Moreover, the standard could not reach the most dangerous offenses. There is no crime in the statute books called "attempted tyranny."

Yet the White House campaign to narrow the definition of impeachment met with immediate success. In March one of the members of the House of Representatives said that before voting to impeach Nixon, he would "want to know beyond a reasonable doubt that he was directly involved in the commission of a crime." To impeach the President for the grave abuse of his powers, lawmakers said, would be politically impossible. On the Judiciary Committee itself the senior Republican, Edward Hutchinson of Michigan, disavowed the staff's view of impeachment and adopted the President's. Until the final days of the crisis, the criminal definition of impeachment was to hang over the country's fate like the sword of Damocles.

The criminal standard buttressed the President's larger thesis: In defending himself he was fighting to protect the "Presidency" from sinister forces trying to "weaken" it. On March 12 the President's lawyer, James D. St. Clair, sounded this theme when he declared that he did not represent the President "individually" but rather the "office of the Presidency." There was even a National Citizens Committee for Fairness to the Presidency. It was America's global leadership, Nixon insisted, that made a "strong" Presidency so essential. Regardless of the opinion of some members of the Judiciary Committee, Nixon told a joint session of Congress, he would do nothing that "impairs the ability of the Presidents of the future to make the great decisions that are so essential to this nation and the world."

I used to listen to statements such as those with deep exasperation. Here was a President daring to tell Congress, in effect, that a lawless Presidency was necessary to America's safety, while a congressional attempt to reassert the rule of law undermined the nation's security.

Fortunately for constitutional government, however, Nixon's conception of a strong Presidency included one prerogative whose exercise was in itself an impeachable offense. Throughout the month of March the President insisted that the need for "confidentiality" allowed him to withhold forty-two tapes that the Judiciary Committee had asked of him. Nixon was claiming the right to limit the constitutional power of Congress to inquire into his impeachment. This was more than Republicans on the committee could afford to tolerate.

"Ambition must be made to counteract ambition," Madison had written in *The Federalist*. On April 11 the Judiciary Committee voted 33 to 3 to subpoena the forty-two tapes, the first subpoena ever issued to a President by a committee of the House. Ambition, at last, was counteracting ambition. This set the stage for one of the most lurid moments in the entire Watergate crisis.

As the deadline for compliance drew near, tension began mounting in the country. Comply or defy? Which would the President do? Open defiance was plainly impeachable. Frank compliance was presumably ruinous. On Monday, April 29, the President went on television to give the American people his answer. Seated in the Oval Office with the American flag behind him, President Nixon calmly announced that he was going to take over to the Judiciary Committee—and the public—"edited transcripts" of the subpoenaed tapes. These transcripts "will tell it all," said the President; there was nothing more that would need to be known for an impeachment inquiry about his conduct. To sharpen the public impression of presidential candor, the transcripts had been distributed among forty-two thick, loose-leaf binders, which were stacked in two-foot-high piles by the President's desk. As if to warn the public not to trust what the newspapers would say about the transcripts, Nixon accused the media of concocting the Watergate crisis out of "rumor, gossip, innuendo," of creating a "vague, general impression of massive wrongdoing, implicating everybody, gaining credibility by its endless repetition."

The next day's *New York Times* pronounced the President's speech "his most powerful Watergate defense since the scandal broke." By May 1 James Reston, the newspaper's most eminent columnist, thought the President had "probably gained considerable support in the country." For a few days it seemed as though the President had pulled off a coup. Republicans on the Judiciary Committee acted accordingly. On the first of May, 16 of the 17 committee Republicans voted against sending the President a note advising him that self-edited transcripts punctured by

Nixon with the transcripts of the Watergate tapes, in their forty-two loose-leaf binders.

hundreds upon hundreds of suspicious "inaudibles" and "unintelligibles" were not in compliance with the committee's subpoena. The President, it was said, had succeeded in making impeachment look "partisan" and consequently discreditable.

Not even bowdlerized transcripts, however, could nullify the destructive power of those tapes. They revealed a White House steeped in more sordid conniving than Nixon's worst enemies had imagined. They showed a President advising his aides on how to "stonewall" a grand jury without committing perjury: "You can say, 'I don't remember.' You can say, 'I can't recall. I can't give any answer to that, that I can recall.'" They showed a President urging his counsel to make a "complete report" about Watergate but to "make it very incomplete." They showed a President eager for vengeance against ordinary election opponents. "I want the most comprehensive notes on all those who tried to do us in. . . . They are asking for it and they are going to get it." It showed a President discussing how "national security grounds" might be invoked to justify the Ellsberg burglary should the secret ever come out. "I think we could get by on that," replies Nixon's counsel.

On May 7 Pennsylvania's Hugh Scott, Senate Republican Minority Leader, pronounced the revelations in the transcript "disgusting, shabby, immoral performances." Joseph Alsop, who had long been friendly toward the President in his column, compared the atmosphere in the Oval Office to the "back room of a second-rate advertising agency in a suburb of hell." A week after Nixon's seeming coup Republicans were once again vainly urging him to resign. On May 9 the

House Judiciary Committee staff began presenting to the members its massive accumulation of Watergate material. Since the presentation was made behind closed doors, a suspenseful lull fell over the Watergate battleground.

Over the next two months it was obvious that the Judiciary Committee was growing increasingly impatient with the President, who continued to insist that, even in an impeachment proceeding, the "executive must remain the final arbiter of demands on its confidentiality." When Nixon refused to comply in any way with a second committee subpoena, the members voted 28 to 10 to warn him that "your refusals in and of themselves might constitute a ground for impeachment." The "partisanship" of May 1 had faded by May 30.

Undermining these signs of decisiveness was the continued insistence that only direct presidential involvement in a crime would be regarded as an impeachable offense in the House. Congressmen demanded to see the "smoking gun." They wanted to be shown the "hand in the cookie jar." Alexander Hamilton had called impeachment a "National Inquest." Congress seemed bent on restricting it to the purview of a local courthouse. Nobody spoke of the larger issues. As James Reston noted on May 26, one of the most disturbing aspects of Watergate was the silence of the prominent. Where, Reston asked, were the educators, the business leaders, and the elder statesmen to delineate and define the great constitutional issues at stake? When the White House began denouncing the Judiciary Committee as a "lynch mob," virtually nobody rose to the committee's defense.

On July 7 the Sunday edition of the *New York Times* made doleful reading. "The official investigations seem beset by semitropical torpor," the newspaper reported in its weekly news summary. White House attacks on the committee, said the *Times,* were proving effective in the country. In March, 60 percent of those polled by Gallup wanted the President tried in the Senate for his misdeeds. By June the figure had fallen to 50 percent. The movement for impeachment, said the *Times,* was losing its momentum. Nixon, it seemed, had worn out the public capacity for righteous indignation.

Then, on July 19, John Doar, the Democrats' counsel, did what nobody had done before with the enormous, confusing mass of interconnected misdeeds that we labeled "Watergate" for sheer convenience. At a meeting of the Judiciary Committee he compressed the endlessly ramified scandal into a grave and compelling case for impeaching the thirty-seventh President of the United States. He spoke of the President's "enormous crimes." He warned the committee that it dare not look indifferently upon the "terrible deed of subverting the Constitution." He urged the members to consider with favor five broad articles of impeachment, "charges with a grave historic ring," as the *Times* said of them.

In a brief statement, Albert Jenner, the Republicans' counsel, strongly endorsed Doar's recommendations. The Founding Fathers, he reminded committee members, had established a free country and a free Constitution. It was now the committee's momentous duty to determine "whether that country and that Constitution are to be preserved."

How I had yearned for those words during the long, arid months of the "smoking gun" and the "hand in the cookie jar." Members of the committee must have felt the same way, too, for Jenner's words were to leave a profound mark on their final deliberations. That I did not know yet, but what I did know was heartening. The grave maxims of liberty, once invoked, instantly took the measure of meanness and effrontery. When the President's press spokesman, Ron Ziegler, denounced the committee's proceedings as a "kangaroo court," a wave of disgust coursed through Congress. The hour of the Founders had arrived.

The final deliberations of the House Judiciary Committee began on the evening of July 24, when Chairman Peter Rodino gaveled the committee to order before some forty-five million television viewers. The committee made a curious spectacle: thirty-eight strangers strung out on a two-tiered dais, a huge piece of furniture as unfamiliar as the faces of its occupants.

Chairman Rodino made the first opening remarks. His public career had been long, unblemished, and thoroughly undistinguished. Now the representative from Newark, New Jersey, linked hands with the Founding Fathers of our government. "For more than two years, there have been serious allegations, by people of good faith and sound intelligence, that the President, Richard M. Nixon, has committed grave and systematic violations of the Constitution." The framers of our Constitution, said Rodino, had provided an exact measure of a President's responsibilities. It was by the terms of the President's oath of office, prescribed in the Constitution, that the framers intended to hold Presidents "accountable and lawful."

That was to prove the keynote. That evening and over the following days, as each committee member delivered a statement, it became increasingly clear that the broad maxims of constitutional supremacy had taken command of the impeachment inquiry. "We will by this impeachment proceeding be establishing a standard of conduct for the President of the United States which will for all time be a matter of public record," Caldwell Butler, a conservative Virginia Republican, reminded his conservative constituents. "If we fail to impeach . . . we will have left condoned and unpunished an abuse of power totally without justification."

There were still White House loyalists of course; men who kept demanding to see a presidential directive ordering a crime and a documented "tie-in" between Nixon and his henchmen. Set against the great principle of constitutional supremacy, however, this common view was now exposed for what it was: reckless trifling with our ancient liberties. Can the United States permit a President "to escape accountability because he may choose to deal behind closed doors," asked James Mann, a South Carolina conservative. "Can anyone argue," asked George Danielson, a California liberal, "that if a President breaches his oath of office, he should not be removed?" In a voice of unforgettable power and richness, Barbara Jordan, a black legislator from Texas, sounded the grand theme of the committee with particular depth of feeling. Once, she said, the Constitution had excluded people of her race, but that evil had been remedied. "My faith in the Constitution is whole, it is complete, it is total and I am not going to sit here and be an idle spectator to the diminution, the subversion, the destruction of the Constitution."

On July 27 the Judiciary Committee voted 27 to 11 (six Republicans joining all twenty-one Democrats) to impeach Richard Nixon on the grounds that he and his agents had "prevented, obstructed, and impeded the administration of justice" in "violation of his constitutional oath faithfully to execute the office of President of the United States and, to the best of his ability, preserve, protect, and defend the Constitution of the United States, and in violation of his constitutional duty to take care that the laws be faithfully executed."

On July 29 the Judiciary Committee voted 28 to 10 to impeach Richard Nixon for "violating the constitutional rights of citizens, impairing the due and proper administration of justice and the conduct of lawful inquiries, or contravening the laws governing agencies of the executive branch. . . ." Thus, the illegal wiretaps, the sinister White House spies, the attempted use of the IRS to punish political opponents, the abuse of the CIA, and the break-in at Ellsberg's psychiatrist's office—misconduct hitherto deemed too "vague" for impeachment—now became part of a President's impeachable failure to abide by his constitutional oath to carry out his constitutional duty.

Lastly, on July 30 the Judiciary Committee, hoping to protect some future impeachment inquiry from a repetition of Nixon's defiance, voted 21 to 17 to impeach him for refusing to comply with the committee's subpoenas. "This concludes the work of the committee," Rodino announced at eleven o'clock that night. Armed with the wisdom of the Founders and the authority of America's republican principles, the committee had cut through the smoke screens, the lies, and the pettifogging that had muddled the Watergate crisis for so many months. It had subjected an imperious Presidency to the rule of fundamental law. It had demonstrated by resounding majorities that holding a President accountable is neither "liberal" nor "conservative," neither "Democratic" nor "Republican," but something far more basic to the American republic.

For months the forces of evasion had claimed that impeachment would "tear the country apart." But now the country was more united than it had been in years. The impeachment inquiry had sounded the chords of deepest patriotism, and Americans responded, it seemed to me, with quiet pride in their country and themselves. On Capitol Hill, congressional leaders reported that Nixon's impeachment would command three hundred votes at a minimum. The Senate began preparing for the President's trial. Then, as countless wits remarked, a funny thing happened on the way to the forum.

Back on July 24, the day the Judiciary Committee began its televised deliberations, the Supreme Court had ordered the President to surrender sixty-four taped conversations subpoenaed by the Watergate prosecutor. At the time I had regarded the decision chiefly as an auspicious omen for the evening's proceedings. Only Richard Nixon knew that the Court had signed his death warrant. On August 5 the President announced that he was making public three tapes that "may further damage my case." In fact they destroyed what little was left of it. Recorded six days after the Watergate break-in, they showed the President discussing detailed preparations for the cover-up with his chief of staff, Bob Haldeman. They showed the President and his henchman discussing how to use the CIA to block the FBI, which was coming dangerously close to the White House. "You call them in," says the President. "Good deal," says his aide. In short, the three tapes proved that the President had told nothing but lies about Watergate for twenty-six months. Every one of Nixon's ten Judiciary Committee defenders now announced that he favored Nixon's impeachment.

The President still had one last evasion: on the evening of August 8 he appeared on television to make his last important announcement. "I no longer have a strong enough political base in Congress," said Nixon, doing his best to imply that the resolution of a great constitutional crisis was mere maneuvering for political advantage. "Therefore, I shall resign the Presidency effective at noon tomorrow." He admitted to no wrongdoing. If he had made mistakes of judgment, "they were made in what I believed at the time to be in the best interests of the nation."

On the morning of August 9 the first President ever to resign from office boarded Air Force One and left town. The "system" had worked. But in the watches of the night, who has not asked himself now and then: How would it all have turned out had there been no White House tapes?

7 Social Change

On August 28, 1963, over 200,000 African Americans and whites gathered for a day-long rally at the Lincoln Memorial to demand an end to racial discrimination. The highlight of the event was Martin Luther King, Jr.'s inspiring "I Have a Dream" speech.

Levittown: The Buy of the Century

Alexander O. Boulton

When World War II ended, many feared that the sudden disruption of the production of planes, tanks, and other weapons as well as the return of millions of soldiers and sailors in search of civilian employment would create another Great Depression. Instead, after a brief period of adjustment, came a great boom.

Of the many causes of this boom was the revolution in the way houses were constructed. This housing revolution was organized by Alfred and William Levitt in suburban Long Island, east of New York City. As the architectural historian Alexander O. Boulton explains, in a little more than a decade beginning in 1947, the Levitts designed, built, and sold more than 17,000 single-family homes, thus creating a new community—Levittown.

This Sprawlig settlement and others like it built by the Levitts and their competitors changed the face of postwar America and altered the way countless Americans lived and thought. Not all these changes were salutary, as Boulton points out, for the residents of the new communities or even for the Levitts.

Years later, after the fall of his financial empire, William Levitt remembered with some satisfaction the story of a boy in Levittown, Long Island, who finished his prayers with "and God bless Mommy and Daddy and Mr. Levitt." Levitt may well have belonged in this trinity. When he sold his company in 1968, more Americans lived in suburbs than in cities, making this the first suburban nation in history, and his family was largely responsible for that.

Jim and Virginia Tolley met William Levitt in 1949 after waiting in line with three thousand other ex-GIs and their families to buy houses. Bill Levitt pointed to a plot on a map spread out on a long table and advised the Tolleys to buy the house he would build on that spot. Thanks to a large picture window with an eastern exposure, the Tolley's home, Levitt promised, would have sunshine in the coldest months of winter, and its large overhanging eaves would keep them cool in the summer. The Tolleys, who lived in a three-room apartment in Jackson Heights, bought the unbuilt house.

Their story was shared by the more than 3.5 million Americans who had lacked new housing in 1946, housing that had not been built during the Depression and the war. People kept marrying and having babies, but for almost two decades nobody was building new homes.

In providing affordable housing for thousands of Americans after the war, the Levitts were following a basic American success formula; they were at the right place at the right time. Abraham, the patriarch of the family, had been a real estate lawyer in Brooklyn. His two sons, William and Alfred, briefly attended New York University before they began to buy land and design and build houses on a small scale. Alfred was the architect, learning his trade by trial and error, while William was the salesman and became the more public figure. The Second World War transformed their business. Encouraged by wartime contracts for large-scale housing projects, they followed the same mass-production principles that earlier in the century had been developed to build automobiles and that in wartime made ships and airplanes, tanks and guns.

Levittown, Long Island, thirty miles east of New York City, was the first of their postwar projects. Levittown was not the earliest planned in the country, but it was certainly the biggest, and it is still considered the largest housing project ever assembled by a single builder. Between 1947 and 1951 the Levitts built more than seventeen thousand houses, along with seven village greens and shopping centers, fourteen playgrounds, nine swimming pools, two bowling alleys, and a town hall, on land that had once been potato farms. In addition, the company sold land for schools at cost and donated sites for churches and fire stations.

Following the course of other American industries, the Levitts expanded both horizontally and vertically. They purchased timberland in California and a lumber mill, they built a nail factory, they established their own construction supply company to avoid middlemen, and they acquired a fleet of cement trucks and grading equipment. Instead of the product moving along a production line, however, the Levitt house stood stationary while men, materials, and equipment moved around it. At its peak of efficiency the Levitt organization could complete a house every fifteen minutes. Although these were not prefabricated houses all the materials, including the preassembled plumbing systems and precut lumber, were delivered to the site ready for construction. Twenty-seven steps were required to build a Levittown house, and each work crew had its specialized task. One man did nothing but move from house to house bolting washing machines to the floor. William Levitt liked to say his business was the General Motors of the housing industry. Indeed, the automobile seems to have inspired many of Levitt's practices. He even produced new house models each year, and a few Levittown families would actually buy updated versions, just as they bought Detroit's latest products.

The first style, a four-and-a-half room bungalow with steeply pitched roof, offered five slight variations on the placement of doors and windows. The result, according to a 1947 *Architectural Forum*, was "completely conventional, highly standardized, and aptly described in the public's favorite adjective, 'cute.'" A couple of years later the same publication moderated its tone of easy scorn to pronounce the style "a much better-than-average version of the darling of the depression decade—builder's Cape Cod."

Levittown houses were not what the popular 1960s song called "little boxes of ticky-tacky." They were exceptionally well built, the product of some of the most innovative methods and materials in the industry. Taking a page from Frank Lloyd Wright's Usonian houses, Levittown homes stood on concrete slab foundations (they had no basements), in which copper coils provided radiant heating. The Tolleys were among the first customers for the 1949 ranch-style houses that replaced the earlier Cape Cod design. The ranches featured Thermopane glass picture windows, fireplaces opening into two rooms, and carports instead of garages. In addition, they had built-in closets and bookcases and swinging shelf units that acted as

Although later mocked as "little boxes made of ticky-tacky," Levittown houses allowed many to realize the dream of owning their own home.

walls to open up or close the space between kitchen, living room, and entry passage. At twenty-five by thirty-two, the houses were also two feet longer than the earlier models, and they offered as standard features built-in appliances that were only just coming into general use; many houses contained Bendix washing machines and Admiral television sets. The fixed price of $7,990 allowed the Levitts to advertise "the housing deal of the century." It was probably true. Levitt and his sons seemed to be practically giving homes away. Thousands of families bought into new Levittowns in Pennsylvania, New Jersey, Illinois, Michigan, and even Paris and Puerto Rico. The techniques that the Levitts initiated have been copied by home builders throughout the country ever since.

Despite its immediate success, from the earliest days Levittown also stood as a metaphor for all the possible failings of postwar America. The architectural critic Lewis Mumford is said to have declared the tract an "instant slum" when he first saw it, and he certainly was aiming at Levittown when he condemned the postwar American suburb for its "multitude of uniform, unidentifiable houses, lined up inflexibly, at uniform distances, on uniform roads, in a treeless communal waste, inhabited by people of the same class, the same age group, witnessing the same television performances, eating the same prefabricated foods, from the same freezers, conforming in every inward and outward respect to the same common mold." Some of the early rules, requiring the neighbors to mow their lawns every week, forbidding fences, or banning the hanging out of laundry on weekends, did indeed speak of the kind of regimentation Mumford snobbishly abhorred.

Today's visitor to the original Long Island Levittown might be surprised by many of those early criticisms. Now almost fifty years old, most of the houses have been so extensively remodeled that it is often difficult to distinguish the basic Cape Cod or ranch inside its Tudor half-timbering or postmodern, classical eclecticism. Greenery and shade trees have enveloped the bare landscape of the 1950s and Japanese sand gardens, Renaissance topiary, and electrically generated brooks and waterfalls decorate many of Levittown's standard sixty-by-one-hundred-foot plots. The place now seems not the model of mass conformity but a monument to American individualism.

Probably Levittown was never the drab and monotonous place its critics imagined. For many early residents it allowed cultural diversity to flourish. Pre-war inner-city neighborhoods often had ethnic divisions unknown in Levittown. Louis and Marylin Cuviello, who bought a one-bathroom house in 1949 and reared eleven children there, found themselves moving in a wider world than the one they had known in the city. She was a German-American married to an Italian-American, and in their Levittown neighborhood most of the householders were Jewish. During their first years there the Cuviellos took classes in Judaism at the local synagogue, and they often celebrated both Passover and Christmas with their neighbors.

But this American idyll was not for everyone. In 1949, after Gene Burnett, like his fellow veteran Jim Tolley, saw advertisements for Levittown in several New York newspapers, he drove to Long Island with his fiancée. The Levittown salesman refused to give him an application form. "It's not me," the agent said. "The builders have not at this time decided to sell to Negroes." This pattern of racial exclusion was set in 1947, when rental contracts prohibited "the premises to be used or occupied by any person other than a member of the Caucasian race." In 1992 Gene Burnett, now a retired sergeant in the Suffolk County, Long Island, Police Department, told a reporter, "I'll never forget the ride back to East Harlem."

There were other such episodes. Bill Cotter, a retired auto mechanic, and his family sublet a house in Levittown in 1953. When his sublet expired, he was informed that he would not be allowed either to rent or to own a house in Levittown. Despite the protests of friendly neighbors, who launched a petition drive in their behalf, Cotter, his wife, and their five children were forced to vacate. These racial policies persisted. As late as the 1980s real estate agents in the area assured white home buyers that they did not sell to blacks, and in 1990 the census revealed that .03 percent of Levittown's population—127 out of more than 400,000—was African-American.

Levittown has been both celebrated and denounced as the fruit of American laissez-faire capitalism. In fact, it may more accurately be described as the successful result of an alliance between government and private enterprise. Levittown and the rise of American suburbia in general could not have happened without attractive loan packages for home buyers guaranteed by the FHA and the VA. Tax breaks, such as the deductibility of mortgages, encouraged suburbanites, who were also helped by a burst of federally funded highway construction. For almost half a century after World War II, the government has played a major role in helping consumers obtain the products of industry—washing machines, television sets, cars, and, especially, houses. For most of us it's been a great ride.

For Bill Levitt it's been a roller coaster. Things started to go sour for him after the sale of his company to ITT in 1968. He received about fifty million dollars in ITT stock and launched a spending spree that did not stop until the courts stepped in. Levitt's agreement with ITT prohibited him from building projects in the United States for ten years, so he turned elsewhere: housing in Nigeria and Venezuela, oil drilling in Israel, and housing and irrigation in Iran—just before the fall of the shah. He invested in rotary engines, recording companies, and pharmacies. Most of the projects failed. Meanwhile, the ITT stock that was his major capital asset plummeted from $104 to $12 a share in the first four years.

Levitt re-entered the housing market in the United States in 1978 with projects in Orlando and Tampa, Florida. Construction and sales moved quickly at first but soon slowed as contractors began to sue for payment. More than two thousand people, some of them original Levittowners who were now ready to retire, paid deposits for houses in the Florida Levittowns that were never built. Levitt, it was later discovered, had been using the funds from his Florida projects to support his expensive habits. Along the way he had removed more than ten million dollars from a charitable foundation that his family had established. These legal and financial problems have made Bill Levitt a virtual hermit, and today he lives in seclusion not far from the Long Island Levittown that bears his name.

Levittown residents have mixed feelings about their unique heritage. Periodically some of them have attempted to redraw the boundaries of their town line so they could have more elegant addresses. More recently, proud members of the Levittown Historical Society have worked to encourage a new appreciation for their community. They are pushing to establish historic landmark districts while they try to preserve the few houses that have remained relatively unchanged over the years. They are also casting a wide net among their neighbors and former neighbors to gather artifacts and memorabilia for a museum. Recently the Smithsonian Institution announced that it was looking for an original Levittown house to add to its American domestic-life collection. Some African-American groups continue to question the virtue of memorializing a policy of exclusion, but the history-minded residents are pressing ahead, and Eddie Bortell, the Historical Society's vice president, is optimistic. If the work of the historical society has helped bring attention to some of these painful questions, he says, then that in itself is a reward for its efforts.

Desegregating the Schools

Liva Baker

Any list of major events in American history and any account of the shifting course of race relations in the United States is bound to include the Supreme Court case known officially as *Brown* v. *the Board of Education of the City of Topeka*. In 1896, in the case known as *Plessy* v. *Ferguson*, the Court had decided that blacks could be segregated from whites in railroad cars (and by implication in schools) provided that their facilities were equal in quality to those of whites. Over the years this "separate but equal" rule determined how the Court dealt with racial questions. Segregation was broken down to some extent, but only after it had been conclusively demonstrated that the facilities provided for blacks were inferior to those available to whites.

Liva Baker's account of how the Court reached the contrary conclusion in *Brown* v. *Board of Education* begins with an earlier case involving voting (*Smith* v. *Allwright*, 1944). She goes on to show how the members of the Court finally came to conclude that separate was inherently unequal and therefore unconstitutional. Beyond this, she explains how the justices dealt with the socially explosive question, "*how* and *when* was desegregation to be achieved?" Baker is the author of *Felix Frankfurter*, a biography of a key actor in the drama she describes here.

On May 17, 1954, the Supreme Court of the United States destroyed the legal basis for racial segregation in public schools. As it almost had to be in a case that stirred elemental passions, the decision was unanimous. It was also, as Chief Justice Earl Warren had told the other justices ten days earlier it must be, "short, readable by the lay public, non-rhetorical, unemotional, and, above all, non-accusatory."

As the Chief Justice read the historic and potentially divisive opinion the nine justices—Justice Robert H. Jackson had left his hospital bed to be present—sat expressionless and calm, the rare picture of august solidarity belying three years of judicial soul-searching that had led to this moment.

. . . The 1954 desegregation decision, which still is attended by controversy, not only altered the nation's educational patterns but also eroded a way of life and touched people's most sensitive nerves.

Like most cases that come to the Supreme Court, *Brown* v. *Board of Education* was begun in a small way by quite ordinary people. Linda Brown, of Topeka, Kansas, in 1951 a fourth-grade student at a public elementary school for Negroes a long walk and a bus trip from her home, wanted to attend a nearby public elementary school for white children. She was turned away. Her father, the Reverend Oliver Brown, and twelve other parents sued the Topeka Board of Education in the local federal court. A special three-judge panel heard the case and decided that since Negro and white schools in Topeka were substantially equal, the Negroes

Linda Brown of Topeka, Kansas, posed for the camera in 1953. She was turned away from her neighborhood white elementary school, an action that set in motion the events leading to the momentous Brown v. Board of Education *decision.*

were not discriminated against and they could not attend white schools. The Browns and the other parents appealed to the Supreme Court.

Since the Constitutional Convention of 1789 the issue of race had either been compromised or evaded, except during Reconstruction. No branch of government had been willing to confront it squarely, and as Justice Jackson commented during the oral argument of *Brown,* "I suppose that realistically the reason this case is here is that action couldn't be obtained from Congress." Beginning in the late 1930s, the Supreme Court had begun gradually but steadily desegregating American life; restrictive covenants that insured residential segregation, the white primary, segregated education in graduate schools, Jim Crow laws—these and others had collapsed before the Supreme Court. Now the court was forced to face the most explosive issue of all: segregation in public elementary schools.

The justices were not unworldly men, however avidly they sometimes seemed to cultivate an aura of monasticism. Before appointment to the Supreme Court each of them had held some public office. During their deliberations they were grimly aware that their decisions—whether they would hear the case or not hear it; whether, if they did hear it, they declared racial segregation in public schools constitutional or unconstitutional—presaged resentment at best, and probably resistance, from a large segment of the population.

They spent an extraordinary amount of time discussing the problem, examining it from historical, legal, political, and social perspectives. When the Brown case first reached the Supreme Court late in 1951, the justices spent seven months discussing whether they would even hear it. Finally, on June 7, 1952, they agreed that the court could note *probable* jurisdiction. . . .

Once that jurisdictional obstacle was hurdled, however, the court added other school segregation cases and combined them for argument until they had a total of five cases: one from the border state of Kansas, one each from rural Virginia and South Carolina, one from North-oriented Delaware, and one from federally administered District of Columbia. Together these cases gave the Supreme Court a detailed picture of racial segregation by law in American public schools. (At the time, state constitutional provisions and laws or local ordinances required the schools of seventeen southern and border states and the District of Columbia to be segregated; in four other states—Arizona, Kansas, New Mexico, and Wyoming—segregated schools were legally permitted on an optional basis.)

The court that was to hear these five segregation cases argued in December, 1952, was judicially unpredictable. At one end were two liberal activists: justices Hugo L. Black, former United States senator from Alabama, and William O. Douglas, former Yale law professor and chairman of the Securities and Exchange Commission. Appointed to the Supreme Court by President Franklin D. Roosevelt, both were quick to use the power of the court in the name of "social justice."

The rest of the court was enigmatic on the issue of racial segregation in public schools. Indianian Sherman Minton had been an administrative aide to President Franklin D. Roosevelt and a close friend of Harry S Truman, with whom he entered the Senate in 1935. He was appointed to the Supreme Court by President Truman in 1949. Nothing in his writings indicated his position in these segregation cases.

The *New York Times* described Justice Harold H. Burton, on his appointment to the Supreme Court in 1945, as a "liberal of marked independence." As a justice, however, he seemed to lean toward a conservative stance; on civil rights he had voted both ways.

Justice Jackson, Solicitor General and Attorney General under Roosevelt, vigorous prosecutor of war criminals at Nuremberg, assumed the mantle of judicial restraint when he was appointed to the Supreme Court in 1941; he was hesitant to overrule state and federal enactments, believing, like his frequent judicial ally Justice Frankfurter, that undesirability could not be equated with unconstitutionality.

At the Senate hearings on his appointment to the Supreme Court in 1949, Justice Tom C. Clark, a Texas protégé of Senator Tom Connally and Representative Sam Rayburn, had been denounced by Negro groups for failing to protect Negro civil rights when he was Attorney General. Yet it was under Clark's stewardship that the Justice Department began to file amicus curiae (friend of the court) briefs defining the administration's legal positions; these consistently argued against racial discrimination and became a significant part of later civil-rights litigation. Clark had also, as president of the Federal Bar Association, demanded admission of Negro lawyers, and in 1950 had written a concurring opinion when the Supreme Court quashed a criminal indictment of a Negro on the grounds that Negroes had been discriminated against in the selection of grand jury panels. Clark's record looked "liberal" in 1952; however, he had not yet had to face the question whether racial segregation in public schools denied "equal protection of the laws."

Justice Stanley F. Reed came from the border state of Kentucky and had been Solicitor General under Roosevelt, arguing for the validity of NRA, TVA, the Wagner Act, and other of the President's measures. Appointed to the Supreme Court in 1938, he had become somewhat conservative but had also written a vigorous defense of Negro voting rights in 1944. How Reed came to write that 1944 opinion reveals not a little of the political consideration that goes into a major decision of the Supreme Court.

At conference on January 15, 1944, the Supreme Court decided to declare the Texas exclusion of Negroes from primary elections unconstitutional. Felix Frankfurter was assigned to write the opinion. The case was called *Smith* v. *Allwright*.

". . . That afternoon," a Frankfurter memorandum reads, "Bob Jackson came to see me. . . . He thought it was a very great mistake to have me write the *Allwright* opinion. For a good part of the country the subject—Negro disenfranchisement—was in the domain of the irrational and we have to take account of such facts. At best it will be very unpalatable to the South and should not be exacerbated by having the opinion written by a member of the Court who has, from the point of view of Southern prejudice, three disqualifications: 'You are a New Englander, you are a Jew and you are not a Democrat—at least not recognized as such.'" Frankfurter replied that he saw Jackson's point; Jackson was free, Frankfurter said, to suggest to the Chief Justice—Harlan Fiske Stone at that time—that the opinion be reassigned. When Stone later asked Frankfurter to suggest a name, Frankfurter declared that "the job required, of course, delicacy of treatment and absence of a raucous voice and that I thought of the Southerners Reed was the better of the two for the job. He agreed to that. . . ."

Thus, on April 3, 1944, in the case of *Smith* v. *Allwright*, the Texas white primary was invalidated. Justice Reed—Southerner, Protestant, and Democrat—spoke for the majority: "The United States is a constitutional democracy. Its organic law grants to all citizens a right to participate in the choice of elected officials without restriction by any State because of race."

In 1952, in addition to these seven justices, there were two crucial men on the court that was to hear the school segregation cases: Chief Justice Fred M. Vinson and Felix Frankfurter. But Vinson died before the school segregation cases were decided, and so what he would have done can only be a matter of speculation.

He was succeeded by Earl Warren, three-term governor of California and Republican candidate for Vice President in 1948. A hearty, amiable man on the surface, he was expected to be, as one of his biographers put it, "the colorless manager of a team of all-stars." No one, including President Dwight D. Eisenhower, who appointed him, expected a courageous, reforming chief justice. Justice Frankfurter wrote his impressions of Warren to a young English friend at the time of the appointment:

> . . . He has not had an eminent legal career, but he might well have had had he not been deflected from the practice of law into public life. He brings to his work that largeness of experience and breadth of outlook which may well make him a very good Chief Justice provided he has some other qualities which, from what I have seen, I believe he has. First and foremost, complete absorption in the work of the Court is demanded. That is not as easy to attain as you might think, because this is a

very foolish and distracting town. Secondly, he must have great industry because . . . for about nine months of the year it is a steady grind. Further, he must have the capacity to learn, he must be alert to the range and complexities of the problems that come before this Court. . . . One more requisite. . . . Intent, open-minded, patient listening is a surprisingly rare faculty even of judges. The new Chief Justice has it, I believe, to a rare degree.

Warren seemed, like most of the court, judicially unpredictable. He had never been able to live down his major role as California attorney general in sending Japanese and Japanese-Americans in the state to detention camps at the outbreak of World War II. But beyond this questionable moment in his career, there was a bold record as crusading district attorney in Alameda County and a progressive governorship during which Warren battled annually against a hostile legislature for social legislation and reforms.

The other crucial man on the Supreme Court in 1952 was Felix Frankfurter. Appointed to the Supreme Court in 1939 by Roosevelt, Justice Frankfurter had eagerly joined in the decisions invalidating legal segregation prior to the Brown case. He had, however, consistently laid a light restraining hand on his brethren.

He was a sworn enemy of racial discrimination; he had served on the legal committee of the NAACP from 1929 until he was appointed to the Supreme Court (when he scrupulously severed connections with all organizations). He was, however, aware of the potential for divisiveness in racial discrimination cases before the court. He wrote in a note to Justice Wiley B. Rutledge regarding a 1948 case of racial discrimination on an excursion boat: ". . . Considerable practical experience with problems of race relations led me to the conclusion that the ugly practices of racial discrimination should be dealt with by eloquence of action but with austerity of speech. . . ." Likewise, when Chief Justice Vinson's draft opinion in a 1950 case involving segregation in graduate schools was circulated among the justices for suggestions—as is customary on the court—Frankfurter urged restraint in the rhetoric. The opinion, he said, ought to accomplish "the desired result without needlessly stirring the kind of feelings that are felt even by truly liberal and high-minded southerners. . . . One does not have to say everything that is so. . . . The shorter the opinion, the more there is an appearance of unexcitement and inevitability about it, the better. . . ."

The school desegregation decisions of 1952–1955 were broken into two parts. The first was *whether* racial segregation in public schools was constitutional or unconstitutional; inherent in this question was whether it was the business of the court or the business of Congress to deal with the problem. The court struggled nearly a year before making up its mind on that question.

The second part of the decisions was the question of remedy: *How* and *when* was desegregation to be achieved? This question was not answered for a full year after the court declared racial segregation in public schools unconstitutional, in May of 1954. The delay—which gave the South a breathing spell—was used to forge a compromise between immediate wholesale desegregation and gradual adjustment to the court's decision; between Negro rights and southern hostility. That year was full of judicial pondering and introspection that scotch any notion that the court arbitrarily exerted its power.

The segregation cases had been argued the first time in December, 1952. Lawyers—mostly from the NAACP—argued for the Negro plaintiffs that state school segregation laws denied to Negroes the equal protection guaranteed under the Fourteenth Amendment of the Constitution. Attorneys for the southern school districts countered that school segregation involved no constitutional rights; it was, they said, strictly a state legislative matter. The court listened, waited six months, and then in June, 1953, scheduled the cases for reargument the following term, with counsel for both sides instructed this time to address themselves to five specific questions.

The first three questions concerned the original intent of the framers of the Fourteenth Amendment regarding racial segregation in public schools.

That amendment, passed by a Republican Congress in 1866 in the heat of post-Civil War passion, says nothing about racial segregation in public schools; but neither does it say anything about housing or transportation or juries, areas in which the Supreme Court had, by 1953, already used it to invalidate discriminatory practices. Like the rest of the Constitution, the Fourteenth Amendment is a vessel into which judges had, over the years, poured many meanings. Its crucial first section merely said: "No State shall . . . deny to any person within its jurisdiction the equal protection of the laws." Section 5 gives Congress the power to enforce the amendment's provisions "by appropriate legislation."

Now in 1953 the Supreme Court wanted to know: Did the authors of the Fourteenth Amendment in fact intend desegregation of public schools either at the time of their writing or in the future? Exhaustive research by the court and the contending parties never revealed a clear answer to that.

Questions four and five asked how desegregation might be achieved, prompting observers to speculate that the court—still headed by Chief Justice Vinson—had already decided to declare racial segregation in public schools unconstitutional.

For the scheduled rehearing the court extended an invitation to the Attorney General of the United States to participate in oral arguments. A Frankfurter memorandum of June 8, 1953, explained that the new administration under Eisenhower "may have the responsibility of carrying out a decision full of perplexities; it should therefore be asked to face that responsibility as part of our process of adjudication. . . ." When the rearguments were heard in December, 1953, their significant portions turned out to be those dealing with the question of a remedy for segregation if deemed warranted.

NAACP lawyers, led by Thurgood Marshall, later to be appointed to the Supreme Court himself, urged immediate admission of Negro children to the schools of their choice, but reluctantly acknowledged that the Supreme Court had the power to effect instead a gradual adjustment. The southern states, whose chief attorney was John W. Davis, 1924 Democratic Presidential candidate, argued that the Supreme Court had the power to order a gradual process, but no effective way of mandating the details. "Your Honors do not sit, and cannot sit, as a glorified Board of Education for the State of South Carolina or any other State," John Davis declared.

At this stage of the proceedings the government's position was anomalous. The brief filed by the Eisenhower administration did not urge the court to hold public school segregation unconstitutional, although its overall tenor supported such a holding. Some of the lawyers who worked on it have said that an original version did include a direct call for the court to declare public school segregation unconstitutional but that it was diluted by either Attorney General Herbert Brownell or President Eisenhower. Brownell has denied this, saying that the brief never contained such a call. But he agreed—and advised Eisenhower—that if J. Lee Rankin, the Assistant Attorney General who was to argue for the government in court, was asked during oral argument for the administration's position, he would answer that the court should hold public school segregation unconstitutional—which was what Rankin actually did.

On the question of how desegregation could be accomplished, the government suggested remanding the cases to the lower courts, where, in the light of local conditions, decrees would be formulated and a gradual adjustment be made.

Shortly after this December reargument and four months before the Supreme Court would officially declare public school segregation unconstitutional, Justice Frankfurter addressed himself, in a memorandum for his associates, to the questions of *how* and *when*. He explained, in a covering note, that he was thinking out loud and that "sometimes one's thinking, whether good or bad, may stimulate good thoughts in others." He added parenthetically that "the typewriting was done under conditions of strictest security."

Whether the court was already thinking in terms of two decisions rather than one and had reached unanimity is not known. The memorandum's cautious restraint seems to indicate, however, that Frankfurter, in an attempt to achieve unanimity, was articulating the concerns of whatever recalcitrant justices remained, and perhaps trying to point out that implementation, while it had major difficulties, was not impossible. Because it introduces the concept of "with all deliberate speed," it is one of the most important pieces of writing on the segregation cases prior to their being decided.

Although, Frankfurter told his brethren, the court had before it only five individual cases, "we are asked in effect to transform state-wide school systems in nearly a score of states," and it was not going to be easy. First the court must define, Frankfurter wrote, exactly what the required result was. For the first time in the written discussions, the word *integration* was used; it has since become the heart of much of the controversy surrounding school racial problems. "Integration," Frankfurter said, "that is, 'equal protection,' can readily be achieved by lowering the standards of those who at the start are, in the phrase of George Orwell, 'more equal'. . . . It would indeed make a mockery of the Constitutional adjudication designed to vindicate a claim to equal treatment, to achieve 'integrated' but lower educational standards."

As to the time factor, the court does its duty, he explained, "if it gets effectively under way the righting of a wrong. When the wrong is a deeply rooted state policy the court does its duty if it decrees measures that reverse the direction of the unconstitutional policy so as to uproot it 'with all deliberate speed.'" This was a phrase Frankfurter had used previously in at least three decisions. Like *integration*, it became a controversial issue in the desegregation process.

Tentatively, Frankfurter preferred some gradual process of desegregation. "The Court does not know," he wrote, "that a simple scrambling of the two school systems may not work. It surely cannot assume that scrambling is all there is to it. . . . One is

Thurgood Marshall (center), then special counsel of the NAACP, with the two other attorneys who successfully argued the landmark case. Marshall was later appointed to the Supreme Court in 1967.

surely entitled to suspect that spreading the adjustment over time will more effectively accomplish the desired end. . . ."

However, he warned, before the court could fashion a decree, it faced an enormous and complex fact-finding task, made more difficult by the various interpretations that could be applied to facts "different in kind than courts usually consider" and "embedded in deep feeling."

"Physical, educational, budgetary, and time factors" must be considered; there would be problems for both teachers and students, and "problems caused by shifts in population which these readjustments may well induce." All these must be ascertained in a complex framework where "the spread of differences in the ratios of white to colored population among the various counties in different States is very considerable."

Awareness of these difficulties accounts for the fact that a remedy for segregated schools did not appear in the May 17, 1954, decision. The justices simply declared racially segregated schools unconstitutional, and the last paragraph of the unanimous opinion read:

> Because these are class actions, because of the wide applicability of this decision, and because of the great variety of local conditions, the formulation of decrees in these cases presents problems of considerable complexity. We have now announced that such segregation is a denial of the equal protection of the laws. In order that we may have the full assistance of the parties in formulating decrees, the cases will be restored to the docket, and the parties are requested to present further argument on questions 4 and 5 [the questions of *how*] previously propounded by the Court for the reargument this Term.

The Attorney General of the United States as well as the attorneys general of the states requiring or permitting segregation in public education were invited to participate as amici curiae. Undoubtedly the court hoped that by inviting participation of the states—most of them southern—that permitted or required segregation, the South itself, at least on an official level, would accept the inevitability of change and join in devising an acceptable remedy.

The justices knew they had touched sensitive nerves, but they were probably not prepared for the widespread resistance their decision drew, largely in the South. Emotion outran reason; invective submerged valid legal debate. Deep South prosegregationist states such as Alabama, Georgia, and Mississippi did not accept the court's invitation to participate in reargument lest they endow the May 17, 1954, decision with recognition. Vacationing in Massachusetts, Frankfurter mused on the problem and, in a letter to Warren, recommended that the court gather data on what "administrative, financial, commonsensical and other considerations legitimately enter" the normal school-districting process so as to have some frame of reference in dealing with southern redistricting. "The Southern States are fever patients. Let us find out, if we can, what healthy bodies do about such things in order to guard against attributing to the fever conduct and consequences that are not fairly attributable to fever. . . ."

Following Frankfurter's suggestion, Chief Justice Warren circulated among the justices in November, 1954, a seventy-nine-page Segregation Research Report containing background information to be referred to by the justices in thinking about implementing their decision of the past May. It included a survey of normal school-districting practices, a summary of southern reaction to the May 17 decision, analyses of previously desegregated schools, proposed plans to abolish public schools, discussion of court jurisdiction over school districting, and maps of school districts showing distribution of white and Negro students. The report pointed up the complexity of the *how* problem facing the Supreme Court: How could nine justices, sitting in their marble palace in Washington, with their limited knowledge of local problems, devise a formula that could be applied to such a diversified collection of school districts? The *when* was equally a problem: "'Forthwith' would either be given a meaning short of immediacy or introduce a range of leeway to render it imprecise," Frankfurter said in a memorandum of February 10, 1955. "And it would most certainly provoke resentment. Yet any limitation allowing a specific number of years in which to achieve compliance could well be treated as a grace period during which nothing need be done."

The segregation cases were reargued from April 11 to 14, 1955. On the last of those days, Frankfurter wrote to his colleagues: "Hamilton Basso is, as I dare say you know, a very perceptive Southern writer, and carries weight, I believe, both North and South. A letter of his in last Sunday's *New York Times* has for me the persuasiveness not of novelty but of emphasis."

Basso's letter, which Frankfurter reproduced, was an urgent *cri de coeur* for understanding of the South's present defiant temper. Segregation, it said, like slavery the century before, "was the foremost preoccupation of the Southern mind" in the press and in conversation. Out of a confusion of opinion, ranging from "logical argument to irrational bitterness," Basso wrote, "that which most clearly emerges is a feeling of deep resentment over what is looked upon as outside pressure. . . . It [the South] has gone far toward convincing itself that it is going to be 'pressured' in a quick reorganization of its whole society . . . and that the rest of the country is almost callously indifferent to the difficulties implicit in such a course."

Two days later, on April 16, 1955, the justices met in conference, still searching—against the background of angry resistance—for answers to the questions they had asked in court. Chief Justice Warren opened the discussion with his admission that he himself had not reached a fixed opinion; perhaps the brethren could talk it over, as they had the original desegregation decision.

There were, Warren began, some things the court should not do. The Supreme Court ought not to tell the lower courts what to do; it should not fix a definite date for completion of desegregation nor even suggest to a lower court that that court should set a date, nor should the Supreme Court dictate any procedural requirement. Clearly, Their Honors were not going to sit as a "super school board."

What appealed to Warren at the time, rather than a formal decree, was an opinion citing factors for the lower courts to consider, with some Supreme Court guidance; it would, he explained, be rather cruel to shift back and let them flounder. There were two ground rules to be observed: (1) these were class actions—that is, as the May 17, 1954, decision had declared, they affected everyone similarly situated, not only the plaintiffs—and (2) the lower courts should be entitled to consider physical factors but not psychological attitudes.

Adhering to conference protocol, the other justices spoke in turn, from the most senior (Black) to the most junior (John Marshall Harlan, who had replaced Robert Jackson on Jackson's death). There was little agreement among them except as to the fact that the final opinion should be unanimous. Justice Black expressed the feeling when he declared that if a unanimous opinion were humanly possible, he would do everything he could to achieve it. Nonetheless, the Alabaman differed with Chief Justice Warren. He knew, he said, every southern district judge on anyone's list, and not one of them was going to be for desegregation. Black advised saying and doing as little as possible; nothing was more important than that the Supreme Court should not issue what it could not enforce. He advised reiterating the unconstitutionality of racial segregation in public schools, formulating a decree affecting only the five cases before the court, and enjoining school boards from refusing to admit these specific Negro students.

Perhaps no one except the justices themselves will ever know exactly how the Warren-Black points of view were reconciled. However, the unanimity so necessary to this kind of decision was in some way achieved, and six weeks after the April 16 conference, on May 31, 1955, Chief Justice Earl Warren read the Supreme Court's unanimous opinion, outlining that court's plan for desegregating the nation's schools. It was very much a Warren opinion, conforming to the points he had made in the April 16 conference.

The court showed that *it* was not "callously indifferent" to the difficulties of reorganizing southern society, as Hamilton Basso had said the South believed most of the nation was. The decision in fact gave every opportunity to the South to itself solve whatever problems accompanied desegregation—and in its own good time.

As the 1954 decision had been clearly for the Negro plaintiffs, this 1955 decision was clearly for the defendant school boards. Together, the two decisions were an attempt to balance the claims of the two parties, to reconcile "public and private needs."

The court solved the *how* of desegregation by attempting to be neither so vague as to invite "confusion and evasion" nor so specific that the court would become the nation's school board. The burden of desegregating was placed on the local school boards, with the lower courts required to consider "whether the action of school authorities constitutes good faith implementation of the governing constitutional principles."

But the lower courts were not left to flounder. As Warren had suggested in the April 16 conference, they were given general guidelines: they were to adjust and reconcile "public and private needs"; they could consider "problems related to administration, arising from the physical conditions of the school plant, transportation system, personnel, revision of school districts and attendance areas into compact units to achieve a system of determining admission to the public schools on a non-racial basis"; and there was to be no gerrymandering. However, as Chief Justice Warren had also said in the April 16 conference, psychological factors were to be disallowed, and the opinion reaffirmed it: "the vitality of these constitutional principles cannot be allowed to yield simply because of disagreement with them."

The crucial question of *when* was reserved until the last paragraph. It was not going to be the beginning of the next school term, as NAACP lawyers had urged. Frankfurter had warned the court in a memorandum against requiring a deadline, because, he said, it would have to be an arbitrary deadline and would be considered "an imposition of our will without the ascertainment . . . of the local situation. And it would tend to alienate instead of enlist favorable or educable local sentiment." Instead, the phrase in Frankfurter's January, 1954, memorandum appeared in the final decision: "the cases are remanded to the District Courts to take such proceedings and enter such orders and decrees consistent with this opinion as are necessary and proper to admit to public schools on a racially nondiscriminatory basis with all deliberate speed the parties to these cases. . . ."

In the years since the desegregation decisions most observers have credited Chief Justice Warren with welding the various individuals together to achieve unanimity. Warren modestly denies it: "It was the most self-effacing job ever written there. . . . Everyone there was so cooperative and so helpful" he has said, going on to give credit to the three Southerners on the court—Clark, Reed, and Black—"not because they developed the legal philosophy of it, but because they had the courage to do what was done." It was, Warren points out, "tough for them to go home" for a time.

Justice Frankfurter had made the same observation, but with an added dimension, in a note he wrote to Justice Reed three days after the 1954 decision. It read:

> History does not record dangers averted. I have no doubt that if the *Segregation* cases had reached decision last Term there would have been four dissenters—Vinson, Reed, Jackson and Clark—and certainly several opinions for the majority view. That would have been catastrophic. And if we had not had unanimity now inevitably there would have been more than one opinion for the majority. That would have been disastrous.
>
> It ought to give you much satisfaction to be able to say, as you have every right to say, "I have done the State some service." I am inclined to think, indeed I believe, in no single act since you have been on this Court have you done the Republic a more lasting service. I am not unaware of the hard struggle this involved in the conscience of your mind and in the mind of your conscience. I am not unaware, because all I have to do is look within.
>
> As a citizen of the Republic, even more than as a colleague, I feel deep gratitude for your share in what I believe to be a great good for our nation.

The Housework Revolution

Ruth Schwartz Cowan

The writing of the history of past events is greatly influenced by the present in several ways, some obvious, some subtle. The modern women's movement, for example, has led historians to investigate the role and activities of women in previous periods, and since the movement has resulted in more women entering the work force and seeking to become professionals of every sort, it has led to a rapid increase in the number of women historians. These historians, in turn, have both been drawn to the study of women's history and been influenced in how they interpret the past by their personal experiences as women.

This essay by Professor Ruth Schwartz Cowan of the State University of New York at Stony Brook illustrates these points. She specializes in women's history, but also in the history of science and technology. So in dealing with the impact of household appliances such as vacuum cleaners and washing machines, she is interested not only in how these "laborsaving" appliances worked but also in how they affected the lives of the women who used them. The automobile, which presumably has made life freer and easier, is for anyone running a household, Professor Cowan explains, just another mechanical appliance, a necessary tool for getting the job done. Perhaps a male historian might have arrived at this conclusion, but Cowan makes clear that personal experience lay behind her insight.

Things are seldom what they seem. Skim milk masquerades as cream. And labor-saving household appliances often do not save labor. This is the surprising conclusion reached by a small army of historians, sociologists, and home economists who have undertaken, in recent years, to study the one form of work that has turned out to be most resistant to inquiry and analysis—namely, housework.

During the first half of the twentieth century, the average American household was transformed by the introduction of a group of machines that profoundly altered the daily lives of housewives; the forty years between 1920 and 1960 witnessed what might be aptly called the "industrial revolution in the home." Where once there had been a wood- or coal-burning stove there now was a gas or electric range. Clothes that had once been scrubbed on a metal washboard were now tossed into a tub and cleansed by an electrically driven agitator. The dryer replaced the clothesline; the vacuum cleaner replaced the broom; the refrigerator replaced the icebox and the root cellar; an automatic pump, some piping, and a tap replaced the hand pump, the bucket, and the well. No one had to chop and haul wood any more. No one had to shovel out ashes or beat rugs or carry water; no one even had to toss egg whites with a fork for an hour to make an angel food cake.

And yet American housewives in 1960, 1970, and even 1980 continued to log about the same number of hours at their work as their grandmothers and mothers had in 1910, 1920, and 1930. The earliest time studies of housewives date from the very same period in which time studies of other workers were becoming popular—the first three decades of the twentieth century. The sample sizes of these studies were usually quite small, and they did not always define housework in precisely the same way (some counted an hour spent taking children to the playground as "work," while others called it "leisure"), but their results were more or less consistent: whether rural or urban, the average American housewife performed fifty to sixty hours of unpaid work in her home every week, and the only variable that significantly altered this was the number of small children.

A half-century later not much had changed. Survey research had become much more sophisticated, and sample sizes had grown considerably, but the results of the time studies remained surprisingly consistent. The average American housewife, now armed with dozens of motors and thousands of electronic chips, still spends fifty to sixty hours a week doing housework. The only variable that significantly altered the size of that number was full-time employment in the labor force; "working" housewives cut down the average number of hours that they spend cooking and cleaning, shopping and chauffeuring, to a not insignificant thirty-five—virtually the equivalent of another full-time job.

How can this be true? Surely even the most sophisticated advertising copywriter of all times could not fool almost the entire American population over the course of at least three generations. Laborsaving devices must be saving something, or Americans would not continue, year after year, to plunk down their hard-earned dollars for them.

And if laborsaving devices have not saved labor in the home, then what is it that has suddenly made it possible for more than 70 percent of the wives and mothers in the American population to enter the work force and stay there? A brief glance at the histories of some of the technologies that have transformed housework during the twentieth century will help us answer some of these questions.

The portable vacuum cleaner was one of the earliest electric appliances to make its appearance in American homes, and reasonably priced models appeared on the retail market as early as 1910. For decades prior to the turn of the century, inventors had been trying to create a carpet-cleaning system that would improve on the carpet sweeper with adjustable rotary brushes (patented by Melville Bissell in 1876), or the semiannual ritual of hauling rugs outside and beating them, or the practice of regularly sweeping the dirt out of a rug that had been covered with dampened, torn newspapers. Early efforts to solve the problem had focused on the use of large steam, gasoline, or electric motors attached to piston-type pumps and lots of hoses. Many of these "stationary" vacuum-cleaning systems were installed in apartment houses or hotels, but some were hauled around the streets in horse-drawn carriages by entrepreneurs hoping to establish themselves as "professional housecleaners."

In the first decade of the twentieth century, when fractional-horsepower electric motors became widely—and inexpensively—available, the portable vacuum cleaner intended for use in an individual household was born. One early model—invented by a woman, Corrine Dufour—consisted of a rotary brush, an electrically driven fan, and a wet sponge for absorbing the dust and dirt. Another, patented by David E. Kenney in 1907, had a twelve-inch nozzle attached to a metal tube attached to a flexible hose that led to a vacuum pump and separating devices. The Hoover, which was based on a brush, a fan, and a collecting bag, was on the market by 1908. The Electrolux, the first of the canister types of cleaner, which could vacuum something above the level of the floor, was brought over from Sweden in 1924 and met with immediate success.

These early vacuum cleaners were hardly a breeze to operate. All were heavy, and most were extremely cumbersome to boot. One early home economist mounted a basal metabolism machine on the back of one of her hapless students and proceeded to determine that more energy was expended in the effort to clean a sample carpet with a vacuum cleaner than when the same carpet was attacked with a hard broom. The difference, of course, was that the vacuum cleaner did a better job, at least on carpets, because a good deal of what the broom stirred up simply resettled a foot or two away from where it had first been lodged.

Whatever the liabilities of early vacuum cleaners may have been, Americans nonetheless appreciated their virtues; according to a market survey taken in Zanesville, Ohio, in 1926, slightly more than half the households owned one. Later improvements in design made these devices easier to operate. By 1960 vacuum cleaners were found in 70 percent of the nation's homes.

When the vacuum cleaner is viewed in a historical context, however, it is easy to see why it did not save housewifely labor. Its introduction coincided almost precisely with the disappearance of the domestic servant. The number of persons engaged in household service dropped from 1,851,000 in 1910 to 1,411,000 in 1920, while the number of households enumerated in the census rose from 20.3 million to 24.4 million. Moreover, between 1900 and 1920 the number of household servants per thousand persons dropped from 98.9 to 58.0, while during the 1920s the decline was even more precipitous as the restrictive immigration acts dried up what had once been the single most abundant source of domestic labor.

For the most economically comfortable segment of the population, this meant just one thing: the adult female head of the household was doing more housework than she had ever done before. What Maggie had once done with a broom, Mrs. Smith was now doing with a vacuum cleaner. Knowing that this was happening, several early copywriters for vacuum cleaner advertisements focused on its implications. The vacuum cleaner, General Electric announced in 1918, is better than a maid: it doesn't quit, get drunk, or demand higher wages. The switch from Maggie to Mrs. Smith shows up, in time-study statistics, as an increase in the time that Mrs. Smith is spending at her work.

For those—and they were the vast majority of the population—who were not economically comfortable, the vacuum cleaner implied something else again: not an increase in the time spent in housework but an increase in the standard of living. In many households across the country, acquisition of a vacuum cleaner was connected to an expansion of living space, the move from a small apartment to a small house, the purchase of wall-to-wall carpeting. If this did not happen during the difficult 1930s, it became more possible during the expansive 1950s. As living quarters grew larger, standards for their upkeep increased; rugs had to be vacuumed every week, in some households every day, rather than semiannually, as had been customary. The net result, of course, was that when armed with a vacuum cleaner, housewives whose parents had been poor could keep more space cleaner than their mothers and grandmothers would have ever believed possible. We might put this everyday phenomenon in language that economists can understand: The introduction of the vacuum cleaner led to improvements in productivity but not to any significant decrease in the amount of time expended by each worker.

The history of the washing machine illustrates a similar phenomenon. "Blue Monday" had traditionally been, as its name implies, the bane of a housewife's existence—especially when Monday turned out to be "Monday . . . and Tuesday to do the ironing." Thousands of patents for "new and improved" washers were issued during the nineteenth century in an effort to cash in on the housewife's despair. Most of these early washing machines were wooden or metal tubs combined with some kind of hand-cranked mechanism that would rub or push or twirl laundry when the tub was filled with water and soap. At the end of the century, the Sears catalog offered four such washing machines, ranging in price from $2.50 to $4.25, all sold in combination with hand-cranked wringers.

These early machines may have saved time in the laundering process (four shirts could be washed at once instead of each having to be rubbed separately against a washboard), but they probably didn't save much energy. Lacking taps and drains, the tubs still had to be filled and emptied by hand, and each piece still had to be run through a wringer and hung up to dry.

Not long after the appearance of fractional-horsepower motors, several enterprising manufacturers had the idea of hooking them up to the crank mechanisms of washers and wringers—and the electric washer was born. By the 1920s, when mass production of such machines began, both the general structure of the machine (a central-shaft agitator rotating within a cylindrical tub, hooked up to the household water supply) and the general structure of the industry (oligopolistic—with a very few firms holding most of the patents and controlling most of the market) had achieved their final form. By 1926 just over a quarter of the families in Zanesville had an electric washer, but by 1941 fully 52 percent of all American households either owned or had interior access (which means that they could use coin-operated models installed in the basements of apartment houses) to such a machine. The automatic washer, which consisted of a vertically rotating washer cylinder that could also act as a centrifugal extractor, was introduced by the Bendix Home Appliance Corporation in 1938, but it remained expensive, and therefore inaccessible, until after World War II. This machine contained timing devices that allowed it to proceed through its various cycles automatically; by spinning the clothes around in the extractor phase of its cycle, it also eliminated the wringer. Although the Bendix subsequently disappeared from the retail market (versions of this sturdy machine may still be found in Laundromats), its design principles are replicated in the agitator washers that currently chug away in millions of American homes.

Both the early wringer washers and their more recent automatic cousins have released American women from the burden of drudgery. No one who has ever tried to launder a sheet by hand, and without the benefits of hot running water, would want to return to the days of the scrub board and tub. But "labor" is composed of both "energy expenditure" and "time expenditure," and the history of laundry work demonstrates that the one may be conserved while the other is not.

The reason for this is, as with the vacuum cleaner, twofold. In the early decades of the century, many households employed laundresses to do their wash; this was

Early washers took some drudgery out of housework, but modern ones have simply made the house-wife a laundress.

true, surprisingly enough, even for some very poor households when wives and mothers were disabled or employed full-time in field or factory. Other house-holds—rich and poor—used commercial laundry services. Large, mechanized "steam" laundries were first constructed in this country in the 1860s, and by the 1920s they could be found in virtually every urban neighborhood and many rural ones as well.

But the advent of the electric home washer spelled doom both for the laun-dress and for the commercial laundry; since the housewife's labor was unpaid, and since the washer took so much of the drudgery out of washday, the one-time expen-diture for a machine seemed, in many families, a more sensible arrangement than continuous expenditure for domestic services. In the process, of course, the time spent on laundry work by the individual housewife, who had previously employed either a laundress or a service, was bound to increase.

For those who had not previously enjoyed the benefits of relief from washday drudgery, the electric washer meant something quite different but equally signifi-cant: an upgrading of household cleanliness. Men stopped wearing removable col-lars and cuffs, which meant that the whole of their shirts had to be washed and then ironed. Housewives began changing two sheets every week, instead of moving the top sheet to the bottom and adding only one that was fresh. Teen-agers began changing their underwear every day instead of every weekend. In the early 1960s, when synthetic no-iron fabrics were introduced, the size of the household laundry load increased again; shirts and skirts, sheets and blouses that had once been sent out to the dry cleaner or the corner laundry were now being tossed into the household wash basket. By the 1980s the average American housewife, armed now with an automatic washing machine and an automatic dryer, was processing roughly ten times (by weight) the amount of laundry that her mother had been accustomed to. Drudgery had disappeared, but the laundry hadn't. The average time spent on this chore in 1925 had been 5.8 hours per week; in 1964 it was 6.2.

And then there is the automobile. We do not usually think of our cars as household appliances, but that is precisely what they are, since housework, as currently understood, could not possibly be performed without them. The average American housewife is today more likely to be found behind a steering wheel than in front of a stove. While writing this article I interrupted myself five times: once to take a child to field-hockey practice, then a second time, to bring her back when practice was finished; once to pick up some groceries at the supermarket; once to retrieve my husband, who was stranded at the train station; once for a trip to a doctor's office. Each time I was doing housework, and each time I had to use my car.

Like the washing machine and the vacuum cleaner, the automobile started to transform the nature of housework in the 1920s. Until the introduction of the Model T in 1908, automobiles had been playthings for the idle rich, and although many wealthy women learned to drive early in the century (and several participated in well-publicized auto races), they were hardly the women who were likely to be using their cars to haul groceries.

But by 1920, and certainly by 1930, all this had changed. Helen and Robert Lynd, who conducted an intensive study of Muncie, Indiana, between 1923 and 1925 (reported in their famous book *Middletown*), estimated that in Muncie in the 1890s only 125 families, all members of the "elite," owned a horse and buggy, but by 1923 there were 6,222 passenger cars in the city, "roughly one for every 7.1 persons, or two for every three families." By 1930, according to national statistics, there were roughly 30 million households in the United States—and 26 million registered automobiles.

What did the automobile mean for the housewife? Unlike public transportation systems, it was convenient. Located right at her doorstep, it could deposit her at the doorstep that she wanted or needed to visit. And unlike the bicycle or her own two feet, the automobile could carry bulky packages as well as several additional people. Acquisition of an automobile therefore meant that a housewife, once she had learned how to drive, could become her own door-to-door delivery service. And as more housewives acquired automobiles, more businessmen discovered the joys of dispensing with delivery services—particularly during the Depression.

To make a long story short, the iceman does not cometh anymore. Neither does the milkman, the bakery truck, the butcher, the grocer, the knife sharpener, the seamstress, or the doctor. Like many other businessmen, doctors discovered that their earnings increased when they stayed in their offices and transferred the responsibility for transportation to their ambulatory patients.

And so a new category was added to the housewife's traditional job description: chauffeur. The suburban station wagon is now "Mom's Taxi." Children who once walked to school now have to be transported by their mothers; husbands who once walked home from work now have to be picked up by their wives; groceries that once were dispensed from pushcarts or horse-drawn wagons now have to be packed into paper bags and hauled home in family cars. "Contemporary women," one time-study expert reported in 1974, "spend about one full working day per week on the road and in stores compared with less than two hours per week for women in the 1920s." If everything we needed to maintain our homes and sustain our families were delivered right to our doorsteps—and every member of the family had independent means for getting where she or he wanted to go—the hours spent in housework by American housewives would decrease dramatically.

The histories of the vacuum cleaner, the washing machine, and the automobile illustrate the varied reasons why the time spent in housework has not markedly decreased in the United States during the last half-century despite the introduction of so many ostensibly laborsaving appliances. But these histories do not help us understand what has made it possible for so many American wives and mothers to enter the labor force full-time during those same years. Until recently, one of the explanations most often offered for the startling increase in the participation of married women in the work force (up from 24.8 percent in 1950 to 50.1 percent in 1980) was household technology. What with microwave ovens and frozen foods, washer and dryer combinations and paper diapers, the reasoning goes, housework can now be done in no time at all, and women have so much time on their hands that they find they must go out and look for a job for fear of going stark, raving mad.

As every "working" housewife knows, this pattern of reasoning is itself stark, raving mad. Most adult women are in the work force today quite simply because they need the money. Indeed, most "working" housewives today hold down not one but two jobs; they put in what has come to be called a "double day." Secretaries, lab technicians, janitors, sewing machine operators, teachers, nurses, or physicians for eight (or nine or ten) hours, they race home to become chief cook and bottle washer for another five, leaving the cleaning and the marketing for Saturday and Sunday. Housework, as we have seen, still takes a lot of time, modern technology notwithstanding.

Yet household technologies have played a major role in facilitating (as opposed to causing) what some observers believe to be the most significant social revolution of our time. They do it in two ways, the first of which we have already noted. By relieving housework of the drudgery that it once entailed, washing machines, vacuum cleaners, dishwashers, and water pumps have made it feasible for a woman to put in a double day without destroying her health, to work full-time and still sustain herself and her family at a reasonably comfortable level.

The second relationship between household technology and the participation of married women in the work force is considerably more subtle. It involves the history of some technologies that we rarely think of as technologies at all—and certainly not as household appliances. Instead of being sheathed in stainless steel or porcelain, these devices appear in our kitchens in little brown bottles and bags of flour; instead of using switches and buttons to turn them on, we use hypodermic needles and sugar cubes. They are various forms of medication, the products not only of modern medicine but also of modern industrial chemistry: polio vaccines and vitamin pills; tetanus toxins and ampicillin; enriched breads and tuberculin tests.

Before any of these technologies had made their appearance, nursing may well have been the most time-consuming and most essential aspect of housework. During the eighteenth and nineteenth centuries and even during the first five decades of the twentieth century, it was the woman of the house who was expected (and who had been trained, usually by *her* mother) to sit up all night cooling and calming a feverish child, to change bandages on suppurating wounds, to clean bed linens stained with excrement, to prepare easily digestible broths, to cradle colicky infants on her lap for hours on end, to prepare bodies for burial. An attack of the measles might mean the care of a bedridden child for a month. Pneumonia might require six months of bed rest. A small knife cut could become infected and produce a fever that would rage for days. Every summer brought the fear of polio epidemics, and every polio epidemic left some group of mothers with the perpetual problem of tending to the needs of a handicapped child.

Cholera, diphtheria, typhoid fever—if they weren't fatal—could mean weeks of sleepless nights and hard-pressed days. "Just as soon as the person is attacked," one experienced mother wrote to her worried daughter during a cholera epidemic in Oklahoma in 1885, "be it ever so slightly, he or she ought to go to bed immediately and stay there; put a mustard [plaster] over the bowels and if vomiting over the stomach. See that the feet are kept warm, either by warm iron or brick, or bottles of hot water. If the disease progresses the limbs will begin to cramp, which must be prevented by applying cloths wrung out of hot water and wrapping round them. When one is vomiting so terribly, of course, it is next to impossible to keep medicine down, but in cholera it must be done."

These were the routines to which American women were once accustomed, routines regarded as matters of life and death. To gain some sense of the way in which modern medicines have altered not only the routines of housework but also the emotional commitment that often accompanies such work, we need only read out a list of the diseases to which most American children are unlikely to succumb today, remembering how many of them once were fatal or terribly disabling: diphtheria, whooping cough, tetanus, pellagra, rickets, measles, mumps, tuberculosis, smallpox, cholera, malaria, and polio.

And many of today's ordinary childhood complaints, curable within a few days of the ingestion of antibiotics, once might have entailed weeks, or even months, of full-time attention: bronchitis; strep throat; scarlet fever; bacterial pneumonia; infections of the skin, or the eyes, or the ears, or the airways. In the days before the introduction of modern vaccines, antibiotics, and vitamin supplements, a mother who was employed full-time was a serious, sometimes life-endangering threat to the health of her family. This is part of the reason why life expectancy was always low and infant mortality high among the poorest segment of the population—those most likely to be dependent upon a mother's wages.

Thus modern technology, especially modern medical technology, has made it possible for married women to enter the work force by releasing housewives not just from drudgery but also from the dreaded emotional equation of female employment with poverty and disease. She may be exhausted at the end of her double day, but the modern "working" housewife can at least fall into bed knowing that her efforts have made it possible to sustain her family at a level of health and comfort that not so long ago was reserved only for those who were very rich.

Cigarettes and Cancer

John A. Meyer

When the first tobacco was shipped to England from Virginia by the Jamestown settlers, King James I himself denounced smoking as a "stinking" custom "dangerous to the lungs." But large numbers of his subjects quickly acquired the smoking habit and tobacco was soon one of the main colonial exports to the mother country and indirectly to the rest of Europe. Most Europeans smoked tobacco in pipes (American Indians preferred cigars or a primitive cigarette, wrapped in a corn husk). By the time of the Civil War, cigarettes were becoming popular and after the development of machines that could mass produce them, demand increased rapidly.

During this period few people considered smoking harmful and those who did were usually considered old fashioned. Children were told that smoking would stunt their growth, and conservatives considered women who smoked wantons or at least unladylike, but decade by decade through the twentieth century, per capita consumption of cigarettes soared.

How the harmful effects of tobacco were discovered and what was done about this knowledge is the subject of this essay by John A. Meyer. Dr. Meyer, a professor of thoracic surgery, is the author of *Lung Cancer Chronicles*.

The patient at Barnes Hospital in St. Louis, in 1919, might have wondered during his last days why all the physicians were so peculiarly interested in his case. When the man died, Dr. George Dock, chairman of the department of medicine, asked all third- and fourth-year medical students at the teaching hospital to observe the autopsy. The patient's disease had been so rare, he said, that most of them would never see it again. The disease was lung cancer.

Dr. Alton Ochsner, then one of the students, wrote years later, "I did not see another case until 1936, seventeen years later, when in a period of six months, I saw nine patients with cancer of the lung. Having been impressed with the extreme rarity of this condition seventeen years previously, this represented an epidemic for which there had to be a cause. All the afflicted patients were men who smoked heavily and had smoked since World War I. . . . I had the temerity, at that time, to postulate that the probable cause of this new epidemic was cigarette use."

At the beginning of this century, most smokers chose cigars; the cigarette was seen as somewhat effete and faintly subversive. Smoking was an almost wholly male custom. In 1904 a New York City policeman arrested a woman for smoking a cigarette in an automobile and told her, "You can't do that on Fifth Avenue!" Smoking by female schoolteachers was considered grounds for dismissal. At an official White House dinner in 1910, Baroness Rosen, wife of the Russian ambassador, asked President Taft for a cigarette. The embarrassed President had to send his military aide, Maj. Archie Butt, to find one; finally the bandleader obliged.

The commercial manufacture of cigarettes had been a cottage industry until 1881, when James A. Bonsack invented a cigarette-making machine. In 1883 James Buchanan Duke, who had inherited his father's tobacco business in Durham, North Carolina, bought two of Bonsack's machines. Within five years Duke's company was selling nearly a billion cigarettes annually, far more than any other manufacturer.

Until World War I, cigarette production in America remained stable. But after the United States entered the conflict, in 1917, Duke's company and the National Cigarette Service Committee distributed millions of cigarettes free to the troops in France, and they became so powerful a morale factor that General Pershing himself demanded priority for their shipment to the front. The war began to fix the cigarette habit on the American people: between 1910 and 1919 production increased by 633 percent, from fewer than ten billion a year to nearly seventy billion. Contemporary literature reflected the change. O. Henry's carefully observed turn-of-the-century stories almost never mention cigarettes. But by the time of Ernest Hemingway's expatriates in *The Sun Also Rises,* published in 1926, men and women alike smoke constantly.

It was the consequences of this growing habit that physicians began to notice in the 1930s. As the first cases of lung cancer began to appear, doctors struggled to find ways to cope with the disease. . . . In 1950 [Dr. Evarts A.] Graham and a medical student named Ernst Wynder published a landmark study of the disease in the *Journal of the American Medical Association.* They found that practically all the victims had been long-time heavy cigarette smokers. An association between lung cancer and smoking had already been suggested by a number of other researchers, and a 1932 paper in the *American Journal of Cancer* had accurately blamed the tars in cigarettes for the formation of cancer. But this was the first major study to make the connection. In 1953 it was followed by the Sloan-Kettering Report, in which researchers at the Memorial Sloan-Kettering Cancer Center, in New York City, announced that they had produced skin cancers in mice by painting the tars from tobacco smoke on their backs.

Graham himself had been a cigarette smoker for more than twenty years, but he quit after his 1950 study and devoted himself after retirement in 1951 to research on the mechanisms of cancer production by tobacco tars. The remainder of the story is one of sad irony. In 1957 he was found to have lung cancer himself, of an especially malignant type called small-cell carcinoma. Graham died that same year; his patient Dr. Gilmore survived him by more than half a decade.

Long before the dangers of smoking became evident, cigarette companies were implying that it was actually beneficial. In 1927 the American Tobacco Company launched an advertising campaign claiming that "11,105 physicians" endorsed Lucky Strikes as "less irritating to sensitive or tender throats than any other cigarettes." Physicians' groups responded angrily, but they were more offended by the commercialization of professional opinion than by the specific claims involved.

In 1946 the R. J. Reynolds Tobacco Company launched its campaign featuring the "T-Zone Test" ("Taste and Throat") with a claim that "more doctors smoke

The figures quoted have been checked and certified to by LYBRAND, ROSS BROS. AND MONTGOMERY, Accountants and Auditors.

The comforting presence of a doctor ratifies Lucky's claim to smoothness in a 1930 advertisement.

Camels than any other cigarette!" Of course, many more doctors did smoke then than now, and Camels were extremely popular. In 1949 Camel advertised its "30-day Test" with a group photograph of "noted throat specialists" who had found "not one case of throat irritation due to smoking Camels!" By the early 1950s, however, as medical studies began demonstrating close links between cigarette smoking and ill health, the manufacturers stopped claiming that smoking was healthful and began instead to insist that no connection with disease had been proved.

In the meantime, cases of—and deaths from—lung cancer among American men had begun a dizzying climb. In 1930 the death rate from lung cancer among men was less than 5 per 100,000 population per year. By 1950 it had quintupled to more than 20; today it is above 70. The numbers of new cases and of deaths have never been very far apart; even today not quite 10 percent of all lung-cancer patients can be cured. In 1989 there were an estimated 155,000 new cases of lung cancer in the United States and 142,000 deaths from the disease, making it far and away the leading cause of cancer deaths in our society, and cigarette smoking is responsible for an estimated 85 percent of the cases. The death rate still continues to rise, but there are definite signs that among men its rate of increase is diminishing, as more men give up smoking.

The rise of lung cancer among women lagged behind that among men by about thirty years. Heavy smoking remained relatively unacceptable socially for women until around World War II. Today women's lung-cancer death rates are skyrocketing the way men's did twenty or thirty years ago. A number of studies indicate that it may be harder for women to quit than for men, and it has been predicted that by the year 2000 more women than men will be dying of lung cancer.

World War II, like World War I, gave cigarette smoking an enormous boost. Cigarettes were sold at military-post exchanges and ships' stores tax-free and virtually at cost—usually for a nickel a pack—and they were distributed free in the forward areas and were packaged in K rations.

The 1950s were the golden age of cigarettes on television. Arthur Godfrey would sign off at the end of his Chesterfield-sponsored variety show, saying, "This is Arthur 'Buy-'em-by-the-carton' Godfrey!" (The message was dropped in 1959 when Godfrey himself was found to have lung cancer. He underwent removal of the lung followed by radiation therapy, made a remarkable recovery, and lived for twenty-four years afterward.) When John Cameron Swayze anchored "The Camel News Caravan" in the early days of television, the sponsor required him to have a burning cigarette visible whenever he was on camera. Likewise, Edward R. Murrow was never seen on air without a cigarette; he died of lung cancer in 1965. But during the 1960s the tide turned against cigarettes on TV.

The change had begun in 1955, when Surgeon General Leroy E. Burney invited representatives of the National Cancer Institute, the National Heart Institute, the American Cancer Society, and the American Heart Association to establish a study group to assess the mounting evidence of links between cigarette smoking and lung cancer. The group concluded that a causal relationship did indeed exist, and late in 1959 Dr. Burney published an article in the *Journal of the American Medical Association* stating the Public Health Service's position: Cigarette smoking caused cancer.

The reports received little notice at the time, but as the 1960s got under way, agitation began to grow for the adoption of an official government position on smoking and health. In May 1962 an enterprising reporter pressured President John F. Kennedy on the subject at a press conference. The President plainly was caught off guard: "The—that matter is sensitive enough and the stock market is in sufficient difficulty without my giving you an answer which is not based on complete information, which I don't have, and therefore perhaps we could—I'd be glad to respond to that question in more detail next week."

Not long afterward Kennedy announced that he was assigning his surgeon general, Dr. Luther Terry, the responsibility for a study of smoking and health. He assured Dr. Terry that he expected an expert scientific review and would allow no political interference.

In July 1962 the surgeon general and his staff met with representatives of various medical associations and volunteer organizations, the Food and Drug Administration, the Federal Trade Commission, the Departments of Agriculture and Commerce, the Federal Communications Commission, the President's Office of Science and Technology, and the industry-backed Tobacco Institute. The representatives were given a list of 150 eminent biomedical scientists, none of whom had taken a major public position on smoking; from this list they were to propose a committee of ten members and to strike any name to which they objected for any reason.

All of the first ten scientists contacted agreed to serve; three were cigarette smokers. They began meeting in November 1962 and worked for fourteen months before submitting their formal report, which was released at a press conference on January 11, 1964. Known ever after as the Surgeon General's Report, it indicted smoking as a major cause of lung cancer in men and as a contributing cause of many forms of chronic lung disease.

After the report came out, the Federal Trade Commission issued the Trade Regulation Rules on Cigarette Labeling and Advertising, which, as of January 1, 1966, required that all cigarette packages carry a warning ("Caution, Cigarette Smoking May Be Hazardous to Your Health"), that cigarette advertising not be directed at people under twenty-five or at schools or colleges, and that no claims be made for the healthfulness of filters or cigarette products.

The industry's Tobacco Institute protested the new rules: "We respectfully submit that in these Trade Regulation Rules the Commission is . . . plainly legislating." Few could deny the substance of the allegation, but a tradition of "delegated authority" had long been emerging between Congress and its administrative agencies, so the legal question became one of the limits of that delegation. It has largely been resolved in favor of the agencies.

The tobacco companies received a further blow in 1970, when after two years of lobbying, the Federal Trade Commission persuaded Congress to pass the Public Health Cigarette Smoking Act. The bill had two main provisions: a stronger warning was to appear not only on cigarette packages but in print advertisements as well ("Warning: The Surgeon General Has Determined That Cigarette Smoking Is Dangerous to Your Health"), and all cigarette advertising was to be banned from radio and television. This time Congress itself issued the restrictive ruling. Challenged in the courts by the tobacco industry, the legislation was upheld by the Supreme Court in 1972. In 1984 the warning was made stronger again, establishing today's four alternating messages: "Cigarette Smoke Contains Carbon Monoxide"; "Quitting Smoking Now Greatly Reduces Serious Risks to Your Health"; "Smoking by Pregnant Women May Result in Fetal Injury, Premature Birth, and Low Birth Weight"; and "Smoking Causes Lung Cancer, Heart Disease, Emphysema, and May Complicate Pregnancy."

In the summer of 1987 the First U.S. Circuit Court of Appeals in Boston ruled that these warnings on cigarette packages are sufficient to protect the tobacco companies against lawsuits claiming injury or death from smoking; the ruling dismissed the case of *Palmer* v. *Liggett Group,* filed in 1983 and seeking damages for $3 million for the death of Joseph C. Palmer from lung cancer in 1980. In the case of *Cipollone* v. *Liggett Group, Lorillard, Inc., and Philip Morris, Inc.,* concluded in New Jersey in 1988, the plaintiff herself was found "80 percent responsible" for her illness and its course, and the Liggett Group "20 percent responsible." The verdict required Liggett to pay the plaintiff's family an award of $400,000. The jury concluded that

Liggett had failed to warn of health risks and had misled the public with its advertising slogans prior to 1966, when the first warning-label rule took effect, but the tobacco companies were exonerated of having conspired to misrepresent the dangers of smoking. The defense called the award "an expression of sympathy by the jury"; it was voided on appeal in January 1990, and then went to the United States Supreme Court. The Supreme Court ruled in June of this year that warning labels did not pre-empt all damage suits, and opened the way for a retrial of the Cipollone case. Moreover, by ruling that Congress had "offered no sign that it wished to insulate cigarette manufacturers from longstanding rules governing fraud," the court threw the door wide open for future damage suits alleging that tobacco companies concealed information about the dangers of smoking or otherwise deceived smokers.

The biggest change in cigarettes themselves since the 1964 Surgeon General's Report has been the proliferation of low-tar, low-nicotine filtered cigarettes. Filters were first added to cigarettes long before there was public concern about the dangers of smoking. Viceroy advertised them in 1939: "AT LAST . . . a cigarette that filters each puff clean! . . . No more tobacco in mouth or teeth." After Wynder and Graham's 1950 report and the 1953 Sloan-Kettering Report, filters came into progressively greater public demand, and by the 1960s they had practically taken over the market.

Unfortunately, the advantages of low-tar and low-nicotine "light" cigarettes have proven to be largely illusory for several reasons: first, while nicotine and tars can be reduced, carbon monoxide is a product of burning, and as long as cigarettes burn, they will produce it; second, confirmed smokers tend to increase their cigarette consumption after switching to lighter brands; and third, studies have found that the risk of heart attack increases with the number of cigarettes smoked per day and does not decline when milder ones replace full-strength brands.

Cigarette manufacturers counter by pointing out that a precise chain of events leading from smoking to cancer has never been established, and that no statistical study of smokers and cancer has been able to rule out every other possible variable—factors such as diet, environment, and alcohol consumption. The industry continues to maintain that its product does not harm its users' health and that it provides pleasurable relaxation. This latter point, at least, is inarguable. Jean Nicot de Villemain, a French ambassador to Lisbon in the late sixteenth century, is said to have sent seeds of the tobacco plant to Catherine de Médicis, Queen of France, around 1556. The product had been brought to Europe from the New World first by Spanish and Portuguese explorers, but it was Nicot who presented it to Catherine and who later achieved immortality when Linnaeus used his name to christen the plant the seeds came from, *Nicotiana tabacum*. Later the active chemical alkaloid in its leaves was named nicotine.

This is the primary addicting substance in tobacco, and it is readily absorbed into the bloodstream from tobacco smoke in the lungs or from smokeless tobacco in the mouth or nose. Once in the blood, nicotine is rapidly distributed to the brain, where it binds to chemical receptors located throughout the nervous system to quicken the heartbeat, raise the blood pressure, relax skeletal muscles, and affect nearly all the endocrine glands.

In regular tobacco users, nicotine levels accumulate in the body during the day and persist at declining levels overnight; as a result, users maintain some degree of exposure to the drug practically around the clock.

For decades there have been organizations that try to help smokers quit, but successive surgeon generals' reports have found that most ex-smokers have quit spontaneously and on their own. A 1985 national survey estimated that of the 41 million Americans who quit smoking, 90 percent had done so without formal treatment programs or smoking-cessation devices. . . .

Surgical removal of the lung, or an appropriate part of it, remains the only real potential cure for lung cancer, and then only when the cancer has not yet begun to spread. Unfortunately, spreading cancer cells may be impossible to identify before the operation and afterward can give rise to recurrence or metastasis, the transmission of the disease to a new site. As a result the surgeon can speak of having effected a cure only in terms of the passage of time. Lung cancer will generally recur within three years or less if it is to recur at all. Among all patients with a new diagnosis of lung cancer, not quite one in ten will live five years. . . .

Probably no other human affliction besides AIDS depends so completely on prevention. Having risen from obscurity in our own century, lung cancer remains the number-one killer among all cancers.

The Rise and Decline of the Teenager

Thomas Hine

Prior to 1941, when the term "teenager" first appeared in print, one referred to "big boys or older girls." During the Depression, as more young people remained in high school for want of job opportunities, they became an increasingly coherent group, and thus required a label of their own: teenager. Historian Thomas Hine found that before teenagers were regarded as a special group, most young people of either sex moved inexorably, and at an early age, toward their adult occupations and roles. The small percentage who remained in school and entered college were destined for professions and elite roles in society. This division of young people by classes began to change early in the twentieth century. Psychologist G. Stanley Hall's tome, *Adolescence* (1904), and the emergence of child-labor laws, caused adolescents to be regarded as somewhat peculiar and especially vulnerable: the passage through the teen years was increasingly regarded as an ordeal, a concept that Erik Erikson later termed an "identity crisis." Hine's basic point is that the role, and indeed, the meaning of teenagers has changed, as has our way of thinking about them. This article is adapted from Hine's *The Rise and Fall of the American Teenager* (1999).

When the anthropologist Margaret Mead journeyed to the South Pacific in 1926, she was looking for something that experts of the time thought didn't exist: untroubled adolescence.

Adolescence, psychologists and educators believed, was inevitably a period of storm and stress. It debilitated young men and women. It made their actions unpredictable, their characters flighty and undependable. And if people who had lived through their teens didn't remember being that unhappy, some said, it was because it had been so traumatic that their conscious minds had suppressed what really happened.

At the age of twenty-five, Mead, who wasn't all that far beyond adolescence herself, simply couldn't believe that this picture of life's second decade expressed a necessary or universal truth. If she could find a place where social and sexual maturity could be attained without a struggle, where adolescence was so peaceful it scarcely seemed to exist, her point would be made. So she went to Samoa.

There are few places left on earth remote enough to give a contemporary observer real perspective on how Americans think about their young people. The teenager, with all the ideas about adolescence that the word encodes, is one of our most potent cultural exports. All around the world, satellites beam down MTV with its messages of consumption, self-indulgence, alienation, angst, and hedonism. The American invention of youth culture has become thoroughly international; it causes consternation and sells products everywhere.

Still, although it is extremely difficult to travel far enough across the earth to escape our culture's ideas about teenagers, one can travel in time. Youth has a history, and since the European colonization of North America, the second decade of life has offered a tremendous diversity of expectations and experiences. They haven't all been good experiences; most were backbreaking, some horrifying. One needn't be nostalgic for those lost forms of youth in order to learn from them. Nobody wants to send young people off to the coal mines, as was done a century ago, or rent them out to neighboring households as servants, as seventeenth-century New Englanders did. Nevertheless, history can be our Samoa, a window into very different ways of thinking and behaving that can throw our own attitudes into sharp relief and highlight assumptions that we don't even know we're making.

Like Mead, who freely admitted that her research in Samoa was shaped by what she viewed as a problem in the American culture of her own time, I have set out on historical explorations spurred by a suspicion that something is deeply wrong with the way we think about youth. Many members of my generation, the baby boomers, have moved seamlessly from blaming our parents for the ills of society to blaming our children. Teenage villains, unwed mothers, new smokers, reckless drivers, and criminal predators are familiar figures in the media, even when the problems they represent are more common among other age groups. Cities and suburbs enact curfews and other laws that only young people need obey, while Congress and state legislatures find new ways to punish young offenders as adults.

The way we think about teenagers is most contradictory. We assume that they should be somehow protected from the world of work, yet many high school students work as much as twenty hours a week. Teenagers form the core of our low-wage retail and restaurant work force, the local equivalent of the even lower-wage overseas manufacturing work force that makes the footwear and other items teens covet.

Yet at the same time as our economy depends on the young, we tend to view teenagers as less than trustworthy. This is a hangover from the attitudes Mead was trying to fight, though nowadays we're likely to ascribe young people's perceived quirks to "raging hormones." Most adults seem to view this conflicted, contradictory figure of the teenager as inevitable, part of the growth of a human being. Yet many people now living came of age before there was anything called a teenager. This creature is a mid-twentieth-century phenomenon. And almost everything has changed since the early 1940s, when it emerged. Are teenagers still necessary?

The word *teenager* initially saw print in 1941. It isn't known who thought up the word; its appearance, in an article in *Popular Science,* was not likely its first use. People had been speaking of someone in his or her teens for centuries, but that was a description of an individual. To speak of someone as a teenager is to make that person a member of a very large group, one defined only by age but presumed to have a lot in common. The word arose when it did because it described something new.

The teenager was a product of the Great Depression. Like other massive projects of the New Deal—the Hoover Dam, the TVA—it represented an immense channeling and redirection of energy. Unlike such public works, however, it was a more or less inadvertent invention. It happened in several steps.

First came the country's general economic collapse and a dramatic disappearance of jobs. As in previous panics and depressions, young people were among those thrown out of work. What was different was that after 1933, when Franklin D. Roosevelt took office, virtually *all* young people were thrown out of work, as part of a public policy to reserve jobs for men trying to support families. Businesses could actually be fined if they kept childless young people on their payrolls. Also, for the first two years of the Depression, the Roosevelt administration essentially ignored the needs of the youths it had turned out of work, except in the effort of the Civilian Conservation Corps (CCC), which was aimed at men in their late teens and early twenties.

There was, however, one very old and established institution available to young people who wanted to do something with their time and energy: high school. The first public high school had opened in Boston in 1821, but secondary education was very slow to win acceptance among working-class families that counted on their children's incomes for survival. Not until 112 years after that first school opened were a majority of high-school-age Americans actually enrolled.

The Depression was the worst possible time for high school to catch on. The American public education system was, then as now, supported primarily by local real estate taxes; these had plummeted along with real estate values. Schools were laying off teachers even as they enrolled unprecedented numbers of students. They were ill equipped to deal with their new, diverse clientele.

For many of these new students, high school was a stop-gap, something one did to weather a bad time. But by 1940 an overwhelming majority of young people were enrolled, and perhaps more important, there was a new expectation that nearly everyone would go, and even graduate.

This change in standards was a radical departure in the way society imagined itself. Before the Depression finishing high school was a clear mark that a youth, particularly a male, belonged to the middle class or above. Dropping out in the first or second year indicated membership in the working class. Once a large majority started going to high school, all of them, regardless of their economic or social status, began to be seen as members of a single group. The word *teenager* appeared precisely at the moment that it seemed to be needed.

Not long before, many young people in their mid-teens had been considered virtually grown up. Now that they were students rather than workers, they came to seem younger than before. During the 1920s "youth" in the movies had meant sexually mature figures, such as Joan Crawford, whom F. Scott Fitzgerald himself called the definitive flapper. Late in the 1930s a new kind of youth emerged in the movies, personified above all by the bizarre boy-man Mickey Rooney and the Andy Hardy movies he began to make in 1937. His frequent co-star Judy Garland was part of the phenomenon too. As Dorothy, in *The Wizard of Oz*, Garland was clearly a woman, not the girl everyone pretended she was. The tension between the maturity she feels and the childishness others see in her helps make the film more than a children's fantasy. It is an early, piquant expression of the predicament of the teenager.

Another less profound but amazingly enduring model for the emerging idea of the teenager was that perennial high schooler Archie, who first appeared in a comic book in 1941. He was drawn by Bob Montana, a teenager himself, who was working for a living as a staff artist at a comic book company. For the last half-century Archie, Jughead, Betty, Veronica, and their circle have appealed more to youngsters aspiring to become teenagers than to teenagers themselves.

Nevertheless, the early popularity of characters like Andy Hardy and Archie indicated that the view of high school students as essentially juvenile was catching on. A far stronger signal came when the draft was revived, shortly before the United States entered World War II. Although married men with families were eligible for induction, in many cases up to the age of forty, high school students were automatically deferred. Young men of seventeen, sixteen, and younger had been soldiers in all of America's previous wars and, more than likely, in every war that had ever been fought. By 1941 they had come to seem too young.

Having identified the teenager as a Frankenstein monster formed in the thirties by high school, Mickey Rooney movies, child psychology, mass manufacturing, and the New Deal, I might well have traced the story through bobbysoxers, drive-in movies, Holden Caulfield, Elvis, the civil rights martyr Emmett Till, top-forty radio, Gidget, the Mustang, heavy metal, Nirvana. Instead I found myself drawn farther into the past. While the teenager was a new thing in 1940, it nevertheless was an idea with deep roots in our culture.

At the very dawn of English settlement in North America, Puritan elders were declaring that they had come to this savage continent for the sake of their children, who did not seem sufficiently grateful. (Like latter-day suburbanites, they had made the move for the sake of the kids.) They were also shocked by the sheer size of their children. Better nutrition caused Americans of European background to reach physical and sexual maturity sooner than their parents had and to grow larger than their parents. No wonder some early settlers fretted that their children were different from them and at risk of going native.

By the middle of the eighteenth century, there was a whole literature of complaint against both apprentices who affected expensive and exotic costumes and licentious young people given to nighttime "frolicks." Jonathan Edwards gave one of the most vivid descriptions of moral decline and then proceeded to deal with it by mobilizing youthful enthusiasm within the church. By the time of the American Revolution, half the population was under sixteen. Young women over eighteen were hard to marry off, as one upper-class observer noted, because their teeth were starting to rot. (Seemingly unrelated issues like dental hygiene have always played an unsung role in the way we define the ages of man and woman.)

Yet as youthful as the American population was, young people stood in the mainstream of social and economic life. They were not the discrete group that today's teenagers are. "In America," wrote Alexis de Tocqueville in 1835, "there is in truth no adolescence. At the close of boyhood, he is a man and begins to trace out his own path."

Things were beginning to change, however. High school, the institution that would eventually define the teenager, had already been invented. By the second quarter of the nineteenth century, it was becoming clear that rapid changes in manufacturing, transport, and marketing meant that the children of merchants, skilled artisans, and professionals would live in a very different world from that of their parents. Adults could no longer rely on passing on their businesses or impart-ing their skills to their children, who would probably need formal schooling. In-creasingly, prosperous Americans were having fewer children and investing more in their education.

At the time, most secondary schooling took place in privately operated acade-mies. These varied widely in nature and quality, and for the most part students went to them only when they had both a need and the time. These schools didn't have fixed curricula, and students and teachers were constantly coming and going, since being a student was not yet a primary job. Students most often stayed at boarding-houses near the academies; they rarely lived at home.

The tax-supported high school, which by the 1860s had displaced the private academy, was based on a different set of assumptions. Attendance at it was a full-time activity, in which the student adjusted to the school's schedule, not vice versa. Whereas academies had been the product of a society in which most economic ac-tivity happened in the home, high school evolved in tandem with the ideal of the bourgeois home, protected from the world of work and presided over by a mother who was also the primary moral teacher. High school students, by definition, led privileged, sheltered lives.

Most academies had enrolled only males, but nearly all high schools were from the outset coeducational. There was some public consternation over mixing the sexes at so volatile an age, but most cities decided that providing separate schools was too costly. High schools were acceptable places to send one's daughter because they were close to home. Moreover, their graduates were qualified to teach ele-mentary school, a major employment opportunity for young women. The result was that females constituted a majority of the high school population. Moreover, male graduates were likely to be upper class, since they included only those who didn't have to drop out to work, while female graduates represented a wider social range.

Some of the early high schools were conceived as more practical and accessible alternatives to college. In a relatively short time, however, high school curricula be-came dominated by Latin and algebra, the courses required by the most selective colleges. Parents looked to win advantage for their children, so a "good" high school became one whose students went on to top colleges.

The earliest high schools treated their students almost as adults and allowed them to make decisions about their social lives. Students organized their own ex-tracurricular activities and played on athletic teams with older men and workers. Toward the end of the nineteenth century, however, high schools increasingly sought to protect their charges from the dangers of the larger world. They orga-nized dances so that their students wouldn't go to dance halls. They organized sports so that students would compete with others their own age. They created cheerleading squads, in the hope that the presence of females would make boys play less violently. They discovered and promoted that ineffable quality "school spirit," which was supposed to promote loyalty, patriotism, and social control. By the turn of the twentieth century, the football captain could escort the chief cheer-leader to the senior prom.

This all sounds familiar, but this high school crowd still accounted for less than 10 percent of the secondary-school-age population. Nearly all the rest were working, most of them with their families on farms, but also in factories, mines, and department stores, in the "street trades" (as newspaper hawkers or delivery boys), in the home doing piecework, or even as prostitutes. If early high school students are obvious predecessors to today's teenagers, their working contemporaries also helped create the youth culture.

One thing the working-class young shared with high school students and with today's teenagers is that they were emissaries of the new. Parents wanted their children to be prepared for the future. Among the working class, a substantially immigrant population, newness was America itself. Throughout the nineteenth century settlement workers and journalists repeatedly observed the way immigrant parents depended on their children to teach them the way things worked in their new country. They also noted a generation gap, as parents tried to cling to traditions and values from the old country while their children learned and invented other ways to live. Parents both applauded and deplored their children's participation in a new world. Youth became, in itself, a source of authority. When contemporary parents look to their children to fix the computer, program the VCR, or tell them what's new in the culture, they continue a long American tradition.

For laboring purposes one ceased to be a child no later than the age of ten. In many states schooling was required until twelve or thirteen, but compulsory attendance laws were rarely strictly enforced. In Philadelphia in the 1880s the standard bribe to free one's child from schooling was twenty-five cents. This was an excellent investment, considering how dependent many families were on their children. In Fall River, Massachusetts, some mill owners hired only men who had able-bodied sons who could also work. In Scranton, Pennsylvania, children's incomes usually added up to more than their fathers'.

The working teenager is, of course, hardly extinct. American high school students are far more likely to have part-time jobs than are their counterparts in other developed countries, and their work hours are on average substantially longer. The difference is that families don't often depend on their wages for their livelihood. Teenagers today spend most of what they earn on their own cars, clothing, and amusement. Indeed, they largely carry such industries as music, film, and footwear, in which the United States is a world leader. Their economic might sustains the powerful youth culture that so many find threatening, violent, and crude.

We can see the origins of this youth culture and of its ability to horrify in the young urban workers of the late nineteenth century. Young people, especially the rootless entrepreneurs of the street trades, were among the chief patrons of cheap theaters featuring music and melodrama that sprang up by the hundreds in the largest cities. (In Horatio Alger's hugely popular novels, the first stage of the hero's reform is often the decision to stay away from the theater and use the admission price to open a savings account.) They also helped support public dance halls, which promoted wild new forms of dancing and, many thought, easy virtue.

Adults are perennially shocked by the sexuality and the physical vitality of the young. There is nevertheless a real difference between the surprise and fear parents feel when they see their babies grow strong and independent and the mistrust of young people as a class. One is timeless. The other dates from 1904 and the publication of G. Stanley Hall's fourteen-hundred-page *Adolescence: Its Psychology and Its Relations to Physiology, Anthropology, Sociology, Sex, Crime, Religion and Education.*

With this book Hall, a psychologist and the president of Clark University, invented the field of adolescent psychology. He defined adolescence as a universal, unavoidable, and extremely precarious stage of human development. He asserted that behavior that would indicate insanity in an adult should be considered normal in an adolescent. (This has long since been proved untrue, but it is still widely believed.) He provided a basis for dealing with adolescents as neither children nor adults but as distinctive, beautiful, dangerous creatures. That people in their teens should be considered separately from others, which seems obvious to us today, was Hall's boldest, most original, and most influential idea.

The physical and sexual development of young people was not, he argued, evidence of maturity. Their body changes were merely armaments in a struggle to achieve a higher state of being. "Youth awakes to a new world," he wrote, "and understands neither it nor himself." People in their teens were, he thought, recapitulating the stage of human evolution in which people ceased to be savages and became civilized. He worried that young people were growing up too quickly, and he blamed it on "our urbanized hothouse life that tends to ripen everything before its time." He believed it was necessary to fight this growing precocity by giving young people the time, space, and guidance to help them weather the tumult and pain of adolescence.

It is hard to believe that a book so unreadable could be so influential, but the size and comprehensiveness of Hall's discussion of adolescents lent weight and authority to other social movements whose common aim was to treat people in their teens differently from adults and children. Among the book's supporters were secondary school educators who found in Hall's writing a justification for their new enthusiasm about moving beyond academic training to shape the whole person. They also found in it a justification for raising the age for ending compulsory school attendance.

Hall's book coincided as well with the rise of the juvenile-court movement, whose goal was to treat youth crime as a problem of personal development rather than as a transgression against society. This view encouraged legislatures and city councils to enact laws creating curfews and other "status offenses"—acts affecting only young people. (A decade earlier women's organizations had successfully campaigned to raise the age of consent for sex in most states, which greatly increased the number of statutory-rape prosecutions.)

Hall's findings also gave ammunition to advocates of child labor laws. Their campaigns were for the most part unsuccessful, but employment of children and teens dropped during the first two decades of the twentieth century anyway, as machines replaced unskilled manufacturing jobs in many industries. In the years after Hall's book came out, manufacturers increasingly spoke of workers in their teens as unreliable, irresponsible, and even disruptive. They had stopped thinking of fourteen-year-olds as young ordinary workers and begun to view them as adolescents.

Each of these movements was seen as a progressive attempt to reform American society, and their advocates certainly had their hearts in the right place. But the price for young people was a stigma of incompetence, instability, and even insanity. Adolescents couldn't be counted on. Hall even argued that female adolescents be "put to grass" for a few years and not allowed to work or attend school until the crisis had passed.

This was the orthodoxy Mead was trying to combat when she wrote *Coming of Age in Samoa*. She wanted to disprove Hall's psychoanalytic assertion that adolescence is inherent to all human development and replace it with the anthropological view that cultures invent the adolescence they need. Maturity, she argued, is at least as much a matter of social acceptance as it is of an individual's physical and mental development. In Samoa, she said, adolescence was relatively untroubled, because it didn't have to accomplish very much. The society changed little from generation to generation. Roles were more or less fixed. Young people knew from childhood what they should expect. American adolescence was more difficult because it had to achieve more, although she clearly didn't believe it had to be quite so horrible as Hall and his followers thought.

Serious questions have been raised about some of Mead's methods and findings in Samoa, and Hall's theories have been thoroughly discredited. These two seminal thinkers on adolescence represented extreme views, and adolescence is of course both biological and cultural. The changes it brings are unmistakable, but countless external factors shape what it means to be a grown-up in a particular place and time. In a dynamic society like that of the United States, the nature of adolescence must inevitably shift over time.

Indeed, Mead's research, which concentrated on young women, was a product of the sexual revolution of the 1920s, in which female sexuality was widely acknowledged for the first time. Prostitution was on the decrease, and the sexual activity of "respectable" young women was rising. In *This Side of Paradise* F. Scott Fitzgerald's young Princetonians were amazed at how easy it was to be kissed. But the protagonist in the novel gives what proved to be an accurate account of what was going on. "Just as a cooling pot gives off heat," she says, "so all through youth and adolescence we give off calories of virtue. That's what's called ingenuousness." Short skirts, bobbed hair, corset checkrooms at dances, and petting parties were seen by people at the time as symptoms of libertinism among the "flaming youth," but when Kinsey interviewed members of this generation three decades later, he learned that the heat had been more finely calibrated than it appeared. Young women had been making their chastity last as long as they needed it to. It turned out that while 40 percent of females in their teens and 50 percent of males petted to orgasm in the 1920s—nearly twice the pre-war rate—petting was most common among those who had had the most schooling. While commentators focused on the antics of the upper classes, working-class young people, who were closer to marriage, were twice as likely to have gone beyond and had sexual intercourse.

Despite enduring popular interest in Mead's findings, Hall's notion that adolescence is an inevitable crisis of the individual has, over the years, been more potent. (Perhaps it speaks more forcefully to our individualistic culture than does Mead's emphasis on shared challenges and values.) Certainly, during the post–World War II era, when the teenager grew to be a major cultural and economic phenomenon, the psychoanalytic approach dominated. J.D. Salinger's

Holden Caulfield, literature's most famous teenager, has an unforgettable voice and great charm, but it is difficult to read *Catcher in the Rye* today without feeling that Holden's problems are not, as he hopes, a phase he's going through but truly pathological. While Salinger doesn't make a judgment in the book, 1950s readers would most likely have thought Holden just another troubled adolescent, albeit an uncommonly interesting one.

When Hall was writing, at the turn of the twentieth century, he generalized about adolescents from a group that was still a small minority, middle-class youths whose main occupation was schooling. In all of his fourteen hundred pages, he never mentioned the large number of young people who still had to work to help support their families. Half a century later American society was more or less as Hall had described it, and just about everyone could afford to have an adolescence.

The twenty-five-year period following the end of World War II was the classic era of the teenager. Family incomes were growing, which meant that more could be spent on each child and educational aspirations could rise. Declining industries, such as radio and the movies, both of which were threatened by television, remade themselves to appeal to the youth market. Teenage culture gave rise to rock 'n' roll. Young people acquired automobiles of their own and invented a whole new car culture.

At the same time, though, teenagers were provoking a lot of anxiety. Congressional committees investigated juvenile delinquency for a decade. High schools and police forces took action against a rising wave of youth crime, a phenomenon that really didn't exist. Moreover, there were indications that not all teenagers were happy in their presumed immaturity. Many, if not most, of the pop icons of the time, from Elvis on down, were working-class outsiders who embodied a style very different from that of the suburban teen.

And many teenagers were escaping from their status in a more substantive way, by getting married. The general prosperity meant that there were jobs available in which the high school dropout or graduate could make enough to support a family. In 1960 about half of all brides were under twenty. In 1959 teenage pregnancy reached its all-time peak, but nearly all the mothers were married.

This post–World War II era brought forth the third key thinker on American adolescence, the psychologist Erik Erikson. He assumed, like Hall, that adolescence was inherent to human development and that an identity crisis, a term he invented, was necessarily a part of it. But he also acknowledged that this identity must be found in the context of a culture and of history. He argued that not only does adolescence change over the course of history but it also is the time when individuals learn to adapt themselves to their historical moment. "The identity problem changes with the historical period," he wrote. "That is, in fact, its job." While earlier thinkers on adolescence had made much of youthful idealism, Erikson argued that one of the tasks of adolescence was to be fiercely realistic about one's society and time.

He did not think that forging an identity in such a complex and confusing society as ours was easy for most people. He wanted adolescence to be what he termed "a psycho-social moratorium," to allow people the time and space to get a sense of how they would deal with the world of which they would be a part. Among

Movies like Rebel Without a Cause, *starring James Dean, depicted the futility and hopelessness of American youth in the 1950s.*

the results would be an occupational identity, a sense of how one would support and express oneself.

And so ideas about the nature of adolescence have shaped our image of teenagers. Reclassifying all people of secondary school age as teenagers wasn't possible until nearly all had some period of adolescence before entering adult life. Still, *teenager* isn't just another word for *adolescent*. Indeed, the teenager may be, as Edgar Z. Friedenberg argued in a 1959 book, a failed adolescent. Being a teenager is, he said, a false identity, meant to short-circuit the quest for a real one. By giving people superficial roles to play, advertising, the mass media, and even the schools confuse young people and leave them disatisfied and thus open to sales pitches that promise a deepening of identity.

Whether you agree with that argument or not, it does seem evident that the challenges of adolescence have been changing rapidly in the last several decades, leaving the label "teenager" as little more than a lazy way of talking about young people. The term encompasses a contradictory grab bag of beliefs, prejudices, and expectations. It can allow us to build a wall around an age group and to assume that its members' problems can safely be ignored.

The generation entering its teens today will be in sheer number, if not as a percentage of the population, the largest in our history. The people in this age group have already emerged as the most significant marketing phenomenon since the baby boom. They have spurred the opening of new teen-oriented clothing stores in

No area of the country appeared immune from the school shootings that shook the nation in the late 1990s and on into the next century. From Kentucky to Oregon, Arkansas to California, Pennsylvania to Colorado, students died, shot by their fellow students. A memorial erected at Santana High School in California, where two students were killed in March 2001, pleads for an end to the violence.

malls and the launching of successful new magazines. They are helping make the Internet grow. They even have their own television network, the WB. They have their own money to spend, and they spend a lot of their families' income too, partly because their mothers are too busy to shop.

But they do not represent any return to the teenage golden age of the 1950s and 1960s. This generation has grown up in a period of declining personal income and increasing inequality. A sizable percentage consists of the children of immigrants. Educational aspirations are very high, and no wonder: You need a college education today to make a salary equivalent to that of a high school graduate in 1970. The permanent occupational identity that was available in the post–World

War II society of which Erikson wrote, one in which lifelong work for large corpora-tions was the norm, has all but disappeared. Many see their parents still striving for the sort of stable identity Erikson thought could be resolved in youth. While it ap-pears to be a great time to be a teenager, it seems a difficult one to be an adolescent.

Throughout history Americans in their teens have often played highly respon-sible roles in their society. They have helped their families survive. They have worked with new technologies and hastened their adoption. Young people became teenagers because we had nothing better for them to do. High schools became cus-todial institutions for the young. We stopped expecting young people to be produc-tive members of the society and began to think of them as gullible consumers. We defined maturity primarily in terms of being permitted adult vices, and then were surprised when teenagers drank, smoked, or had promiscuous sex.

We can no longer go to Samoa to gain perspective on the shape of our lives at the dawn of the third millennium, nor can we go back in time to find a model for the future. What we learn from looking at the past is that there are many different ways in which Americans have been young. Young people and adults need to keep reinventing adolescence so that it serves us all. Sometimes what we think we know about teenagers gets in our way. But just as there was a time, not long ago, before there were teenagers, perhaps we will live to see a day when teenagers themselves will be history.

———————

Educational Change

Gerald W. Bracey

The golden era of American education did not exist, or so Gerald Bracey asserts. Whatever the qualitative merits of secondary school education in 1900, and these can be debated, only a tiny percentage of Americans attended such schools. If the purpose of education in a democracy is not to educate an elite superbly but to educate the great majority decently, then the modern American educational system, which graduates over four-fifths of the nation's teenagers, is far, far better than what came before it. Why, then, does nearly every complain of the state of American education? Bracey contends that educators and their critics have repeatedly made common cause in denouncing American education, the former to squeeze more funding from politicians and the public, and the latter, to exploit widespread anxieties over the purposes of education in a modern democracy. This article is adapted from Bracey's book, *Setting the Record Straight* (1997).

At one point in his 1988 book *The Thirteenth Man*, the former Secretary of Education Terrel Bell speaks of the decline of secondary education in America. "If we are frank with ourselves," he writes, "we must acknowledge that for most Americans . . . neither diligence in learning nor rigorous standards of performance prevail. . . . How do we once again become a nation of learners, in which attitudes towards intellectual pursuit and quality of work have excellence as their core?"

With these words Bell echoes two qualities common to educational reformers since World War II: nostalgia and amnesia. They look back through a haze to some imagined golden era of American education when we were "a nation of learners," forgetting that a century ago the high school graduation rate was about 3 percent, and it didn't exceed 50 percent until mid-century, whereas today it is 83 percent. . . .

Between 1910 and 1945, secondary schools expanded rapidly, the graduation rate rising from 10 percent to 45 percent. Their growth did not however, mean any greater coherence. . . . By the end of the war, secondary school enrollments approached 90 percent. A conference was held in 1945 to discuss how to cope with this expanding clientele. At the time, educators were strongly influenced by the emerging field of psychometrics—aptitude, achievement, and intelligence testing. Many test makers believed that intellectual ability was inherited and was distributed throughout the population in a normal curve. On the basis of this assumption, the conference decided that no more than 20 percent of high school students would ever go to college. Another 20 percent could be served by the recently developed vocational programs. That left 60 percent of students with no appropriate curriculum.

The conference decided to build a curriculum for this "forgotten 60 percent" around the "needs of students," and this led to the development of what was called

Life Adjustment Education. Life Adjustment Education was a genuine attempt to make schools serve an increasingly diverse population, but it assumed that the students couldn't be challenged academically. It was intellectually weak and open to easy ridicule. How would the "needs of students" be determined? In many instances, by questionnaires filled out by the students themselves. But teenagers were as likely then as ever to see their needs in terms of making friends, getting along with the opposite sex, and so on.

Liberal arts universities had already looked down on schools of education. When these schools now started promoting Life Adjustment Education, the liberal arts professors exploded in derision. Foremost among these critics was Arthur Bestor, a professor of history at the University of Illinois, who in 1953 wrote a popular book titled *Educational Wastelands: The Retreat From Learning in Our Public Schools.* Note the word *retreat.* This appears to be the first time a critique of the schools harked back to a previous time when things were better.

Bestor loaded *Wastelands* with statistics to demonstrate the schools' decline. He observed, for instance, that "fifty years ago, *half* of all students in public schools were studying Latin; today less than a quarter . . . are enrolled in courses in *all* foreign languages put together." He failed to add that fifty years before, only 50 percent of students had been enrolled in *any* school and only 7 percent of all students graduated from high school. A quarter of the current crop of students was actually far more of them.

Thus the sense of failure actually reflected the success of the schools in reaching out to what were called "new learners." But, perhaps more important, it also reflected America's changed role in the world. The Cold War and the space and weapons races were heating up. According to the Committee on the Present Danger, a group of thirty-three powerful leaders from business, industry, the military, and universities, in 1951, "We need both a reservoir of trained men and a continuing advance on every scientific and technical front."

The most vocal advocate of an educated work force as the front line in the Cold War was Adm. Hyman G. Rickover, the father of America's nuclear navy. "Let us never forget," Rickover said, "that there can be no second place in a contest with Russia and that there will be no second chance if we lose." Armed with statistics from the Director of Central Intelligence, Allen Dulles, Rickover stumped the country and harangued members of Congress on the need for more scientists, engineers, and mathematicians. The Russians, Dulles said his statistics showed, were outstripping us in these vital areas.

Where would we get the manpower we needed? Where else but from the schools? For the first time, schools were expected to play a role in national security. And they weren't good enough at it.

When the Russians launched *Sputnik,* the first man-made satellite to circle the globe, the schools' critics took the event as proof that they had been right. The schools were failing. *Sputnik* went up in October 1957; by the following spring *Life* magazine had readied a five-part series, *Crisis in Education.* The cover of the March 24, 1958, edition showed two students: a stern-looking Alexei Kutzkov in Moscow and a relaxed, smiling Stephen Lapekas in Chicago. Inside, photographs showed Kutzkov conducting complex experiments in physics and chemistry and reading *Sister Carrie* out loud in English class. Lapekas was depicted walking hand in hand with his girlfriend and rehearsing for a musical. In the one American classroom picture, Lapekas retreats from a math problem on the blackboard, laughing along with his classmates. The caption explains that "Stephen amused the class with wise-cracks about his ineptitude."

Life engaged Sloan Wilson, author of *The Man in the Gray Flannel Suit,* a success-ful novel that had become known as something of a social critique, for a two-page essay titled "It's Time to Close Our Carnival." Like Bestor, Wilson saw only decline and failure. "The facts of the school crisis are all out and in plain sight and pretty dreadful to look at," he wrote. "A surprisingly small percentage of high school stu-dents is studying what used to be considered basic subjects. . . . People are com-plaining that the diploma has been devalued to the point of meaninglessness. . . . It is hard to deny that America's schools, which were supposed to reflect one of his-tory's noblest dreams and to cultivate the nation's youthful minds, have degener-ated into a system for coddling and entertaining the mediocre."

In 1983 the government study *A Nation at Risk* would discover a "rising tide of mediocrity." Wilson had found the same swelling current almost precisely twenty-five years earlier. But when Wilson was writing, precious little data existed about school performance, and what there was contradicted the novelist's message. Al-though the number of people taking the SATs had increased from 10,654 in 1941 to 376,800 in 1957, their scores had remained at the same levels as in 1941, the year SAT standards had been set. And scores on achievement tests had been steadily rising.

American schools have often been faulted for not solving social problems, and in the sixties they were condemned for failing to achieve racial integration soon enough. While they were taking the blame for continued segregation, the verdict arrived on the grand curriculum reforms that had followed *Sputnik:* They had failed.

Reformers held out great hopes for the new math and its attendant innovations in other fields. That the new curricula were being developed by some of the finest minds at some of our finest universities was initially thought to be their greatest strength. Later it was recognized as their greatest weakness. Although eminent in their fields, the scholars had no sense of how a classroom works. They tried to cre-ate materials that "would permit scholars to speak directly to the child" and be "teacher-proof," observed Robert J. Schaefer, dean of Teachers College, Columbia University. This in itself guaranteed failure.

At about the same time as the new curricula were being pronounced dead, a spate of books was appearing with titles like *Death at an Early Age, 36 Children,* and *The Way It Spozed to Be.* Most described how schools were failing to serve minority students, but some, like *How Children Fail,* contained more general indictments of public schools, contributing to a growing feeling that they were simply not good places for children to be. "Free schools" and "alternative schools" began to spring up around the country. The antischool feeling was summed up in Charles Silber-man's authoritative book *Crisis in the Classroom.*

Crisis in the Classroom appeared in 1970. The red menace still hung over our heads. Domestic events—assassinations, Vietnam, urban uprisings, Chicago, Kent State—had created the sense that nothing was secure. In this milieu Silberman ob-served the malaise that pervaded our schools and wondered why. He pointed out that in a review of 186 then-and-now studies (which compare achievement at two points in time) devoted to education, all but 10 had favored now. He asked, "Why, then, the pervasive sense of crisis? How to explain the fact that an educational system that appears to be superbly successful from one standpoint appears to be in grave trouble from another?" He clearly had the social unrest of both urban blacks and suburban whites in mind when he suggested that "the question cannot be answered with regard to education alone; it is in fact the central paradox of American life. In almost every area, improvements beyond what anyone thought possible fifty or twenty-five or even ten years ago have produced anger and anxiety rather than satisfaction."

But improvements in schools, Silberman concluded, did not mean there was no crisis: "The test of a society, as of an institution, is not whether it is improving, although certainly such a test is relevant, but whether it is adequate to the needs of the present and of the foreseeable future. Our educating institutions fail that test." Thus he rejected nostalgia but saw a crisis nonetheless in the appalling quality of life in schools.

"Because adults take the schools so much for granted," he wrote, "they fail to appreciate what grim, joyless places most American schools are, how oppressive and petty are the rules by which they are governed, how intellectually sterile and aesthetically barren the atmosphere, what an appalling lack of civility obtains on the part of teachers and principals, what contempt they consciously display for children as children."

However accurate Silberman's characterization may have been, it fitted well with the descriptions found in many of the other books of the time. Silberman offered as a cure the same prescription that the journalist Joseph Featherstone had suggested three years earlier in a series of articles that ran in *The New Republic:* open education, a British import that involved making the classroom more informal and that was originally intended only for five- to seven-year-olds.

Whatever currency Silberman's message had was lost seven years later when the College Board called attention to what was then a little-attended fact: SAT scores had been falling for fourteen years. The board formed a panel, headed by former Secretary of Labor Willard Wirtz, to study the decline, and the panel attributed most of it to changes in who was taking the test: more women, more minorities, more students with low high school grades. Noting that the decline stemmed largely from easier access to college, the vice-chair of the panel, former U.S. Commissioner of Education Harold Howe II, wrote an article titled "Let's Have Another SAT Decline." He contended that the civil rights agenda of equal access to education was unfinished, that the doors needed to be opened wider, and if this caused the scores to drop further, so be it.

The Wirtz panel emphasized the complexity of the decline. One of its background papers simply listed the number of hypotheses brought forward to explain the fall: There were eighty-seven of them, not including one from a physicist blaming the radioactive fallout from nuclear testing programs in the fifties. The media and the public had a simpler interpretation. While the developers of the SAT still called their test a "mere supplement," the public now saw it as the platinum rod for measuring school performance. And that performance was getting worse.

Beginning in 1980 a new diagnosis of what was wrong with American schools appeared, and a new prescription was produced for curing the ailment. Policy papers written for the presidential candidate Ronald Reagan concluded that American schools were declining at the hands of a force heretofore seen as positive in public education: the federal government. Building on arguments made by Milton Friedman in his 1962 book *Capitalism and Freedom,* Reagan's advisers recommended abolishing the U.S. Department of Education, which only recently had been elevated to cabinet status. In addition, tuition tax credits and vouchers should be provided to parents to permit them to choose where to send their children to school. In the free-market environment that would then develop, good schools would flourish and bad schools would go out of business. Previous perceptions of educational decline had led to increased federal involvement. That involvement, the new view contended, had been part of the problem.

In his book about life with a boss who is trying to do away with your job, Reagan's Secretary of Education, Terrel Bell, reports that he heard constant criticisms about the state of American education and began to long for an event that, like *Sputnik,* would shake the nation out of its complacency. No such event was forthcoming, and Bell fell back on establishing yet another blue-ribbon panel, the National Commission on Excellence in Education.

The commission's report, *A Nation at Risk,* may well rank as one of the most selective uses of data in the history of education. After its opening statement about the "rising tide of mediocrity" and how if an unfriendly foreign power had foisted our schools on us we might have considered it an act of war, the document goes on to list thirteen indicators of dangerous trouble. These indicators seem to have been carefully picked to give as negative a view as possible.

For instance, one of them is: "There was a steady decline in science achievement scores of U.S. 17-year-olds as measured by national assessments of science in 1969, 1973 and 1977." This statement, as far as it goes, is true. But why seventeen-year-olds? Why science? Because only the trend of science scores for seventeen-year-olds supports the crisis rhetoric. The science scores of the other two age groups measured, nine- and thirteen-year-olds, do not. The reading and math scores of nine-, thirteen-, and seventeen-year-olds do not; they were either steady or rising. Of nine trend lines, only one supported the crisis rhetoric. That was the one the commission reported.

The findings should have been challenged by educational organizations, but they had their own reason to accept them: Often their policies are influenced by how an event will affect the availability of funds. Since *A Nation at Risk* depicted grave problems, it seemed likely to generate money to fix those problems. Educational organizations accepted the report enthusiastically.

Risk embraced a new and powerful assumption: that the schools are tightly linked to the performance of the U.S. economy and our ability to compete in the global marketplace. In fact, competition in the global marketplace became the goad for the eighties that the Cold War had been three decades earlier. When a recession arrived late in 1990, this putative link allowed people to blame the schools.

Starting three years ago, however, newspaper headlines began heralding a recovery, and the Geneva-based World Economic Forum pronounced the U.S. economy the most competitive of any among twenty-five developed nations in both 1994 and 1995. In 1996 the forum changed its formula and the United States fell to fourth place; the International Institute for Management and Development retained a formula similar to the forum's old one and found the country still number one.

Larry Cuban, a professor at Stanford University, has pointed out that though people blamed schools for the recession of the late eighties, they gave them no credit for the recovery of the nineties, and he dismisses the idea of a strong direct link between educational and economic performance in advanced nations. He points out, for example, that critics of American public education generally argue that Germany and Japan have superior schools. Yet in recent years those two countries have been mired in long-term recessions, their worst since World War II.

Meanwhile the debate over schools and their relationship to the economy has been accompanied by a shift in talk about the purposes of schooling. The goals of building citizens or broadly educated or well-rounded adults have been left behind in favor of the need to prepare students to get jobs and to provide skilled workers for business.

People have never agreed about the purpose of education in this country—or anywhere else. Aristotle already knew why when he observed that education dealt with "the good life" and people would always differ on what the good life was. To see it principally in terms of getting and keeping a job, though, is rather new to America.

One of our pre-eminent educational influences, Thomas Jefferson, saw education as having two purposes. On one hand, it would act as a great sorting machine with which "the best geniuses will be raked from the rubbish annually" to form an "aristocracy of worth and genius," as opposed to the aristocracies of blood that afflicted Europe. On the other hand, Jefferson thought, all citizens' "minds must be improved to a certain degree" so they could protect the nation from the "germ of corruption."

Even Jefferson's more practical peer Benjamin Franklin did not support vocational training. He realized that people building a new nation would need many skills, but he believed a school's job was to leave them "fitted for learning any business calling or profession." In this he sounds surprisingly like former Secretary of Labor Robert Reich contending that the most valuable skill to learn in school today is "flexibility." In any case, specific vocational goals entered educational discussions early in this century, as secondary schooling began its rapid expansion. When *A Nation at Risk* appeared, it emphasized the preparation of a skilled work force as no one had before.

A Nation at Risk has served the purposes of both those who want to provide more resources for the schools and those who want to overhaul the system and introduce privatization. Both sides have appeared to welcome only bad news about the schools. Thus, when a large, federally funded report concluded that there was no crisis in American education, the Bush administration suppressed it; it was ultimately published by the Clinton administration under the title *Perspectives on Education in America*. And the Bush Department of Education held a press conference to publicize an international study that found American students ranking low in math and science . . . but made no attempt to tell anyone when another study found American students' reading skills the second best of any of thirty-one countries.

That study was eventually discovered by *Education Week;* when *USA Today* subsequently reported it, the paper also quoted a deputy Assistant Secretary of Education dismissing the finding.

In 1993 former Secretary of Education William Bennett released numbers purporting to show that there is no relationship between states' SAT scores and the money those states spend on education. This report was widely disseminated by the Heritage Foundation, and the table summarizing its results was reproduced in *The Wall Street Journal.* Yet people have known for years that the principal source of differences among states lies in the proportion of seniors taking the SAT. In Utah and Mississippi only 4 percent of the seniors take the test, and this tiny elite does well. In Connecticut, which spends far more per pupil on education, 81 percent of the senior class huddles in angst on Saturday mornings to fill in the answer sheets. With the vast majority of its seniors taking the test, Connecticut is digging much deeper into its talent pool, and that excavation shows up in lower scores.

Whether elements of free-market competition would improve schools is not a question for this article, but it seems clear that those who support the notion have sometimes been overzealous in their search for evidence that the current system does not work. The resulting stream of negativity has created a climate in which the media accentuate the negative, sometimes inaccurately. For instance, in 1993 the usually reliable *Education Week* conducted a ten-year retrospective on what had happened since *A Nation at Risk* appeared. The answer, essentially, was not much: The "proportion of American youngsters performing at high levels remains infinitesimally small. In the past ten years for instance the number and proportion of students scoring at or above 650 on the verbal or math section of the Scholastic Aptitude Test has actually declined." But the numbers that confirmed the fall were for scores between 650 and 800 in 1982 but only for scores between 650 and 690 in 1992. When the higher scores were added in for the later year, they showed clearly that, in fact, more students were doing well than ever.

In the three years since, the proportion of high scorers has continued to rise. Denis Doyle, a Heritage Foundation visiting fellow, voiced a popular belief in *Issues '96: The Candidate's Briefing Book, 1996,* when he ascribed the rise in scores to Asian-American students. It is true that Asian-American students score much higher on the math SAT than do other ethnic groups, but they cannot account for most of the growth. In fact, there has been a 74 percent rise in the proportion of students scoring above 650 since 1981. Omit Asian students, and you still see a 57 percent increase.

Today most statistics continue to show what Silberman found twenty-five years ago: Now is better than then. . . . The biggest threat to the American educational system may come not from within our schools but from the depth of our divisions over what exactly they should accomplish and how best to get them to accomplish it. And our divisions will not be healed as long as we ignore the history of the accomplishments that have already been made. We should begin improving our schools by appreciating how well they have, in most places and at most times, done so far.

TEXT CREDITS

"Thirteen Books You Must Read to Understand America" by Arthur M. Schlesinger, Jr., *American Heritage*, February/March 1998. © 1998 by American Heritage, Inc. Reprinted by permission of American Heritage Inc.

"The Making of Men: Fraternal Orders in the Nineteenth Century" by Mark C. Carnes from *American Heritage*, September 1993. Copyright © 1993 by American Heritage, Inc. Reprinted by permission of American Heritage Inc.

"Butte America" by Dan Baum. Reprinted by permission of International Creative Management, Inc. Copyright © 1997 by Dan Baum.

"The Age of the Bosses" by William V. Shannon, *American Heritage,* 20, 4, June 1969: 26–31. Copyright © 1969 by American Heritage, a division of Forbes, Inc.

"Learning to Go to the Movies" by David Nasaw, from *American Heritage,* November 1993. Copyright © 1993 by David Nasaw. Reprinted by permission of William Morris Agency, Inc. on behalf of the author.

"A Road They Did Not Know" (*American Heritage* article), from *Crazy Horse* by Larry McMurtry, copyright © 1999 by Larry McMurtry. Used by permission of Viking Penguin, a division of Penguin Putnam, Inc.

"A Little Milk, A Little Honey" (reprinted under the title "The Diaspora in America: A Study of Jewish Immigration") by David Boroff, *American Heritage,* October 1966: 12–21, 74–81. Copyright © 1966 by American Heritage, a division of Forbes, Inc.

"The Reluctant Conquerors: How the Generals Viewed the Indians" (reprinted under the title "Reluctant Conquerors: American Army Officers and the Plains Indians") by Thomas C. Leonard, *American Heritage,* 27, 5, August 1976: 34–40. Copyright © 1976 by American Heritage, a division of Forbes, Inc.

"Saint Jane and the Ward Boss" (reprinted under the title "Jane Addams: Urban Crusader") by Anne Firor Scott, *American Heritage,* December 1960: 12–17, 94–99. Copyright © 1960 by American Heritage, a division of Forbes, Inc.

"Inventing Modern Football" (reprinted under the title "Reforming College Football") by John S. Watterson, *American Heritage,* 39, 6, September/October 1988: 102–113. Copyright © 1988 by American Heritage, a division of Forbes, Inc.

"Father of the Forests" (reprinted under the title "Gordon Pinchot: Father of the Forests") by T. H. Watkins, *American Heritage,* 42, 1, February/March 1991: 86-98. Copyright © 1991 by American Heritage, a division of Forbes, Inc.

"Our War with Spain Marked the First Year of the American Century" by John Lukacs from *American Heritage,* May/June 1998. Copyright © 1998 by American Heritage, Inc. Reprinted by permission of American Heritage Inc.

"Yesterday, December 7, 1941" by Richard M. Ketchum. Originally appeared in *American Heritage,* 40, 7 November. All rights reserved. Copyright © 1989 by Richard M. Ketchum. Reprinted by permission of Brandt & Hochman Literary Agents, Inc.

"Holocaust" by William J. Vanden Heuvel, from *American Heritage,* July/August 1999. Copyright © 1999 by American Heritage, Inc. Reprinted by permission of American Heritage Inc.

From *All the Laws but One* by William H. Rehnquist, copyright © 1998 by William H. Rehnquist. Used by permission of Alfred A. Knopf, a division of Random House, Inc.

"The Biggest Decision: Why We Had to Drop the Bomb" by Robert James Maddox, *American Heritage,* May/June 1995. Copyright © 1995 by American Heritage Inc. Reprinted by permission of American Heritage Inc.

"The Big Picture of the Great Depression" by John A. Garraty, *American Heritage,* 37, 4, August/September 1986: 90–97. Copyright © 1986 by American Heritage, a division of Forbes, Inc.

"The Case of the Chambermaid and the 'Nine Old Men'" by William E. Leuchtenburg, *American Heritage,* 38, 1, January/February 1987. Copyright © 1987 by American Heritage, a division of Forbes, Inc.

"FDR: The Man of the Century" by Arthur Schlesinger, Jr. *American Heritage*, May/June 1995. Copyright © 1994 by American Heritage Inc. Reprinted by permission of American Heritage Inc.

ILLUSTRATION CREDITS